Contents

Print Estimator's Handbook

Hugh M Speirs

Published by
Pira International Ltd
Randalls Road, Leatherhead
Surrey KT22 7RU
UK

T +44 (0) 1372 802080
F +44 (0) 1372 802079
E publications@pira.co.uk
W www.piranet.com

© Copyright
Pira International Ltd 2004

ISBN 1 85802 922 8

Head of publications
Philip Swinden
philips@pira.co.uk

Customer services manager
Denise Davidson
publications@pira.co.uk
T +44 (0)1372 802080

Typeset in the UK by
Jeff Porter, Deeping St James,
Peterborough, Lincs

List of tables

List of figures

The central role of estimating

1

Although estimating has an increasingly central and wide-ranging role in printing administration, its main purpose remains evaluation of the possible range of options available to produce a given job and the variations thereof. This information is used to decide the method of working that is the most cost-effective for each printing company against all the criteria considered appropriate to that enquiry. This information and detail, in the form of production times, materials, outwork and other related costs, are then extended at the appropriate cost factor rates to produce an estimate, from which a firm price and quotation are prepared for the customer.

Preparation of an estimate is the starting point for the production and control systems and processes that initially create and establish production instructions and data used to record the job. These will then be used to control and monitor the passage of the job through its different stages once the quotation is confirmed as an order. An integrated computerised management information system (MIS) makes it easier to transfer data from estimating through the complete cycle of a job, including works instruction, production, stock control and costing. Cost comparisons based on estimated figures and actual production records can be used to record variances and performance levels, and by monitoring performance it is possible to manage and improve company performance.

Estimating has developed into the major administrative role of a printing organisation, responding to the bespoke nature of the industry. Specialisation and the growing recognition of different discrete print markets, increased competitiveness brought about by customer pressure on pricing, quality and levels of service have ensured that print management no longer views estimating as simply a price-creating process. Properly managed and supported, estimating can provide invaluable information on the company's competitiveness, activity, productivity and benchmark targets using technical, commercial and financial criteria.

Estimating considerations

Print-buying customers, or parties working on their behalf, will generally require a firm price before placing an order. As printed goods are essentially bespoke, they do not easily fall into a standardised pattern or narrow range of work. Cost estimates for most printed jobs are therefore worked out individually in advance. Consider the suitability of the work in relation to each printer's equipment base, capability and expertise. Before the quotation is prepared, the anticipated contribution and profit margin need to be established commensurate with company policy and specific factors relevant to when the quotation is submitted.

A further factor influencing how estimates are prepared is where an increasing number of printers are becoming increasingly specialised, producing relatively standardised ranges of work. Examples include a large section of digital printing, including on-demand stationery, plus other major sectors such as magazines, periodicals, books, cartons and business forms. The resultant database of established times and costs that can then be built up enables such organisations to move towards market-based pricing. Often this requirement is customer-driven. With their experience and knowledge of the jobs being considered, printers and print-related companies can react speedily and readily to new print specifications and permutations.

Competitive markets require accurate estimating. To overestimate on one job may cause the loss of an order, but persistent overestimating will result in the loss of the customer. To underestimate will result in financial loss and the danger of establishing inaccurate figures for future pricing calculations. Contrary to this, however, there is a growing acceptance by printers and print buyers in certain sectors of print that prices and details for the same job can and often will change over short periods of time. This is mainly due to printing being increasingly seen as a commodity in certain types of work and circumstances, such as regularly ordered transactional print, where printers applying contribution as their major yardstick vary their prices. This will depend on how busy they are when certain job enquiries and jobs are offered.

Web-based print auctions are a case in point. Here job enquiries and specifications are posted on the web, either on a completely open basis to all printers, or restricted to approved suppliers. On a closed basis, prices are submitted without any indication of other prices that have been submitted; with an open system, from the first price submitted, each subsequent price can be viewed by anyone given access to the website or system, to decide if they wish to submit a price lower than the lowest current bid. There is a cut-off for close of bidding, and most bidding takes place very close to the cut-off, with prices falling quite dramatically or remaining relatively unchanged. When quoting for new customers it is important to check their credit ratings in the early stages of an enquiry. This normally means getting satisfactory bank and trade references. It is usually the responsibility of senior management to approve new trading credit in accordance with company policy.

Variations in prices quoted by different companies for the same job are often considerable, partly due to the reasons already covered. Although some of the variation is due to inaccurate estimating, there are many factors that affect the prices submitted. No two printers have identical equipment, costing systems or methods of working, and outputs from similar machines vary across the industry, as per the other factors already covered. Studies of submitted quotations have found that differences of over 100% do occur, although they are relatively uncommon, but there are frequently differences of up to 25% or more.

Technical and commercial knowledge

An estimator needs sound technical knowledge and good awareness, and this cannot be overemphasised. In particular, estimators should fully understand working practices, printing processes, equipment, materials and methods of working applicable to their own organisation. Although estimators are obviously not expected to do the job, e.g. in prepress or machine printing, they need to visualise each job, breaking it into its component stages from beginning to end. Besides sound technical knowledge, it is increasingly necessary for estimators to have good commercial knowledge and customer service skills. The days are gone when print was priced solely on a cost-plus basis, with increasing emphasis on other financial criteria such as value added and contribution, plus production-related matters such as ongoing and forward loading of capacity and capability.

Printers also have to be far more customer-centred and focused to be successful, so they have to be responsive to customer needs and requirements. Such a customer-centric approach leads to much better customer and supplier relationships, increased market knowledge and the opportunity of being recognised by customers as offering a high-quality added-value service. This should create a working relationship or partnership that is profitable and beneficial to both parties, often confirmed through being appointed as an approved or preferred print supplier of goods and services. Computer-assisted estimating is fast, it can retain records and it can integrate with other management systems. It is therefore becoming essential, but this does not lessen the need for competent estimators skilled in print and estimating techniques and well-versed in commercial knowledge and customer service skills.

Production records

An estimate is an opinion and a forecast of costs that should be based on reliable facts, so it is essential that accurate production records of previous job costs are maintained by each printing organisation. These records must be updated regularly with information established from more recent job records and production targets.

When compiling average outputs, consider as wide a range of work as necessary. Similar types of work should be grouped together to give output figures applicable to that particular range and quality of work. Examples include different prepress workflow times applicable to simple work, such as leaflets and standard booklets. By contrast, complex graphic-rich brochures can involve a mixture of files created and/or received, preflighting, a proofing cycle, make-up, trapping and imposition as required to approved press-ready files downloaded for computer-to-plate (CTP). Press and postpress make-ready times will tend to vary from job to job, but consistent average times for similar work will occur. Factors that cause significant variations should be highlighted and included in the estimate, such as waiting for wet work and applying a coating or varnish.

The time spent in recording and producing accurate data and output tables like those included in this book will be amply repaid by increased accuracy and much speedier compilation. The tables in this book are based on a wide cross section of data prepared from machinery manufacturers, printing companies and organisations. Although they can be taken as reasonably representative of the average, they are no substitute for 'speed tables' and data compiled from your own production records.

Decide on the operations for which you will compile the time, cost/price and speed tables. If necessary, the range can easily be extended and broken down more precisely. When compiling data for estimating, decide which operations should be included in the set-up and make-ready times and also the machine running speed ranges, from slow start-up to maximum level. This will involve a range of speeds based on different factors influencing the net completed copies per hour. Remember that the calculations will need to allow for the total quantity of paper, board or other substrate, including overs and waste copies.

Carefully consider your staffing levels. These are the staffing levels needed to complete the range of operations involved and the method of recovering the costs. For example, most cost centres will include machine and labour elements, but some operations or cost centres have a cost rate or charge that covers the machine element only, with the labour element applied separately, depending on the number of people required. This situation is particularly relevant in print finishing and postpress operations where, for example, the number of people required to complete a certain operation or operations varies with the number of sections, hoppers or units to be fed. Staffing levels will normally be negotiated and agreed, along with working practices, to suit each organisation's own circumstances and estimators should reflect these circumstances in their calculations. When any changes affect staffing levels and/or working practices, it is essential that estimators are informed so that they can adjust their calculations.

Production records and related costs should be prepared for all work and processes completed in-house, i.e. within the host organisation. In addition, records should be kept of goods and services supplied by trade houses, which will need to be updated regularly to reflect changes in pricing structure and the range of services offered. Draw up production records to match your own specific requirements. The items in Box 1.1 would be relevant to a wide cross section of printing companies and some will coincide with your own organisation.

| **Production records for a wide range of printing and print-related operations** | ▶ Design cycle: from initial concept to final approval of digitally created artwork and files.
▶ Prepress workflows: recorded in one integrated combined state from initial stage or stages to production of press-ready image data for downloading and queuing to digital printing devices, computer-to-plate (CTP) for conventional printing processes. Alternatively as a series of itemised activities or stages as set out in the next seven points.
▶ Receipt, creation and processing of files: from a range of sources and stages, including hard copy, direct keying, word processing files, raw and final finished desktop publishing (DTP) files, press-ready PDF files, etc.
▶ Scanning: time- and/or cost-based records depending on size and complexity, such as cut-outs and retouching.
▶ Preflighting, disk conversion and certified file approval stages.
▶ Proofing cycle: time- and/or cost-based records from visual to target or contract stages.
▶ Final prepress preparation stages: trapping, imposition and planning.
▶ Rasterising and downloading to different output devices and stages: such as B3, B2 and B1, in the form of computer-to-film (CTF), computer-to-plate (CTP) computer-to-press (CTPr) and digital printing. The range of work covers simple bookwork, tabular work, complex line and tone combined, and four-colour process. |

▶ Miscellaneous times: such as camera and contact times, film output, planning and assembly, conventional platemaking.

▶ Press or machine printing make-ready and set-up times: sheet-fed and web-fed presses cover a wide range of single- and multicolour configurations, as well as technological enhancements.

▶ Press or machine printing speed tables: based on different quantity breaks, print and substrate type.

▶ Postpress inline finishing: consider the impact on press make-ready and set-up and printing machine speed tables.

▶ Postpress online, nearline and off-line finishing times: combined in automated workflows, such as gather, stitch, trim (GST) machine and case bookbinding lines; alternatively as add-on digital printing and finishing capabilities, or as a series of itemised activities and stages as set out in the next seven items.

▶ Guillotine times: cover basic and programmatic machines, also three-knife trimmers, based on the number of cuts and/or products cut per hour.

▶ Folding machine make-ready: cover set-up, based on size of sheet and number of folds; also the impact of additional processes such as inline gluing, perforating and slotting.

▶ Folding machine speed tables: based on sheet size, number of folds, type of material.

▶ Separate off-line gathering, collating, stitching lines, plus operations such as bookletmakers.

▶ Specialist postpress, print finishing and converting make-ready times and speeds: cover operations such as cutting-and-creasing and making up cartons, collating and making up business forms and sets, label die-cutting, embossing, and foil blocking.

▶ Ancillary hand- and benchwork operational times.

▶ Packing and dispatch.

Paper and board, plus other materials and consumables, often account for up to 40% or more of the overall job cost, so take care to clearly identify and account for them. A common and major error in estimating the amount of material required is to confuse leaves and pages, hence doubling or halving the correct material usage. This error can be made at several points in the estimating process, rendering some or all of the subsequent calculations inaccurate, often by a considerable amount. Guillotine calculations of bound publications are another common source of error where leaves and pages are mixed up, resulting in half or double the correct cutting time being used in the estimate.

The grouping and linking of different job workflows or stages is also an increasingly common feature on computerised estimating systems, leading to faster compilation of estimates and reduced incidence of errors. All production records used in estimating and production planning records should be regularly checked by comparing estimated times with actual times taken. Major discrepancies should be investigated and the speed tables should be amended if circumstances have changed.

With the agreement of the relevant parties, the estimating department can allow for improved working practices and economies within a printing company. In machine printing, for example, economies can be realised through reduced overall make-ready times by running jobs or parts of jobs sequentially that require the same facilities such as common ink colours, size and type of sheet or web, numbering, perforating and varnishing. The same principle applies to print finishing operations where grouping of common factors, such as arranging the same or very similar formats to run in sequence on finishing lines, will reduce make-ready times to a minimum.

The ultimate control of the running sequence lies with the production planning and control staff, where delivery dates and customer requirements play a crucial role. Nevertheless, estimators, production planners and production controllers should work closely together to agree strategy in achieving the right balance between the highest level of cost-effectiveness, sequencing of jobs and meeting customer requirements. When working methods are likely to be more costly than indicated by the estimated work plan, then the estimator should be informed, as it may be possible to charge the customer for this increase. An example is where the customer has changed the agreed specification or timetable for that particular job.

Continual improvements in the productivity of prepress, press and postpress equipment and in MIS functionality, along with far-reaching developments such as Job Definition Format (JDF) are having a profound impact on the structure and pattern of estimating standards. A new range of equipment can now produce printed products and print-related services in a large number of ways. When faced with such variety, the estimator must establish a unit for estimating accurate costs or times. The unit could be the time taken to complete an operation, the machine speed per hour recorded in running an operation, or even the production of a set unit such as an A4 page or a B2 spread.

An efficient factory or operation is always in a constant state of change, especially the areas described in this book, such as speed tables, operational times and unit prices, which need regular checking and revision to keep them accurate and up to date. Proposed changes in production equipment or working practices should be communicated immediately to the estimating department so that they can be assessed and factored into future calculations. At all times the estimating department should be in close contact with the sales and production departments to allow for special considerations and requirements.

Administrative functions

Although printing has changed dramatically in recent years, improved customer satisfaction and service should be a common goal through the support and cooperation of all parties involved in the printing production chain. As each piece of printing is bespoke, it presents a fresh challenge. Ambiguous instructions in any part of the communication or interaction chain, from the inception of an idea to finished printed product can lead to costly mistakes, frustration among all the parties concerned and lost customers. Correct, efficient and orderly instructions help to prevent or at least minimise jobs going wrong and ensure they are produced to everyone's satisfaction. The role of the administrative functions is to act as a chain of communication between the customer and the production departments. The print communication chain starts when the customer or print buyer passes print enquiries or orders to one of the members of the sales and marketing or customer service team.

Customers

Without customers there would be no business. Every customer must therefore be seen not only for their current order, but as potential for future business. Fulfilling the customer's needs every time will help secure the next order, or at least enquiry. Some customers will only order print very infrequently, e.g. a catalogue published once a year or batches of stationery every few months. At the other end of the spectrum is the professional print buyer or publisher who has an annual print-buying budget of hundreds of thousands or millions of pounds. Infrequent buyers of print will rely heavily on the printer's staff to guide them through the stages of printing and the onus is very much on the customer service staff, such as estimators or account executives, to maintain close contact and provide prompt and reliable advice at all stages. In the case of experienced or professional print buyers, the printer is dealing with customers who work with and through a wide range of printing and print-related companies. They will lay down well-documented instructions and procedures, in return expecting the printer to understand them and to respond positively to a well-structured relationship.

Sales

Sales staff make and maintain contact with customers and create demand for the company's products and production capacity by attending to customer requirements and enquiries. Their main function is to create and attend to existing and potential customers' enquiries by visiting the clients regularly and on request, and ensuring the correct interpretation of each enquiry or order is passed on to the estimator or account executive. Whenever possible, they should also seek feedback on the competitiveness of the quotations submitted and the service quality provided by the printing company.

Account executives

To streamline and improve communications with customers, account executives are now often part of a customer service team or group, consisting of sales personnel, account executives and estimators, representing particular market sectors or dedicated to one large customer base. The account executive is ostensibly the inside works contact for the customer and it is generally their responsibility to progress and service each enquiry and order for the customer. This is a good arrangement because account executives become thoroughly familiar with the particular requirements of each customer. Account executives that have been trained as estimators or production progress chasers are often used to carry out these duties when required. Customers find it very beneficial when contacting the printing company to have one point of contact handling their work through the complete job cycle.

Estimating

Estimating entails preparing estimates and, in conjunction with sales representatives, account executives and senior management, preparing and servicing the quotations submitted. The estimator has to calculate all the cost elements of an enquiry and prepare a draft estimate. Apart from senior estimating staff, estimates are normally reviewed by another member of senior management who decides the actual selling price. The final quotation is then prepared and submitted to the customer for consideration.

Purchasing

Purchasing can be carried out by a specialised purchasing department, estimators or account executives, depending on the specific arrangements within an organisation. Efficient purchasing and procurement policies ensure the right material and goods are available at the right time on the best possible terms.

Production planning and control

Production planning and control is one of the most difficult and challenging roles in a printing organisation. It is the responsibility of this department to plan, control and monitor production through the respective processes to ensure that jobs recover their costs to meet financial targets and meet customers' requirements. Production planning involves translating the customer's requirements into instructions for the satisfactory completion of each job, laying plans for the production departments and arranging or managing the supply of materials and outwork. The control element ensures the close monitoring of production programmes, altering and amending them as required within the constraints that time and facilities permit.

Costing

Costing is concerned initially with finding the costs of running a business and from this calculating cost recovery rates and/or prices that will be used for estimating, control and pricing. A cost-based management information system, such as the one introduced by the British Printing Industries Federation (BPIF), is used by many printing organisations in the UK as the basis of their own costing systems, enabling them to identify and monitor all aspects of costs and cost recovery.

Pricing and invoicing

Pricing is the determination of the price to be charged to the customer at the time a quotation is requested, or after a job has been delivered and the cost of its production is known. It is essential that the quotation and actual job records are periodically compared and used as a source of feedback for the estimator. The specification in the quotation should agree with the production of the finished job, or where variations have taken place, as they often do in production, these must be taken into account when arriving at the price to be charged.

Additional requirements and services beyond those contained in the quotation, including amendments and alterations to the original files supplied, e.g. author's corrections, overtime premium charges, additional sets of proofs and excess carriage, will normally be charged as extras to recover their costs. If the job has not been estimated, the completed cost record of the job will be prepared for pricing. This will involve scrutinising the costs and fixing the price in accordance with the policy of the printing company. Historical costs and an analysis of pricing on work of a similar nature will be used as a basis for establishing prices on the jobs before the invoice is prepared and submitted to the customer.

Computerised estimating

2

The process of producing an estimate, or series of related estimates, can be laborious and time-consuming, particularly when even the simplest printed job can be carried out in so many different ways. This can involve different methods of working, different sizes of material and selecting from a variety of machines and operations. The difficulty is compounded by customers regularly requesting estimates that are 'variations on a theme', where permutations based on varying print quantities and format need to be prepared separately, starting from a base estimate involving complex calculations and extensions such as run-ons. Here are some examples of different format permutations, showing variations per product type:

▶ 1000 letterheadings, size A4, printed in (a) two colours, black plus PMS 302, (b) three colours, black plus PMS 302 and 408 and (c) four-colour process.

▶ Letterheadings printed as above, but additionally in a range of different quantities: 500, 1000 and 2000.

▶ 20,000 brochures, size A4, printed throughout in four-colour process, consisting of (a) 32 pages plus cover, (b) 48 pages plus cover and (c) 56 pages plus cover.

▶ Brochures printed as above, but additionally covers matt laminated outside spread only with pocket and gusset on back page.

▶ 100,000 catalogues, size 280mm × 220mm printed 96 pages self-cover in (a) black only, (b) black and one spot colour and (c) four-colour process throughout.

▶ Catalogues printed as above, but 96 pages plus cover, with and without overall gloss UV varnishing on outer spread only.

▶ 10,000 business forms, size 11in deep × 216mm wide, printed black plus two specials on one side, light blue on reverse, consisting of (a) two-part, (b) three-part and (c) four-part sets.

▶ Business forms printed as above, but additionally in a range of different quantities: 5000, 20,000 and 25,000.

▶ 100,000 labels, size 100mm × 200mm wide printed in (a) four-colour process, (b) four-colour process plus one special colour and (c) four-colour process plus two special colours, trimmed flush on guillotine.

▶ Labels printed as above, but die-cut to irregular shape, rather than guillotine trimmed.

▶ 200,000 cartons, to master style D, printed in (a) four-colour process, (b) four-colour process plus one special colour and (c) four-colour process plus two special colours. All plus overall UV varnish one side only.

▶ Cartons printed as above, but additionally in a range of different quantities: 150,000, 300,000 and 500,000.

Print-buying customers are now much more cost-conscious and will request several quotations from a larger number of printers and suppliers. This has increased the number of quotations submitted by a printer without a corresponding increase in print orders. The swift and accurate submission of quotations to customers helps to secure a higher percentage of jobs. A great many potential jobs are lost because the quotation is submitted too late to be considered. Constant pressure is therefore put on printers to turn round quotations quickly and efficiently, often by email or fax, often within an hour and certainly within 12–24 hours of the enquiry being placed. A computerised estimating system helps to address this problem by producing accurate, complex and well-presented quotations with a very quick turnaround. Manual estimating cannot cope with the speed and complexity of modern business requirements.

Advantages

Speed

Computers can calculate at a much faster rate than a manual system. This is especially advantageous with complex quotations.

Ease of operation

Most of the computerised estimating systems are easy to follow after initial training, whereas a manual system normally requires a much higher level of estimating skill.

Accessibility

Once the data is input into the computerised estimating system and the database is created, it can then be accessed by any authorised personnel. Data can be retrieved almost instantaneously when a customer makes an enquiry or raises a query over the telephone, and it can be amended or altered during the telephone call.

Improved uniformity and accuracy

Having several estimators use the same computerised estimating system ensures they will be using the same hourly cost rates and underlying calculations. The problem when estimates are produced manually is that all estimators tend to have their own individual way of thinking. This can result in rates and production speeds being changed often in an unpredictable manner, which makes it difficult for someone else to follow and amend if required. Customers receive inconsistent quotes and records are not always easily available.

Powerful database

Modern computer systems have very large storage capacity with sophisticated and continually improving software, so it is quick and easy to compile estimates, recall estimates and compare them with previous submissions.

Integration

Estimating is no longer a stand-alone function. Apart from accounts, it is often the first management function to be computerised by a printing company. However, as an integrated management information system (MIS) is developed within an organisation, all the major functions, such as sales and marketing, order processing, costing and invoicing, production planning, stock control and financial accounts, can be linked together into one system driven by one master database. This allows the estimator and other 'approved' members of staff to have simple and speedy access to job costs and other information, ensuring the calculation parameters within the system are as up to date and accurate as possible. Then current material and outwork prices, plus availability of stock material, should always be readily to hand.

Some assistance, no replacement

A computerised estimating system is a tool to assist the estimating function, not to replace it. There may be a degree of deskilling in the basic elements of preparing calculations but, overall, computerisation provides an estimator with the opportunity to learn and apply new skills. It is the combination of the competent, technically and commercially aware estimator and the computerised estimating system that enhances and extends the estimating function to a higher level than could ever be achieved by just a manual system. One of the main challenges faced by printing companies before installing a new computerised MIS or estimating system is to plan for as smooth a changeover as possible from the existing system to the new one. Ideally there should be an overlap period when both systems coexist before all the records and data can be transferred to the new system. This transition period will differ from company to company, depending on the complexity of the computer system being installed, the quality of the existing records, and the systems that are being replaced.

Types of system

Computerised estimating systems when first introduced tended to fall into two main groups: off-the-shelf or standard, and bespoke or customised. Off-the-shelf systems normally involve a relatively standard package that only allows minor customising to the preset configurations in the host system. This does not present a problem to most mainstream printers, as most suppliers regularly enhance the features and flexibility of their systems in response to feedback from users. Practically all the currently available systems developed for the printing and print-related areas are modular and allow a certain amount of tailoring to a specific user's needs. Figure 3.1 (page 58) shows how the estimating module fits into a fully configured MIS.

Bespoke systems are written specifically to suit the needs and requirements of a particular organisation. The systems normally streamline the estimating process by presenting the estimator with a greatly simplified and modified estimating operation, based on the existing working practices of the host company or on a new workflow pattern to coincide with a major new development in the company. This could be the introduction of CTP, an on-demand digital printing facility or print facilities management, etc. The bespoke system will generally determine the optimum method of working, presenting various permutations, times and costs of materials. Alternatively the system will be automated to produce a price or series of prices in response to different job specifications and details that are entered into the system.

Increasingly, however, there is a large middle ground where the two systems merge into one. Although printers can simply buy a stand-alone computerised estimating package, especially in the initial stages, the vast majority of estimating systems are bought as part of a MIS, with the estimating module often being the first module installed. A considerable amount of bespoking is now available as most off-the-shelf or standard systems have a range of estimating modules supported by one master MIS.

Sheet-fed and web-fed or reel-fed estimating modules are available covering different printing processes and their variations, such as sheet-fed offset litho, heatset web offset and reel-fed, plus digital and screen printing. Also catered for are general and commercial printing, labels, business forms and direct mail, cartons, digital, on-demand stationery, reprographics, etc. MIS suppliers encourage innovation and system improvement by issuing upgrades on a regular basis. User meetings and regular news-sheets are common ways to keep system users up to date. Internal product development, plus suggestions from printers and user groups, have helped most well-established MIS and computerised estimating systems to develop into very powerful and comprehensive tools.

Outline of a system

A computerised estimating system operates from a database of production and costing information, containing data such as types of operation, prepress activities, presses, production speeds, print finishing operations, hourly cost rates, material cost and ink usage formulae, plus other production, operational and cost-related areas. All this information is made available to the estimator during the estimating process. An instruction manual and/or a computer helpline are available to help the estimator resolve any problems they may encounter. The estimator is guided through the data entry process by on-screen instructions at each stage, and by working from a fully functioning estimating module within a MIS, the estimator will be able to start from existing data in preparing estimates. Three main approaches to computerised estimating are in general use, although most estimators will tend to use all three approaches at some time or other, to suit the type of work, presentation of estimates and/or estimating service required by different customers.

The historical approach

The historical approach builds an archive or history of previous enquiries and jobs. This provides a mechanism to match new enquiries as closely as possible to work already held in the system. Alphanumeric or other types of coding allow the estimator to search in a structured manner, so that estimates can be accessed on a wide range of criteria, including successful, unsuccessful or failed, pending, unused, ready-to-price, product type, title of job, representative and raised between dates. An alphanumeric product code system, which may be adopted by a company, could result in the following example. Product code BA4PCAJ016S represents a brochure (B), finished size A4 (A4), printed four-colour process throughout (PC), on art paper (A), 115gsm (J), 16 pages (016) plus folded, saddle-stitched and trimmed (S).

The template approach

The template approach is based on setting up or constructing a number of 'model' estimates of typical jobs that provide the basis for preparing estimates from typical specifications and enquiries. Apart from creating template estimating data from new data, many printers save existing jobs, in their original form or an amended form, as examples of template estimates.

The scales approach

The scales approach uses reference tables to find the costs of standard products or services. The system is also popular where goods and services are sold mostly on a price list basis, such as book printers, bulk stock form printers, trade printers and printers offering a targeted range of printed products such as on-demand stationery. Scales-based estimating data is often prepared in a spreadsheet form, initially using software such as Microsoft Excel.

Historical plus template

Most computerised estimating systems combine the historical and template approaches. In the early stages of a computerised estimating system, the template approach helps inexperienced estimators to be up and running faster, and it builds their confidence in working with the system. As time progresses, archiving of past jobs tends to become more significant. The scales approach lends itself to pricing work produced on an ongoing basis for a regular customer, e.g. a publisher placing enquiries for magazines or books with a printer to a set format will often be quoted set charges or scales for the work. Examples would be prepress as price per page, with various different components, such as types of file supplied, with and without scanning and make-up, plus printing and binding per 8-, 16- or 32-page section, etc.

Normal sequence of operations

Job description

Customer details are entered or recalled from within the system, with a description of the job created, including dimensions and quantities. Set-up templates of a range of work regularly undertaken by the organisation, or historical estimate details, can be recalled and modified as necessary, if required.

Methods of working

Based on the job details and the suitability and availability of presses to do the job, the system chooses the most economic method of working, such as sheetwork, multiple-image, 16-page or 32-page sections. The estimator has the option to override the method of working chosen by the system, but this will generally happen on just a few specific occasions.

Materials

Paper, board and other relevant materials held in stock are displayed, often based on the chosen method of working. Some computerised estimating systems will calculate the most cost-effective working size relative to available material sizes and printing presses, as well as working out the total cost of the chosen substrates. Ink is calculated from predetermined formulae or entered manually by the estimator, and then extrapolated at the cost per kilogram or using some other appropriate unit.

Prepress

Each of the prepress operations or departments is displayed using the set production records entered in the system, allowing the estimator to override the master data to accommodate specific job differences and complexities. Prepress materials, such as proofing substrates, film and plates are highlighted, amended or agreed as applicable.

Press and machine printing

The range of presses available and their specifications are displayed, including number of units (one-, two- or four-colour, etc.) and sizes with related set-up times for make-ready, wash-up, plate changes, etc. Within the system, speed tables reflect the wide range of running speeds influenced by the length of run, stock to be printed, press type and general quality-related circumstances. Some estimating systems work from preset data, where the calculations are made automatically in the background, presenting the estimator with fully costed subtotals and totals; the estimator can drill down to check and/or amend the parameters set up in the system.

Postpress and print finishing

Because so many variables are associated with postpress operations, estimating systems will often highlight the full range of operations and associated equipment available, or they will only identify the equipment and processes relevant to each particular enquiry or category of work. Either way the estimator works through the operational stages, accessing a wide range of make-ready times, speed tables and related costs, just as with printing.

Outwork

Regular trade and outwork suppliers, with a description of their services and prices, are often set up in the system, giving the estimator easy access through an on-screen display. Costs are normally split into set-up and volume-related costs. This ensures that run-on prices are calculated correctly. When all operational times have been calculated, they are totalled automatically at the current hourly cost rates.

Summary

Summary screens are displayed on the system with subtotals and totals for each department or cost centre. A preset mark-up percentage is often applied, department by department or overall, to arrive at the projected price based on the company's target level. Increasingly, however, total costs are compared against a range of prices, margins and other indices computed to reflect predicted market prices or prices that will yield the projected best available return set by the organisation.

Additional reports

When operated correctly and efficiently, computerised estimating systems generate estimates with a much higher level of information and data, well in excess of anything that can be achieved manually. But this is only part of the savings gained from generating estimates on a computerised MIS. From the data created by the estimator in producing an estimate, there are additional reports and associated documentation generated by the system. Here are some of them:

▶ Quotation letter and shortened quotation details giving summary totals only, which are ideal for quick reference checks and analysis.
▶ Job or works instruction ticket along with other associated order-handling documentation such as materials release slip, purchase orders and acknowledgement of order.
▶ Work plan of each job for production control purposes with operational times and materials requirements.
▶ Analytical reports detailing cost, profit, value added, contribution, etc.
▶ Detailed operational times and costs for each section or department.
▶ Cost and estimate comparisons.

Major benefits   Facilities offered on most computerised estimating systems can include automatic recall of previous estimates by various criteria, including customer's name, type of product, main line of business, market sector, size and number of colours, all of which make it much easier and quicker to estimate and compare similar jobs and repeat jobs. Computerised estimating systems have given the estimating function a much higher profile, changing its significance considerably from being just one of the administrative functions to the major, pivotal role in the control and monitoring processes of management information systems.

Computerised estimating systems have developed a much wider role than merely providing a fast quotation service. The data created in producing an estimate is stored in a database, where it can be manipulated for control and information purposes. For example, representatives' activity can be compared to establish the success rate of quotations to orders. Estimates can also be classified into different categories of work to establish the return from each sector. If the quotation is accepted and becomes an order, it can be tracked through the MIS. As daily production data and material usage are booked through the recording and costing system, an up-to-date record can be maintained as a production control measure, comparing estimated times with actual times, and as a cost control measure, comparing estimated material and outwork costs with actual costs.

Most printing organisations raise estimates through their computerised estimating system, even when orders are placed without a request for a quotation. This is partly to log job details on to the system, so the required job-related documentation can be generated, but also to provide a way to carry out estimate versus job comparison for monitoring and control.

Estimating examples   To assist the appreciation and understanding of computer-generated estimating, screen presentations and other related information have been included, based on the two job enquiries covered by Figure 5.2 (page 86) and boxes 12.1 and 12.2 (pages 294–297), produced on the i.teba SolPrint MIS, pages 18-42 and DDS Accura MIS, pages 43-56.'

CD accompanying this publication   The CD contains information and/or estimate examples covering the two job enquiries in Figure 5.2 (page 86) from the following MIS companies: Accura, Imprint, Optimus, Printpak, Shuttleworth and SolPrint.

FIGURE 2.1 Example of 'Celebrate Print' labels and 'The future of printing MIS' booklets estimate details, consisting of quotation breakdown, quotation letter and screen shots in sequence produced on the i-teba SolPrint MIS

Figure 2.1 comprises the images on pages 18–42

QUOTATION BREAKDOWN

Quote Number	11,856	Estimate Number	12,481/1		Title	Celebrate Print Label			Quote Date	15/12/2003
Customer	46	Test Customer			Contact	Test contact	Tel 999999	Fax 883888		

Quantity	300,000		Title				Printing	Printed 4 process colours plus 2 special colours on the face, plus spot (95% area) gloss seal coating.
Estimator	NEIL		Extent				Binding	Guillotine, pack in cartons
Salesrep	House Account		Trimmed				Delivery	Delivery to one London address.
Account Exec	NEIL		Origination				Extra details	

Customer to supply press-ready PDF file of one-up label to printer'specifications with single image high quality digital colour proof.
Printer to submit multiple-image wet proofs produced from proposed press plates on job stock to the customer for approval before proceeding to print.
one-sided label paper 90gsm

Technical Note			Paper				Price	

Working

Title	Method	Cols	Side	Press	Speed	M/R	Run	Total	Rate	R/O per 1,000
1) label	1 off 2pp - 20 up 1 side only	7/0	1	Speedmaster	8,000	2.43	2.05	4.48	190.00	1.30

Extra ink washup time 1.50 Extra work & turn m/r time 0.00 Extra plate change 0.00

					2.43	2.05	4.48		851.83	1.30

Paper

Title	Name			Size	gsm	Sheets	£/1000	£/Tonne	Tonnes	R/O per 1,000
1) label	one-sided label paper 90gsm			720 x 1,020	90	16,400	£67.00	1,013.68	1.084	3.55
						16,400			1.084	3.55

Price Breakdown

				Dept		% margin	margin	R/O per 1,000
Total Cost		£3,024.89		Paper		10%	£109.88	£1,098.80
Profit/Loss	10.00%	£302.48		Repro		0%	£0.00	£0.00
Selling Price		**£3,327.37**		Printing		0%	£0.00	£851.83
				Finishing		0%	£0.00	£158.90
Gross Profit	9.09%			Outwork		10%	£41.03	£410.32
Markup	10.00%							
Total Value Added	1,599.85							

Printed: 04 March 2004 -SolPrint-

Page 1 of 2

Quote No 11,856 - Celebrate Print Label Quantity 300,000 AIC No 46

Dept A: Paper

Part	Side	Description		Speed	M/R	Run	Qty/Time	Rate	300,000	R/O per 1,000
1) label	1	one-sided label paper 90gsm	W				16,400		1,098.80	3.55
									1,098.80	**3.55**

Dept B: Repro

Part	Side	Description		Speed	M/R	Run	Qty/Time	Rate	300,000	R/O per 1,000
1) label	1	Wet proofs	Subcontract				7	0.03	210.00	
		(7 x wet proofs per colour @ £210.00)								
		Digital Pre-press	Labour	1		6.00	6.00 hrs	20.00	120.00	
		(6 x Enter number of hours)								
		Planning per page	Labour	50		0.04	0.04 hrs	20.00	0.80	
		(2 x Number of Pages)								
		Metal Plates	Labour				0.23 hrs	101.43	23.33	
									354.13	**0.00**

Dept C: Printing

Part	Side	Description		Speed	M/R	Run	Qty/Time	Rate	300,000	R/O per 1,000
1) label	1	Speedmaster	Ink Washups				1.50 hrs	190.00	285.00	
		Speedmaster	Job M/R					0	0.00	
		Speedmaster	Plate M/R				0.93 hrs	190.68	177.33	
		Speedmaster	Run				2.05 hrs	190.00	389.50	1.30
									851.83	**1.30**

Dept D: Finishing

Part	Side	Description		Speed	M/R	Run	Qty/Time	Rate	300,000	R/O per 1,000
1) label	1	Guillotine	Labour			4.30	4.30 hrs	35.00	150.50	0.48
finishing		Cartons	Material				30	3.57	8.40	0.03
									158.90	**0.51**

Dept E: Outwork

Part	Side	Description		Speed	M/R	Run	Qty/Time	Rate	300,000	R/O per 1,000
1) label	1	Ink Cost					7		254.90	0.85
		Metal Plates	Material				7		54.46	
finishing		Delivery	Subcontract				841	8.33	100.96	0.34
		(841 x Delivery @ £100.96)								
									410.32	**1.19**

Print Arena

Caxton House

Bedford Row

London

WC1

Estimate No.   11856/1
Date   01/06/2004

Dear Mr Williamson

We thank you for your recent enquiry and have pleasure in quoting you as follows:-

Title   Celebrate Print Label

Trimmed   190 x 164mm

Origination   Customer to supply press-ready PDF file of one-up label to printer'specifications with single image high
                           quality digital colour proof.
                           Printer to submit multiple-image wet proofs produced from proposed press plates on job stock to the
                           customer for approval before proceeding to print.

Paper   one-sided label paper 90gsm

Printing   Printed 4 process colours plus 2 special colours on the face, plus spot (95% area) gloss seal coating.

Binding   Guillotine, pack in cartons

Delivery   Delivery to one London address.

Extra details

Prices   300,000   £ 3,327.37

Yours sincerely

Neil Nicholson
Commercial Manager

Initial estimate header screen

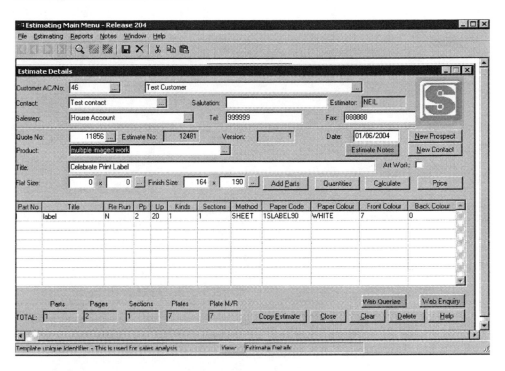

Printing and imposition details: part 1 – label

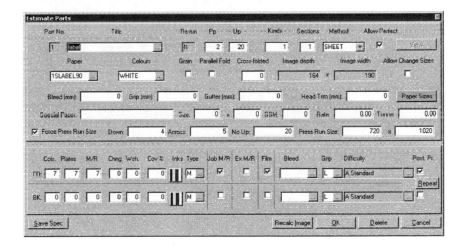

Quantities

Calculations

Prepress, printing and part finishing

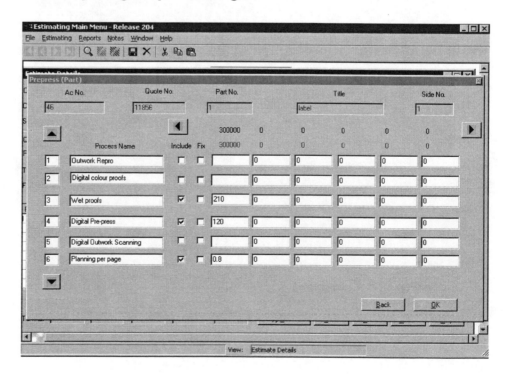

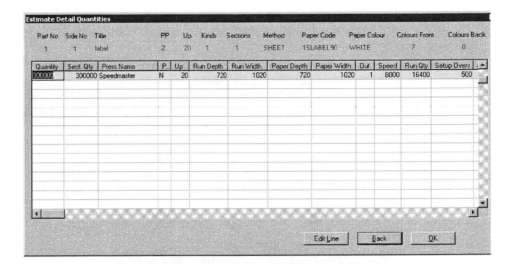

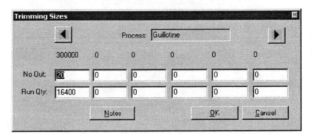

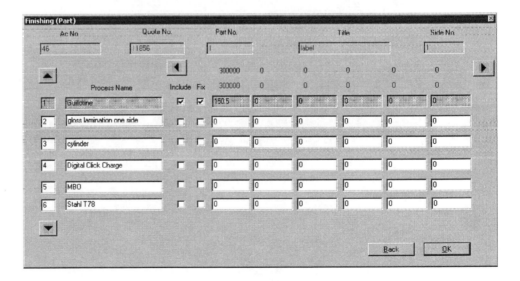

Job finishing

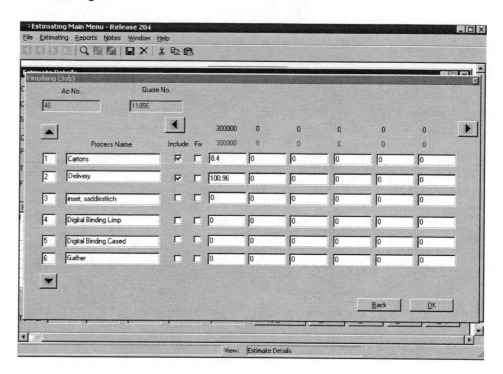

Pricing

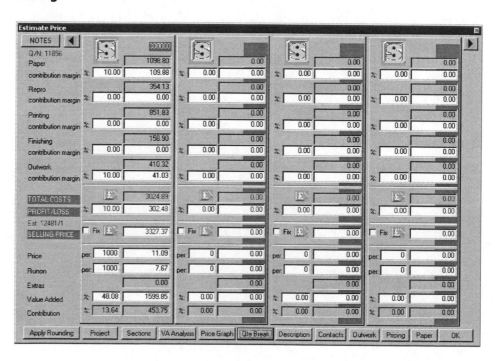

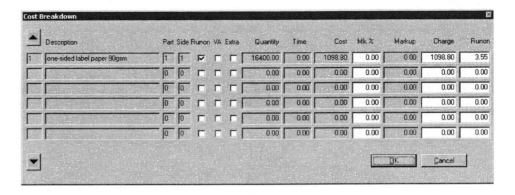

Quotation description text

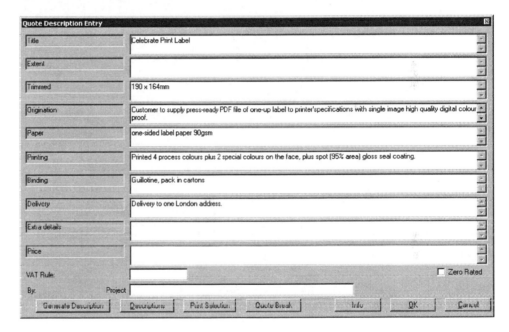

QUOTATION BREAKDOWN

Quote Number	11,855	Estimate Number	12,477/1	Title	'The future of printing MIS' booklet		Quote Date	15/12/2003
Customer	46	Test Customer		Contact	Test contact		Fax	888838

Quantity 5,000

Title

Tel 999999

Printing: cover: Printed 4 process colours throughout, overall seal coated and gloss laminated outside spread only. 8pp text: Printed 4 process colours throughout, plus overall seal coated. 4pp text - 2 kinds: Printed black and one common PMS colour throughout.

Estimator NEIL

Extent 4pp cover / 8pp text / 4pp text - 2 kinds / 297 x 210mm

Binding: Folded, inserted, saddle-stitched and trimmed two wires. Packed in boxes

Salesrep House Account

Account Exec NEIL

Trimmed

Origination Customer to supply press-ready PDF files to the printer's specification with colour laser visual proofs. Printer to supply contract digital colour proofs to the customer for approval before proceeding to print.

Delivery Delivery to one address in London

Extra details

Paper cover: two-sided matt coard board 250gsm / 8pp text: matt coated paper 115gsm / 4pp text - 2 kinds: different coloured uncoated GP 80gsm

Price

Technical Note

Working

Title	Method	Cols	Side	Press	Speed	M/R	Run	Total	Rate	5,000	R/O per 1,000
1) cover	1 off 4pp - 2 up Sheet work	5/5	1	Speedmaster	8,000	1.91	0.40	2.31	191.00	441.34	15.44
			2	Speedmaster	8,000	0.66	0.40	1.06	192.00	203.84	15.44
	Extra ink washup time 1.25 Extra work & turn m/r time 0.00 Extra plate change 0.00										
2) 8pp text	1 off 8pp - 1 up Sheet work	5/5	1	Speedmaster	8,000	0.66	0.72	1.38	192.00	264.41	27.55
			2	Speedmaster	8,000	0.66	0.72	1.38	192.00	264.41	27.55
	Extra ink washup time 0.25 Extra work & turn m/r time 0.00 Extra plate change 0.00										
3) 4pp text - 2 kinds	2 off 4pp - 1 up W/Turn	2/2	1	Speedmaster	0	0.78	0.00	0.78	191.00	148.83	0.00
	Extra ink washup time 0.00 Extra work & turn m/r time 0.00 Extra plate change 0.00										
						4.67	2.24	6.91		1,322.83	85.97

Paper

Title	Name	Size	gsm	Sheets	£/1000	Tonnes	£/Tonne	5,000	R/O per 1,000
1) cover	two-sided matt coard board 250gsm	450 x 640	250	3,250	£60.00	0.234	833.33	195.00	31.80
2) 8pp text	matt coated paper 115gsm	450 x 640	115	5,800	£30.00	0.192	905.80	174.00	31.20
3) 4pp text - 2 kinds	coloured uncoated GP 80gsm	450 x 640	80	5,050	£30.00	0.116	1,302.08	151.50	30.30
				14,100		0.542		520.50	93.30

Printed: 04 March 2004 -SolPrint-

Page 1 of 5

Quote No 11,855 - The future of printing MIS' booklet Quantity 5,000 A/C No

Price Breakdown

Total Cost		£3,549.12
Profit/Loss	10.00%	£354.91
Selling Price		**£3,904.03**
Gross Profit		9.09%
Markup		10.00%
Total Value Added		2,398.26

Dept	% margin	margin	5,000	R/O per 1,000
Paper	10%	£52.05	£520.50	£93.30
Repro	0%	£0.00	£427.97	£0.00
Printing	0%	£0.00	£1,322.83	£85.97
Finishing	0%	£0.00	£311.38	£41.88
Outwork	10%	£83.12	£831.27	£128.91

Printed: 04 March 2004 -SolPrint-

Quote No 11,855 - 'The future of printing MIS' booklet Quantity 5,000 A/C No

Dept A: Paper

Part	Side	Description		Speed	M/R	Run	Qty/Time	Rate	5,000	R/O per 1,000
1) cover	1	two-sided matt coand board 250gsm	w				3.250		195.00	31.80
2) 8pp text	1	matt coated paper 115gsm	w				5.800		174.00	31.20
3) 4pp text - 2 kinds	1	coloured uncoated GP 80gsm	b				5.050		151.50	30.30
									520.50	**93.30**

Dept B: Repro

Part	Side	Description	Speed	M/R	Run	Qty/Time	Rate	5,000	R/O per 1,000
1) cover	1	Digital colour proofs Labour	3		0.66	0.66 hrs	30.00	20.00	
		(2 x digital col proof)							
		Digital colour proofs Material				2	0.10	20.00	
		Digital Pre-press Labour	1		1.00	1.00 hrs	20.00	20.00	
		(1 x Enter number of hours)							
		Planning per page Labour	50		0.08	0.08 hrs	20.00	1.60	
		(4 x Number of Pages)							
		Metal Plates Labour				0.16 hrs	104.13	16.66	
	2	Metal Plates Labour				0.16 hrs	104.13	16.66	
2) 8pp text	1	Digital colour proofs Labour	3		1.33	1.33 hrs	30.00	40.00	
		(4 x digital col proof)							
		Digital colour proofs Material				4	0.10	40.00	
		Digital Pre-press Labour	1		1.00	1.00 hrs	20.00	20.00	
		(1 x Enter number of hours)							
		Planning per page Labour	50		0.16	0.16 hrs	20.00	3.20	
		(8 x Number of Pages)							
		Metal Plates Labour				0.16 hrs	104.13	16.66	
	2	Metal Plates Labour				0.16 hrs	104.13	16.66	
3) 4pp text - 2 kinds	1	Digital colour proofs Labour	3		2.66	2.66 hrs	30.00	80.00	
		(8 x digital col proof)							
		Digital colour proofs Material				8	0.10	80.00	
		Digital Pre-press Labour	1		1.00	1.00 hrs	20.00	20.00	
		(1 x Enter number of hours)							
		Planning per page Labour	50		0.16	0.16 hrs	20.00	3.20	
		(8 x Number of Pages)							
		Metal Plates Labour				0.13 hrs	102.54	13.33	
								427.97	**0.00**

Dept C: Printing

Part	Side	Description	Speed	M/R	Run	Qty/Time	Rate	5,000	R/O per 1,000
1) cover	1	Speedmaster Ink Washups				1.25 hrs	190.00	237.50	
		Speedmaster Job M/R					0	0.00	
		Speedmaster Plate M/R				0.66 hrs	191.91	126.66	

Printed: 04 March 2004 -SolPrint-

Quote No 11,855 - 'The future of printing MIS' booklet Quantity 5,000 A/C No

Part	Side		Description		Speed	M/R	Run	Qty/Time	Rate		R/O per 1,000
		Speedmaster	Run					0.40 hrs	192.95	77.18	15.44
	2	Speedmaster	Plate M/R					0.66 hrs	191.91	126.66	
		Speedmaster	Run					0.40 hrs	192.95	77.18	15.44
2) 8pp text	1	Speedmaster	Job M/R							0.00	
		Speedmaster	Plate M/R					0.66 hrs	191.91	126.66	
		Speedmaster	Run					0.72 hrs	191.32	137.75	27.55
	2	Speedmaster	Plate M/R					0.66 hrs	191.91	126.66	
		Speedmaster	Run					0.72 hrs	191.32	137.75	27.55
3) 4pp text - 2 kinds	1	Speedmaster	Ink Washups					0.25 hrs	190.00	47.50	
		Speedmaster	Job M/R							0.00	
		Speedmaster	Plate M/R					0.53 hrs	191.19	101.33	
		Speedmaster	Run							0.00	
										1,322.83	**85.97**

Dept D: Finishing

Part	Side	Description		Speed	M/R	Run	Qty/Time	Rate		R/O per 1,000
1) cover	1	cylinder	Labour	3,000	0.49	1.67	2.16 hrs	40.00	86.67	13.33
		(5,000 x one score)								
2) 8pp text	1	Stahl T78	Labour	6,018	0.67	0.96	1.63 hrs	40.00	65.22	7.71
		(5,800 x Folding)								
3) 4pp text - 2 kinds	1	Guillotine	Labour	8,003	0.33	0.63	0.45 hrs	35.20	15.84	1.77
		Stahl T52	Labour				0.96 hrs	10.00	9.65	1.26
		(5,050 x Fold)								
finishing		Cartons	Material				50	3.57	14.00	2.80
		inset, saddlestitch	Labour	4,000	0.75	1.25	2.00 hrs	60.00	120.00	15.00
		(5,000 x one up)								
									311.38	**41.88**

Dept E: Outwork

Part	Side	Description		Speed	M/R	Run	Qty/Time	Rate		R/O per 1,000
1) cover	1	Ink Cost					5,000		42.38	8.48
		Metal Plates Material					5		38.90	
		gloss lamination one side	Subcontract				5,000	20.00	250.00	50.00
		(5,000 x 450 x 640 @ £250.00)								
	2	Ink Cost					5		42.38	8.48
		Metal Plates Material					5		38.90	
2) 8pp text	1	Ink Cost					5		75.63	15.13
		Metal Plates Material					5		38.90	
	2	Ink Cost					5		75.63	15.13
		Metal Plates Material					5		38.90	
3) 4pp text - 2 kinds	1	Ink Cost					2		38.78	7.76
		Metal Plates Material					4		31.12	
finishing		Delivery	Subcontract				369	3.33	119.75	23.95
									831.27	**128.91**

Quote No 11,855 - 'The future of printing MIS' booklet Quantity 5,000 A/C No

(399 x Delivery @ £119.75)

Print Arena

Caxton House

Bedford Row

London

WC1

Estimate No.	11857/2
Date	01/06/2004

Dear

We thank you for your recent enquiry and have pleasure in quoting you as follows:-

Title	'The future of printing MIS' booklet
Trimmed	297 x 210mm
Origination	Customer to supply press-ready PDF files to the printer's specification with colour laser visual proofs. Printer to supply contract digital colour proofs to the customer for approval before proceeding to print.
Paper	cover: two-sided matt coard board 250gsm 8pp text: matt coated paper 115gsm 4pp text - 2 kinds: different coloured uncoated GP 80gsm
Printing	cover: Printed 4 process colours throughout, overall seal coated and gloss laminated outside spread only 8pp text: Printed 4 process colours throughout, plus overall seal coated. 4pp text - 2 kinds: Printed black and one common PMS colour throughout.
Binding	Folded, insetted, saddle-stitched and trimmed two wires. Packed in boxes
Delivery	Delivery to one address in London
Extra details	
Prices	5,000 £ 3,904.03 Run on £ 171.75 per 1,000

Yours sincerely

Neil Nicholson
Commercial Manager

Overview of the SolPrint estimating package

The SolPrint Estimating module has been designed to take the user/estimator through the estimate in a logical manner, which emulates the production process for the job being estimated.

After inputting the known detailed information about the job (quantities, sizes, number of colours, materials, etc.), the system first offers the user the option to choose processes in the prepress area before moving on to the press and then finishing operations. This is achieved by presenting the user with a list of installed options for each area, thereby giving them the opportunity to choose which ones are required for the particular job.

It is a 'parts' driven system which allows individual parts of the job to be calculated and recalculated without affecting other parts of the job. This then allows different quantities and processes to be applied to each part of the job. For example, an A4 brochure with a 4pp cover and 8pp text can be considered a two-part job with the cover being Part 1 and the text Part 2. During the estimate this gives the option to apply a gloss laminate to the outer cover without having to apply it to the 8pp text.

In the same way, a bigger than A4 4pp folder with a pocket on page three could be Part 1 and the A4 data sheets which go in the pocket could be designated Part 2. This would allow the estimator to include a larger quantity of data sheets (as the customer may wish to use them on their own without the folder) in the estimate, simply by applying the larger quantity to Part 2, thereby not affecting the required quantity of folders.

At the completion of the estimate, a price screen gives an overview of the estimate costed calculations, and allows the estimator to override any of the prices included as well as the final selling price.

The following screens illustrate the sequence of estimate details in the form of screen shots as presented to the estimator from the specimen Quotation 11857/2, 'The future of printing MIS' booklets.

Initial estimate header screen

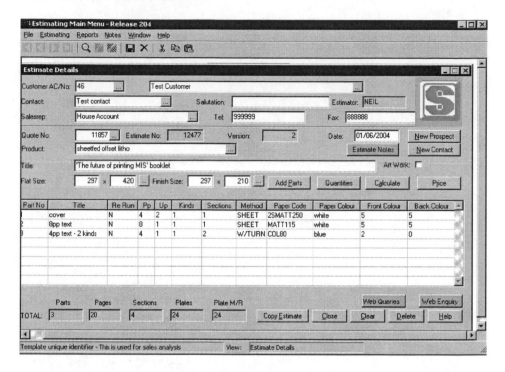

Print and imposition details: part 1 – cover

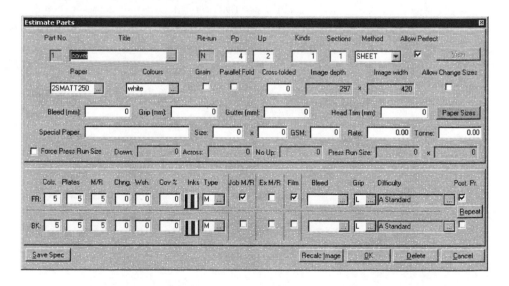

Part 2 – 8pp text

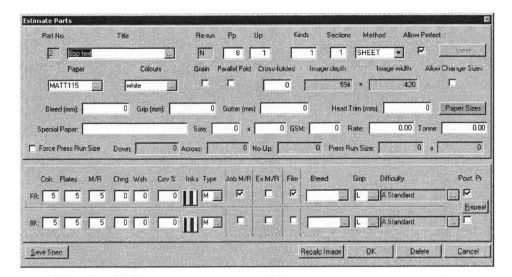

Part 3 – 2 x 4pp text

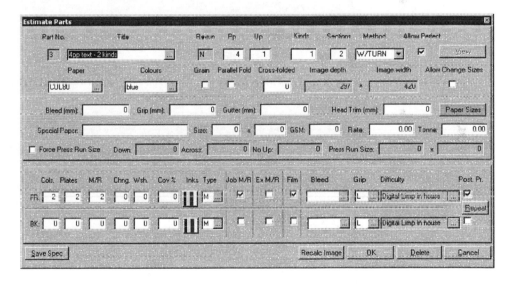

Quantities

Calculations

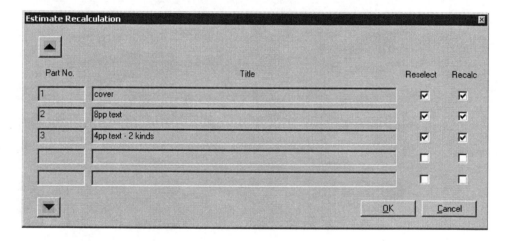

Prepress, printing and part finishing details: part 1

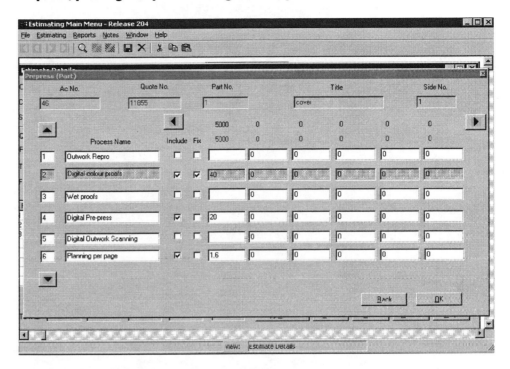

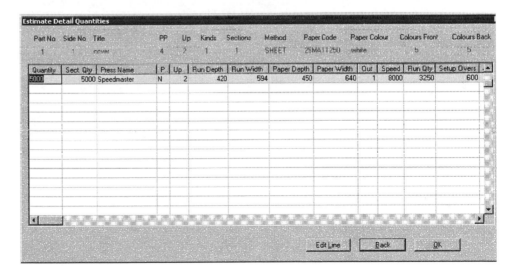

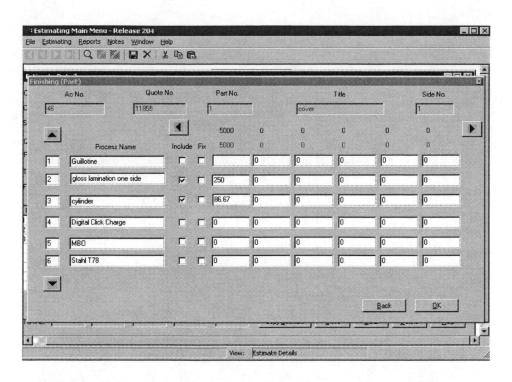

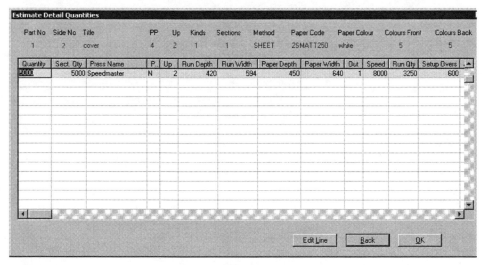

Part 2

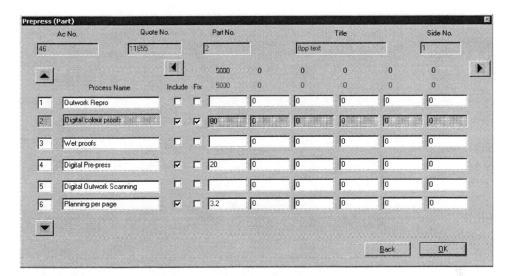

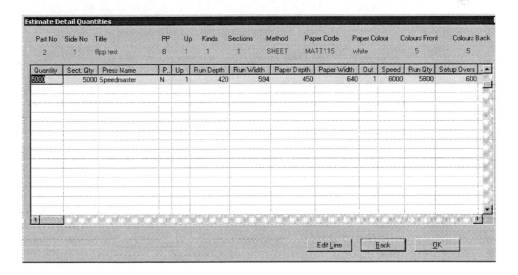

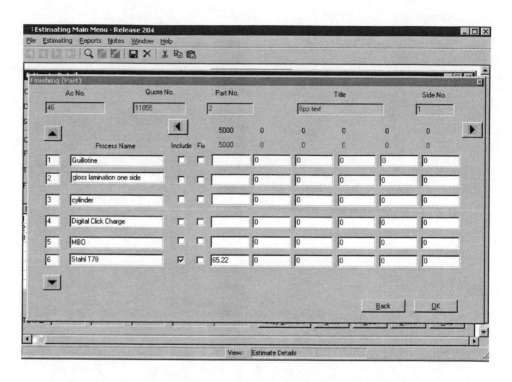

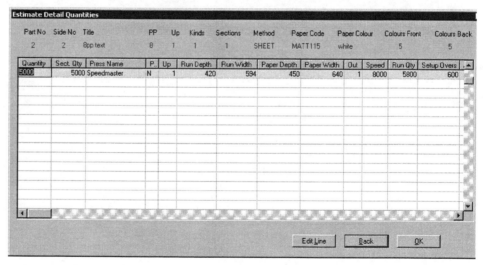

Part 3

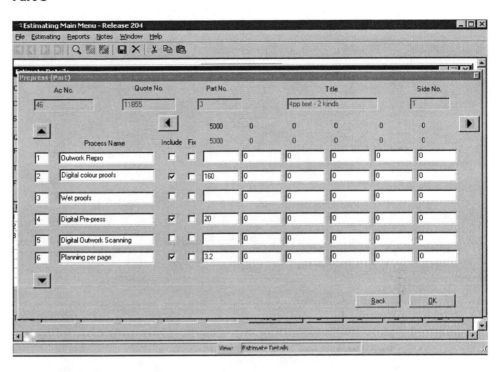

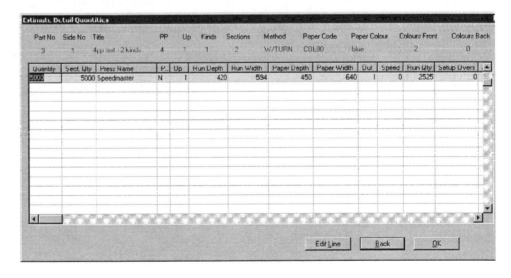

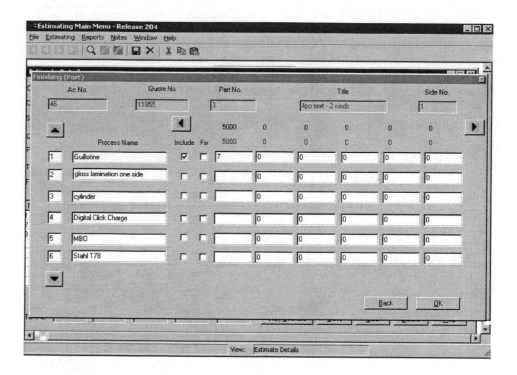

Job finishing

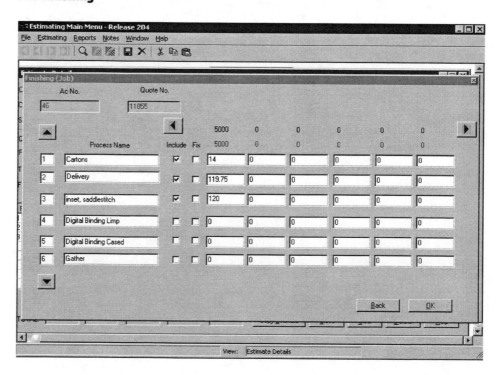

Pricing

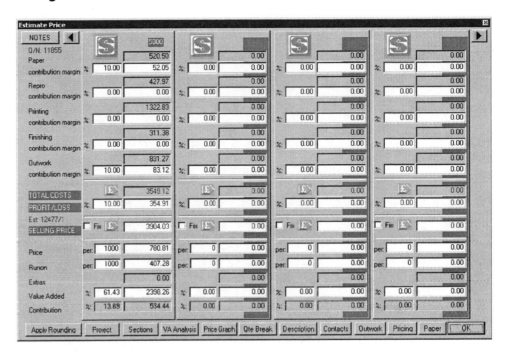

Drill down on paper costs

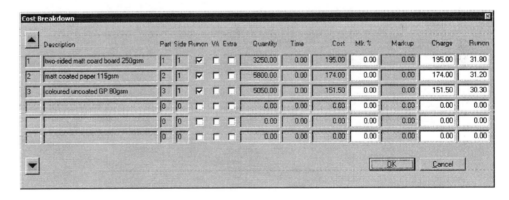

Quotation description text

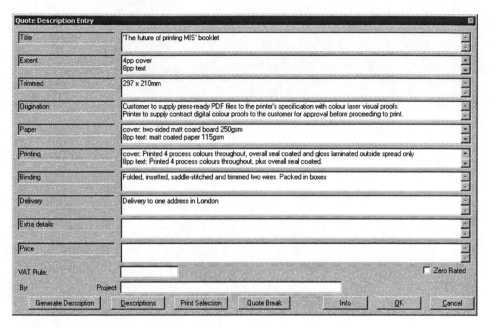

Source: i·teba

FIGURE 2.2 Example of 'Celebrate Print' labels and 'The future of printing MIS' booklets estimate details, consisting of estimate analysis and quotation letter produced on the DDS Accura MIS

Table 2.2 comprises pages 43–56

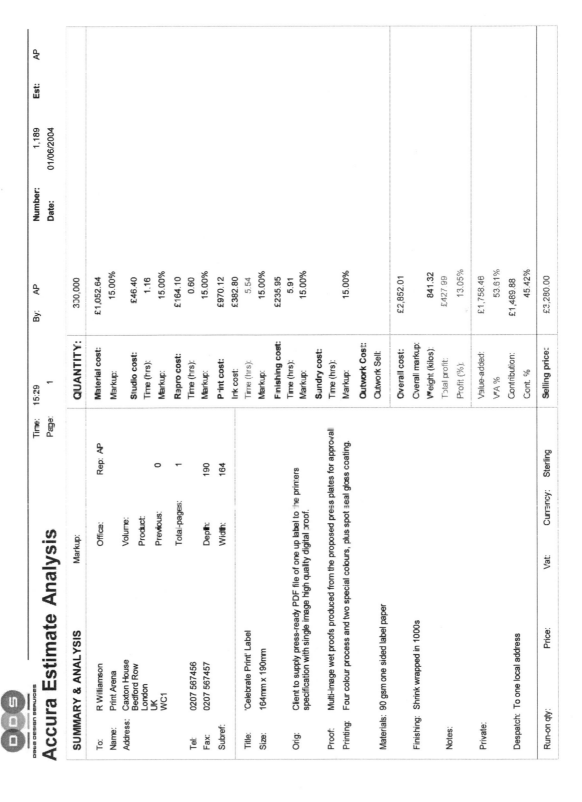

Accura Estimate Analysis		Time:	15:29		By:	AP	Number:	1,189	Est:	AP
		Page:	1				Date:	01/06/2004		

SUMMARY & ANALYSIS Markup:

					QUANTITY:	330,000		
To:	R Williamson	Office:	Rep: AP		**Material cost:**	£1,052.64		
Name:	Print Arena	Volume:			Markup:	15.00%		
Address:	Caxton House	Product:			**Studio cost:**	£46.40		
	Bedford Row	Previous:	0		Time (hrs):	1.16		
	London				Markup:	15.00%		
	UK				**Rapro cost:**	£164.10		
	WC1	Total pages:	1		Time (hrs):	0.60		
Tel:	0207 567456				Markup:	15.00%		
Fax:	0207 567457	Depth:	190		**Print cost:**	£970.12		
Subref:		Width:	164		Ink cost:	£382.80		
					Time (hrs):	5.54		
Title:	'Celebrate Print' Label				Markup:	15.00%		
Size:	164mm x 190mm				**Finishing cost:**	£235.95		
					Time (hrs):	5.91		
Orig:	Client to supply press-ready PDF file of one up label to the printers specification with single image high quality digital proof.				Markup:	15.00%		
					Sundry cost:			
					Time (hrs):			
Proof:	Multi-image wet proofs produced from the proposed press plates for approval				Markup:	15.00%		
Printing:	Four colour process and two special colours, plus spot seal gloss coating.				**Outwork Cost:**			
					Outwork Sell:			
Materials:	90 gsm one sided label paper				**Overall cost:**	£2,852.01		
					Overall markup:			
Finishing:	Shrink wrapped in 1000s				**Weight (kilos):**	841.32		
					Total profit:	£427.99		
Notes:					Profit (%):	13.05%		
					Value-added:	£1,758.46		
Private:					VA %	53.61%		
					Contribution:	£1,489.88		
Despatch: To one local address					Cont. %	45.42%		
Run-on qty:		Price:		Vat:	Currency: Sterling		**Selling price:**	£3,280.00		

Accura Estimate Analysis

Time: 15:29 Page: 2 By: AP Number: 1,189 Date: 1/06/2004 Est: AP

SECTION

Types: 1 Sheet . **QUANTITY:** 300,000

MATERIAL

Code	Depth	Width	Wgt	Supplier	Pages	No.out	Colour
LAB90	720.00	1,020.00	90	PAPER	2	20	White

Label paper 90 gsm

☐ Round to nearest whole unit of: 0

Tool: Qty: 1 Gear 0

Image depth: 190.00
Image width: 164.00
☐ Use standing charge

Overs-profile: LABEL
Qty (no overs): 15,000.00
Overs-qty: 925
Sheet-qty: 15,925.00
Unit-qty: 15,925.00
Rate/1000: £66.10
Per: 1,000.00

TRIMMING

	Pocket	Flap	Imposition
	0	0	Portrait
		No. out (horiz):	5
Size: Depth: 1,020 Width: 720		No. out (vert):	4

Cost: £1,052.64

Weight (kilos): 1,052.58

INKS

Description	Coverage	Face	Reverse	Sq. m/kilo	Rate
Process inks + 2 special colours	15.00%	6	0	350.0000	90.00

☐ Allow ink drying time

Area (sq. m) 1,488.6690
Quantity (kilos) 4.25

PRINTING B1 6 colour

Cols.	Rate	M-readies	Sub-m/r	Washups	Method	No.up	Horiz	Vert.
6	£175.00	6.00	0.00	0.00	S	20	5	4

Cost: £382.80

Press: B16
Running sheets: 15,925
Impressions: 15,925
Speed: 6,261
Hours: 5.54

Options

☐ Plates are supplied on this section	☐ Use standing plate charge
☐ Film is supplied	No.cols: 0
☐ This section should be perfected	☒ Use converting unit
☐ Use on-line numbering	☐ Rewind reel after printing
☐ Use on-line perforating	

Cost: £970.12

PLATES

Plate	Description	Price	Per	Min-charge	Quantity
B1PL	B1 CTP plate	14.35	1	0.00	6

Cost: £86.10

Accura Estimate Analysis

DDS Data Design Services

Time:	15:29	By:	AP	Number:	1,189	Est:	AP
Page:	3			Date:	1/06/2004		

LABOUR

Description	No.up	Group	Per	Cycles	Min.	Method	Quantity		300,000
Pre Flight checking	1	1	1.00	1		Fixed	Quantity/time:	0.50	
							Speed:	1	
					Supplier:		Rate:	£40.0000	
					Lead-time:		**Cost:**	**20.00**	
Planning and final check	1	1	1.00	1		Fixed	Quantity/time:	0.66	
							Speed:	1	
					Supplier:		Rate:	£40.0000	
					Lead-time:		**Cost:**	**26.40**	
Run B1 Film from CTP	1	1	1.00	6		Fixed	Quantity/time:	0.60	
							Speed:	1	
					Supplier:		Rate:	£130.0000	
					Lead-time:		**Cost:**	**78.00**	
B1 makeready	1	1	1.00	6		Fixed	Quantity/time:	3.00	
							Speed:	1	
					Supplier:		Rate:	£175.0000	
					Lead-time:		**Cost:**	**525.00**	
B1 print run	1	1	1.00	1		User	Quantity/time:	2.54	
							Speed:	6,261	
					Supplier:		Rate:	£175.0000	
					Lead-time:		**Cost:**	**445.12**	
Trimming complex	20	1,000	1.00	1		Machine	Quantity/time:	3.91	
							Speed:	4	
					Supplier:		Rate:	£45.0000	
					Lead-time:		**Cost:**	**175.95**	
Shrink wrap	1	1,000	1.00	1	£2.00	Machine	Quantity/time:	2.00	
							Speed:	150	
					Supplier:		Rate:	£30.0000	
					Lead-time:		**Cost:**	**60.00**	

MATERIALS

Description	No.up	Group	Per	Cycles	Min.	Method	Quantity
							300,000

Accura Estimate Analysis

DDS design services

			Time:	15:29		Page:	4
		By: AP	Number: 1,189	Est: AP			
		Date: 1/06/2004					

Label paper 90 gsm 1 1,000.00 1 Variable
Supplier: 1
Lead-time:
Quantity/time: 15,925.00
Speed: 1
Rate: £66.1000
Cost: 1,052.64

Process inks + 2 special colour 1 350.00 1 £5.00 Variable
Supplier: 1
Lead-time:
Quantity/time: 1,488.67
Speed: 1
Rate: £90.0000
Cost: 382.80

B1 CTP plate 1 1.00 1 Fixed
Supplier: 1
Lead-time:
Quantity/time: 6.00
Speed: 1
Rate: £14.3500
Cost: 86.10

Data Design Services Ltd
Lakesbury Mews
Hiltingbury Road
Chandlers Ford
Eastleigh

Data Design Services

Tel: 023 8024 0470
Fax: 023 8025 2573

URGENT ESTIMATE

To:	Print Arena	**From:**	Alan Potter
Attention:	R Williamson	**Date:**	16/03/2004
Fax no:	0207 567457	**Quote ref:**	1,189 / AP

Subject: Re: Your recent enquiry, please accept the following quotation to meet your requirements

Title: 'Celebrate Print' Label

Size/spec: 164mm x 190mm

Origination: Client to supply press-ready PDF file of one up label to the printers specification with single image high quality digital proof.

Proof: Multi-image wet proofs produced from the proposed press plates for approval before printing

Printing: Four colour process and two special colours, plus spot seal gloss coating.

Materials: 90 gsm one sided label paper

Finishing: Shrink wrapped in 1000s

Quantity	Price (£)
300000	3,280.00

Delivery: To one local address

Comments:

Terms: All prices exclude vat (where applicable), are valid for 30 days, and are subject to sight of artwork or disk. Material prices may be subject to change at time of order placement. All orders are placed subject to our terms & conditions, available on request.

I trust our estimate meets with your approval, and look forward to receiving your instructions in due course. If I can be of any further assistance, please do not hesitate to contact me.

Assuring you of our best attention

Alan Potter
Sales Director

Accura Estimate Analysis

				Time:	15:29	By:	AP	Number:	1,188	Est:	AP
		Markup:		Page:	1			Date:	1/06/2004		

SUMMARY & ANALYSIS

		QUANTITY:	5,000
To:	R Williamson		
Name:	Print Arena	Office:	Rep: AP
Address:	Caxton House	Volume:	
	Bedford Row	Product:	
	London	Previous:	0
	UK		
	WC1	Total-pages:	1
Tel:	0207 567456		
Fax:	0207 567457	Depth:	297
Subref:		Width:	210

Title:	The future of printing MIS A4 booklets 16 pages plus cover	
Size:	A4 - 297 x 210	
Orig:	Client to provide Press ready PDF files to the printers specification with colour laser visuals	
Proof:	Digital colour proofs to be provided for approval before printing	
Printing:	Cover printed four colour process throughout plus seal coat 2 kinds of 4 page text printed black and one common PMS colour	
Materials:	Cover - 250gsm matt coated board Inner - 8 pages printed on 115gsm matt coated	
Finishing:	Folded, insetted, saddle stitched and trimmed 2 wire	
Notes:		
Private:		
Despatch:	To one local address	

Material cost:	£522.53	
Markup:	10.00%	
Studio cost:	£240.40	
Time (hrs):	3.16	
Markup:	10.00%	
Repro cost:	£122.40	
Time (hrs):	1.60	
Markup:	10.00%	
Print cost:	£1,942.96	
Ink cost:	£19.52	
Time (hrs):	12.69	
Markup:	10.00%	
Finishing cost:	£15.50	
Time (hrs):	0.52	
Markup:	10.00%	
Sundry cost:	£104.00	
Time (hrs):	5.00	
Markup:	10.00%	
Outwork Cost:	£150.00	
Outwork Sell:	150.00	
Overall cost:	£3,117.31	
Overall markup:		
Weight (kilos):	442.83	
Total profit:	£296.69	
Profit (%):	8.69%	
Value-added:	£2,567.95	
V/A %:	75.22%	
Contribution:	£2,132.19	
Cont. %:	62.45%	

Run-on qty:	Price:	Vat:	Currency:	Sterling
			Selling price:	£3,414.00

Accura Estimate Analysis

DDS
Data Design Services

Time:	15:39	By:	AP	Number:	1,188	Est:	AP
Page:	2			Date:	1/06/2004		

SECTION	Cover		Types:	1	Sheet	**QUANTITY:**	5,000

MATERIAL

Code	Depth	Width	Wgt	Supplier	Pages	No. out	Colour			Covers-profile:	4COLPIR
MATT250	450.00	640.00	250	PAPER	4	2	White			Qty (no overs):	2,500.00

Matt coated 250gsm

					Image depth:	297.00		Covers-qty:	843

☐ Round to nearest whole unit of: 0 Image width: 420.00

Sheet-qty: 3,343.00

Tool:		Qty:	1	Gear	0	☐ Use standing charge	Unit-qty:	3,343.00

Rate/1000: £60.00

TRIMMING

			Pocket	Flap		Imposition		Per:	1,000.00
			0	0		Portrait		**Cost:**	**£200.58**

No. out (horiz): 2

Size:	Depth:	640	Width:	450		No. out (vert):	1	Weight (kilos):	240.70

INKS

Description	Coverage	Face	Reverse	Sq. m/kilo	Rate		Area (sq. m)	125.1017
Process inks	15.00%	4	4	350.0000	15.00		Quantity (kilos)	0.36

☐ Allow ink drying time

Cost: **£5.36**

PRINTING B2 10 colour convertible p

Cols.	Rate	M-readies	Sub-m/r	Washups	Method	No.up	Horiz	Vert	Press	B2
3	£190.00	8.00	0.00	0.00	S	2	2	1	Running sheets	3,343

Impressions: 13,372

┌─ Options ────────────────────────────┐

☐ Plates are supplied on this section	☐ Use standing plate charge		Speed:	6,000
☐ Film is supplied			Hours:	3.83
☐ This section should be perfected	No.cols:	0	**Cost:**	**£727.45**
☐ Use on-line numbering	☒ Use converting unit			
☐ Use on-line perforating	☐ Rewind reel after printing			

└──────────────────────────────────────┘

PLATES

Plate	Description	Price	Per	Min-charge	Quantity		Cost:	£24.00
B2	B2 CTP plate	3.00	1	0.00	8			

Accura Estimate Analysis

Time: 15:29	By: AP	Number: 1,188
Page: 3		Date: 1/06/2004 Est: AP

SECTION Text Types: 1 Sheet

QUANTITY: 5,000

Overs-profile:	4COLPIR
Qty (no overs):	5,000.00
Overs-qty:	1,050
Sheet-qty:	6,050.00
Unit-qty:	6,050.00
Rate/1000	£25.00
Per:	1,000.00

MATERIAL

Code	Depth	Width	Wgt	Supplier	Pages	No.out	Colour
MATT115	450.00	640.00	115	PAPER	8	1	White

Matt coated 115gsm
Image depth: 594.00
Image width: 420.00
Round to nearest whole unit of: 0
Tool: Qty: 1 Gear 0 Use standing charge

Cost: £151.25

TRIMMING

Pocket 0 Flap 0 Imposition Portrait 1
No. out (horiz): 1
No. out (vert): 1

Size: Depth: 640 Width: 450

Weight (kilos): 200.38

INKS

Description	Coverage	Face	Reverse	Sq. m/kilo	Rate
Process inks	15.00%	4	4	350.0000	15.00

Allow ink drying time

Area (sq. m): 226.4031
Quantity (kilos): 0.65

Cost: £9.70

PRINTING B2 10 colour convertible ρ

Cols.	Rate	M-readies	Sub-m/r	Washups	Method	No.up	Horiz	Vert.
3	£190.00	8.00	0.00	0.00	S	1	1	1

Press	B2
Running sheets	6,050
Impressions:	24,200
Speed:	6,001
Hours:	5.63

Cost: £1,070.21

Options
☐ Plates are supplied on this section ☐ Use standing plate charge
☐ Film is supplied
☐ This section should be perfected No.cols: 0
☐ Use on-line numbering ☒ Use converting unit
☐ Use on-line perforating ☐ Rewind reel after printing

PLATES

Plate	Description	Price	Per	Min-charge	Quantity
B2	B2 CTP plate	3.00	1	0.00	8

Cost: £24.00

Accura Estimate Analysis

DDS Design Services

Time: 15:29	By: AP	Number: 1,188
Page: 4		Date: 1/06/2004	Est: AP

SECTION Inner   Types: 2   Sheet

QUANTITY:
Overs-profile:	1COL
Qty (no overs):	5,000.00
Overs-qty:	690
Sheet-qty:	5,690.00
Unit-qty:	5,690.00
Rate/1000:	£30.00
Per:	1,000.00
Cost:	**£170.70**

Quantity: 5,000

MATERIAL

Code	Depth	Width	Wgt	Supplier	Pages	No. out	Colour
ART80C	450.00	640.00	115	PAPER	4	2	White

80gsm coloured paper   Image depth: 297.00   Image width: 420.00

Round to nearest whole unit of: 0

Tool: Qty: 1   Gear 0   Use standing charge

Weight (kilos): 188.45

TRIMMING

Pocket 0   Flap 0   Imposition Portrait

No. out (horiz): 2
No. out (vert): 1

Area (sq. m): 141.9541
Quantity (kilos): 0.41

Size: Depth: 640   Width: 450   Rate 11.00

Cost: £4.46

INKS

Description	Coverage	Face	Reverse	Sq. m/kilo	Rate
Black jobbing ink	10.00%	1	1	350.0000	11.00

Allow ink drying time

Press	SPM4
Running sheets:	5,690
Impressions:	11,380
Speed:	4,500
Hours:	3.23

PRINTING Speedmaster 4 colour

Cols.	Rate	M-readies	Sub-m/r	Washups	Method	No.up	Horiz	Vert.
5	£45.00	2.00	2.00	0.00	S	2	2	1

Cost: £145.30

Options

- Plates are supplied on this section
- Film is supplied
- This section should be perfected
- Use on-line numbering
- Use on-line perforating

- Use standing plate charge
- No.cols: 0
- ☒ Use converting unit
- Rewind reel after printing

PLATES

Plate	Description	Price	Per	Min-charge	Quantity
SMP	Speedmaster plate	5.00	1	0.00	4

Cost: £20.00

Accura Estimate Analysis

Time: 15:29 By: AP Number: 1,188 Est: AP
Page: 5 Date: 1/06/2004

LABOUR

Description	No.up	Group	Per	Cycles	Min.	Method			Quantity
Pre Flight checking	1	1	1.00	1		Fixed	Quantity/time: 0.50 Speed: 1 Rate: £40.0000 **Cost:** 20.00	Supplier: Lead-time:	5,000
Planning and final check	1	1	1.00	1		Fixed	Quantity/time: 0.66 Speed: 1 Rate: £40.0000 **Cost:** 26.40	Supplier: Lead-time:	
4 col high res SRA2 proof	1	1	1.00	4		Fixed	Quantity/time: 1.00 Speed: 1 Rate: £60.0000 **Cost:** 60.00	Supplier: Lead-time:	
4 col high res SRA2 proof	1	1	1.00	4		Fixed	Quantity/time: 1.00 Speed: 1 Rate: £60.0000 **Cost:** 60.00	Supplier: Lead-time:	
RIP, image & check A2 film	1	1	1.00	4		Fixed	Quantity/time: 1.60 Speed: 1 Rate: £29.0000 **Cost:** 46.40	Supplier: Lead-time:	
B2 makeready	1	1	1.00	8		Fixed	Quantity/time: 1.60 Speed: 1 Rate: £190.0000 **Cost:** 304.00	Supplier: Lead-time:	
B2 print run	1	1	1.00	4		User	Quantity/time: 2.23 Speed: 6,000 Rate: £190.0000 **Cost:** 423.45	Supplier: Lead-time:	
B2 makeready	1	1	1.00	8		Fixed	Quantity/time: 1.60 Speed: 1 Rate: £190.0000 **Cost:** 304.00	Supplier: Lead-time:	

DDS Data Design Services

Accura Estimate Analysis

Time: 15.29 By: AP Number: 1,188
Page: 6 Date: 1/06/2004 Est: AP

B2 print run	1	1	1.00	4		User
				Supplier:		Quantity/time: 4.03
				Lead-time:		Speed: 6,001
						Rate: £190.0000
						Cost: 766.21

Speedmaster makeready	1	1	1.00	2		Fixed
				Supplier:		Quantity/time: 0.50
				Lead-time:		Speed: 1
						Rate: £45.0000
						Cost: 22.50

Speedmaster subsequent make	1	1	1.00	2		Fixed
				Supplier:		Quantity/time: 0.20
				Lead-time:		Speed: 1
						Rate: £45.0000
						Cost: 9.00

Speedmaster print run	1	1	1.00	2		User
				Supplier:		Quantity/time: 2.53
				Lead-time:		Speed: 4,500
						Rate: £45.0000
						Cost: 113.80

Trimming simple	1	200	1.00	1		Machine
				Supplier:		Quantity/time: 0.52
				Lead-time:		Speed: 60
						Rate: £30.0000
						Cost: 15.50

Delivery by our van	1	1	1.00	1		User
				Supplier:		Quantity/time: 5.00
				Lead-time:		Speed: 1
						Rate: £20.0000
						Cost: 100.00

MATERIALS

Description	No.up	Group	Per	Cycles	Min.	Method	Quantity
Cromalin SRA2 2 colour	1	1	1.00	1	£1.00	Fixed	5,000
				Supplier:			Quantity/time: 4.00
				Lead-time:			Speed: 1
							Rate: £3.5000
							Cost: 14.00
Cromalin SRA2 4 colour	1	1	1.00	1	£1.00	Fixed	
				Supplier:			Quantity/time: 4.00
				Lead-time:			Speed: 1
							Rate: £15.0000
							Cost: 60.00

Accura Estimate Analysis

					Time:	15:29	By:	AP	Number:	1,188	Est:	
					Page:	7			Date:	1/06/2004		AP

Packing Boxes
1 1 125.00 Fixed
Supplier: 1
Lead-time:
Quantity/time: 20.00
Speed: 1
Rate: £25.0000
Cost: 4.00

Matt coated 250gsm
1 1,000.00 £5.00 Variable
Supplier: 1
Lead-time:
Quantity/time: 3,343.00
Speed: 1
Rate: £60.0000
Cost: 200.58

Process inks
1 350.00 £5.00 Variable
Supplier: 1
Lead-time:
Quantity/time: 125.10
Speed: 1
Rate: £15.0000
Cost: 5.36

B2 CTP plate
1 1.00 £1.00 Fixed
Supplier: 1
Lead-time:
Quantity/time: 8.00
Speed: 1
Rate: £3.0000
Cost: 24.00

Matt coated 115gsm
1 1,000.00 Variable
Supplier: 1
Lead-time:
Quantity/time: 6,050.00
Speed: 1
Rate: £25.0000
Cost: 151.25

Process inks
1 350.00 £5.00 Variable
Supplier: 1
Lead-time:
Quantity/time: 226.40
Speed: 1
Rate: £15.0000
Cost: 9.70

B2 CTP plate
1 1.00 £1.00 Fixed
Supplier: 1
Lead-time:
Quantity/time: 8.00
Speed: 1
Rate: £3.0000
Cost: 24.00

80gsm coloured paper
1 1,000.00 Variable
Supplier: 1
Lead-time:
Quantity/time: 5,690.00
Speed: 1
Rate: £30.0000
Cost: 170.70

Black jobbing ink
1 350.00 Variable
Supplier: 1
Lead-time:
Quantity/time: 141.95
Speed: 1
Rate: £11.0000
Cost: 4.46

DDS Data Design Services

Accura Estimate Analysis

		Time: 15:29	By: AP	Number: 1,188	Est: AP
		Page: 8		Date: 1/06/2004	

Speedmaster plate

No.up	Group	Per		
1	1	1.00		Fixed

Supplier:	Quantity/time:	4.00
	Speed:	1
Lead-time:	Rate:	£5.0000
	Cost:	**20.00**

A2 imagesetter film

No.up	Group	Per		
1	1	1.00		Fixed

Supplier:	Quantity/time:	4.00
	Speed:	1
Lead-time:	Rate:	£2.0000
	Cost:	**8.00**

OUTWORK

Description	No.up	Group	Per	Cycles	Min.	Method
Laminating	1	1	1.00			Adhoc

Supplier: SURLAM	Quantity	5,000
	Quantity/time:	1.00
	Speed	1
Lead-time:	Rate:	£150.0000
	Cost:	**150.00**

Data Design Services Ltd
Lakesbury Mews
Hiltingbury Road
Chandlers Ford
Eastleigh

Data Design services

Tel: 023 8024 0470
Fax: 023 8025 2573

URGENT ESTIMATE

To:	Print Arena	**From:**	Alan Potter
Attention:	R Williamson	**Date:**	1/06/2004
Fax no:	0207 567457	**Quote ref:**	1,188 / AP

Subject: Re: Your recent enquiry, please accept the following quotation to meet your requirements

Title: The future of printing MIS A4 booklets 16 pages plus cover

Size/spec: A4 - 297 x 210

Origination: Client to provide Press ready PDF files to the printers specification with colour laser visuals

Proof: Digital colour proofs to be provided for approval before printing

Printing: Cover printed four colour process throughout plus seal coat
2 kinds of 4 page text printed black and one common PMS colour

Materials: Cover - 250gsm matt coated board
Inner - 8 pages printed on 115gsm matt coated
Inner - 2 kinds of 4 page sections printed on 80gsm uncoated general paper

Finishing: Folded, insetted, saddle stitched and trimmed 2 wire

Quantity	Price (£)
5000	3,414.00

Delivery: To one local address

Comments:

Terms: All prices exclude vat (where applicable), are valid for 30 days, and are subject to sight of artwork or disk. Material prices may be subject to change at time of order placement. All orders are placed subject to our terms & conditions, available on request.

I trust our estimate meets with your approval, and look forward to receiving your instructions in due course. If I can be of any further assistance, please do not hesitate to contact me.

Assuring you of our best attention

Alan Potter
Sales Director

Source: DDS (Data Design Services)

Management information systems

3

Computerised estimating plays a central role in a management information system (MIS); it is continually being developed and improved. Figure 3.1 (overleaf) is a flow diagram of a fully integrated and comprehensive MIS. Once the estimator receives the customer enquiry and related customer details, the information and data created in the system are used to inform, control and manage all functions of the organisation. A MIS is a network of computers linked to an organisation's central database. It is used for recording, accessing, storing, manipulating and processing information, helping all users to work more effectively. All organisations are increasingly bombarded with information. If this information is not carefully harnessed and controlled, the organisation cannot achieve its best performance and will fail to deliver the service its customers now require. Manual and non-integrated systems cannot cope effectively with this information explosion, but a properly functioning MIS can receive, store and analyse information in a constructive and meaningful way.

Main features of a MIS

Computerised

Computers can store vast amounts of information in structured form, calculate at incredibly fast speeds and present data in a wide variety of formats that offer tremendous benefits to all managers. A MIS has all these features.

Integrated

At its most effective, the MIS contains elements that interact and automatically update related data within the system, alleviating the need for multiple inputs and alterations. For example, hourly cost rate changes only need to be updated once, so estimating, costing and accounts departments can be confident they are using the same rates at any moment.

Management information

Management information that is accurate, accessible and concise forms the lifeblood of any organisation. Therefore it needs to be sufficiently extensive and relevant to allow short-term operational and long-term planning decisions to be relied upon. A well-maintained MIS meets these requirements.

Range of functional tasks

Once installed, a MIS should be able to do a wide range of functional tasks, especially those most likely to be required by the organisation that installed it. To meet the extremely fast new developments in web-based communication and business opportunities, MIS companies continually develop and introduce web functionality to their systems.

Recording and monitoring

To gain the maximum benefit of operating a MIS in a modern business environment, information needs to be recorded in real time, i.e. processing information through all the required stages immediately it is available. The most effective means of achieving real-time recording is by introducing electronic links between the production facilities and the MIS. Automatic recording devices are the ideal way, but they are not always possible or practical. If automatic recording is not possible, try to make the recording of time and

FIGURE 3.1 Modular configuration of a MIS illustrating the important and central role played by estimating

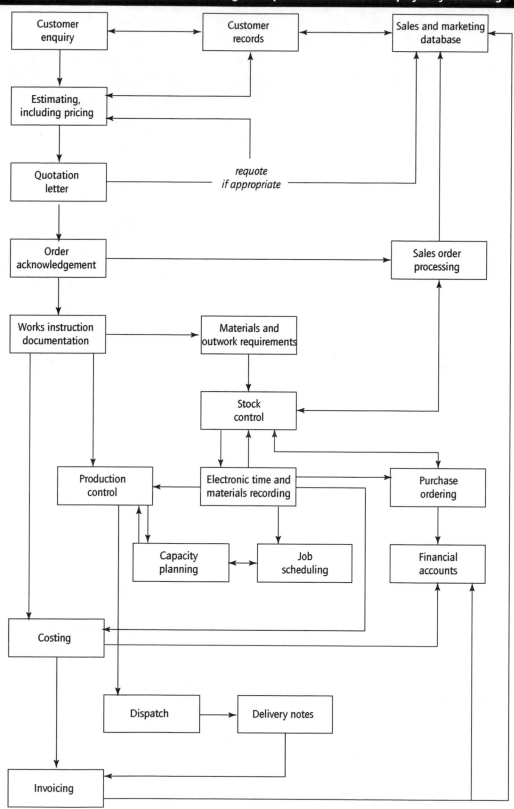

Source: H. M. Speirs

processes as simple as possible to ensure a fast and efficient system with integrity of information.

Very few MIS companies have so far offered direct links to presses, as it requires considerable investment to develop gateways covering the wide range of printing equipment, and up to now there has been relatively little interest from printers. Instead MIS companies offer their own range of interfaces to presses and other equipment, where operators enter production data manually via a keypad hooked up to the host MIS. Alternatively a bar code reader is used as the interface, where the operator swipes the appropriate bar code, initially identifying themselves to the system and then entering the relevant operation and time taken on a particular job, along with the recorded time for production data such as press malfunction, breakdown and substrate problems.

Benefits of operating a MIS

Estimating is not the only function to benefit from a MIS, as against a manual non-integrated system. Other beneficiaries are sales and marketing, administration, production planning and control, and financial and cost control.

Sales and marketing

▶ A MIS identifies markets that produce the best results for the organisation. It analyses previous sales data and breaks it down into different job types and market sectors as required.

▶ A MIS helps to plan sales campaigns by month, by product, by industry sector and by geographical area. Target marketing based on historical data can be easily built up in the system, from inputted data and records.

▶ A MIS can predict several possible prices using different criteria. It can project and identify important criteria and guidelines from the system, such as value added, target mark-up and projected market rate. This tells printing companies how they are performing and ensures the best possible return for the work carried out.

▶ A MIS improves the success rate of estimates through quicker turnaround and ease of access to previous quotation conversion and success rates. Some systems also record customer feedback.

▶ A MIS improves measurement and control of sales, including marketing processes, by providing a wide range of data built up from sales prospects, market research and penetration factors. These statistics can be used to direct and monitor the marketing and sales mix.

Administration

▶ A MIS improves internal communications by having a centralised information store. This increases interaction and feedback as all users work from the same database.

▶ A MIS provides data validation and standardisation, giving tighter control over data. Individuals and departments take much greater care when they enter data as everyone using the MIS relies on its accuracy and conformance to standards.

▶ A MIS enhances customer service by giving wider access and availability of information. Much wider-ranging and higher-quality customer information is available from historical data.

▶ A MIS improves documentation by presenting its information in a consistent way.

▶ A MIS supports quality management systems by implementing disciplined procedures and audit trails. It improves traceability.

▶ A MIS improves efficiency and this leads to long-term time savings. The considerable benefits begin when the system is installed and get larger as more and more data is processed, analysed and acted on.

Production planning

▶ A MIS optimises production resources through improved scheduling of available work. The production scheduling module allows 'what if' scenarios to be investigated and generates lists of jobs that indicate the most effective working methods across a wide range of machines and operations.

▶ A MIS improves control of materials, purchasing and usage by generating documentation and verification systems, including electronic recording of stock receipts, issues, usage and returns.

▶ A MIS uses shop-floor information to give early identification of potential bottlenecks. Production controllers receiving real-time reports can respond quickly to discrepancies between estimated and actual times by rearranging current and future work plans. Forward loading can be spread out much more realistically with real-time reporting.

▶ A MIS improves customer service through better prediction and fulfilment of delivery dates. Up-to-date reporting gives better feedback and control over production activities.

Financial and cost control

▶ A MIS improves credit control through current work-in-progress and debtor information. Bringing together all production, materials, administration and financial data into one common system makes it quicker to establish accurate information on any matter.

▶ A MIS improves collection and analysis of costing and charging. It replaces manual time sheets or daily dockets with electronic means such as keypads and terminals; this improves the data accuracy, the data entry rate and the reconciliation of costing and pricing.

▶ A MIS allows speedier billing, which improves cash flow. It considerably reduces the long delays associated with end-of-month charging. Invoicing can be done at any time on a job once it has been completed and all relevant costs have been booked.

▶ Where there are links to financial ledgers, a MIS eliminates multiple inputs of the same transaction. Ideally it should be able to do all the financial operations required by a printing company within its integrated financial/accounts module or it should link to a compatible financial package.

▶ A MIS improves purchasing and control for materials and outwork as it provides more accurate job requirements forecasting, then monitors and records any stock movements.

Impact on the organisation and its staff

A MIS allows the different functions of an organisation, especially customer services, including estimators and account executives, to work in a much more effective and informed way. This improves the response and service given to the customer. With a fully functioning MIS, the whole is greater than the sum of its parts, i.e. the collective benefit to everyone using the system is greater than the individual inputs of each user.

The information available to each organisational function is invaluable in completing its specific role more effectively, but the two-way flow of data also helps to reveal how all users interact with each other. The ISO 9000 quality assurance standard encourages 'internal customers', where every individual is seen as a link in the quality chain and is responsible for ensuring that their product or service meets the required standard and specification before being passed on to the next part of the chain. This self-supporting aspect of individuals and organisational functions is central to the philosophy of a MIS. Consequently, a MIS can only reach its full potential, if it receives the full cooperation and understanding of all users.

All management and administrative staff, including estimators, and all shop-floor operatives must ensure their recording and inputting of data are correct and accurate – the system is only as good as the data it contains. When using a MIS, the estimator has a much wider and much more crucial role than when working separately to produce manual. As can be seen from Figure 3.1 (page 58), estimating is at the very beginning of all administrative, commercial and management functions, creating the main platform of the database, from which all other functions operate.

Operational stages following the estimate
Pricing

The pricing to be quoted to the customer is calculated and decided on from the estimated costs, anticipated market price and company policy.

Quotation letter

The quotation letter is generated automatically by the system and is generally available in hard copy as a letter or in soft copy as an email.

Order acknowledgement

Order acknowledgement, if required, and job bag or works instruction documents are generated automatically to the required format in hard or soft copy.

Costing, invoicing, dispatch

The initial data for costing, invoicing and dispatch will be partly generated from the estimate or compared with data taken from the estimate. But these details may have to be amended if changes are made to the specification and general instructions when the order is placed.

Purchase ordering

On some MIS the requirements and costs for materials and outwork are linked automatically to stock control and approved suppliers' details. Purchasing procedures are flagged up and automatically generated as directed by the system.

Production control

Production control, linking electronic time and materials recording, job scheduling and capacity planning will use the estimated data such as methods of working and production times to help plan, monitor and control jobs by comparing estimated times and costs with actual times and costs.

Sales, marketing, customer records

Sales order data, sales and marketing data, and customer data will be picked up from estimates and resultant orders to ensure, for example, that any stock-in-hand is allocated automatically, leaving out-of-stock items to be placed on a back order. Based on the data input for the estimate using alphanumeric coding, etc., marketing staff receive an invaluable and current database on types of job, customers and conversion rates from estimates to orders.

Financial accounts

Financial accounts will feed off details generated from costing, invoices and purchase orders, etc., all of which are related to the estimate, if only indirectly.

MIS used by printers

Most of the MIS used by printers are available on a modular basis. The printer initially purchases a selected range of modules – typically estimating, job bag documentation and pricing – and uses them to set up the system before deciding whether to add further modules. Some printers install a complete system with most if not all the available modules. Figure 3.2 is a typical complete MIS used by printers; it shows the integrated nature of the functions or modules from the initial job enquiry to delivery and invoicing.

The main platform of a printers' MIS is the Windows PC, although Apple Mac and Unix are also used. Some systems only offer their system on a PC platform, others PC and Mac, with a few PC, Mac and Unix. No system significantly dominates the UK scene in terms of units sold and maintained. There are a wide range of management information systems serving the UK printing industry, including Accura, Cabbell, EstiMate for Windows, Focus Advantage, Imprint, Optimus 2020, Pecas, EFI/PrintCafe Logic, Prograph and Printsmith, Printcost for Windows, Printpak, Prism Enterprise and Win, Sanderson, Shuttleworth, Solprint and Tharstern. Most systems cover a wide range of print sectors, particularly through different estimating modules, such as sheet, narrow-reel and web-fed offset litho, flexo, screen and repro. Other systems are only suitable for specific areas of the industry.

FIGURE 3.2 EFI/PrintCafe's fully integrated Logic MIS

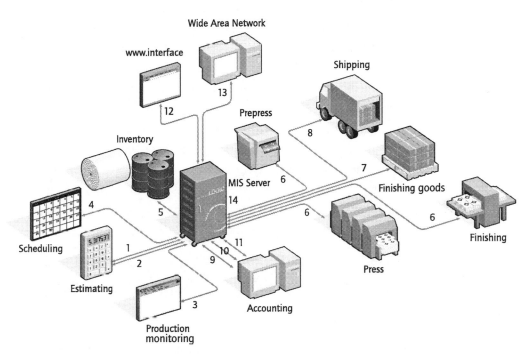

1. Estimating/quoting
2. Production planning
3. Order entry/job tracking
4. Integrated scheduling
5. Inventory management
6. Shop-floor data exchange/ electronic forms
7. Finishing goods inventory/ fulfilment
8. Shipping and receiving
9. Costing/invoicing
10. Purchasing, A/P, G/L
11. Financial reporting
12. Web interface/e-services
13. Multi-company/multi-division
14. Centralised database/ employee, machine & process analysis/ management reporting archives

Source: EFI/PrintCafe

New developments in MIS

Until recently, printers' MIS were predominantly closed, internal systems used mainly for administrative functions such as estimating, job order documentation, costing, pricing and invoicing. This has largely changed over the past few years with the introduction of more feature-rich systems using the latest Windows or Windows-type operating systems. There has also been a shift from the old client/server model to a standard browser client and web server model, allowing remote access, and thereby increasing the functionality and usefulness of the systems for all users.

Management information systems are now being seen as the ideal vehicle to provide effective and mutually beneficial service to printers, print-buying customers and all other parties in the print supply and demand chain. The incorporation of a web browser means that online e-commerce features are now taking MIS to a new level of integration, with a wide sender and user base, passworded as appropriate. Since the boom and bust of many dotcom companies, printers are beginning to reconsider the benefits of online services, particularly alongside the new facilities offered by MIS companies. The level of available services and facilities varies from the simple emailing of enquiries and orders, to controlled access to the printer's MIS, where customers can reorder items, call off stock with automatic billing, access job progress details, etc.

Although the early days of print procurement through a plethora of dotcom companies was certainly not an overwhelming success, the legacy for printers is that many print-buying customers are increasingly demanding the streamlined print-buying processes they were introduced to by the early online services. Consequently, printers have lost considerable business to a layer of online print-based solutions offered by third parties, if not in terms of overall business, certainly in terms of overall profits.

In response, MIS companies have introduced a range of e-commerce or online add-on modules to meet the needs of the printer and the services increasingly being demanded by print-buying customers (Figure 3.3). In 2004 the add-on e-commerce module, or series of modules, are typically installed by printers serving the corporate sector, such as banks, building societies, insurance companies and telecoms. A further expanding area is printers offering or planning to offer print-on-demand services. Owing to the diversity of their

FIGURE 3.3 Range of established modules forming the main core of a MIS, with a selection of add-ons for online e-commerce

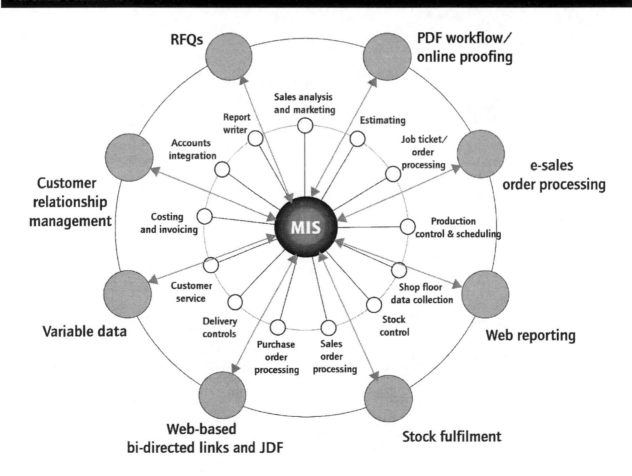

Source: Pira International Ltd

work, general commercial printers have not embraced e-commerce to the same extent, but they are increasingly recognising the importance of online proofing, online quotations and online ordering.

Online e-commerce
modules

Figure 3.3 shows an example of the integration between the inner core of mainstream and established functions and the outer core of web-based functions. Notice the bidirectional links. The inner core contains the functional areas outlined earlier in this chapter. Here is a brief round-up of the outer core. The request-for-quote (RFQ) enables print buyers to raise quote requests, receive pricing details online and place orders. On some systems the product specification entered online is automatically transferred to the host MIS, where complete estimates are generated using the input entered by the customer. The sales price is then automatically sent direct to the website, where the print buyer views the information and places an order, when everything is satisfactory.

FIGURE 3.4 TharsternSQL Customer On-line screen showing menu options and selected RFQs page

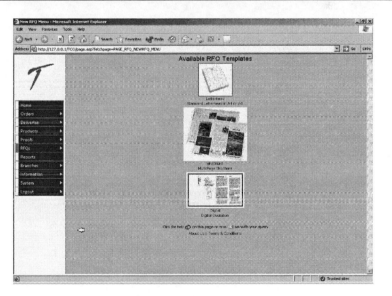

Source: Tharstern

As well as RFQs, PDF workflow and online proofing have become an increasingly popular way to simplify and improve the print-buying process (Figure 3.5, overleaf). PDF is Portable Document Format and a PDF workflow allows for online soft proofing. The print buyer can also use it to place orders by providing the order details and the content of the print job. A preview of the order in PDF will then generally be provided for validation and proofing. Once the order is validated and completed, the job can be created automatically as a print-ready PDF.

FIGURE 3.5 Optimus b2b PDF preview online proofing screenshot

Source: Optimus

E-sales order processing

E-sales order processing is a well-established online facility, offered particularly by digital printers, through the use of mainly template-based printing, covering standard prices and printed products such as stationery, leaflets, folders and booklets in established formats, where the host website is used as a portal for printer and print buyer.

Web reporting

Each report created by the host MIS can be exported to the web for access by customers, remote employees, sales representatives and others with relevant access rights. This allows for all relevant parties to be automatically kept up to date.

Stock fulfilment

Stock fulfilment enables the print buyer to place orders for finished goods and call off stock online. Additional facilities include online access to current stock levels and prices, with orders raised automatically on the MIS.

Web-based links and JDF

To retain the loyalty of current users and to attract new ones, MIS companies must build on their current developments and keep pace with the technological and structural changes in the printing industry. This will mean improving system functionality to satisfy printers and print-buying customers. Job Definition Format (JDF) is a standard based on XML; it is designed to facilitate information interchange between customer and supplier. JDF will become the norm, as will the constant need to follow future standards designed to improve and streamline the print chain and workflow in its widest context.

Variable data

In addition to modules such as e-sales order processing, variable data functionality allows the print-buying customer flexibility to amend and update their copy online, particularly to a range of standard products such as stationery.

Customer management

Customer relationship management (CRM) and customer service modules are growing in popularity as printers seek to streamline and improve the interface between themselves and their customers. CRM often includes swift response and support to a printer's customer base by recording the full history of activities with prospective and current clients. It may also offer tagging of important notes to quotes and jobs for easy identification by production staff, plus automatic linking of relevant communications to prospects and customers, including sales executives' diaries, emails and other activities. Customer service modules will generally enable print buyers to view their estimate and job history records, track active jobs and check the status of proofs and deliveries in real time.

New features for future systems
Customer support

One future driver of MIS development will be a need for tools to help printers become outward-facing and customer-centric, through the faster take-up and implementation of online e-commerce solutions.

JDF compliance

To make the printing cycle more streamlined and integrated, it requires an open standard such as JDF, rather than the present 'islands of technology', i.e. fragmented prepress, press and postpress equipment and processes. Its application, right from when data is first created, used and received by printers, will form the central hub of a user-friendly workflow and communication channel with customers, suppliers and partners. Without an open standard such as JDF, it will be impossible to achieve an integrated and efficient bidirectional workflow combining customer contact and service, administration, management and production, centred across the host MIS.

Increased functionality

The future should see MIS further extend their functionality and take-up of existing facilities that have been underutilised, such as shop-floor data collection and machine monitoring, as real-time production monitoring becomes more crucial in response to the need for greater efficiency controls and keeping customers better informed.

Alliances and partnerships

There is likely to be a reduction in the number of available MIS through takeovers, amalgamations and partnerships with other suppliers in the print chain. This is unlikely to be dramatic, but it could affect funding of R&D required to keep pace with users' aspirations.

Central role in extended workflow

MIS have now established themselves as a major component of a printer's workflow, combining internal and external processes and communications through their web server. As a result, the quality and depth of the information generated and monitored will increase, providing all MIS users with a higher level of information and a better platform for planning and action.

Automated estimating

The main missing link from an efficient e-commerce, online, simple-to-use, integrated workflow, using the MIS as a focal point, is an automated, intelligent estimating system. A user would be able to describe their job in non-technical terms and the system would automatically carry out the calculations. To operate like this, the system would require an automated intelligent engine that would access the required parameters of the printer's MIS, work out the optimum production strategy, cost it and apply a customer-specific mark-up to arrive at a price.

At least some of the MIS companies have been working towards automated estimating for some time. One of the main protagonists is currently Printpak. Printpak users can take their own specific costing data, unintelligible to anyone else, upload it to the network and decide which customers can access it. The chosen customers then use a simple wizard to arrive at a price or series of prices. If the price is agreed, the job details automatically appear in the printer's database, ready to print the job sheet.

The timescale for further development and take-up of online higher-feature facilities and capabilities will be driven by printers and print-buying customers, and this will largely depend on the market sectors where they operate. Certainly the next five to ten years should see significant activity.

Costing and pricing

4

The main task for an estimator is to assess the cost and methods of producing different jobs. Therefore it is essential for the printing company to have a sound cost accountancy system and for the estimator to be familiar with it. The estimator needs at least an understanding of what hourly cost rates are and how they should be applied to different operations and circumstances, along with the costing and pricing policies applied by the company. The main purpose of any costing system is to furnish management and administrative staff with the information they need to achieve company objectives and to provide data for day-to-day monitoring and decision-making.

The most valuable costing information for the estimator is the hourly cost rates and cost recovery rates, along with comparisons between estimated and costed figures on a job-by-job basis and an ongoing basis. The varied composition of the printing industry makes it extremely difficult to choose a single costing system. Traditionally, the printing industry has predominantly used job costing, but in recent years a growing number of companies, especially in specific or targeted market sectors, have adopted more of a marginal costing approach, identifying value added and contribution as key areas in measuring the overall performance of a company.

Marginal costing and job costing

Two costing approaches are most relevant to the printing industry: marginal costing and job or full absorption costing. Marginal costing depends on the distinction between fixed costs and variable costs. Fixed costs do not vary with a company's activity and are incurred even if the company has no work at all. Examples of fixed costs are rent and rates, plus most administrative and management salaries. Variable costs vary with the scale of production and the amount of activity. Examples are direct materials such as paper, board and ink.

Do not confuse marginal costing with pricing at the margin, which is used in the printing industry to mean estimating or pricing jobs very keenly. Here are some of the main occasions when this may occur:

▶ Where costs are trimmed down, when quoting for a very large order with a high contribution value, in an effort to get such a high-volume job against stiff competition from other printers.

▶ Where it is calculated that all overhead and fixed costs are already covered in the work, which is already booked ahead for a particular period. Any additional work completed during this time could in certain circumstances be tightly priced and looked upon as pricing at the margin.

Marginal costing is a particular costing discipline based on the fact that changes in the volume of output result in changes in unit cost. The more units are produced, the more the overheads can be spread. This economies of scale principle is particularly relevant to marginal costing in trying to achieve as large a contribution as possible. When the revenue for a particular job exceeds its variable costs, i.e. the cost of consumables such as paper, board, ink and other direct costs such as outwork, then it is said to make a contribution to the fixed costs or overheads of the business. Absorption or job costing differs from marginal costing in that it concentrates on finding the full absorbed cost of a job by including its variable costs and its proportion of fixed costs.

Most general and jobbing printers find that marginal costing is of limited value to their business, i.e. where it is difficult to determine market prices. But specialist printers operating in a much narrower market sector may adopt the marginal costing system as the most appropriate and suitable to their line of business.

Absorption job costing

In the UK the great majority of printing companies use an absorption job costing system, which is at least loosely based on the British Printing Industries Federation (BPIF) costing system. A brief outline of the system is given below and illustrated in Figure 4.1.

FIGURE 4.1 Flow diagram based on the BPIF costing system

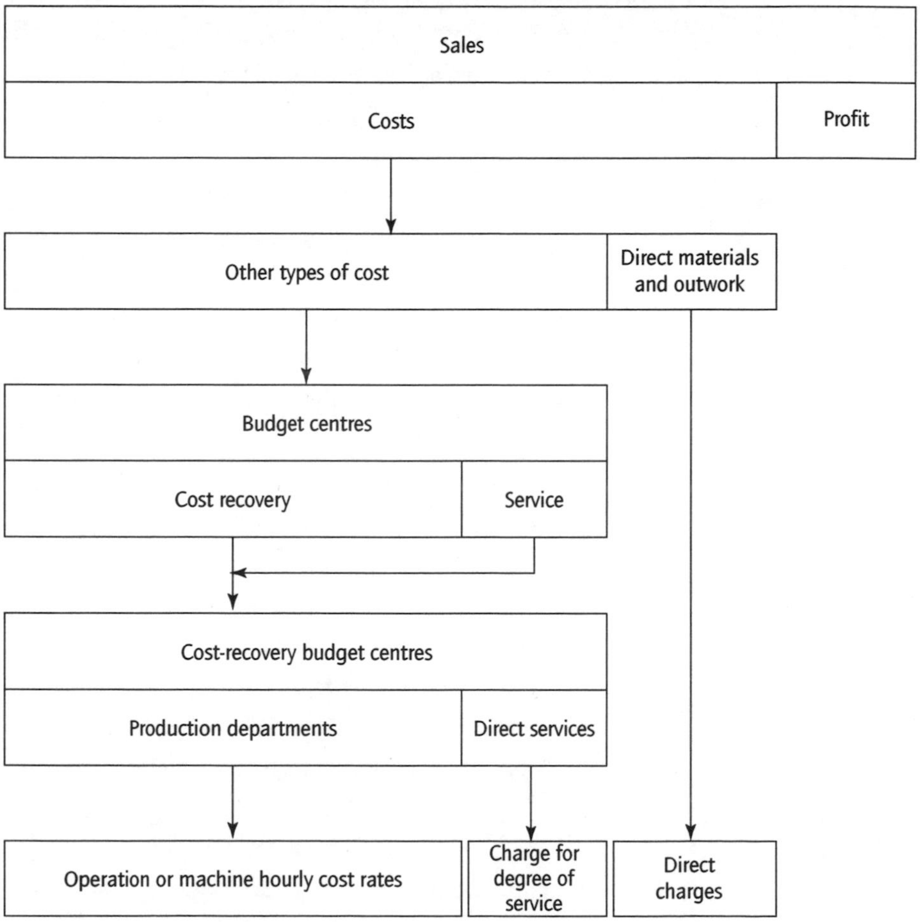

Source: Pira International Ltd

The financial and costing plan

Initially a financial and costing plan is drawn up by the printing company, for a given period ahead, normally a year, including the following areas:

▶ an assessment of the profit or trading position

▶ a forecast of sales

▶ the expected utilisation of factory facilities

▶ assessment of the forecast or planned costs.

An ideal and logical approach to devising the plan is where the sales turnover is projected for the year ahead, with costs controlled so as to yield the required profit. Unfortunately, this approach is unrealistic for most printers as there are normally too many variables. The plan or budget is therefore normally based on the best practical use of the facilities available and the selling effort is directed towards achieving this.

Even in these circumstances an early assessment of the likely demands of regular customers, broken down into different kinds and types of work, will be of great help to management. This will indicate how the sales effort should be directed towards providing a full and balanced use of all facilities during the period ahead. Having a sales and marketing database and historical data on a MIS greatly improves the accuracy of any projections. Various options can then be prepared and considered, highlighting the alternatives available and the probable outcomes of the actions considered.

Budgeting costs

The next part of the plan is to budget costs for the period ahead. Previous expenditure can be a very useful starting point in the budgeting process, but each item must be examined critically to establish whether it was incurred at a reasonable level.

Budget centres

The trading account, the profit and loss account and the balance sheet, plus other records from previous trading years, will reveal figures that help in preparing the budget. They represent the full cost of operating the business in a reasonable and efficient manner. A method now has to be found to relate this cost to budgeted output.

Several operations

Each job may pass through several operations and processes and will make varying demands on the production facilities provided. In addition, certain direct services will be provided by printers, either to aid the production processes or to meet customers' requirements, which can be directly related to jobs. The business is therefore divided into two types of budget centre, production departments and direct services. Here are some examples of production department budget centres:

▶ Prepress, e.g. preflighting, proofing and CTP

▶ Machine printing, e.g. multicolour sheet-fed machines in B2 and B1 sizes

▶ Print finishing, e.g. guillotines, folding machines and automated binding lines.

Here are some examples of direct services budgets:

▶ Materials expenses, e.g. costs relating to storage, handling and provision of raw materials.

▶ Orders received, e.g. administration costs directly related to jobs received.

After the budget centres have been established, find an efficient and effective method of distributing the total budgeted costs. Items of expenditure that can be related directly to individual jobs, e.g. raw materials and outwork, such as laminating, do not need to be distributed. For all other forms of expenditure, find a fair and equitable cost distribution.

It is possible to allocate some items directly to a budget centre, e.g. the wages paid to the operator of a printing press would be allocated to the printing machines budget centre. Other items of expenditure, such as rent and rates must be apportioned to budget centres on an equitable basis, e.g. based on area. Distinguish between allocating and apportioning costs or expenses. Allocation is the allotment or charging of an expense or group of expenses solely to one cost or budget centre. To be able to allocate an expense correctly, it must meet two criteria:

▶ The cost or budget centre must have caused the expense, or that particular part of the expense, to be incurred.

▶ The exact amount and/or cost must be known.

Apportionment is charging a fair share or proportion of an expense or overhead to a cost or budget centre. Bases of apportionment have to be established to distribute the expenses, e.g. rent and rates may be apportioned on the basis of area. After this has been completed, the total forecast cost of each budget centre will have been determined, and the next task is to apportion the total of each service budget centre to the cost recovery budget centres using suitable bases of apportionment.

Calculation of hourly cost rates

Cost recovery rates provide information that is vital to three main functions:

▶ assessing costs for pricing purposes

▶ measuring the recovery of costs for control purposes

▶ managing production and selling resources effectively.

The cost recovery rates in a job-costing system need to be related to a unit of output. For the production processes, time taken at each stage is the obvious basis for relating costs to individual jobs. In calculating these hourly cost rates, production departments are divided into two classes:

▶ Single operation, such as scanning

▶ Multiple operation, such as the pressroom, including sheet-fed and web-fed machines.

With a single operational department, simply divide the total cost by the number of hours for the selected optimum use of the facilities. With multiple operational departments, the situation is more complex. For example, among the presses in the printing machines department there may be small single-colour presses and large multicolour presses. The purchase prices of these machines will be vastly different and the wages paid to their operators will also be very different.

When a fixed asset such as a printing machine is purchased by an organisation, it is really buying so many proposed years of effective service. This will be influenced in many ways:

▶ how much it is used

▶ whether it will operate under single-, double-, treble- or continental-shift working

▶ how it is used

▶ how it is maintained

▶ its construction and the distinct possibility that it may become obsolete before it is physically worn out.

To recover the cost of such a purchase, the organisation must work out an annual depreciation rate that will be charged or set aside for the life of the asset. When the item comes to be replaced, an adequate amount of money will have been created, by the depreciation charges over the period, to buy a similar machine at an appropriate time in the future, if that is considered the correct decision.

It is not possible to relate cost equitably to individual jobs by using cost recovery rates that are simply obtained through dividing the total cost of the department by an optimum number of hours. The technique is therefore to break down these budget centres into several different cost centres – such as individual machines, groups of similar machines and hand operations – and to relate the budgeted costs to these cost centres. The budgeted cost of each cost centre can then be divided by the assumed achievable productive hours.

Basis hours　Production-based employees are normally paid for a set number of hours each week per year, but not all this time can be related to jobs. Each employee will receive annual and statutory holidays and, during each working week, time will be spent in ways that cannot be directly related to jobs. The approach, then, must be to determine the number of direct hours that ought to be achieved at each cost centre, taking account of unavoidable indirect time and holidays.

From the 52 weeks in a year, most printing employees have more than six weeks of holiday, made up of annual holiday and bank holidays. This non productive time must be recovered in the hourly cost rates. Suppose the total holiday per year is six weeks and four days, then the annual cost of any operation or machine would be divided by the remaining 45 weeks and one day, or 45.2 weeks, to find the weekly cost, assuming a five-day working week. Although hourly cost rates are calculated in this way, it is common for essential operations or machines to be staffed throughout the holiday periods, by operators working overtime as cover, or by moving or splitting crews from one machine to another. Here are some examples of indirect, or non-chargeable, time:

▶ Maintenance of machines, including general wash-up

▶ Waiting for any reason, unless this is essential to meet customer requirements. Management using costing information for control purposes as well as for pricing will consider how much indirect time is unavoidable and will set standards for direct, or chargeable, hours on that basis. Another management option is to use the average number of direct hours the company has achieved in the past.

Depending on the circumstances, there are widely differing computations for the range of operations in a printing organisation. Where a steady flow of regular work is expected, such as on printing machines, then 30–32 hours out of a 37.5 hour shift can be a realistic figure, i.e. 80–85% utilisation. But where the workflow can be unpredictable with regular slack periods, such as on the perfect binding line of a magazine printer, then perhaps a weekly average of 20–25 hours per shift can be expected. The number of direct hours achieved from an operation is crucial in the profitability of any organisation. Regularly under-recording on the budgeted figures will lead to under-recovery and loss in a department or operation. Over-recording, i.e. regularly achieving more than the budgeted figure, will lead to a more profitable department and perhaps a readjustment to more competitive hourly cost rates.

Here are some typical examples of cost-absorbing factors used when measuring hourly cost rates:

▶ cost per square metre of space;

▶ cost per £100 of capital employed;

▶ cost per kilowatt-hour consumed by productive facilities;

▶ overall cost per £1 of wages paid;

▶ other areas where adequate records are kept; for example, machine maintenance would allow separate costs to be established for this area.

Example 4.1 The following figures are weekly costs for a printing machine. They are for illustration purposes only.

	£
Area	55.00
Capital	700.00
Power	45.00
Wages (includes employer's National Insurance contribution)	544.00
Maintenance and overheads	456.00
Total	1,800.00

If the machine works only a single shift and there are 32 budgeted direct hours per week, then the hourly cost rate is £1800/32 = £56.25. If the budgeted direct hours per week drop to 30, then the hourly cost rate has to rise to recover the costs; it becomes £1800/30 = £60.00.

Other costs

Direct materials and outwork

Direct material costs such as paper and board are normally recovered by applying a percentage mark-up or handling charge per kilogram, or both, applied to the weight of materials used, including those supplied by customers. Outwork, inks and plates, etc., are normally recovered by adding a percentage handling charge on to the base purchasing price.

Direct services

Direct services, other than direct materials and outwork, are recovered according to the services offered. A system of applying an appropriate charge can be used, for example, to recover an order expense applied on each works order received. The expenses involved in packing and delivering completed jobs can be recovered by a variety of set packing rates depending on circumstances, with delivery charges applied as per set rates or individually as incurred. Without a system of relating costs to activities, it is impossible to estimate the cost of an individual job.

Different costing models

Digital printing is generally costed in a completely different manner to conventional printing processes such as offset litho, mainly due to the different ways conventional and digital printing processes have evolved. Whereas conventional printing processes mainly use hourly cost rates, digital printing processes mainly use click rates and cost per copy to recover the machine printing cost elements of jobs and as a basis for pricing.

Hourly cost rates model

Most printing companies using conventional printing processes have a long tradition of purchasing or at least retaining the use of their major capital assets, such as printing presses, for relatively long periods of time. A particular example is printing presses, which are generally acquired for at least seven, ten or more years. Based on previous experience the equipment at the end of the planned depreciation period or agreement will still generally retain a relatively good trade-in or resale value to the benefit of the printer, if this arrangement was part of the purchase terms.

Although digital printing technology is expanding at an incredibly fast pace, conventional printing processes are at a mature level, giving relative stability to the planned depreciation and use of press equipment. There is also a wide and long-established infrastructure to conventional printing processes, so printers have a very big choice of suppliers for presses and consumables. This includes inks and plates that can be interchanged and used on any generic group of printing presses, such as sheet-fed offset litho, heatset or coldset. Another major difference between conventional printing processes and digital printing is that conventional printing processes vary greatly in their range of net average running speeds between short runs and long runs by as much as 300% variance. Digital printing systems, by contrast, run at a fixed rate regardless of the quantity printed. As a result, the price per copy, in terms of press running time with conventional printing processes, will vary considerably depending on the print quantity. For digital printing it remains the same whatever the print quantity.

These points, coupled with the bespoke and variable nature of conventional printing processes plus the wide variety of printing products and services, mean that conventional printers have found hourly cost rates are the most accurate and appropriate way of costing. But because digital printing presses have a fixed and/or predictable cost structure, they are mainly costed and priced using the click rate and cost per copy model.

Click rate model

Compared with conventional printing, digital printing was established much more recently as a major printing process, during the past 10–20 years. Therefore digital printing is largely in its infancy, and although it is growing at a faster rate than any other printing process, it does not have the stability of the conventional printing processes.

The exceedingly fast rate of change and development of digital printing systems is a dual-edged sword, for manufacturers and for users. This is because increased productivity and quality are taking digital printing to a higher level, but they are quickly making existing equipment out of date, if not obsolete, reducing its competitive life cycle. A further factor is that each type or series of digital printing copier/printers and presses have generally been developed as independent and different from other digital systems with their own specific toner or ink. This is partly to conform to their specific designs and requirements, but also perhaps to protect their market position. Hence the same synergy that exists with the more stable and established conventional printing processes does not exist with digital printing.

Existing digital press users and prospective users are generally reluctant to make an outright purchase of expensive digital printing equipment without a clear picture of its probable competitiveness and capabilities during its life cycle. As a result, although digital printing equipment as a straightforward capital purchase is available on most machines, it is more likely to be acquired on a lease or contract basis for a minimum set period. This is generally over three to five years for colour systems and up to seven years for monochrome systems. Digital press manufacturers and equipment suppliers offer a wide range of available contract options to suit the buyer's requirements on length of contract, projected usage and cost.

Here are the major factors and issues related to digital press contracts, click rates and cost per copy:

▶ finance in the form of capital purchase, lease or rental
▶ choice of RIP, software, add-on inline functions and features
▶ ink or toner
▶ maintenance, service and call-outs.

As most digital press equipment contracts are bespoke to each user's specific requirements and financial considerations, the details of each contract will differ depending on the actual mix of the goods and services covered. The major and central factors to be considered are the length and related costs of the contract, plus the number of copies expected to be produced during this period. From this information it is possible to calculate the cost per copy.

Here are some other factors that have to be considered in the contract mix:

▶ The majority of suppliers now work on a single charge per drum revolution, A4 or A3, creating the click rate per copy, i.e. the price is the same per single revolution of the machine whether the user runs an A3 sheet or an A4 sheet through the machine. Some operate a different charge for A4 and A3 copies.

▶ Most inclusive contracts are structured with a minimum billing arrangement to recover the capital element of the equipment, assuming the user has not separately purchased the equipment. The result of this type of contract is the use of stepped pricing, as in Examples 4.2 and 4.3, where the first band of pricing includes the capital financing of the equipment.

▶ Where the digital printing presses have been purchased, a lower click rate is applied covering, for example, the toner, maintenance and service elements of the contract.

▶ Contracts do not normally allow for carrying forward or balancing usage of machine or number of copies over a period of time such as a year.

Example 4.2 This example illustrates a high-volume contract for a high-speed A3 monochrome copier/printer over a five-year period.

500,000 copies per month, covering financing of the machine, toner, service and maintenance	Click rate at 1p per copy, A4 or A3
500,001 copies and above per month, covering basically toner, service and maintenance	Click rate at 0.55p per copy, A4 or A3

Example 4.3 This example illustrates a high-volume contract for a high-speed SRA3 four-colour copier/printer over a three-year period.

20,000 copies per month, covering financing of the machine, toner, service and maintenance	Click rate at 17p per copy, A4 or A3
20,001 copies and above per month, covering basically toner, service and maintenance	Click rate at 10p per copy, A4 or A3

Costing model for a digital printing printer/copier or press
Step 1

Calculate a separate hourly cost for the operator when the machine is not running, such as set-up, planning jobs and preparatory work.

Step 2

Calculate the full recovery cost of the machine, including all related costs, such as finance, capital lease, ink or toner, maintenance, service and call-outs and operator costs. In addition, other costs such as the machine's share of premises, power and overheads. The total figure should then be divided by the projected number of copies to be generated in a chosen period, such as per year, to arrive at the cost per copy. Previous records of copies produced will normally be used whenever they are available, plus any appropriate adjustment to take account of expected changes in the coming period. Where there are no previous records or experience, it is normal to establish lowest and highest projected figures. From this the risk must be considered between achieving the most economical rate per copy, without falling short of the agreed quantity break, otherwise cost will be incurred for the outstanding number of copies not produced.

Inclusive cost

The inclusive cost per copy is established by adding the result of step 1 to the result of step 2. The costs established in step 1 will often be charged per job, e.g. 5–10min make-ready and set-up per reasonable-sized job at the calculated hourly cost rate, or as a set charge per job. This is illustrated in Table 10.14 (page 248).

Costing and pricing policy

As conventional printing is essentially bespoke in nature, it has traditionally been a cost-plus production-driven industry. However, due to increased product specialisation, the focus has moved at least partly towards a market-driven approach. This changes a printing organisation's approach from being predominantly a passive order taker with fairly standard profit mark-ups, to identifying printing product areas where its equipment and expertise lead to market-sensitive pricing – at a level where higher contributions and profits can be achieved along with more sustained workflow.

If a company adopts a market-driven approach, it will become more aware of opportunities and threats in pursuing a policy of obtaining any type of work as long as it keeps the presses running. This policy often leads to low prices, costing losses and unbalanced resource use, plus expensive overtime and/or expensive outwork charges. To be successful and profitable, besides identifying with its own markets and products, a company needs to identify equally as much with its customers' markets and products, perhaps even more so. If a printing company only sees itself as putting ink on paper, no matter what the potential of the finished item, then it is probably missing opportunities for higher profitability.

Adopting market pricing results in different profit margins, depending on the specific printed product, e.g. labels, magazines, cartons, continuous stationery, with the result that identifying areas of growth and the benefits of specialisation will improve the company's profitability. A planned mix of work is preferable and more predictable than relying on entirely ad hoc orders. A review of a company's cost statement will reveal the type of work previously undertaken, broken down into product types. This will reveal surplus on job costs, also sales total and value added. By actively pursuing a selected policy and a directed approach to customers and product areas that yield the best possible returns, a company can increase its market share in areas which maximise its profitability and use of resources.

If an organisation adopts entirely the full absorption costing approach then cost plus a percentage profit often determines the quoted price, especially in the absence of any further information on the job in question. An estimate is an opinion or forecast of what the job is likely to cost in labour and materials, with the price often fixed by a senior member of management applying company policy on required return, etc. Full absorption costing is often criticised for being relatively inflexible in supposedly recommending a standard mark-up on all jobs and in being unresponsive to market pricing. However, the mark-up can and should be varied to suit the circumstances of each individual job.

Marginal costing separates out fixed and variable costs, encouraging prices to be seen as making a contribution to the company. Once the variable costs have been covered, the balance is set against the fixed costs. Pricing with marginal costing tends to be more flexible, often leading towards specialisation where the higher the volume, the wider the spread of fixed cost recovery. To gauge how a business is performing and to provide a useful means of measurement and target setting, some companies try to establish their break-even point, i.e. where total costs, fixed and variable, equal the achieved level of sales. Any reduction in sales from this basis will result in a loss; conversely, above the break-even point all the contribution is profit.

Value added

Value added is calculated by deducting the cost of direct materials and outwork from sales. It is has become popular in establishing a more cost-effective pricing policy. Value added differentiates between in-company and outwork costs, so as to identify and highlight the extra value of work done within the company. Pricing will then reflect this balance when considering whether it is viable to take on jobs at a certain price level. Suppose the overall possible market price for a job works out at £10,000, including £5500 of outwork and material costs. Then the value added is £4500, or 45%. This is a low percentage value added, leaving only a relatively small contribution with very little room for manoeuvre in price reduction.

Now suppose the overall market price is £10,000, but the material costs are £2500. This time the value added is £7500, or 75%. This is a much higher percentage value added and it allows greater room for price adjustment, emphasising the point that value added is a more positive measure of efficient trading than turnover. It is a sound policy to use value added as a target and guide when assessing the real worth of an enquiry.

Hourly charge rate

Hourly charge rates have become relatively common in recent years, especially where prices are given direct to customers for services such as design and repro work. Hourly charge rates are hourly cost rates with inbuilt mark-ups to reflect the overall return required by the printing company. An hourly cost rate for design at £45.50 with an average 10% mark-up converts to an hourly charge rate of £50.

Estimating and pricing indicators

Computerised estimating allows estimators to calculate estimating and pricing indicators. Estimating is no longer a stand-alone function; it has become part of management control and decision-making. It is easy to store computer data – previous estimates and jobs, information and feedback from customers and representatives, conversion or success rates, and estimated costs versus actual costs – then manipulate it to present management with a wide range of estimating and pricing indicators and performance ratios. It is possible to calculate estimating and pricing indicators during manual estimating, but apart from some simple indicators, it requires too much number crunching to be practical. Once the estimator has completed an estimate up to calculating the full cost of producing the jobs in question, the next process is to price the work. Here are some indicators in regular use for identifying the best or most appropriate return to a printing company based on current circumstances and previously considered parameters and targets.

Estimated price

Estimated price is the calculated price quoted to the customer based on an assessment of the estimated cost/value to the printer and/or the value of the job to the customer.

Estimated percent profit
Estimated percent profit is the percentage allowed for on top of the estimated cost of producing a job.

Mark-up
Mark-up is the uplift applied to certain elements of an enquiry or job; the elements will depend on company policy.

Value added and value added per hour
Value added is calculated by deducting the cost of materials and outwork from the total job costs. Value added per hour is calculated by taking value added and dividing it by the actual number of hours to produce the job.

Contribution and contribution per hour
Contribution is calculated by deducting direct productive wages from value added. Contribution per hour is calculated by taking contribution and dividing it by the actual number of hours to produce the job.

Target
Target is the required return over a period of time. It is often established from the annual budget drawn up by a company.

Target price
The target price is the price that allows the company to achieve its objectives. The target price for one sector of work may be a mark-up of 15% over cost, whereas for another type of work the target price may be a mark-up of 5% over cost.

Target value added and target value added per hour
Target value added and target value added per hour are guides that reflect the required return for a company to meet its objectives. For example, a company may set its target value added per hour at £75.

Predicted price
Predicted price is a price that reflects the average returns recorded for a customer over a previous period of time.

Predicted value added per hour
Predicted value added per hour reflects the average value added per hour recorded for a customer over a previous period of time.

Selected price
Selected price is a price chosen from a combination of specific customers and job types previously submitted or charged.

Selected value added per hour
Selected value added per hour is a value added per hour chosen from a combination of specific customers and job types previously submitted or charged.

Performance and efficiency ratios
The overall performance of any commercial organisation is measured by its profitability; the more efficiently it uses its capital, manpower, equipment and materials, the more it will improve its ability to trade. Although any company or organisation can compare its trading results from year to year using its own profit and loss accounts and balance

sheets, it is a much more meaningful exercise if it is able to compare and contrast its performance on a regular basis with other organisations operating in similar market sectors. A wide range of performance and efficiency ratios help organisations to benchmark themselves. Here are some of the most popular ones; the possible targets are for illustration only. Performance and efficiency ratios can be retrieved from a MIS, just as estimating and pricing indicators are generated through the computerised estimating software.

Sales per head
Sales per head is the gross value of sales, excluding VAT and sale of fixed assets, divided by the number of employees. Possible target £65,000.

Sales per £1 of wages
Sales per £1 of wages is the gross value of sales divided by the total wage bill. Possible target 2.85.

Value added per head
Value added per head is value added divided by the number of employees. Possible target £42,000.

Value added per £1 of wages
Value added per £1 of wages is found by taking value added and dividing by the total wage bill. Possible target 1.85.

Value added as a percentage of sales
Value added as a percentage of sales is found by taking value added, dividing it by sales then multiplying by 100%. Possible target 65%.

Job descriptions and specifications

5

On receiving an enquiry, it is very important to prepare a clear, concise and accurate job description and job specification. Failure to establish the customer's requirements accurately at the beginning of an enquiry can lead to misunderstanding, additional costs to the printer, loss of the job, or worse still, loss of the customer. The more detailed and complete the job specification, the greater the chance for the printer to prepare an accurate and comprehensive quotation and the greater the chance of the job being done to the customer's satisfaction. It is much better for both parties if the estimator receives estimate enquiries by email or in the post instead of verbally; where appropriate, they should be accompanied by a dummy, a layout or a similar type of print sample.

The prepared enquiry with all other relevant details should be checked to ensure a full and clear understanding of the requirements. Figure 5.2 (page 86) shows a typical estimate enquiry for two separate jobs, 'The Future of MIS' booklets and 'Celebrate Print' labels, covered on pages 18-56, also boxes 12.1 and 12.2 (pages 294–297). Figure 2.1 is job 1, 'Celebrate Print' labels produced on the Tharstern SQL v2.0 MIS, and Figure 2.2 is job 2, 'The Future of MIS' booklets produced on the i·teba Solprint MIS. On receipt of such comprehensive details, the estimator will be able to process the enquiry with confidence that the estimate and quotation produced will accurately reflect the customer's requirements. However, there may still be some areas which need further clarification, even allowing for the customer supplying full estimate enquiry details. This is especially true with a new customer. Lack of clarity or conflicting instructions should be noted and raised with the customer where appropriate.

Where there is any doubt about the detail or instructions, it is best practice to refer the unclear items back to the customer or their representative. Do not proceed with the estimate until everything has been made clear. Customers generally welcome the opportunity to discuss and check their job specifications at an early stage of an enquiry. It shows an interest and awareness by the printer and can lead to an excellent working relationship. The customer expects a firm, competitive quotation from a dependable printing company and the printer expects to produce a quality product yielding a satisfactory return.

Setting out the job specification

The style and content of the job description will depend on the organisation and the type of work, but all job descriptions should be clear and consistent. However the estimate enquiry details are presented to the estimator, the details and calculations used to prepare the estimate must be structured so that the data can be entered logically into a computerised estimating system or MIS. The ideal scenario is to have the customer prepare the job descriptions and job specifications in an easily understandable format. Figure 5.1, overleaf, is an example of an enquiry form used for recording job description and job specification details. A list of the major areas to cover when establishing job specifications is given on page 85. Figure 5.2 (page 86) is an example of a typical estimate enquiry received from a customer. Modifications to the customer's specifications could produce considerable cost savings, so always be alert to submitting alternative specifications that would lower the overall job cost and/or improve the job quality.

FIGURE 5.1 Example enquiry form

Enquiry form

Customer: Account no.

Contact name:

Address:

Job title:

Quantity/run-on:

Size flat/folded:

Description/print details:

Paper/board:

Ink colours:

Finishing details:

Estimate no.

Date estimate required by:

Price quoted:

Company rep:

Fax/phone/letter/email:

Date:

Customer tel:

Customer fax:

Customer email:

Sample attached: Yes/No   Job previously printed for this client: Yes/No   Enquiry previously quoted for: Yes/No

Previous job/quote refs where applicable:

Origination:

We to create, scan and make up from the following details/instructions and details as attached:

Word files supplied _   Quark XPress files supplied _   Press-ready PDF files supplied _

Details:

Proofs required – type and number:

Date proofs required: Sent by: Soft proofs/email _____   Fax _____   Post _   Rep _

Printing process and details: Litho _____   Digital _____   Outwork _____

Details:

Finishing details:

Outwork details:

Delivery details:

Special instructions/comments:

Price required by: Email _____   Phone _____   Fax _____   Post _____   Rep _____   Production schedule Yes/No

Source: Pira international Ltd

Job specification details	▶	Customer's name and address.
	▶	Enquiry details for reference: by representative, email, telephone, fax and letter.
	▶	Date received and allocated estimate number.
	▶	Previous job numbers or enquiries, where applicable.
	▶	Job title for identification and reference.
	▶	Page size, e.g. 297mm × 210mm.
	▶	Extent, e.g. 128 pages plus cover.
	▶	Technical specification: outlining prepress, press, postpress and material usage as follows.

We, the printer, to plan and make plates from print-ready PDFs prepared in line with our specification and instructions. Job title: 'Printing in the 21st Century' brochure, size 297mm × 210mm, 64 pages self-cover printed throughout in four-colour process on 100gsm silk coated paper. Folded sections, insetted, saddle-stitched two wires and trimmed flush to size. Shrink-wrapped in 100s and delivered to one address in central London.

▶ Quantity: state the total quantity or the range of quantities requested, plus run-on and run-back copies.

▶ Pagination: itemise any changes to the set pagination of 64 pages text and resultant price adjustments, such as plus or minus a four-page or eight-page section.

▶ Material: state whether paper and board prices are inclusive in production prices or quoted as a separate item. If the material is to be supplied by the customer, then the size, type, grammage and quantity, including specified overs, have to be stated, as well as delivery dates and handling instructions. For example, ream-wrapped, bulk-packed on pallets not exceeding 1000kg.

FIGURE 5.2 Example estimate enquiry

Estimate enquiry

Email/fax message from:

Ref no. 4321   Date: 4 06 2004

Word attachment/number of pages: 1

Creative Design & Print Ltd

Baskerville House

122 Hillside Road

Mansewood

Glasgow G43 1BU

Attention of:

Jonathan G. MacNeill, Commercial Manager

MSPrint Ltd

Reply required by: Friday 18 06 2004

Job descriptions

Please supply price(s) based on the following details.

Job 1: 5000 copies 'The Future of Printing MIS' booklets, size 297mm × 210mm, 16 pages plus cover, printed sheet-fed offset litho. Cover printed four-colour process throughout on two-sided matt coated board 250gsm, overall seal-coated and gloss-laminated on outside spread only. Eight pages of text printed throughout in four-colour process on matt coated paper 115gsm, plus overall seal-coated. Two kinds of four pages of text printed black and one common PMS colour on different coloured uncoated general printing paper 80gsm, with light text and tint-based ink coverage. Product folded, insetted, saddle-stitched and trimmed two wires. Packed in boxes and delivered to one address in London. We to supply press-ready PDF files to your specifications with colour laser visual proofs. Printer to submit contract digital colour proofs for approval before proceeding to print.

Job 2: 300,000 labels 'Celebrate Print', size 164mm × 190mm (long grain), trimmed to bleed, printed sheet-fed offset litho one side only in four-colour process and two special colours, plus spot (95% area) gloss seal coating on 90gsm one-sided label paper. We to supply press-ready PDF file of 1-up label to your specifications with single-image high-quality digital colour proof. Printer to submit multiple-image wet proofs produced from proposed press plates on job stock for approval before proceeding to print.

Source: Pira international Ltd

Data exchange and workflows

Here are some of the major issues and developments affecting prepress and the interchange of data between the different parties in the print supply chain, and with major implications for the time taken, hence costs, to complete the different stages of a job.

Data exchange formats

PostScript PostScript is used almost universally in printing, so PostScript-based workflows have proved to be a highly popular choice. As the de facto standard page description language, PostScript is used in all areas of digital print preparation. The open and accessible nature of PostScript is one of its great advantages, but flexibility is one of its main disadvantages. This is due to the inconsistency and unpredictability in how PostScript is interpreted by the wide range of available DTP applications and raster image processors (RIPs). The adoption of the rip once, output many (ROOM) approach helps to overcome this problem as the interpretation of PostScript into a raster file is split into two stages: production of the master RIP data then device-specific bitmap for output requirements. By adopting the ROOM approach, the same rasterised file is used to generate proofs as well as to drive the final output device such as computer-to-press or computer-to-print.

PDF PostScript files are converted to PDF mainly by Adobe's Acrobat Distiller; Acrobat Reader, the other part of the Acrobat software, is used to read or view the PDF files. PDF is a very secure and compact, but flexible, file format. Device independent, it is increasingly used in a wide range of multimedia options. It is a much more compressed and efficient file format than PostScript. Distiller creates PDF files by printing to a PostScript driver, or virtual printer, then distilling into PDF. Many of the established software packages such as Quark XPress, InDesign and PageMaker can print to PDF. PDF is used as a means of converting a file by turning the data into a digital file that can be viewed and printed out by anyone, even though they may not have access to the application software, fonts or graphics from which the file was originally created.

But as with PostScript, flexibility can cause problems. PDF files created by different parties initially for their own internal use often need correcting and/or amending by the receiver, such as the service bureau, repro company or printer, to suit their specific requirements. As a result, the receivers of the digital data often supply their customers with a guide on how to create PDF files, along with a copy of their printer drivers and/or settings to streamline the process and ensure uniformity to an agreed standard. Now that PDFs have a central role in workflow solutions, they can be created from a range of supplier equipment and processes.

Proprietary Dedicated proprietary systems and workflows tend to lock users into a closed environment, making them reliant on a single supplier or system; this is the main disadvantage. Besides that, there is generally the high cost of the system, along with support and maintenance. The main advantage of a proprietary system is the use of a secure workflow developed and constructed for a specific purpose and outcome. Proprietary systems tend now to be mainly used for very specific areas and applications such as CADCAM (computer-aided design, computer-aided manufacture), plus production areas with special features such as security printing, complex full-colour work, and complex work with many features and a high graphics content. Most proprietary systems now have import/export interfaces, since no workflow can really survive for very long unless it can integrate with the major systems in general use. To accelerate this trend, software is now becoming available to open up the closed environment of proprietary systems.

TIFF TIFF is an open but proprietary standard developed jointly by Aldus and Microsoft for importing scanned data into DTP software. TIFF files do not depend on any specific software or hardware. The TIFF data is interpreted by the relevant software through the tags used to identify them, hence the name TIFF, Tagged Image File Format.

TIFF/IT TIFF/IT is an open file format specification with ISO standard specification. A TIFF/IT workflow integrates into any existing PostScript-compatible workflow. It avoids the interpretation inconsistency of PostScript but results in very large files, creating a trade-off between large file sizes with high resolution and smaller file sizes with lower resolution. TIFF/IT produces good quality predictable data, where only screening and other output-specific requirements need to be added before final output. It is also reliable and predictable – the proof always matches the final output.

Workflow developments

With the move towards more extensive and integrated workflows, along with the development of Job Definition Format (JDF) and the International Cooperation for the Integration of Processes in Prepress, Press and Postpress (CIP4), the number of operations and stages in a typical comprehensive workflow has grown considerably. To this end, efficient, well-planned and well-constructed workflows are assuming a greater and more central importance.

JDF JDF is the new open standard based on Extensible Markup Language (XML) that is increasingly being adopted by a wide range of organisations and users when creating and exchanging data as it provides a universal interface between incompatible systems. A feature of XML is that once data is marked up and saved in XML, it can be reused and repurposed in a wide range of multimedia options such as digital print, e-books and websites.

JDF increases workflow automation by creating a digital job bag that contains the information and data to control a print job from start to finish. It acts as a universal electronic job ticket that can describe a print job in all its stages. Many manufacturers and developers are now committed to developing an interface between their own code and JDF, thereby supporting a universal standard for exchanging production data between JDF-compliant systems. However, as JDF is extensible, it is inevitable that, at least in the relatively early stages, some manufacturers and developers will come up with JDF variants, causing possible conflicts and inconsistencies.

JDF has been called the 'missing link' in workflow systems, enabling disparate elements of the printing process to communicate with each other and creating a fully compatible system that includes prepress, press, postpress plus MIS and print buying.

CIP4 CIP4 is an international standards body based in Switzerland. Its main purpose is to develop and encourage digital standards and links between all users and suppliers in the print chain. Its predecessor, CIP3, covered the three Ps – prepress, press, postpress – and developed the Print Production Format (PPF) that includes the benefits of once-only data acquisition including administrative and job set-up data, preview images for each colour separation to facilitate presetting of the ink zones on the printing press, transfer functions, colour and density measuring information, register mark, cutting data and folding procedures. In addition, specific data can store application- or vendor-specific information, e.g. machine settings for repeat jobs.

CIP4 has added the fourth P of processes as it extends its activities to develop and promote vendor-independent standards for the graphic arts industry such as JDF. As more and more administrative, management and production operations are created, controlled and operated from an increasingly digital platform, including e-commerce and MIS, there is an ever greater need to develop links between all players in the printing chain without having to repurpose the data in different formats to suit different applications or standards. The ultimate objective is a fully automated and integrated workflow. To this end, JDF has been designed to include a detailed description of the creative, prepress, press, postpress and delivery processes associated with any job, and Job Management Format (JMF) has been developed as a communications standard for production machinery.

The integration of CIP3, CIP4 and MIS has been slow to take off, although it has the potential to create a very effective and streamlined workflow. A likely pattern in the future will be where the MIS identifies the most cost-effective job route and generates the control data then JMF ensures it is followed in the most efficient manner.

Points to note on job specifications

Prepress

Prepress is a very complex area as a wide range of materials are supplied to printers and/or prepared by printers in digital, mixed-media and analogue forms, so most printers issue comprehensive instructions and information on how prepress material should be supplied. Customers, prepress service suppliers such as repro companies and printers incur extra costs unless all prepress instructions are followed and all material exchanged between parties is prepared to an agreed specification and format.

Printing processes, inks and varnishes

Clearly state the printing processes and ink colours to be used. This will include deviation from normal trade practice, such as non-process colours, specials, metallic inks or overall coatings and varnishes, which will involve additional work and extra wash-ups, incurring extra costs.

Print finishing   Specify how the job is to be finished. For example, a bound publication may be saddle-stitched, perfect bound, slotted, notched, edition case bound, thread sewn, comb or spiral wire bound, etc.

Packing   Specify how the job is to be packed. For example, in cartons, shrink-wrapped, individually wrapped for mailing or bulk packed.

Carriage   State delivery arrangements. For example, ex works, bulk to one address, or dispatched as per dispatch list to various addresses.

Terms   State company policy. For example, net monthly or 30 days from date of invoice.

Extras   There should always be a clear understanding of what potential extras may appear on the final invoice. This is often an area of contention between printer and customer since it falls outside the agreed specification as understood by the estimator and reflected in the quotation submitted by the printer. Here are the most common extras to be charged:

▶ Files and/or other material not supplied to specification; an example is word processing files supplied instead of press-ready PDFs.

▶ Extra proofs, where the customer has requested proofs beyond those quoted for.

▶ Additional deliveries, where further instructions are received which include expedited and extra delivery destinations.

▶ Materials supplied by the publisher or customer, including paper and board; extra costs may be incurred to cover a materials shortfall if insufficient materials are supplied.

▶ Film supplied not as quoted; perhaps unplanned film is supplied instead of plate-ready one-piece film.

▶ Author's corrections and amendments made on the files supplied.

▶ Additional services to quotation such as mailing and postal charges.

▶ Premium rates, such as for overtime caused by late approval of proofs.

Any costs that are extra to the quotation should, where possible, be agreed with the customer before production of the job or before the process incurring the extra. The invoice submitted for each job should be based on the quotation submitted to the customer; departures from the quotation should be clearly itemised. Extra costs should only be charged when the customer has deviated from the original specification and/or production schedule. When the printer deviates from the agreed plan to suit their own working arrangements and incurs extra costs, then the printer should absorb these costs and should not pass them on to the customer.

Penalty clauses   Printers working on time-critical items, such as periodicals or publicity for a new product launch, may incur a penalty for late delivery. Printers accepting this kind of work must be sure they can do the job on time and must be certain the customer will take responsibility for customer delays.

Normal estimating procedure

1. Create a full job description or specification from the information and detail supplied.
2. Decide on the method of working, e.g. multiple-image working, sheetwork, half-sheetwork, 16-page, 32-page sections, etc. This quickly establishes whether the enquiry is suited to the company's processes and equipment, perhaps by comparing sheet-fed to web offset, offset litho to screen printing, heatset web offset to gravure, sheet-fed to reel-fed, and so on.
3. Calculate the size, quantity and costs of paper and board. Include materials-handling expenses.
4. Calculate the ink quantities required and any related costs.
5. Estimate the times and costs for each operation, along with any directly chargeable items such as proofs, plates, dies, cutting-and-creasing formes.
6. Establish the cost of any necessary outwork, including handling charges.
7. Re-read the enquiry details carefully and check the completed estimate thoroughly.
8. Check over the calculations and target parameters, e.g. value-added return and mark-up for type of work.
9. Once the quotation is produced in its final form, check it against the estimate and customer requirements before submitting it to the customer.

Points to note on quotations

In theory the estimator's responsibility finishes when the estimate has been prepared. Depending on company policy, the estimated cost will often be considered by a senior member of management, who then decides on the selling or quotation price. In practice the experienced estimator will often possess sufficient knowledge of the company's work and pricing policies to complete the majority of quotations on their own. Several factors govern the profit margin to be added when preparing a quotation. Here are some of them.

How important is a certain type of work for the company at this particular time? A healthy balance of work throughout all service and production departments is very difficult to achieve. If one area is fully committed for a period ahead, additional work of the same type will incur overtime premium costs. If practical, this would normally be reflected in a higher mark-up at least to recover these extra costs. A shortage of work in any area would have the opposite effect, lowering the profit margin to obtain the job and help balance the workflow.

How suited is any job to a company's particular equipment and expertise?
An enquiry that could lead to a job outside the scope of work regularly produced by the company will influence the price submitted. Printers gain expertise and operational efficiency by concentrating on certain classes of work; for example, general jobbing and commercial work, stationery, magazines, printing on plastic or direct mail. To deviate from

the core business increases the risk element and therefore the costs for the printer. This again would normally be reflected in a higher margin, if the company considered undertaking the work themselves or placing it with another printer.

What price is the customer prepared to pay? Establish an accurate market price or customer price. Then the profit margin will be the difference between the total estimated costs and the price assessed to be the current market price for that job.

Are there any special considerations when submitting a particular quotation? Certain customers expect extended credit terms well above the normal custom and practice. The cost of financing this credit may have to be absorbed by the printer, so keep a careful check on the true return of these jobs. If the printer has to buy a lot of paper to print a large job, for example, it will negotiate prepayment by the customer on mutually beneficial terms.

Run-on and run-back figures

When submitting quotations, it is always useful to calculate run-on and run-back figures, even if they have not been requested by the customer. Printer and customer normally benefit from the economies of scale that come from longer print runs in conventional printing, reflected in the different prices for different print quantities. To avoid misunderstanding, it is common practice to provide stepped quotations that start with a minimum base figure then quote for additional quantities. Here are three examples; notice how the run-on price changes for different print quantities.

(a) 5,000 copies	£6,000
per 1,000 copies (run-on up to 9,999 copies)	@ £335
(b) 10,000 copies	£7,350
per 1,000 copies (run-on up to 14,999 copies)	@ £285
(c) 15,000 copies	£8,400

The cost per 1000 copies is £1200 for 5000 copies, £735 for the 10,000 copies and £560 for 15,000 copies. Each of these totals includes the cost for the fixed cost set-up of the job, whereas the run-on per 1000 copies does not. Another approach practised by some printers is to introduce a run-back figure per 1000 copies based on a lower rate than the 1000 run-on rate. This is to ensure that the printer recovers the fixed cost set-up charges of the job at varying print quantities. Providing the order conforms to the quotation, the run-on and run-back figures are a great help to the costing and pricing function when it has to calculate a charge for overs or shortages on the final quantity delivered. Note that run-on and run-back figures will only be reliable where the method of working does not change and the cost of materials is not adversely affected by the final quantity ordered.

Quotation letter

The quotation letter, or its equivalent, such as a quotation email, normally follows a set pattern. This will take the form of recording the customer's details, job specifications and details, plus pricing and any other information relevant to the quotation conditions. Pages 20 and 30 illustrate estimate examples in line with the estimate enquiry, Figure 5.1, on page 86. Printers often include additional comments at the foot of the quotation to clarify items, emphasise and draw things to the attention of the buyer or customer. Here are a selection.

▶ The above prices are given subject to sight of copy, films, files and other materials supplied to us.

▶ The above prices are as at today's date and are subject to review after 30 days from the date of the quotation, if not confirmed as an order.

▶ This estimate is valid for all work charged within six months of the date of the estimate, excluding VAT. However, any unforeseen material increases could result in additional costs and we reserve the right to increase charges without normal notice.

▶ Author's corrections to be charged extra.

▶ This estimate is given subject to the conditions which are overleaf and such conditions shall be deemed to be embodied in any contract arising out of this estimate and the acceptance thereof, unless otherwise provided.

▶ Prices allow for all materials, originals, files, film, etc., when supplied to us, to be as specified in the correct sizes, quantities and quality.

▶ We respectfully draw your attention to our conditions of sale as printed overleaf.

Most printers reproduce their standard terms and conditions on the reverse of the quotation and/or supply it in soft-copy form plus a separate printed form when requested. Most printers base their conditions of contract on those issued by the British Printing Industries Federation (BPIF) on behalf of its members. The standard conditions of contract were produced after discussions with the Office of Fair Trading. They are reproduced below with the kind permission of the BPIF. They are provided as suggestions only; it is not obligatory for BPIF members to use these terms. These conditions are regularly reviewed and are therefore subject to change. A review is scheduled in 2004.

BPIF standard conditions of contract

For the standard conditions to have full legal force in any individual case, it is essential that they should be drawn to the customer's attention. It is not sufficient merely to print the conditions on the back of the estimate form. There must also be wording on the face of the form making reference to the printing on the back. This wording must be sufficiently prominent to prevent a customer alleging that they did not see it, and it is suggested that it should be printed as part of the estimate or quotation letter, i.e. above the signature, rather than printing it at the foot of the form. Here is a suggested wording:

This estimate is given subject to the standard conditions of contract issued by the British Printing Industries Federation and printed overleaf which conditions shall be deemed to be embodied in any contract based on or arising out of this estimate except as may be otherwise indicated herein or subsequently agreed in writing.

Where a firm wishes to use its own special conditions in addition to the standard conditions (or some of them), these special conditions may be printed on the face of the estimate, preferably above the signature, or on the reverse of the estimate underneath the standard conditions, provided it is made clear that the additional clauses are not part of the standard conditions. It is not essential to print a copy of the standard conditions on the reverse of every estimate. Sometimes this may not be practical, such as when an estimate is faxed to a potential customer. Provided it is stated that the estimate is subject to the conditions and they are clearly identified, the conditions will apply if the estimate is accepted by the customer. Then it is good practice to state that a copy of the conditions will be supplied on request, or to forward a copy separately by post.

The unconditional acceptance by a customer of a printer's estimate constitutes a contract on the printer's conditions. Some customers, however, specify in their orders certain conditions of their own. A conditional acceptance of a printer's estimate is not binding on the printer until they confirm or accept it in writing or by conduct. If the printer accepts such a counter-offer, the conditions it contains become added to or, where in conflict, substituted for those in the printer's original estimate. Where appropriate, for 'printer' read 'binder'.

The standard contract

1. Price variation
Estimates are based on the printer's current costs of production and, unless otherwise agreed, are subject to amendment on or at any time after acceptance to meet any rise or fall in such costs.

2. Tax
The printer reserves the right to charge the amount of any value added tax payable whether or not included on the estimate or invoice.

3. Preliminary work
All work carried out, whether experimentally or otherwise, at the customer's request shall be charged.

4. Copy
A charge may be made to cover any additional work involved where copy supplied is not clear and legible.

5. Electronic files
(a) It is the customer's responsibility to maintain a copy of any original electronic file.
(b) The printer shall not be responsible for checking the accuracy of supplied input from an electronic file unless otherwise agreed.

(c) Without prejudice to clause 15, if an electronic file is not suitable for outputting on
equipment normally adequate for such purposes without adjustment or other corrective
action the printer may make a charge for any resulting additional cost incurred.

6. Proofs

Proofs of all work may be submitted for customer's approval and the printer shall incur no
liability for any errors not corrected by the customer in proofs so submitted. Customer's
alterations and additional proofs necessitated thereby shall be charged extra. When style,
type or layout is left to the printer's judgement, changes therefrom made by the customer
shall be charged extra.

7. Colour proofs

Due to differences in equipment, paper, inks and other conditions between colour
proofing and production runs, a reasonable variation in colour between colour proofs and
the completed job will be deemed acceptable unless otherwise agreed.

8. Variations in quantity

Every endeavour will be made to deliver the correct quantity ordered, but estimates are
conditional upon margins of 5% for work in one colour only and 10% for other work being
allowed for overs or shortage (4% and 8% respectively for quantities exceeding 50,000)
the same to be charged or deducted.

9. Delivery and payment

(a) Delivery of work shall be accepted when tendered and thereupon, or if earlier on
notification that the work has been completed, payment shall become due.
(b) Unless otherwise specified the price is for delivery of the work to the customer's
address as set out in the estimate. A charge may be made to cover any extra costs
involved for delivery to a different address.
(c) Should expedited delivery be agreed an extra amount may be charged to cover any
overtime or any other additional costs involved.
(d) Should work be suspended at the request of or delayed through any default of the
customer for a period of 30 calendar days the printer shall then be entitled to
payment for work already carried out, materials specially ordered and other additional
costs including storage.

10. Ownership and risk

(a) The risk in all goods delivered in connection with the work shall pass to the customer
on delivery.
(b) Goods supplied by the printer remain the printer's property until the customer has paid
for them and discharged all other debts owing to the printer.

(c) If the customer becomes insolvent (as set out in clause 16) and the goods have not been paid for in full the printer may take the goods back and, if necessary, enter the customer's premises to do so, or to inspect the goods.

(d) If the customer shall sell the goods before they have been paid for in full he shall hold the proceeds of sale on trust for the printer in a separate account until any sum owing to the printer has been discharged from such proceeds.

11. Claims

Advice of damage, delay or loss of goods in transit or of non-delivery must be given in writing to the printer and the carrier within three clear days of delivery (or, in the case of non-delivery, within 28 days of notification of despatch of the goods) and any claim in respect thereof must be made in writing to the printer and the carrier within seven clear days of delivery (or, in the case of non-delivery, within 42 days of notification of despatch). All other claims must be made in writing to the printer within 28 days of delivery. The printer shall not be liable in respect of any claim unless the aforementioned requirements have been complied with except in any particular case where the customer proves that (i) it was not possible to comply with the requirements and (ii) advice (where required) was given and the claim made as soon as reasonably possible.

12. Liability

(a) The printer shall not be liable for indirect loss or third party claims occasioned by delay in completing the work or for any loss to the customer arising from delay in transit, whether as a result of the printer's negligence or otherwise.

(b) Insofar as is permitted by law where work is defective for any reason, including negligence, the printer's liability (if any) shall be limited to rectifying such defect. Where the printer performs its obligations to rectify defective work under this condition the customer shall not be entitled to any further claim in respect of the work done nor shall the customer be entitled to treat delivery thereof as a ground for repudiating the contract, failing to pay for the work or cancelling further deliveries.

(c) Nothing in these conditions shall exclude the printer's liability for death or personal injury as a result of its negligence.

13. Standing material

(a) Metal, film and other materials owned by the printer and used by him in the production of type, plates, film-setting, negatives, positives and the like shall remain his exclusive property. Such items when supplied by the customer shall remain the customer's property.

(b) Type may be distributed and lithographic or photogravure film and plates, tapes, disks or other work effaced immediately after the order is executed unless written arrangements are made to the contrary. In the latter event, rent may be charged.

(c) The printer shall not be required to download any digital data from his equipment or supply the same to the customer on disk, tape or by any communication link unless written arrangements are made to the contrary.

14. Customer's property

(a) Customer's property and all property supplied to the printer by or on behalf of the customer shall while it is in the possession of the printer or in transit to or from the customer be deemed to be at customer's risk unless otherwise agreed and the customer should insure accordingly.

(b) The printer shall be entitled to make a reasonable charge for the storage of any customer's property left with the printer before receipt of the order or after notification to the customer of completion of the work.

15. Materials supplied by the customer

(a) The printer may reject any film, disks, paper, plates or other materials supplied or specified by the customer which appear to him to be unsuitable. Additional cost incurred if materials are found to be unsuitable during production may be charged except that if the whole or any part of such additional cost could have been avoided but for unreasonable delay by the printer in ascertaining the unsuitability of the materials then that amount shall not be charged to the customer.

(b) Where materials are so supplied or specified, the printer will take every care to secure the best results, but responsibility will not be accepted for imperfect work caused by defects in or unsuitability of materials so supplied or specified.

(c) Quantities of materials supplied shall be adequate to cover normal spoilage.

16. Insolvency

Without prejudice to other remedies, if the customer becomes insolvent (namely, being a company is deemed to be unable to pay its debts or has a winding up petition issued against it or has a receiver, administrator or administrative receiver appointed to it or being a person commits an act of bankruptcy or has a bankruptcy petition issued against him) the printer shall have the right not to proceed further with the contract or any other work for the customer and be entitled to charge for work already carried out (whether completed or not) and materials purchased for the customer, such charge to be an immediate debt due to him. Any unpaid invoices shall become immediately due for payment.

17. General lien

Without prejudice to other remedies, in respect of all unpaid debts due from the customer the printer shall have a general lien on all goods and property in his possession (whether worked on or not) and shall be entitled on the expiration of 14 days' notice to dispose of such goods or property as agent for the customer in such manner and at such price as he thinks fit and to apply the proceeds towards such debts, and shall when accounting to the customer for any balance remaining be discharged from all liability in respect of such goods or property.

18. Illegal matter

(a) The printer shall not be required to print any matter which in his opinion is or may be of an illegal or libellous nature or an infringement of the proprietary or other rights of any third party.

(b) The printer shall be indemnified by the customer in respect of any claims, costs and expenses arising out of any libellous matter or any infringement of copyright, patent, design or of any other proprietary or personal rights contained in any material printed for the customer. The indemnity shall include (without limitation) any amounts paid on a lawyer's advice in settlement of any claim that any matter is libellous or such an infringement.

19. Periodical publications

A contract for the printing of a periodical publication may not be terminated by either party unless 13 weeks notice in writing is given in the case of periodicals produced monthly or more frequently or 26 weeks notice in writing is given in the case of other periodicals. Notice may be given at any time but wherever possible should be given after completion of work on any one issue. Nevertheless the printer may terminate any such contract forthwith should any sum due thereunder remain unpaid.

20. Force majeure

The printer shall be under no liability if he shall be unable to carry out any provision of the contract for any reason beyond his reasonable control including (without limiting the foregoing): Act of God; legislation; war; fire; flood; drought; inadequacy or unsuitability of any instructions, electronic file or other data or materials supplied by the customer; failure of power supply; lock-out, strike or other action taken by employees in contemplation or furtherance of a dispute; or owing to any inability to procure materials required for the performance of the contract. During the continuance of such a contingency the customer may by written notice to the printer elect to terminate the contract and pay for work done and materials used, but subject thereto shall otherwise accept delivery when available.

21. Law

These conditions and all other express and implied terms of the contract shall be governed and construed in accordance with the laws of England (Scotland in the case of Scottish Printers).

Methods of working

6

Having written the job description and studied the print specification, the estimator's next step is to consider how the job can be produced in the most cost-effective manner. This calls for a balance between the specific type of work, variations in how the job can be done, the range of equipment, processes and suitable materials available. It is generally known as methods of working.

The first task for the estimator is to consider the type of work to be produced. There are many types of work, but most can be grouped under the general headings of jobbing work, bookwork, magazines, general commercial high-quality colour printing and specialist work such as heatset and coldset web printing, continuous stationery and business forms, direct response and direct mail marketing, reel-fed self-adhesive labels, folding box cartons, flexible packaging and digital printing. The following checklists deal with some of the main considerations.

Checklists

Jobbing work

1. Quantity to be produced? Format and size?
2. Files, copy, artwork, film supplied? If so, in what form?
3. Type and number of proofs to be supplied?
4. Is the work printed on one side or both sides?
5. How many colours? Overall or common colours only on certain pages?
6. Process or non-standard inks? Seal, varnish, IR or UV drying facilities required?
7. Types of materials requested? Cost, availability?
8. Which presses – sizes and configurations – are available?
9. If printed both sides, print sheetwork or half-sheetwork?
10. Is multiple-working most cost-effective?
11. Print finishing requirements?
12. Any special requirements, e.g. cover with pockets and gussets, laminating?
13. Production and delivery schedules to be supplied?
14. Packing requirements?

Bookwork

1. Quantity to be produced? Format and size?
2. Files, copy, artwork, film supplied? If so, in what form?
3. How many text pages?
4. Type and number of proofs to be supplied?
5. Number and breakdown of sections? Imposition and flat plans to be supplied?
6. Type of cover? Dust jacket?
7. Treatment of illustrations? Integrated with text or separately printed sections?
8. How many colours on printed cover? Varnish, coating or laminating required?
9. How many colours on text pages? Spot or process? Colour fall?
10. Types of materials requested? Cost, availability?
11. Which presses – sizes and configurations – are available?
12. Method of binding? Hardback and softback versions?

13. Special arrangements for method of binding, e.g. additional trim in backs for comb and perfect binding or folder fitted for slot or burst binding?

14. Production and delivery schedules to be supplied?

15. Packing requirements?

16. Stock management arrangements – printed products to be delivered or retained for call-offs?

Magazines

1. Quantity to be produced? Format and size?

2. Files, copy, artwork, film supplied? If so, in what form?

3. Type and number of proofs to be supplied?

4. How many colours on cover? Outside and inside spread?

5. Type of cover – 4-page, 6-page or 8-page gate fold cover?

6. How many text pages? Colour fall and flat plans to be supplied?

7. How many colours on text pages? Spot or process?

8. Types of materials requested? To be supplied?

9. Which presses – sizes and configurations – are available on a regular basis?

10. Method of binding? Saddle-stitched, perfect bound or slotted bound?

11. Any special arrangements for covers? UV varnished, laminating, cover mounts?

12. Any inserts? Size, number?

13. Production and delivery schedules to be supplied?

14. Packing requirements?

15. Distribution arrangements?

General commercial high-quality colour printing

1. Quantity to be produced? Format and size?

2. Files, copy, artwork, film supplied? If so, in what form?

3. Type and number of proofs to be supplied?

4. Is the work printed on one side or both sides?

5. Number of colours? Four-colour process inks or specials? IR or UV drying required?

6. Types of material requested? Cost, availability?

7. Types and sizes of presses available?

8. Is multiple-working most cost-effective?

9. Any special finishes? Coating, varnishing, laminating, UV spot varnish?

10. Print finishing requirements?

11. Production and delivery schedules to be supplied?

12. Packing requirements?

Heatset and coldset web offset printing

1. Quantity to be produced? Format and size?

2. Files, copy, artwork, film supplied? If so, in what form?

3. Type and number of proofs to be supplied?

4. Number of colours? Mono, two-, four-colour process inks or specials?

5. Types of material requested? Cost, availability? To be supplied?

6. Colour fall and flat plans to be supplied?

7. Which presses are available? Single- or multi-web? Number of units? Cut-off sizes?

8. Available press folding configurations? Finished size formats?

9. Additional in-line finishing operations required apart from folding? Spine gluing, inkjet personalisation, final trimming?

10. Printed sections or products delivered as collect or non-collect?

11. Off-press finishing requirements?

12. Production and delivery schedules to be supplied?

13. Packing requirements?

14. Distribution arrangements?

Continuous stationery and business forms

1. Quantity to be produced? Format and size?

2. Files, copy, artwork, film supplied? If so, in what form?

3. Type and number of proofs to be supplied?

4. Number of colours? Mono, two-, four-colour process inks or specials?

5. Types of material requested? Cost, availability?

6. Continuous or cut set forms?

7. Which presses are available? Single- or multi-web? Number of units?

8. Fixed- or variable-cylinder presses? Available cylinder circumferences and widths?

9. Presses to finish as reel-to-reel, reel-to-pack, pack-to-pack or reel-to-sheet?

10. Additional in-line finishing operations to sprocket hole punching, numbering and perforating required? Inkjet personalisation, bar coding, block-out decarbonising?

11. Offline finishing and conversion requirements? Collating, numbering – crash or conventional – perforating, crimping, gluing, tab fastening?

12. Packing requirements?

13. Stock management arrangements – printed products to be delivered or retained for call-offs?

Direct response and direct mail marketing

1. Product type to be produced? Dummy or sample to be supplied by the customer or printer?

2. Quantity to be produced? Format and size?

3. Files, copy, artwork, film supplied? If so, in what form?

4. Type and number of proofs to be supplied?

5. Number of colours? Mono, two-, four-colour process inks or specials?

6. Types of material requested? Cost, availability?

7. Which presses are available, size and configurations? Sheet-fed or web-fed? If web-fed, single- or multi-web? Number of units?

8. Presses to finish as complete product or are further operations necessary?

9. Are in-line finishing facilities available on web presses? Examples are folding, gluing application – hot-melt remoistenable gum and/or cold-impact glue lines – personalising, die-cutting and making-up into finished product?

10. Offline finishing facilities required? Folding, gluing – hot-melt remoistenable gum and/or cold impact glue lines – patch carbonising, personalising, die-cutting and making up into finished product?

11. Requirement for data preparation management? Also for sheet-fed and reel-fed offline inkjet and/or laser printing systems?

12. Packing requirements?

13. Stock management arrangements – printed products to be delivered or retained for call-offs?

Reel-fed self-adhesive labels

1. Quantity to be produced? Label shape, type and size?

2. Files, copy, artwork, film supplied? If so, in what form?

3. Gap between labels across web and around cylinder?

4. Type and number of proofs to be supplied?

5. Number of colours? Special colours and/or four-colour process inks? UV drying required?

6. Types of self-adhesive material requested? Cost, availability?

7. Printing process? Flexo? Letterpress? Screen?

8. Which presses are available? Cylinder sizes and configurations? Flatbed or rotary?

9. In-line finishing facilities available on presses? UV varnish, embossing, foil blocking, laminating, die-cutting and waste stripping, plus delaminating and relaminating for printing on the adhesive-backed side?

10. Flatbed or rotary cutters to be used?

11. Offline finishing facilities required? Label inspection, bar code reading, counting, slitting and re-reeling to suit customer requirements?

12. Packing requirements?

13. Stock management arrangements – printed products to be delivered or retained for call-offs?

Folding box cartons

1. Quantity to be produced? Overall finished size and carton style, e.g. tuck top, claw lock base?

2. Files, copy, artwork, film supplied? If so, in what form?

3. Dummy samples to be supplied or prepared? Quantity and type?

4. Forme making, laser cut or conventional die-cutting board – with or without knives?

5. Type and number of proofs to be supplied?

6. Is the work printed on one side or both sides?

7. Number of colours? Four-colour process inks or specials? IR or UV drying required?

8. Types of material requested? Cost, availability?

9. Types and sizes of presses available? Number of printing units?

10. In-line aqueous coating, conventional or UV varnish finish required?

11. Print finishing requirements apart from cutting-and-creasing, waste stripping and folding box gluing? Embossing? Foil blocking? Window patching? Bar coding?

12. Production and delivery schedules to be supplied?

13. Packing requirements?

14. Stock management arrangements – printed products to be delivered or retained for call-offs?

Digital printing products

1. Quantity to be produced?
2. Suitability to digital printing?
3. Files supplied to specification?
4. Type and number of proofs to be supplied?
5. Is the work printed on one side or both sides?
6. How many colours? Monochrome or four-colour process?
7. Types of materials requested? Suitability for digital printing?
8. Do the available presses offer the quality and capability required by the work?
9. Personalisation, versioning capabilities required? Suitability of data supplied?
10. Print finishing requirements? Creasing? Laminating?
11. Any special requirements?
12. Packing, dispatch requirements?

Unfamiliar work

Sometimes estimators receive enquiries for printed work that is outside their company's normal line of business. Then the company needs to consider whether it is set up for this type of work and whether it is interested in taking the job. Does the company have the knowledge and the equipment to produce it? If the answer is no, then the estimator has the opportunity of obtaining a quotation from a specialist or trade printer/finisher. But the enquiry may be part of a trend and it may be an opportunity to diversify into other printed products.

Imposition

Imposition is the arrangement and assembly of printed images into a predetermined format so that, when bound, each printed page will appear in the correct sequence and position. Alternatively it relates to the laydown of multiple-image work. The approach to imposition applies equally to all the major printing processes, except that offset litho requires a right-reading offset litho plate, whereas conventional letterpress, flexography and gravure require wrong-reading printing plates or cylinders. Screen printing operates from a right-reading stencil mesh, emulsion side down. All imposition schemes work backwards from the finished printed product. As there are considerable practical differences between sheet and web printing, this chapter covers them in separate sections.

When planning how a job will be printed, one of the first things to ensure is that the available finishing equipment can complete the work in the desired way, because once a job is printed, it is difficult or impossible to correct a mistake in the imposition and laydown. If in doubt about any job, consult the finishing department of the printing company, especially if an outside supplier is involved. The printer will generally decide on the imposition schemes, but on regular publications, such as periodicals, magazines and journals, it is common for the printer and publisher to work together on the imposition. An agreed range of impositions will often be drawn up between both parties that allow flexibility in the use of colour and mono pages while keeping within budget.

Multiple images

For printed work such as labels, leaflets, cartons and stationery, including letterheadings and compliment slips, which are not bound in any way, then imposition is not appropriate, as the finished product is a single, separate or self-contained item. The most popular method of working for this type of product is multiple-image working, but for very short runs, single or one-up working is often used. Label and carton printing are particularly suitable where one label or carton of the same kind is planned a multiple number of times on the overall designated working area, or as a series of labels or cartons printed in common colours on a common substrate. Figure 6.1 shows a multiple-image working for a series of four labels, printed together in groups of 16 on the same sheet in common ink colours. Suppose the customer required 200,000 each of the four kinds of label in size A5, then the printer will need 12,500 sheets, plus overs, of sheet size 630mm × 880mm or SRA1. Like imposition, planning and laydown aim to achieve the most economical and practical method of working.

FIGURE 6.1 64-up multiple-image laydown of a series of four labels printed as four blocks of 16 labels

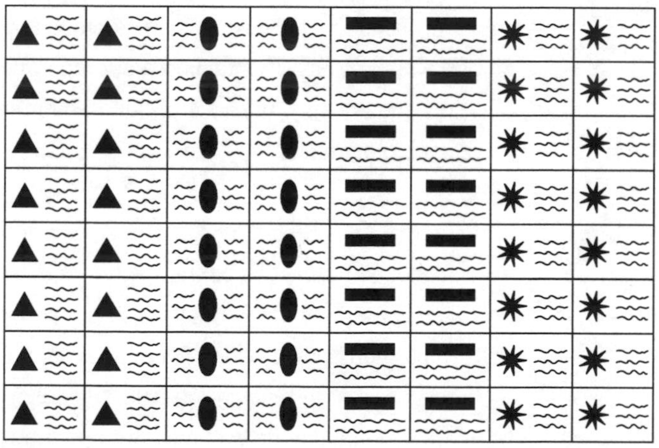

Source: Pira International Ltd

Methods of working: influential factors

▶ Available press sizes: these will determine the minimum and maximum sheet and product sizes that can be produced on a particular press, e.g. 8- or 16-page section, five or ten cartons to view.

▶ Printed product printed on one or both sides: if jobs are printed on one side only, the chosen method will tend to be single- or multiple-image working. Two-sided printed work has a wider range of effective options.

▶ Press configurations: sheet and web presses are available in different configurations; some presses are designed to print one side only, some both sides only, and some can print one or both sides in one press pass. A particular press configuration, or a series of presses with different configurations, will be chosen for a complex job such as a multi-page catalogue with a mixture of mono or single-colour sections and colour sections, matching the capabilities of the presses with the requirements of each job.

▶ Colour fall of printed pages: many bound publications arrange certain pages to fall into a predetermined arrangement so that the grouping of colour pages can be printed together in an economic manner. Tables 6.1 and 6.2 (pages 109 and 110) outline the colour fall for a 32-page publication with 16 pages in four-colour process and 16 pages in black only.

▶ Quantity to be printed: the higher the quantity required of any particular job, the greater the likelihood of multiple-image working and/or the use of larger press sizes.

▶ Stock material sizes: most sheet-fed offset litho printers predominantly use materials in stock sizes, e.g. paper and board in SRA2 (450mm × 640mm), B2 (520mm × 720mm), SRA1 (640mm × 900mm) and B1 (720mm × 1040mm) sheet sizes, which determine the number of pages or images out of a particular sheet size and effectively the method of working.

▶ Method of finishing: bound work is made up with gathered or insetted sections, and this affects the laydown and arrangement of pages. Tables 6.1 and 6.2 are based on the same job specification, but laid out separately as insetted and gathered sections. On bound publications, cutting, folding and binding are the three finishing operations with the greatest impact on the method of working. The laydown of the pages on the printed sheet or web must be capable of being cut or slit and/or subsequently folded into the correct sequence by the equipment available.

Sheet-fed imposition

In sheet-fed printing there are three main methods of working: work-and-turn, work-and-tumble and sheetwork. Work-and-turn and work-and-tumble are also known under the collective term of half-sheetwork. Half-sheetwork uses one set of plates that backs itself to produce two copies out. In work-and-turn the sheet turns on the axis of the short edge; in work-and-tumble the sheet tumbles on the axis of its long edge. Only one set of plates, and therefore make-ready, are required for half-sheetwork, as all the page numbers to complete a printed sheet are included on that single set, which backs itself to complete the printing operation.

To maintain accurate register with work-and-turn, i.e. the correct position of images on the sheet, the side lay on the printing press is changed on back-up from left to right to ensure the same short edge of the sheet is used while printing both sides of the sheet. Work-and-tumble differs in that both long edges of the sheet are used in the printing process, one for printing each side of the sheet; therefore it requires two gripper margins. Figure 6.2 (overleaf) shows a 4-page portrait work-and-turn imposition and Figure 6.3 (overleaf) shows a 4-page landscape work-and-tumble imposition.

FIGURE 6.2 4-page work-and-turn imposition

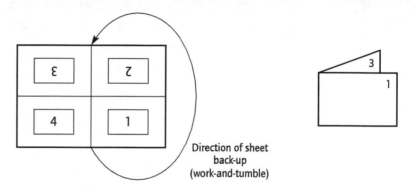

Source: Pira International Ltd

FIGURE 6.3 4-page work-and-tumble imposition

Source: Pira International Ltd

With sheetwork, two sets of plates are required to complete an imposition, inner and outer. The outer always contains the first and last pages of the imposition, and the inner always contains the second and penultimate pages; therefore, unlike half-sheet work, sheetwork requires two sets of plates, resulting in two make-readies, but it only produces one copy out for single-set working. Figure 6.4 illustrates a 4-page sheetwork imposition.

FIGURE 6.4 4-page sheetwork imposition

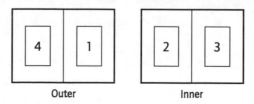

Source: Pira International Ltd

Half-sheetwork requires twice the sheet size used for sheetwork, but only half the quantity, e.g. 40,000 copies of a 16-page A5 booklet printed single-section sheetwork would require

40,000 sheets plus overs of sheet size SRA2 based on eight pages of A5 out of each side of the sheet. Using the same example, but printing by work-and-turn would require 20,000 sheets plus overs of sheet size SRA1 based on 16 pages of A5 out of the sheet.

Selecting the method of working

Sheetwork is the most popular method of working for multisection work printed by sheet-fed offset litho, such as books, magazines and journals, as the perfected sheets can be folded without the additional cutting in half required for half-sheetwork. It is also regularly used where different colours are printed on each side of the printed sheet. Short-run work printed on both sides of the sheet with a straight litho press, i.e. a press that can only print one side at a time, is very much suited to sheetwork. This is because, after the first side of the sheet has been printed, the operator can leave the printed sheets undisturbed to dry while the second set of plates is put on and registered, allowing back-up without too much delay. Work that is printed on one-sided material, such as MG poster or carbonless paper, is always printed sheetwork.

Half-sheetwork is most popular on relatively low-pagination jobs with common colours printed both sides, especially long-run work allowing time for the initial printed sheets to dry before back-up; a further advantage here is that it only requires one set of plates compared to two for sheetwork. Work-and-tumble is most suited to long narrow-shaped work such as gate- and roll-fold work, which would be impractical for work-and-turn. With the development of convertible multicolour sheet-fed offset litho presses up to 14 colours, perfecting has become a popular practice where, for example, a ten-colour convertible press with the appropriate conversion configuration can print five colours both sides in one press pass. This method of working is technically work-and-tumble, as with most presses of this type the sheet has to be tumbled over after printing the first group of colours, before passing through the last group of printing units to complete the back-up.

Figures 6.2 and 6.3 (page 106) show that work-and-turn produces an upright or portrait 4-page section, whereas work-and-tumble produces a landscape 4-page section. This is due to the different way the sheet is turned or tumbled over for back-up. All methods of working can be printed more than 1-up; for example, 2-up work-and-turn or work-and-tumble would result in four copies out, whereas 2-up sheetwork would result in only two copies out.

Flat plans

When producing periodicals such as magazines, journals and other structured-format work, it is common practice for the publisher or customer to supply the printer with a flat plan, indicating the required pagination for editorial and advertising pages, or other matter. The flat plan can also simply be used to indicate the sequence of copy or colour to be used on a publication such as an annual report. As an alternative, a production dummy may be supplied as a made-up copy or series of folded sections. The dummy will normally be produced from plain paper folded to the finished bound size, with details of page numbers, copy, illustrations, numbers of colours, etc.

The publisher, designer or customer, in consultation with the printer, has the task of juggling and manipulating the overall contents into a coherent and cost-effective publication. The printing of most periodical publications is done under contract, where the printing company quotes various options of colour usage within certain cost parameters, e.g. the contract for a monthly magazine of 64 pages text, excluding cover, may state that the publication is to be saddle-stitched, and that the text is to be printed in four 16-page sections, with 32 pages in four-colour process and 32 pages in black only, split evenly throughout the publication. Figure 6.14 (page 116) shows a typical 16-page heatset web offset press cylinder configuration.

Figure 6.5 illustrates a flat plan for the centre 16-page section of the text, i.e. pages 25 to 40; the tinted areas – pages 25, 28, 29, 32, 33, 36, 37 and 40 – indicate four-colour process and the untinted areas – pages 26, 27, 30, 31, 34, 35, 38 and 39 – indicate black only. A careful study of the flat plan will reveal that the outer section pages are in four-colour process and the inner section pages are in black. Any deviation from the specification, including the use of colour outside the agreed flat plan, will incur extra costs. The flat plan is used by the printer as a guide to the colour fall of pages, which has a major impact on deciding the method of working.

FIGURE 6.5 Flat plan covering the colour fall of pages 25 to 40, the 16-page centre spread of a 64 page book

25	26	27	28
29	30	31	32
33	34	35	36
37	38	39	40

Source: Pira International Ltd

How binding affects imposition

With bound work there are two major methods of binding folded sheets or sections together, insetted and gathered. Insetted is where folded sections are placed inside each other and is the most common form of binding associated with saddle stitching. Gathered sections by contrast are placed on top of each other to create a group or block of sections which are typically bound together by adhesive or thread sewn. To help illustrate how binding affects imposition an example job specification is included below and in Tables 6.1 and 6.2 (pages 109 and 110).

Example 6.1 The specification for a job is 32 text pages, excluding cover, of a report printed with pages 1 to 4, 13 to 20 and 29 to 32 in four-colour process, with all remaining pages in black only. The job is to be printed in 8-page sections as insetted sections (Table 6.1) and gathered sections (Table 6.2, overleaf). Table 6.1 lays out the pagination to suit insetted sections, which follows the rule of the sequence of pages running down to the centre spread and back again, with all pairs of pages adding up to one more than the total number of pages, 33 in this case. This common total of 33 results from matching printer's pairs consisting of first number and last number, second number and second last number, and so on, up to pages 16 and 17, the centre spread. The first section containing pages 1 to 4 and 29 to 32, and the fourth section, containing pages 13 to 20 (italicised in Table 6.1) are in four-colour process and therefore require four plates for each section. The second section, containing pages 5 to 8 and 25 to 28, and the third section, containing pages 9 to 12 and 21 to 24, are in black only and therefore require two plates, making a total of ten plates.

TABLE 6.1 4 × 8-page insetted sections

Pages		
1	*32*	
2	*31*	
3	*30*	
4	*29*	*Section 1 in four-colour process*
5	28	
6	27	
7	26	
8	25	Section 2 in black only
9	24	
10	23	
11	22	
12	21	Section 3 in black only
13	*20*	
14	*19*	
15	*18*	
16	*17*	*Section 4 in four-colour process*

Source: Pira International Ltd

Table 6.2 represents four independent gathered sections, where the numbers run in uninterrupted printer's pairs sequence with the first section, pages 1 to 8, adding up to 9; the second section, pages 9 to 16, adding up to 25; the third section, pages 17 to 24, adding up to 41; and the fourth section, pages 25 to 32, adding up to 57. Because each section contains four pages in four-colour (italicised in Table 6.2) and four pages in black, a total of 16 plates are required. The most cost-effective method of working with this job specification would be based on using insetted sections as in Table 6.1.

TABLE 6.2 4 × 8-page gathered sections		
Pages		
1	8	
2	7	
3	6	
4	5	Section 1 – mix of four-colour process and black
9	*16*	
10	*15*	
11	*14*	
12	*13*	Section 2 – mix of four-colour process and black
17	24	
18	23	
19	22	
20	21	Section 3 – mix of four-colour process and black
25	*32*	
26	*31*	
27	30	
28	29	Section 4 – mix of four-colour process and black

Source: Pira International Ltd

Insetted and gathered sections

For periodical work such as magazines, journals, catalogues and more general work, such as brochures, parts lists and manuals, there is the option of using insetted sections for saddle-stitched binding, or gathered sections for mainly adhesive or thread-sewn binding (Figures 6.6 to 6.13, pages 111–115). In bookwork, where pagination is normally well over a hundred pages on bulky stock, gathered sections is the chosen method of binding. Publications thicker than 10mm are unlikely to be suitable for insetted, saddle-stitched work. The methods of calculating the pagination, i.e. page numbers, in the two types of bound section are quite different and are outlined below.

Insetted sections

Figures 6.6 to 6.9 (on the next three pages) illustrate four examples of insetted bound work, covering 16-, 24-, 32- and 64-page publications, split up into 8-page sections as follows:

▶ 16 pages (Figure 6.6): pages 1 to 4 and 13 to 16, pages 5 to 12.

▶ 24 pages (Figure 6.7): pages 1 to 4 and 21 to 24, pages 5 to 8 and 17 to 20, pages 9 to 16.

▶ 32 pages (Figure 6.8): pages 1 to 4 and 29 to 32, pages 5 to 8 and 25 to 28, pages 9 to 12 and 21 to 24, pages 13 to 20.

▶ 64 pages (Figure 6.9): pages 1 to 4 and 61 to 64, pages 5 to 8 and 57 to 60, pages 9 to 12 and 53 to 56, pages 13 to 16 and 49 to 52, pages 17 to 20 and 45 to 48, pages 21 to 24 and 41 to 44, pages 25 to 28 and 37 to 40, pages 29 to 36.

FIGURE 6.6 Insetted 16-page laydown

1	16
2	15
3	14
4	13
5	12
6	11
7	10
8	9

Source: Pira International Ltd

FIGURE 6.7 Insetted 24-page laydown

1	24
2	23
3	22
4	21
5	20
6	19
7	18
8	17
9	16
10	15
11	14
12	13

Source: Pira International Ltd

FIGURE 6.8 Insetted 32-page laydown

1	32
2	31
3	30
4	29
5	28
6	27
7	26
8	25
9	24
10	23
11	22
12	21
13	20
14	19
15	18
16	17

Source: Pira International Ltd

FIGURE 6.9 Insetted 64-page laydown

1	64
2	63
3	62
4	61
5	60
6	59
7	58
8	57
9	56
10	55
11	54
12	53
13	52
14	51
15	50
16	49
17	48
18	47
19	46
20	45
21	44
22	43
23	42
24	41
25	40
26	39
27	38
28	37
29	36
30	35
31	34
32	33

Source: Pira International Ltd

Gathered sections   Figures 6.10 to 6.13 illustrate four examples of gathered bound work. The imposition rules for insetted work do not apply to gathered work. Notice that the pagination of gathered sections is much easier to establish; namely in 8-page consecutive sections as 1 to 8, 9 to 16, 17 to 24, 25 to 32, 33 to 40, 41 to 48, 49 to 56 and 57 to 64.

FIGURE 6.10 Gathered 16-page laydown

1	8
2	7
3	6
4	5
9	16
10	15
11	14
12	13

Source: Pira International Ltd

FIGURE 6.11 Gathered 24-page laydown

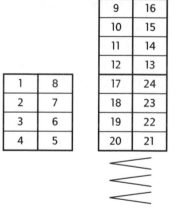

Source: Pira International Ltd

FIGURE 6.12 Gathered 32-page laydown

1	8		17	24
2	7		18	23
3	6		19	22
4	5		20	21
9	16		25	32
10	15		26	31
11	14		27	30
12	13		28	29

Source: Pira International Ltd

FIGURE 6.13 Gathered 64-page laydown

1	8	9	16	17	24	25	32	33	40	41	48	49	56	57	64
2	7	10	15	18	23	26	31	34	39	42	47	50	55	58	63
3	6	11	14	19	22	27	30	35	38	43	46	51	54	59	62
4	5	12	13	20	21	28	29	36	37	44	45	52	53	60	61

Source: Pira International Ltd

Web-fed imposition

Web-fed printing is fundamentally different to sheet-fed printing in that a continuous web of substrate is printed rather than a sheet. There are two types of web-fed or reel-fed presses, large-width and narrow-width.

Large-width web-fed presses

Almost all large-width presses have a fixed-cylinder construction, i.e. the cylinder sizes cannot be changed. In addition the presses are mainly perfector presses, where the web is printed on both sides simultaneously, known as printing topside of web or deck and bottom side of web or deck. The exception to this is the satellite-constructed press, where only one side of the web is printed at a time and perfecting takes place by the web going through a second satellite unit. Another major difference between web-fed and sheet-fed printing is that web-fed printing allows in-line folding and other finishing operations that cannot be achieved with sheet-fed presses.

Large-width web machines come in a range of configurations, including 8-page, 16-page, 32-page, 48-page and 64-page, single- and multi-web. The numbers associated with each press type indicate the number of A4 pages out from one full-width web and cylinder cut-off. Variations in the number of pages from one cylinder cut-off can be obtained by running with say a half or three-quarter width web of paper. As an example, a full-width web on a 16-page press will give 16 pages A4 per cut-off, 12 pages A4 on a three-quarter width web and 8 pages on a half-width web. Figure 6.14 illustrates a typical 16-page press cylinder configuration, showing the 630mm circumference or cut-off, out of which two 297mm lengths are taken, using A4 as an example, with four times 210mm out of the web width. Two sections or jobs can be run together and separated on or off press to add variation to the output configurations, such as the production of two separate 8-page A4 jobs on a 16-page press.

FIGURE 6.14 Typical 16-page heatset web offset press cylinder configuration

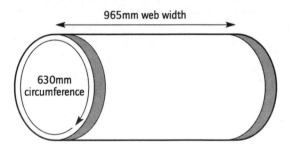

965mm web width

630mm circumference

Source: Pira International Ltd

Table 6.3 indicates a page laydown for a 32-page section, pages 1 to 32, to be printed on a five-unit, twin-web heatset web offset press, with 16 pages in four-colour process, C1 and C2, and 16 pages in black only, B1 and B2. C1 (pages 1, 32; 8, 25; 9, 24; 16, 17) represents the top side of the web or deck of the first web, and C2 (pages 2, 31; 7, 26; 10, 23; 15, 18) represents the bottom side, the equivalent of the outer form in sheetwork printing. B1 (pages 3, 30; 6, 27; 11, 22; 14, 19) represents the top side of the web or deck of the second web, and B2 (pages 4, 29; 5, 28; 12, 21; 13, 20) represents the bottom side, the equivalent of the outer form in sheetwork. Note that all pairs of pages add up to 33. An alternative to producing a 32-page section using the twin-web facility would be to produce one single 16-page section in five colours from a single-web configuration.

TABLE 6.3   A 32-page section produced as 2 × 16-page sections, with one 16-page section covering pages C1 and C2 in four-colour process and pages B1 and B2 in black only

Page 1	four-colour	(C1)	Page 32	four-colour	(C1)
2	four-colour	(C2)	31	four-colour	(C2)
3	black	(B1)	30	black	(B1)
4	black	(B2)	29	black	(B2)
5	black	(B2)	28	black	(B2)
6	black	(B1)	27	black	(B1)
7	four-colour	(C2)	26	four-colour	(C2)
8	four-colour	(C1)	25	four-colour	(C1)
9	four-colour	(C1)	24	four-colour	(C1)
10	four-colour	(C2)	23	four-colour	(C2)
11	black	(B1)	22	black	(B1)
12	black	(B2)	21	black	(B2)
13	black	(B2)	20	black	(B2)
14	black	(B1)	19	black	(B1)
15	four-colour	(C2)	18	four-colour	(C2)
16	four-colour	(C1)	17	four-colour	(C1)

Source: Pira International Ltd

Narrow-width web-fed presses

Most narrow-width web-fed presses are used for a wide range of work, including continuous stationery and business forms, direct mail, labels, tickets and vouchers. Besides reel-to-sheet, the presses are configured to produce a wide range of products, including single-part or multi-part, reel-to-reel or reel-to-pack. When considering different methods of working on narrow-width web-fed presses, it is generally a matter of deciding, for example, how many printed items the press can accommodate, working backwards from the finished size of the job, taking into account the additional processing equipment the job will pass through. The presses can have a fixed cylinder size or a variable cylinder size. The narrow-width and larger-width presses can be 1-wide, (around 394mm or 15.5in wide), 2-wide (around 520mm or 20.5in wide) and 3-wide (around 825mm or 32.5in wide). The width of flexographic and letterpress presses can be as small as 100mm.

Narrow-width presses also often come with the option of variable-size cylinders so that the cut-off or diameter of the cylinder can be changed to suit the requirements of the job, as long as the printing company has the required cylinder sizes and tooling, plus the appropriate finishing or processing facilities. On the larger presses, suitable for continuous business forms and direct mail, the most popular cylinder sizes are 24.75in, 24in, 23.5in, 22in, 20in and 17in. Business forms and other related work are designated in inches because computer stationery still relies on sprocket holes exactly half an inch apart and half-inch tear-off stubs. Variable cylinder circumferences give the opportunity of producing variable product depths, e.g. a 22in cylinder produces a range of depths such as 2in × 11in, 3in × 7.33in, 4in × 5.5in. Figure 6.15 (overleaf) illustrates a 24in circumference, maximum web width 520mm cylinder producing two deep by two wide, 12in × 250mm mailers.

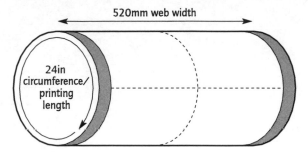

FIGURE 6.15 Narrow-width continuous web-fed press with 520mm maximum web width
and 24in cylinder printing two wide by two deep mailers

520mm web width

24in circumference/ printing length

Source: Pira International Ltd

**Designer's spreads
and printer's spreads**

When arranging for finished artwork, film or digital data to be sent to a printer, the customer should ideally have the work prepared in printer's pairs, rather than designer's pairs. Better still, if multiple pages such as imposed four or eight pages are to be supplied, these should be commensurate with the imposition agreed and supplied by the printer, with appropriate margin allowances. Figure 6.16 illustrates pairs of pages appropriate to an 8-page saddle-stitched booklet as designer's and printer's pairs. When designing and laying out pages, the designer will naturally lay pages out in pairs as they appear in the final printed copy, i.e. appearing as double-page spreads. The printer, however, lays out pages to the required imposition, so that when printed, folded and bound, the pages will fall into the correct sequence.

FIGURE 6.16 Designer's and printer's spreads: two pairs are the same and two are
different

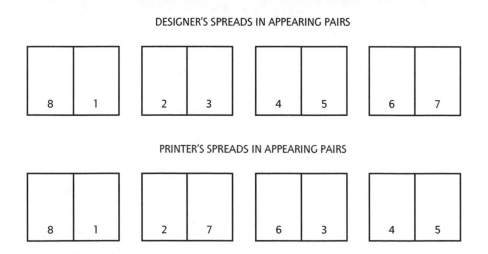

DESIGNER'S SPREADS IN APPEARING PAIRS

| 8 | 1 | | 2 | 3 | | 4 | 5 | | 6 | 7 |

PRINTER'S SPREADS IN APPEARING PAIRS

| 8 | 1 | | 2 | 7 | | 6 | 3 | | 4 | 5 |

Source: Pira International Ltd

Electronic imposition

As we move closer to all-digital prepress workflows, electronic imposition becomes an increasingly accepted practice in generating selected impositions and multiple-image laydowns within a Mac, PC or workstation. Electronic imposition is the process of arranging electronic files into the selected planned format and placement for subsequent outputting in analogue form as planned film, or digital form as plate-ready computer-to-film (CTF) or computer-to-plate (CTP). Briefly, the process consists of the operator calling up the electronic files created on DTP, or dedicated proprietary make-up software, alternatively importing them from other sources such as disk, ISDN and modem. The files and images are then placed into an electronic imposition software package, where the operator selects the facilities required to create the desired finished result, including accessing imposition, Open Prepress Interface (OPI) and trapping options as required. On some electronic imposition software, several versions have been developed to suit the circumstances and requirements of the user, e.g. a simple or cut-down version and a full-featured or multi-licence client/server version. Often electronic imposition will take place on a workstation server handling all the heavy processing for less powerful clients on the network.

Margin allowances in imposition

When preparing an imposition, allowances for margins must be included to ensure the job can be trimmed or cut out to the required final size. With electronic imposition this often means laying the images or pages out so that complete CTF or CTP is carried out. Figures 7.4 to 7.7 (pages 134 and 135) and the accompanying text explain the allowances for trims and other factors.

Paper and board

7

When preparing an estimate, the estimator should always try to establish details of paper, board and other substrate requirements before considering other costs. There are two main reasons for this:

▶ Substrates represent a high proportion of the cost of any finished printed job.
▶ The stock sizes of substrates considerably influence the method of working.

For simplicity, I will often use the term 'paper' to cover all the varieties of material used for printing and processing, including boards and other substrates, cut cards, envelopes and tags, normally issued by the white paper warehouse to the production departments. Here 'white paper' means unprinted paper.

Practical knowledge

It is quite common for a customer to provide a sample swatch or previously printed material sample and expect the printer to match it. In response to this, estimators need to develop their knowledge of different substrate types as much as possible, establishing the most appropriate materials for each job and circumstance. Relatively inexperienced estimators will need to experiment with different kinds of paper and board by getting the feel of them between thumb and forefinger, and by matching one piece of paper with another. The experienced estimator can judge fairly accurately the substance (measured in gsm) and thickness (measured in microns) by sight and feel, but this only comes from hard work and perseverance. Sample swatches or books from paper merchants and mills will help in identifying different types of paper and board.

To ensure accurate colour or shade matching of substrates such as paper and board, use a purpose-built viewing cabinet with a standard natural light source. The viewing booths for inspecting and comparing colour proofs and machine passes are ideal for this. An estimator should also make full use of the information sheets and technical support literature produced by paper merchants and mills. These give hints, tips and recommendations on the use of specific materials, e.g. matt coated, carbonless and recycled paper, and also general recommendations on the printability of a wide range of substrates, as well as suitability of certain substrates for each of the major printing processes. Swatches, price lists and other information from suppliers should be kept for reference and comparison. It is vital to keep them up to date as paper specifications change over time.

The paper and board industry has been generally restructured into large international groups. The most advanced technology for controlling the papermaking process now enables constant testing of required characteristics, specifications and quality. Printers receive much improved, more consistent and higher-specification substrates to print from, allowing them to gain maximum benefit from their ever-improving, modern and fast-running printing presses. Most printing companies have a white paper warehouse where they hold stock of their most commonly used paper and board. In today's very competitive business climate, this can be as low as a buffer stock. Paper merchants will normally deliver stock orders to a printer within 6–24 hours of receiving an order, which aids printers considerably as they cannot afford to tie up a lot of capital in materials, costing interest and excessive storage charges.

Identifying samples

Required abilities

▶ Identify the particular type and quality of paper or board, e.g. gloss or matt coated, smooth uncoated printings.

▶ Establish the gsm or thickness of samples.

▶ Identify any unusual characteristics of the sample, e.g. coloured stock, one-sided material, sandgrain finish, carbonless or folding boxboard.

▶ Identify the source, e.g. paper mill or merchant.

▶ Establish the stock sizes in which the material is available.

▶ Check on availability.

Microns and gsm

The abbreviation gsm stands for grams per square metre. It is a unit for indicating the substance of paper and board, whatever its size, on the basis of weight. The weight of any sample of paper or board expressed in gsm is derived from one single sheet of size A0 (841mm × 1189mm) of that material. Although board weight can be expressed in gsm, it is more common for its caliper thickness to be expressed in microns; one micron, denoted 1μm, is one-thousandth of a millimetre.

Useful test equipment
Paper weighing scales

Paper weighing scales weigh a predetermined sample size of paper or board, generally a square 10cm × 10cm, and express it in gsm.

Micrometer

A micrometer is used to measure paper and board samples in microns. Modern micrometers give a digital read-out of the material thickness, avoiding the possibility of human error in reading the figures on traditional micrometers.

Ordering paper and board

A paper merchant or mill cannot be supplied with too much information on a paper or board order. Unfortunately, some printers will give the minimum information possible and complain when a problem arises. Frequently the problem is due to the incorrect paper or board being used for the job, especially where particular properties are required, e.g. the use of standard bond paper when high-quality laser-guaranteed paper was required. Comprehensive details help the paper merchant or mill to supply paper and/or board that can be expected to perform well; indeed, the onus is then on the supplier to meet the required conditions of the job. The provision of adequate information is the printer's safeguard.

Ordering information

Quality and type Give a full description, including brand name if known, colour, finish, furnish and volume, where appropriate.

Grammage or thickness State the material substance and/or thickness in gsm or in microns, as appropriate.

Format State the sheet dimensions in millimetres, such as the standard size SRA1 (640mm × 900mm) or the non-standard size 630mm × 880mm. With material in reel form, the order specification should exactly match the requirements of the machines for which it is intended, e.g. reel width in millimetres or centimetres, maximum weight of reel, overall diameter or length of paper on reel, correct core diameter, agreed number of mill joins.

Intended use of material State the details of printing processes to be used, e.g. sheet-fed offset litho, heatset or coldset web offset, reel-fed flexography, web-fed gravure, screen or digital. State the type of work to be printed, single-sided or perfected/double-sided work, number and type of colours to be printed, types of ink to be used, plus any subsequent processes such as varnishing or laminating, types of finishing, binding and converting. Give details of any special properties required in the finished print product such as being acid-free or light-fast.

Dimensions and weights of paper and board

Paper and board are manufactured and supplied to printers in sheet, web and reel form to suit the wide range of press sizes that are available, along with other requirements. Apart from local variations and exceptions, the vast majority of the world uses the metric system of measurement and the International Organisation for Standardisation (ISO) range of paper and board sizes. The US and some other countries, however, use the imperial system of measurement, along with paper and board sizes based, somewhat loosely, on the old UK paper sizes still used reasonably extensively by the UK book and related publications industry.

International paper and board sizes

The three main standard size ranges for paper and board are A, B and C; there are also size ranges D, E and G. Range A contains the smallest sizes. Derivatives based on A sizes are generally the most popular for finished printed products, e.g. A4 or A5. In between the sizes in the A range come sizes in the B range – B1 is larger than A1 but smaller than A0 – used mainly for posters, wallcharts and larger-format publications that cannot be obtained from A sizes.

The C range, larger than the A range but smaller than the B range, is mainly for envelope and folder sizes to contain A-sized items. The A, B and C sizes, like all sizes in the ISO series, are proportional to each other (Figure 7.1, overleaf). The basis of the international series of paper sizes is a rectangle, having an overall area of one square metre and sides in the ratio $\sqrt{2} = 1.414$. This basic A size is A0, 841mm × 1189mm. It satisfies the conditions as $1189/841 = 1.414$ and $841\text{mm} × 1189\text{mm} = 999{,}949\text{mm}^2 = 1\text{m}^2$.

The ratio of the sides has the unique property of being retained each time the longer side is halved or the shorter side doubled, making it the ideal shape for graphic reproduction. But note that when the size of paper or board is halved, by cutting the largest dimension in half, the grain direction changes, so B1 long-grain paper cut in half produces B2 short-grain, which halves to produce B3 long-grain, and so on.

FIGURE 7.1 The ISO series of A, B and C sizes are proportional to each other, as shown by the dotted line

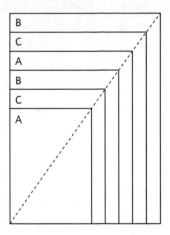

Source: Pira International Ltd

Multiples and subdivisions The basic size in each range of the main international paper and board sizes is A0, B0 or C0. 2A0 has double the shorter dimension and double the area of the basic A0 sheet. A1 has half the longer dimension and half the area of the basic A0 sheet. Similarly, A2 is half A1, A3 is half A2, A4 is half A3, etc., as indicated by Figure 7.2. Table 7.1 lists a range of multiples and subdivisions covering the A, B and C size ranges.

FIGURE 7.2 The range of A sizes obtained by halving or doubling the size above or below in the range from A0 to A7

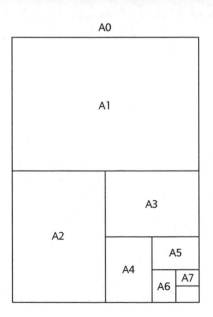

Source: Pira International Ltd

TABLE 7.1 Multiples and subdivisions covering the A, B and C range of sizes (mm)					
A range		**B range**		**C range**	
2A0	1,189 × 1,682	2B0	1,141 × 2,000		
A0	841 × 1,189	B0	1,000 × 1,414		
A1	594 × 841	B1	707 × 1,000		
A2	420 × 594	B2	500 × 707		
A3	297 × 420	B3	353 × 500		
A4	210 × 297	B4	250 × 353	C4	229 × 324
A5	148 × 210	B5	176 × 250	C5	162 × 229
A6	105 × 148	B6	125 × 176	C6	114 × 162

Source: Pira International Ltd

Untrimmed stock sizes of paper and board

To produce an 8-page A4 booklet or an A1 folded map, the printer requires a working size greater than the overall trimmed size of A1 to allow for bleed and colour bar, etc. To accommodate trimmed A sizes, RA and SRA ranges have been introduced. The RA range is only suitable where the minimum trim allowances are required, whereas the larger SR range generally includes most of the additional allowances required by printers when producing A-size products. If an SR size is not large enough, then the appropriate B size will generally be used. This is illustrated in Table 7.2, which shows a range of A, RA, SRA and B sizes.

TABLE 7.2 Selection of A, RA, SRA and B range of sizes in mm							
A sizes		**RA sizes**		**SRA sizes**		**B sizes**	
A0	841 × 1,189	RA0	860 × 1,220	SRA0	900 × 1,280	B0	1,000 × 1,414
A1	594 × 841	RA1	610 × 860	SRA1	640 × 900	B1	707 × 1,000
A2	420 × 594	RA2	430 × 610	SRA2	450 × 640	B2	500 × 707
A3	297 × 420	RA3	305 × 430	SRA3	320 × 450	B3	353 × 500

Source: Pira International Ltd

Popular non-standard and trimmed sizes

Apart from the sizes in Table 7.2, other sizes have become popular to suit specific circumstances, such as 335mm × 640mm, which is the equivalent of 2/3 SRA2 and is used mainly for 6-page A4, or 12-page A5 jobs. The size 640mm × 650mm falls into a similar category, only its main use is for 12-page A4 or 24-page A5 jobs. Due to the increasing use of digital printing devices, such as sheet-fed copier/printer systems, trimmed sizes of A4 and A3 have also become very popular, making this sector a huge growth area. Pre-cut or trimmed and collated sets of carbonless papers are also popular, so the printer chooses the required combination of top, middle and bottom copies, along with the appropriate colours, without needing any prepress cutting.

Rigid box cartons are another sector that tends to use non-standard stock sizes, such as makings or special makings, due to the high volume of material normally ordered, as well as the wide variation in size of carton products. Paper and board sizes are often available from suppliers in variations of the standard sizes in Table 7.2. This is due to rounding up or down, plus general custom and practice, e.g. B1 as 720mm × 1020mm and B2 as 520mm × 720mm.

Traditional UK paper and board imperial sizes

Although the UK has adopted the ISO range of sizes, it still retains some of the old imperial-based paper and board sizes. The UK book publishing sector, for example, continues to use the traditional sizes to a wide extent. Unlike the ISO sizes, the traditional UK paper and board sizes are known by name and there is no proportionality relationship between them. Similarly, multiples and subdivisions are named, whereas in the ISO system they are numbered. Due to the sizes originally being in imperial measurements, there has been a rounding up and down when converting to metric size equivalents. Table 7.3 gives the most common metric approximations of the traditional UK paper and board imperial size ranges.

TABLE 7.3 Range of sizes in mm representing the metric equivalent of traditional UK paper and board imperial system

Printings	
Quad crown	768 × 1,008
Double crown	504 × 768
Quad demy	888 × 1,128
Double demy	564 × 888
Quad royal	960 × 1,222
Double royal	611 × 960
Boards	
Royal	520 × 640
Postal	570 × 730

Source: Pira International Ltd

US paper and board sizes

US paper and board sizes are based on an imperial system rather like the traditional UK system. Apart from having a range of imperial sizes, there is a basis weight for each size expressed in pounds per ream of 500 sheets in its basic size. There are six main paper grades, each with their own basis weight, as indicated by Table 7.4. Table 7.5 outlines the basis weight for the most common paper grade and size, i.e. book papers, along with the equivalent weight for the other paper grades, plus related gsm.

TABLE 7.4 US paper grades, sizes and basis weight range in lb per ream of 500 sheets

Grade of paper	Size (in)	Basis weight (lb) per 500 sheets
Book	25 × 28	30, 40, 45, 50, 60, 70, 80, 90, 100, 120
Bond	17 × 22	13, 16, 20, 24, 28, 32, 36, 40
Cover	20 × 26	50, 60, 65, 80, 90, 100
Bristol	22.5 × 28.5	67, 80, 100, 120, 140, 160
Index	25.5 × 30.5	90, 110, 140, 170
Tag	24 × 36	100, 125, 150, 175, 200, 250

Source: Pira International Ltd

TABLE 7.5 US paper grades, using the basis weight for book papers as the reference grade, highlighted in italics, along with the equivalent weight in lb per ream of 500 sheets for the other paper grades, plus overall gsm

Book	Bond	Cover	Bristol	Index	Tag	gsm
30	12	16	20	25	27	44
40	16	22	27	33	36	59
45	18	25	30	37	41	67
50	20	27	34	41	45	74
60	24	33	40	49	55	89
70	28	38	47	57	64	104
80	31	44	54	65	73	118
90	35	49	60	74	82	133
100	39	55	67	82	91	148
120	47	66	80	98	109	178

Source: Pira International Ltd

Subdivisions of UK and US sizes

Whatever its size, every sheet of paper expressed using UK and US traditional imperial paper and board sizes has a number of subdivisions that are common to all sizes, as shown in Figure 7.3. The reference size of a sheet is known as its basic size; twice basic size is called double size and four times is called quad size. Folding in half along the longer dimension of the basic sheet size gives two equal leaves, or four pages, having folio size. If the folio sheet is folded in the middle of its longer dimension, it will create four leaves, or eight pages; this is called quarto (4to). Further folds will produce octavo (8vo), sextodecimo (16mo), etc.

FIGURE 7.3 Subdivisions of UK and US traditional imperial paper and board sizes from quad to 32mo

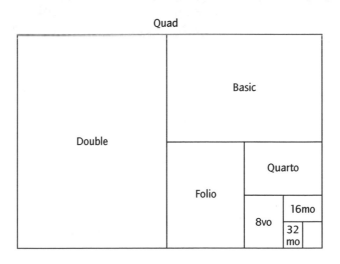

Source: Pira International Ltd

Following the same pattern as described above, each fold halves the superficial area and doubles the number of leaves or pages obtained by the previous fold. The names are used not only when sheets are being folded, but also when being cut. Other less common subdivisions are 6mo, when the long dimension is divided by three and the short dimension by two, to give 6 leaves or 12 pages. Plus ordinary 12mo, when the long dimension is divided by three and the short dimension by four to give 12 leaves, or 24 pages. Untrimmed crown 8vo, for example, is 192mm × 126mm, calculated as 8 × 126mm out of the 1008mm dimension and 4 × 192mm out of the 768mm dimension. Note that a piece of paper, when cut to size, is described as a single leaf that consists of two pages, made up of one page on each side of the leaf. Hence a book consists of a number of pages that is double the number of leaves.

Envelope sizes

Envelopes are available in a variety of sizes to accommodate the wide range of ISO and imperial printed and related products. The ISO C sizes, such as C4, 229mm × 324mm and C6, 114mm × 162mm, are ideal to enclose A4, 210mm × 297mm and A6, 148mm × 105mm, respectively. DL, 110mm × 220mm, is also a very popular envelope size, enclosing one-third A4, 99mm × 210mm.

Supply and purchase of paper and board

When paper or board is required in sufficiently large quantities, it will generally be purchased direct from the mill. For quantities in several tonnes – depending on each mill's minimum quantity, such as 2–5 tonnes – the printer can order a making of any size, i.e. a special size requested by the printer rather than the available stock sizes. An example would be a non-standard paper size of 760mm × 1050mm.

Cutting from mill reels is also common to accommodate special sizes, especially for smaller orders. Some merchants and mills also stock reels for narrow- or wide-web presses in a restricted range of sizes and quantities. It is more common to order webs and reels in makings, rather than sheets, as the tonnages are frequently higher. Special makings, which require a variation of grammage, size and possibly furnish and colour, will require a larger minimum order, such as 5 tonnes or above. Paper and board, when delivered to printers, is normally packed ream-wrapped in 500s for paper, and centums (100s) for board. It is packed in special protective wrappings and/or bulk-packed on pallets (BPOP) and stored at a humidity close to its expected use humidity.

The paper or board should be kept intact by the printer, in the appropriate wrappings, to reach the equivalent temperature of the pressroom before unpacking. Another example of good housekeeping is to cover and protect the paper and board with plastic covers between operations, to minimise the adverse effects caused by changes in temperature and humidity. If the pressroom atmosphere is colder and damper than the unprotected stack of paper, then the paper will gain moisture and expand, creating wavy edges. Conversely, if the surrounding atmosphere is warmer and drier, then it will lose moisture and shrink, creating tight edges.

Paper and board specifications

Paper suppliers now provide a wide range of technical data on paper and board in price lists and promotional literature. The performance of a paper or board is governed by the sum of its properties related to a specific purpose or use. The printer has to consider the runnability of the paper and/or board to ensure the highest possible machine running speed, hence the highest possible productivity. The printer must also ensure the required print quality is achieved. The main properties that affect print quality include grammage, thickness, bulk, smoothness, brightness, gloss, opacity, sheet formation, dimensional stability, tensile strength and moisture content.

Description of papers and boards

A correct description for any substrate should indicate the type of paper or board, colour and finish, size, grammage or caliper; for example, white art, SRA1, 135gsm. Boards may be sold by gsm or by caliper, such as 200, 230, 250, 380 microns (0.2, 0.23, 0.25, 0.38mm), plus sheet thickness, such as two-sheet, three-sheet and four-sheet.

Dimension convention

When stating the dimensions of unprocessed paper or board as delivered, the first dimension is the cross direction. The shorter measurement is only given first for long-grain sheets. For processed paper, the depth, or vertical measurement in relation to the print, should be stated first and the width, or horizontal measurement, should be stated last. When the depth is the longer dimension, the sheet is described as portrait or upright; when the depth is the shorter dimension, the sheet is described as landscape or oblong. For ISO sizes, the basic reference, e.g. A4, implies portrait shape, the letter L denotes landscape formats. Here are some typical examples.

A4	297mm × 210mm (upright)
A4L	210mm × 297mm (landscape)
Metric crown 12mo	126mm × 128mm (square)
Metric crown 4to	384mm × 126mm (long upright)

Paper in web and reel form

Large reel or web material

In recent years the availability and suitability of materials in large reel and web form, including improved quality and range of substrates, have increased considerably for web offset printing grades. They have also increased for gravure and other printing processes, including digital. For coldset web offset, the main types of material are newsprint, improved newsprint and part mechanical uncoated, with the available range of web widths covering from under 600mm to over 1000mm.

Heatset web offset grades are available in a much wider range, from ultra lightweight coated and uncoated at around 39gsm up to 200gsm. The jumbo reels made by some paper mills are up to 8m wide. These are cut down to to suitable web widths to fit available presses, e.g. 440, 450, 620, 870, 880 and 960mm. To reduce wastage, press cut-offs are beginning to change from the standard 630mm to 625mm and 620mm, as well as 590mm and 598mm. Reels are most frequently supplied in around 1000mm diameter and 1 tonne weight.

Direct orders from the mills are 5–10 tonnes minimum, often higher. Combination orders are often placed with the mills by paper merchants for 20–50 tonne lots, made up of smaller orders from a group of printers or publishers. Container and transporter lorries hold approximately 20–50 tonnes and paper mills try to supply in full lorry loads.

Reel-fed self-adhesive label material

A wide range of material comes in roll and reel form for conversion by self-adhesive roll label printers. Apart from the different types of paper and other printing substrates available, there are also different types of backing adhesive and backing paper for particular applications. Most roll- and reel-fed self-adhesive materials are made 1–2m wide. Suppliers of roll- and reel-fed self-adhesive materials will slit down the required size from the full available widths. For example, 4 × 250mm or 12 × 165mm from 1m wide material to suit the printer. Some mills and merchants stock a limited range of cut reel material suitable for reel-fed self-adhesive labels or roll ticket printing; examples include 165mm, 200mm, 250mm and 330mm.

Carbonless reel material

Carbonless reel materials used mainly for business forms are available in a wide range of reel widths, including these millimetre sizes: 184, 203, 216, 230, 235, 241, 255, 267, 280, 305, 310, 330, 345, 368, 380, 405, 432, 470, 482.

Digital reel material

The range of reel material suitable for digital printing is increasing all the time in response to the new market sectors that are being established. Digitally suitable materials include self-adhesive, matt, gloss, satin and silk coated, plus coloured stock from 80gsm to 300gsm in reel widths of 315, 320 and 500mm. Inkjet papers cover a much wider range of reel widths, including 610, 914, 1068, 1270, 1372 and 1524mm.

Buying paper by length or area

When paper is bought in webs and reels, and by weight, there is an unusable portion to each web. This consists of the wrapping, any damaged outer windings, the inner windings too close to the core, the core itself and the reel-end protectors. The weight of these can vary from web to web and, if there are grammage variations in the making, there will be a different length of paper on each web. This is not very serious as mill controls have substantially reduced grammage variations. However, the effect is in marked contrast to sheet sales, where a variation in the making substance will not result in a different number of sheets being included in a ream or on a pallet. Undersize reels cause particular problems where multi-section jobs are being printed. If the last web on a job is shorter than the others, the result will be fewer copies from that web, or any other short web. If the material is from a special order, this could result in the whole job being short or in the production of unsaleable overs of the earlier sections.

Weight and price calculations

Paper is normally sold by weight, either at a price per 1000 sheets or, for larger quantities, at a price per 1000kg or per tonne. Price per kilogram is also quoted. Board prices are quoted per kilogram, per tonne or per 100 boards. If only the grammage (gsm) quantity is required and the price per kilogram is known, it is necessary to calculate the cost of standard quantities from this information. Here are some popular paper and board formulae. The basis of paper weight calculations is an Ao sheet, which has an area of one square metre, expressed as 1000mm × 1000mm here. The actual dimensions of the A0 sheet are 841mm × 1189mm.

To calculate the weight of 1000 sheets of a given paper of a given size and substance

$$\frac{\text{Area (mm}^2\text{) of required sheet} \times \text{gsm}}{1000 \times 1000} = \text{weight (kg) per 1000 sheets}$$

Example 7.1 What is the weight of 1000 sheets of white matt coated paper, 630mm × 880mm in 90gsm?

$$\frac{630 \times 880 \times 90}{1000 \times 1000} = 49.90\text{kg per 1000 sheets}$$

The final figure is often rounded up or down. The price of a given quantity of paper or board is calculated by multiplying the weight in kilograms by the rate per kilogram.

To calculate the number of boards per 100kg of a given sheet size and grammage

$$\frac{100,000,000,000}{\text{gsm} \times \text{sheet dimensions (mm)}} = \text{number of boards per 100kg}$$

Example 7.2 What is the board count of a 420gsm board in size 800mm × 1000mm?

$$\frac{100,000,000,000}{420 \times 800 \times 1000} = 298 \text{ boards per 100kg}$$

To calculate book thickness given the paper's volume basis, grammage and pagination

$$\frac{\text{Volume basis} \times \text{gsm} \times \text{pagination}}{20,000} = \text{book thickness (mm)}$$

Example 7.3 What would be the spine thickness of a book using text paper of volume basis 18 in 95gsm with a total of 160 pages?

$$\frac{18 \times 95 \times 160}{20,000} = 14\text{mm}$$

To calculate the length of paper on a reel or web, given its weight, grammage and width

$$\frac{\text{Weight (kg)} \times 100,000}{\text{gsm} \times \text{width (cm)}} = \text{length (m) of paper on a web}$$

Example 7.4 What is the length in metres of a web of paper weighing 950kg in 70gsm and 880mm wide?

$$\frac{950 \times 100,000}{70 \times 88} = 15,422\text{m}$$

Printing processes and substrates

Each of the printing processes requires certain characteristics in a substrate to function effectively and to meet the required price and/or quality standard:

▶ Sheet-fed offset litho requires an uncoated paper that is well surface-sized, with a firm surface and little loose fibre. Coated stocks do not normally present any problems with loose surface fibres. Long-grain papers give fewer problems with dimensional stability. However, low grammage short-grain paper will often run better than long-grain paper.

▶ Heatset web offset has an upper grammage limit of around 135gsm when the paper is to be folded, with little limitation on sheeted work. Coated paper ideally should have a low moisture content, as blistering of the paper surface may occur when the paper passes through the drying oven.

▶ Coldset web offset requires a soft-sized absorbent paper.

▶ Flexography prints equally well on coated, uncoated and plastic film.

▶ Letterpress requires a compressible, smooth, gloss-coated surface to print fine halftones.

▶ Gravure is well suited to the cheaper grades of paper such as SC mechanicals, as long as they have a satisfactory smoothness. Web ribbon folding is often restricted to 90gsm and below.

▶ Screen printing can print on almost any substrate, including paper, board, plastic, glass, metal and fabric.

▶ Digital printing has been identified by paper mills and merchants, as well as paper and board merchants, as an increasingly important sector that has tremendous growth potential. Digital papers and boards are therefore being developed, and the range extended to meet the demand for a wide spectrum of substrates in sheet and web form.

One of the main properties required in a paper or board suitable for laser digital printing is low moisture content. This should be around 3–5% rather than the 5–8% associated with conventional paper and boards. The substrate needs to be smooth to ensure the toner is distributed evenly. Substrates must also be able to hold a controlled level of resistance, due to the high electrical charges they experience in the digital printing system. Traditionally the major problems associated with digital substrates include coated stock which, due to the intense heat generated during laser printing and electrophotography, tends to blister and crack when folded and emit a strong, distinctive smell.

Digital processes are often set up, or calibrated, to suit the properties of the substrate, often identified by a grading system. In one system, 1A represents the top grade of substrate. This has the highest printing specification and prints to a high level under most circumstances and machine settings. Most digital press manufacturers issue a list of approved substrates that have been found suitable to run on their equipment. Lists are constantly being updated and modified to reflect users' experiences. The range of approved papers and boards cover a range from around 80gsm to 300gsm and above. Sheet sizes of papers and boards specifically made for digital printing range from A4, A3, RA3 and SRA3, plus SRA2 and SRA1 mainly for cutting down to smaller sizes for specialist use.

A range of papers and boards have been developed to suit the wide spectrum of printer systems now used in the modern office environment. Paper and boards are identified as being suitable or guaranteed, covering for example photocopiers, high-volume copiers, colour copiers, laser printers, plan printers, thermal wax printers, mono and colour inkjet, thermal fax and plain paper fax.

Factors affecting size   The available paper sizes of the desired quality should be one of the first considerations when preparing an estimate. The most economical method of working is usually the deciding factor; choose the nearest appropriate standard size. However, where jobs defy economic cutting from a standard sheet, it is sometimes more prudent to assess the size of paper which gives the lowest waste, even though this may adversely affect the most cost-effective printing method. A further consideration is that the quantity and volume required for the job may justify a making in a special size. It can sometimes be the most cost-effective solution to cut to waste the paper in a book or magazine on, say, an odd 12-page section printed on a sheet capable of producing 16 pages, so retaining a common size which qualifies for a making.

It is also advisable to consider a making quantity if the amount required is just under the minimum order quantity since the financial savings can be considerable. When doing this, the full minimum making cost should be included, but estimate handling only for the sheets that are used. When calculating the size required, make allowance for trimming, bleeds, printing machine gripper and side margins. On solid work or where bleeds occur on all edges, gutters should be left down the sheet to accommodate feeder wheels. If these fall across the image on the second pass, they may cause marks. Work to be laminated or varnished may require additional grip on the short edge or even extra allowance all round.

When printing by work-and-tumble and on most convertible presses, e.g. on an eight-colour machine printing as 4/4, there often needs to be an allowance for two gripper margins. Estimators should keep up-to-date records of all presses and machines in an organisation, showing print areas, grips and margins. Note that the amount of gripper space on sheet-fed machines will vary with different types of press.

Allowance for trims

An allowance for trim of 3mm should be made on all edges for single-leaf work, and on head, foredge and tail for bound work. For bled work, printed by offset litho, a further amount is often allowed for on the two side edge margins, plus a 6mm plain margin should be left on the back edge of the sheet to avoid excess water on the leave edge of the sheet encroaching on to the printed image. Six millimetres on each of the three edges is therefore required, making a total of 12mm for the two sides and 6mm for the leave edge. A special allowance, possibly up to 12mm, may be necessary for some subsequent operations, such as graining, varnishing, acetate lamination and for binding lap on automated binding machines.

For small forms and labels, take special care over the allowances to ensure that the maximum number are printed on the sheet. Some bled work, such as sheet-fed labels, cards, leaflets and folders for quality work, may require double cutting, as the outward portion of the substrate on the guillotine always shows a burred edge after cutting. Jobs which are to be punched out, such as shaped labels, also require extra space. Dovetailing is the butting together of irregularly shaped items, such as cartons and labels, to gain the maximum number out of the material used. An extra allowance of 6mm – 3mm for each leaf – must be made in the back margins of folded sections to be perfect bound. Figures 7.4 to 7.7 illustrate a range of margin allowances for different types of work. The tinted areas in the figures represent a 3mm trim allowance.

FIGURE 7.4 Example of margin allowances for work trimmed on all four edges to form the finished size

Source: Pira International Ltd

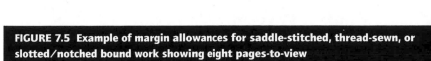

FIGURE 7.5 Example of margin allowances for saddle-stitched, thread-sewn, or slotted/notched bound work showing eight pages-to-view

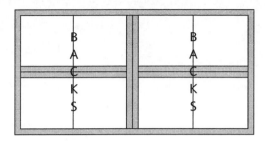

Source: Pira International Ltd

FIGURE 7.6 Example of margin allowances for work that is typical multiple-image working such as 8-up leaflets to view trimmed four sides and single inner cuts to size

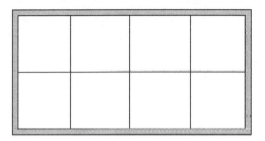

Source: Pira International Ltd

FIGURE 7.7 Example of margin allowances for perfect bound work or multiple-image working, where the equivalent of inner double cuts is required

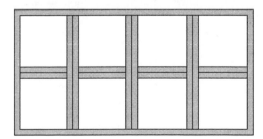

Source: Pira International Ltd

Allowance for grippers	An allowance for gripper margin on sheet-fed printing must be made on bled work. Bleed is where the printed image is extended beyond the trimmed size without sufficient white margin space that can be used as the gripper margin. For small offset machines this can be as low as 6–8mm, whereas for larger sheet-fed machines the allowance is normally 10–12mm. A standard gripper margin allowance of 12mm is often adopted.
Binding lap	A binding lap is often required on folded sections to help maintain their fast and accurate pick-up on modern binding lines. Then the foredge margins have to be increased by up to 9mm to allow for a lap on the foredge of the section.
Colour control strip	When printing multicolour process work, make an allowance of around 10mm for colour control strips on the back edge of the sheet.
Register control strip	On modern fast-running presses, register control devices are often used for measuring, displaying and storing register deviations. Allowances to accommodate these strips vary and often they can be included in existing margin allowances.
Special allowances	A special allowance, possibly up to 12mm, may be necessary for some subsequent finishing operations, such as lamination. An extra 6mm (3mm for each leaf) must be allowed for the built-in back margins of folded sections to be perfect bound. This is to allow for the spine to be trimmed into single leaves for adhesive binding. Most quality bled work will require double cutting. Cards for quality work require a double cut, as the outward portion of boards on the guillotine shows a burred edge after cutting (Figure 7.7, page 135). For forms and labels, take special care in making the proper allowances to ensure that the maximum number is printed on the sheet. Jobs which are to be punched out to shape also require extra space, ranging from 3mm to 6mm, between designs, but dovetailing or interlocking to suit the design can economise on materials, e.g. label and carton work.
Register and grain direction	The grain direction of the paper or board is very important in multicolour close-register work, especially in sheet-fed offset litho when several press passes through the machine are required to complete the job; for example, to complete a four-colour job on a two-colour press will take two passes. To keep substrate stretch to a minimum, it is advisable to print long-grain, i.e. with the grain running parallel to the impression cylinder as used in sheet-fed offset litho. If the grain is short, the tension of the paper or board may cause it to whip, resulting in marking or creasing, and also making it hard to obtain register. When sheets are folded, the grain should ideally run parallel to the main folds to assist accuracy and ease of folding, as well as to ensure correct opening in bookwork.

The grain direction for labels may be either vertical or horizontal to suit labelling machines, so find out the customer's requirements before planning the most economical working method. In carton work, the grain normally runs at right angles to the folds to achieve square corners and maximum rigidity and to suit carton-gluing machines. Most |

papers and boards are stocked long-grain. Paper mills and merchants will supply paper and board short-grain when available or for a special making. Short-grain paper can be obtained by doubling the size of the stock paper and cutting in half, e.g. SRA1 (640mm × 900mm) long-grain cut in half becomes SRA2 (450mm × 640mm) short-grain. Long- and short-grain paper or board are identified using a recognised and uniform means of description, e.g. long-grain SRA2 is described as 450mm × 640(m)mm and short-grain as 450(m)mm × 640mm, where m indicates the grain direction.

Makings and special makings

A making is a non-standard size in a standard grammage and material, e.g. 650mm × 870mm in 90gsm. A special making is a non-standard size in a non-standard grammage and/or material, e.g. 650mm × 870mm in 98gsm. The minimum quantity for a making is usually 2 tonnes for standard papers; special making orders can be as high as 50 tonnes. In either case the mill should be contacted for minimum tonnage and delivery dates. Where print-buying customers are demanding exact quantities of print, i.e. with no unders or overs, and as papermakers' technical control of variables have increased over time, printers are demanding far tighter making tolerances. This is especially true of making quantities. Some mills apply the plus or minus percentage margin figures in the table below, but on large orders many printers are looking for ±1–2%, or in practical terms, no unders and with overs restricted to the nearest reel or pallet. Buyers and makers of paper and board are at liberty to agree specific conditions of sale for individual orders, including making quantities.

	Makings	**Special makings**
	Standard stock quality and grammages in special sizes	Non-standard paper, for example, by reason of quality and/or grammages
Up to and including 1 tonne	10.00%	15.00%
Over 1 tonne and not exceeding 5 tonnes	5.00%	10.00%
Over 5 tonnes and not exceeding 10 tonnes	5.00%	7.50%
Over 10 tonnes and not exceeding 20 tonnes	3.75%	5.00%
Over 20 tonnes	2.50%	2.50%

Double tolerance

If with a making or special making, a printer specifies that they will not accept any tolerance in one direction, double tolerance will normally apply in the other direction. Using the percentage variances previously listed, a printer ordering 'not less than 6 tonnes' would fall into the category of minus 0%, plus 2 × 7.5% (15%), i.e. 6 tonnes to 6 tonnes 150kg. The papermaker is not required to deliver more than the minimum quantity, but the printer must accept the maximum quantity within these tolerances in these circumstances. There are also paper and board manufacturing variations covering measurements in sheets and reels. Here are some examples:
▶ Where paper is guillotined or precision cut, the permissible tolerance is often to be not more than ±2mm.

▶ Grammage should not vary from the ordered grammage by more than ±7.5% under 40gsm, or 5% for 40gsm and above.

▶ Thickness should not vary from the ordered thickness by more than ±10% up to and including 100 microns, or 7.5% for over 100 microns.

It is in the printer's interest to try to negotiate more advantageous terms and conditions than those laid down in the current paper and board trade customs. The printer can submit their own conditions and specifications which, if accepted by the paper mill or merchant, will form the conditions of contract for that particular order or for as long as the arrangement has been agreed.

Breakage charges

Where the quantity of paper or board required for a job is less than the amount normally packed in a parcel, e.g. paper in 500 sheets or board in 100s, the paper supplier will normally break parcels only of unusual or non-standard stock. Then there is an additional cost for splitting and repacking, known as a breakage charge.

Handling customers' paper

In certain classes of work, such as periodicals, bookwork and cartons, the paper and board used may amount to large tonnages per year. These tonnages are often ordered and paid for by the publisher or print buyer as makings and special makings, and delivered direct to the printer. Records must be kept by the printer of all receipts and issues, and a notification sent to the publisher or print buyer, showing the stock balances, after every issue has been made. Where the paper or board is to be supplied by the customer, it is advisable to arrange for samples to be checked by the printer before the paper or board is dispatched by the customer, paper merchant or mill, in case the material is found to be unsuitable for any reason. The material supplied should always allow for overs. When paper or board has been held in stock for a long period, it should be thoroughly examined on receipt. Seriously damaged edges or the effect of dampness could cause a great deal of trouble at a later stage. These matters must be immediately taken up with the customer.

Materials-handling expenses

In addition to the estimated cost of the paper for a job, the estimator will make an allowance to recover the cost and expense of storing and managing paper, board and other materials. These expenses are normally recovered on estimates by adding a percentage of the value of the materials, e.g. 10%; the percentage will vary depending on the volume and value involved. An alternative materials-handling expense is a weight-based charge. Special packing and transport are not covered by this expense and should be added as a further cost to the job.

Calculating the quantity of material required

The number of sheets, or cylinder circumference and cut-offs on web-fed and reel-fed work, required for each printed finished copy is multiplied by the number of printed copies to calculate the total quantity of material required for the job. Take care not to calculate half or double the quantity required by confusing leaves with pages. And remember there are two copies out when printing one-set work-and-turn and on reel-fed work, where variable-sized cylinders are used, to take account of the correct number of copies out, across and around the cylinder. Here are some examples of paper quantity calculations showing the most economical method of working.

Magazine: sheet-fed 10,000 copies consisting of 64 pages self-cover, trimmed size A4, printed sheetwork on 630mm × 880mm paper size.

16 pages out of 630mm × 880mm sheet	
64 pages/16	= 4 sheets per copy
10,000 copies × 4	= 40,000 sheets of 630mm × 880mm, excluding overs

Stationery: sheet-fed

▶ Mixed planning of jobs, printed common colours on common stock.

▶ 500 A4 letterheadings and 1500 compliment slips, size 99mm × 210mm, printed one letterheading to view and three compliment slips to view on RA2, 430mm × 610mm, paper size.

1 × A4 letterheading plus 3 × 1/3 A4 compliment slips out of one RA2 sheet	
	= 500 sheets of 430mm × 610mm, excluding overs

Bookwork: sheet-fed 3500 copies consisting of 320 pages metric crown 8vo, printed sheetwork on metric quad crown 770mm × 1010mm paper size.

64 pages out of 770mm × 1,010mm sheet	
320 pages/64	= 5 sheets per copy
3,500 copies × 5	= 17,500 sheets of 770mm × 1,010mm, excluding overs

Continuous business forms: reel-fed 18,000 single-part forms, finished size A4, worked on cylinder size 24.75in (629mm) with 26in (660mm) reel width

2 × 297mm out of 629mm cylinder circumference and 3 × 210mm out of 660mm reel width	
	= 6 out of reel cut-off
18,000/6	= 3,000 full cylinder cut-offs, excluding overs

Multiple-image leaflet: sheet-fed 360,000 copies of an A4 mailing leaflet printed one side only, without bleed and generous white margins all round. Stock size to be used is SRA1, 640mm × 900mm. The job is printed in black only, does not bleed and has generous white margins, so there is no need for gripper margins. Assume that only single cuts are required.

640mm /210mm = 3 out	900mm/297mm = 3 out	= 9 out in total
360,000/9	= 40,000 sheets of 640mm × 900mm, excluding overs	

Multiple-image leaflet: sheet-fed 360,000 copies of an A4 mailing leaflet, trimmed to bleed, printed both sides in four-colour process. Stock size to be used is SRA1, 640mm × 900mm. As the job is printed in four-colour process and bleeds, it will require a gripper margin and colour control bar as well as an allowance for double cuts. Figure 7.8 shows that the maximum number of A4 leaflets to bleed, with double cuts, out of SRA1 is 8.

360,000/8   = 45,000 sheets of 640mm × 900mm, excluding overs

FIGURE 7.8 Paper calculation for the laydown of an 8-up A4 leaflet

mm		mm	Trimmed sized
297		210	
+ 6		+ 6	trim
= 303	×	= 216	
× 2	×	4	8-up leaflets
= 606	×	= 864	
+ 6		+ 12	sides and leave edges
+ 10			colour bar
+ 12			gripper margin
634	×	876	working size

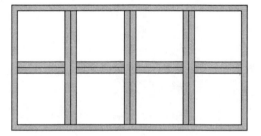

Source: Pira International Ltd

Overs and spoilage allowances

Extra amounts must be added to the basic quantity of paper and board required for a job to allow for wastage and overs during press and postpress operations, as well as to allow for samples and house files. The total quantity of paper required for a job, including wastage and overs, will depend on several things: the number of colours or workings, class of work, closeness of register, class of substrate, type of machine and length of run, plus additional allowances for any binding and outwork processes. Short runs require a higher proportion as a number of sheets or web lengths are wasted in the preliminary stages of machining, whatever the length of the run. With the increasing cost of materials, especially major expensive items such as paper and board, printers are focusing on cutting waste as waste costs must be borne by the company, eating into profits.

Improved press design and electronic controls, as well as substrates having more consistent and predictable printability and runnability, have considerably helped in the drive for reduced spoilage and overs, leading to a 50% reduction or more, compared to the requirements of older, more basic presses. There has also been an overall improvement in the accuracy and consistency of prepress and postpress equipment, which has led to an overall improvement in material usage, covering consumables as well as substrates, plates, ink and print finishing materials.

Allowances for spoilage and methods of calculation undoubtedly vary from company to company, but the allowances in Table 7.6 are representative of the average or middle ground, reflecting the use of modern equipment and current working practices on good quality commercial printing standards, i.e. not fine art work. Yet press and postpress equipment come in a wide range of capabilities, qualities and levels of sophistication, hence printers apply a wide range of wastage and overs allowances. Highly advanced sheet-fed offset litho presses, for example, are often run with allowances half those in Table 7.6.

TABLE 7.6 Spoilage allowances, including press and general finishing/binding operations

Sheet-fed offset litho: straight or convertible presses

Number of colours or print units	1	2	4	5	6	8
Make-ready and set-up waste per press pass (no. of sheets); second side of work-and-turn charged at 50% of first side	100	150	400	500	550	600
Running waste (%)	3	4	5	6	7	8

Web offset: perfector press

Number of colours or print units	1	2	4
Make-ready and cut-off set-up waste per press pass (no. of sheets)	2,000	3,500	4,000
Running waste up to 9,999 copies 30%, 10,000–19,999 copies 20%, 20,000–29,999 copies 15%, 30,000 copies and above 10%			

Narrow reel-fed presses: used for self-adhesive labels, roll tickets and continuous business forms, direct mail, etc.

Number of colours or print units	1	2	4	5	6
Make-ready and set-up waste per press pass (m)	200	300	500	600	850
Running waste (%)	5	6	8	9	10

Web-fed gravure: perfector presses

Number of copies in ('000s)	< 500	501–750	751–1,500	1,501–2,500	> 2,500
Combined make-ready and running waste (%)	> 10	10	9	8	7

Sheet-fed screen

Average make-ready, set-up and running waste (%)	10

Digital printing: monochrome

Make-ready and set-up waste per press pass (no. of sheets/cut-offs)	minimal
Running waste (%)	1–2

Digital printing: colour

Make-ready and set-up waste per press pass (no. of sheets/cut-offs)	5–10
Running waste (%)	up to 10

Source: Pira International Ltd

Notes on Table 7.6 The figures given in Table 7.6 are for guidance only and they vary throughout the industry. This is because no two printing companies have exactly the same range of equipment, working practices and/or work within the same market sectors. Here are some of the factors which cause this variation.

Equipment and working practices A printing company operating with direct digital links and JDF between their prepress, press and postpress equipment – with CTP, presses with high levels of automation, plus automated finishing and binding systems – will have a much lower spoilage rate than other printers using older equipment having a lower specification and mainly manually operated and controlled.

Configuration and number of colours Presses which can complete work in one pass will record much lower overall spoilage than presses which need several passes. A four-colour job printed both sides on a B1 sheet would involve four passes on a two-colour B1 press, two passes on a four-colour B1 press and one press pass on an eight-colour (4/4) convertible B1 press.

Print quantity Smaller print orders will require proportionally greater spoilage allowances, due to the same minimum make-ready and set-up allowances for short and long runs. For example, in heatset web offset for a quantity of 10,000 copies printed four-colour process, the overs required could easily be 60% or more, whereas for over 1 million copies of the same job, the allowance could be under 10%.

Type and weight of substrates Certain types of substrate, such as lightweight, heavyweight and low-quality recycled, will generally require a higher level of spoilage than standard grammage and stock quality.

Range and type of finishing Each additional finishing, binding and converting process applied to a printed sheet or reel will increase the total overs required, so that the correct quantity will be delivered to the customer. Additional finishing processes, such as varnishing, laminating, cutting-and-creasing and foil blocking will each add a further 1–5% to the wastage figures in Table 7.6. When outwork is involved, allow sufficient wastage to cover the work involved. Advice on spoilage allowances should always be sought from the suppliers.

Purchasing paper and board

Paper and board in sheet form are offered for sale in a variety of ways:
▶ price per kilogram (pence/kg);
▶ price per tonne (£/tonne);
▶ price per 1000 or 100 sheets of the selected size and grammage as (£/1000s or £/100s).

Paper and board pricing is mainly based on weight, whereas printers' requirements are mainly related to area. A sheet-fed printer looks at the cost for an area of material, so price per 1000 sheets is often the most useful information. The cost per 1000 sheets can be calculated in the following ways:

$$\frac{£/tonne \times kg/(1000\ sheets)}{1000}$$

$$\frac{pence/kg \times kg/(1000\ sheets)}{1000}$$

If paper is purchased in reel or web form, then the price can be given as follows:
- ▶ price per tonne (£/tonne)
- ▶ price per square metre (£/m^2)
- ▶ price per 1000m^2 (£/1000m^2)
- ▶ price per 1000m of the width ordered.

Here are three invaluable formulae for commercial reel or web printers:

$$Cost\ per\ 1000m^2 = \frac{£/tonne \times gsm}{1000}$$

$$Number\ of\ metres = 1000 \times web\ width\ (mm) \times gsm$$

$$Length\ (m)\ of\ paper\ on\ a\ reel = \frac{reel\ weight\ (kg) \times 100{,}000}{gsm \times width\ (cm)}$$

Sheet-fed printing paper calculations

Example 7.5 Calculate the stock size, quantity and cost of paper required for 5000 copies of an 8-page booklet, size 210mm × 148mm, to be printed sheet-fed offset litho four-colour process throughout on a B2 four-colour press on 100gsm white gloss art at £695 per tonne. Folded, insetted, saddle-stitched two wires, trimmed flush to bleed.

Method of working: 8 pages work-and-turn on SRA2 (450mm × 640mm), two copies out

Net number of sheets required	= 5,000 /2	= 2,500 SRA2 sheets
Make-ready and set-up	= 400 + 200	= 600
Running waste, 2,500 × 5% × 2		= 250
Number of sheets, inclusive of overs		= 3,350 SRA2
Weight per 1,000 sheets	= 0.45 × 0.64 × 100	= 28.8kg
Total cost of paper	= 28.8 × 3.35 × £0.695	= £67.05

Example 7.6 Calculate the quantity and cost of material for 80,000 copies for a saddle-stitched magazine, size 280mm × 220mm, 48 pages self-cover, to be printed by sheet-fed offset litho in four-colour process throughout on an eight-colour B1 press 4/4. Allow for a making of paper in a special size, 80gsm matt coated at £650 per tonne.

Paper size calculation

mm		mm	Trimmed size
280		220	
+ 6		+ 3	trim
= 286	×	= 223	
× 2	×	× 4	8 pages sheetwork
= 572	×	= 892	
+ 6		+ 12	sides and leave edges
+ 10			colour bar
+ 12			gripper margin
600	×	904	working size

Method of working: 8 pages sheetwork on special size 600mm × 904mm, one 16-page section

Net number of sheets required	= 80,000 × 3	= 240,000 sheets
Make-ready and set-up	= 600 × 3	= 1,800
Running waste, 240,000 × 8%		= 19,200
Number of sheets, inclusive of overs		= 261,000 600mm × 904mm
Weight per 1,000 sheets	= 0.60 × 0.904 × 80	= 43.39kg
Total cost of paper	= 43.39 × 261 × £0.65	= £7,361.11

Example 7.7 Calculate the stock size, quantity and cost of paper required for 3.5 million labels, size 100mm × 80mm deep, trimmed to bleed with double cuts. To be printed by offset litho in six colours one side only on a six-colour B1 machine with aqueous coater. Allow for a making of paper in a special size, 75gsm one-sided coated label paper at £890 per tonne.

Paper size calculation

mm		mm	Trimmed size
100		80	
+ 6		+ 6	trim
= 106	×	= 86	
× 9	×	× 8	72-up labels
= 954	×	= 688	
+ 6		+ 12	sides and leave edges
+ 10			colour bar
+ 12			gripper margin
982	×	700	working size

Method of working: 72-up on special size 700mm × 982mm

Net number of sheets required	= 3,500,000 + 72	= 48,611 sheets
Make-ready and set-up	= 550 + 100 (coating)	= 650
Running waste, 240,000 × 8%		= 3,403
Number of sheets, inclusive of overs		= 52,664 700 mm × 982mm
Weight per 1,000 sheets	= 0.70 × 0.982 × 75	= 51.55kg
Total cost of paper	= 51.55 × 52.664 × £0.890	= £2,416.20

Reel-fed and web-fed printing

The approach to paper calculations for reel-fed and web-fed printing is quite different from the approach for sheet-fed printing. Reel-fed or web-fed printing machines come in three main types.

Small-width reel-fed or web-fed machines

Small-width reel-fed or web-fed machines are available in a wide selection of formats and can produce a very comprehensive range of printing and print-related products. The two main areas are continuous stationery products and self-adhesive label products.

Presses for continuous stationery and business forms

Presses for continuous stationery and business forms can be single-part or multi-part, reel-to-reel or reel-to-pack. They can be fixed-cylinder size presses or variable-cylinder size presses. Popular cylinder sizes are 24.75in, 24in, 22in, 20in and 17in circumferences as well as 28in, 26in and 18in. A 24in cylinder press would be able to produce forms in derivatives of 24in, e.g. 24in, 12in, 8in, 6in and 4in deep. A 22in cylinder press could produce 22in, 11in, 7.33in and 5.5in deep forms. It is essential for any company supplying continuous business stationery and/or cheques to have a wide range of cylinders and ancillary equipment.

Self-adhesive label machines

Self-adhesive labels in reel form can be for machine application or hand application by the customer. The way the customer applies the label to the bottle or container is very important. It governs how the job is laid down to suit the customer and the requirements of the printer's machine. Labels can be top or bottom, right- or left-hand edge leading and can be wound on the inside or the outside of the reel. If a front and back label are required, they may be produced alternately on the same reel.

Generally speaking, for small-width self-adhesive machines, 180mm is the maximum reel width, including wastage, but models having reel widths of 200mm and 250mm are also available. Labels can be printed one wide to view on the web, or if printed more than one wide, a slitter unit can cut the number of labels across down to one wide, if required. The more sophisticated machines used for printing self-adhesive labels are capable of printing up to six colours or more, varnishing, die-cutting to shape, foil blocking, numbering, laminating, embossing, perforating and printing on the adhesive side as well as the face side. Attachments to the basic equipment are required to perform some of these operations. A wide range of cylinder circumferences are available; the spacing between labels can vary and it depends on the choice of cylinder size.

Various types of material can be used and in different finishes, e.g. gloss label, cast-coated, clear vinyl. Adhesive backing may be permanent, removable or semi-permanent; semi-permanent labels can be repositioned within a certain time should it be applied slightly out of position. It is possible to produce tube laminates such as toothpaste tubes on reel-fed machines. Flat or rotary cutters can be used; the length of the label and the quantity ordered determine whether flat or rotary cutters are used. Material calculations for small-width reel machines, producing forms or labels, are based on the number out from the width of the printing web and the relevant cut-off for the printing cylinder, e.g. printing A4 forms on a 24.75in (629mm) cylinder press with a web paper 26in (660mm) wide will give six A4 forms out of one complete cylinder circumference. Similarly, the number of labels out will depend on how many labels can be obtained out of the web width and full cylinder circumference.

Paper calculations for heatset web offset printing

Heatset web offset machines

Mini- or narrow-web offset machines Mini- or narrow-web offset machines are used mainly for producing four-colour process covers of magazines and leaflets, folders and small booklets. There are also machines designed or modified for a range of special products, including online facilities such as spot gluing, cutting out to shape, strip gumming and inkjet personalisation for direct mail and special promotions. The presses normally have a maximum web width of between 508mm and 673mm, and a fixed cut-off at between 451mm and 630mm. The standard mini-web produces work commonly based on 8 pages A4 printed four-colour process on both sides.

Large-format web machines Large-format web machines are used mainly for long-run, high-pagination magazines and supplements, mainly in four-colour process. The machines have varying combinations of maximum web width and fixed cut-offs producing output products having 16, 32, 48 or 64 pages, size A4 or its equivalent, printed four-colour process on both sides Twin-web running doubles the output of a single-web machine. For example, a twin-web 16-page press will produce 32 pages. Complex folder arrangements allow a range of formats varying from broadsheet (A2) and tabloid (A3) to permutations of A4 and A5.

The web width required in heatset web offset printing, accommodating adequate trim and binding lap allowances, varies according to the method of binding. The following examples illustrate relatively common practices in the printing industry.

Example 7.8 Example paper width calculation for saddle-stitched work, insetted sections.

Web width = number of pages wide × trimmed width (mm) + 25mm

An A4 job on a 4 × A4 wide web press gives a web width of

4 × 210mm + 25mm = 865mm

Example 7.9 Example paper width calculation for perfect bound work, gathered sections.

Web width = number of pages wide × trimmed width (mm) + 32mm

An A4 job on a 4 × A4 wide web press gives a web width of

4 × 210mm + 32mm = 872mm

As with sheet-fed printing, estimators should build up calculation scales based on the practices in their own organisation.

Example 7.10 How to calculate paper quantity and cost for web offset printing.

Step 1: weight of paper

$$\text{Paper quantity (tonnes)} = \frac{\text{cut-off (mm)}}{1000} \times \frac{\text{web width (mm)}}{1000} \times \frac{\text{gsm}}{1}$$

$$\times \frac{\text{number of pages in job}}{\text{number of pages out}} \times \frac{\text{quantity}}{1000} \times \frac{1}{1000}$$

Step 2: spoilage allowance
Add the appropriate spoilage to the weight of paper established in step 1.

Step 3: cost of paper
Multiply the total weight of paper, including spoilage, by the price per tonne.

Example 7.11 Calculate the size, the web width, the weight and cost of paper for the following job to be printed by heatset web offset in four-colour process on a 16-page, four-wide A4 size press with a 630mm cut-off. 250,000 copies of a 96-page self-cover holiday brochure size A4, saddle-stitched two wires, trimmed to bleed. The paper to be used is part mechanical 80gsm at £640 per tonne. Note a four-wide × A4 size press with a 630mm cut-off will produce 16 pages A4 from one cut-off.

Step 1: weight of paper

$$\frac{630}{1000} \times \frac{865}{1000} \times \frac{80}{1} \times \frac{96}{16} \times \frac{250,000}{1000} \times \frac{1}{1000} = 65.394 \text{ tonnes}$$

Step 2: spoilage allowance

Weight of paper without wastage (tonnes)	=	65.394
Cut-offs		
based on 4,000 cut-offs + 10% running waste		
= 4,000 × 6 = 24,000 = 24 × 0.63 × 0.865 × 80	=	1.046
Running waste		
250,000 × 6 × 10% = 150,000 = 150 × 0.63 × 0.865 × 80	=	6.539
Total weight of paper required (tonnes)	=	**72.979**

Step 3: cost of paper

72.979 tonnes × £640 per tonne = £46,706.56

Example 7.12 Calculate the size, width of web, weight and cost of text paper only for the following job to be printed by heatset web offset in four-colour process on an 8-page, two-wide A4 press with a 630mm cut-off. 20,000 copies of a monthly magazine, 88 pages plus cover, size 220mm × 286mm, perfect bound, trimmed to bleed. The paper to be used is white art 100gsm at £660 per tonne. Note a two-wide × A4 size press with 630mm cut-off will produce 8 pages A4.

Step 1: weight of paper

$$\frac{630}{1000} \times \frac{472}{1000} \times \frac{100}{1} \times \frac{88}{8} \times \frac{20,000}{1000} \times \frac{1}{1000} = 6.542 \text{ tonnes}$$

Step 2: spoilage allowance

Weight of paper without wastage (tonnes)	=	6.542
Cut-offs		
based on 4,000 cut-offs + 15% running waste		
= 4,000 × 11 = 44,000 = 44 × 0.63 × 0.472 × 100	=	1.308
Running waste		
20,000 × 11 × 10% = 22,000 = 22 × 0.63 × 0.472 × 100	=	0.654
Total weight of paper required (tonnes)	=	**8.504**

Step 3: cost of paper

8.504 tonnes × £660 = £5612.64

Inks and toners

8

Estimating the ink quantities and/or ink prices to be used on a range of jobs is not an easy or quick process, and this leads some printing organisations to adopt a simpler and quicker alternative to calculating ink usage for each job. A common example is on small-format jobs with very short runs and light ink coverage. Here ink represents only a small charge to the overall cost of the printed job that could well be exceeded by the administrative cost of the ink calculation. Further examples are where printers regularly undertake predictable types of printing work, applying a price- or weight-based formula calculated from their previous experience and historical records of ink consumption, as illustrated by Tables 8.4 and 8.5 (pages 162 and 164 respectively). As a result, ink calculations are often greatly simplified by one of the following approaches:

▶ Applying a minimum or set charge of, 50p, £1, £5 or £10, depending on the size and type of job, coverage and colours used, to recover the cost of the ink.

▶ Charging a minimum amount of ink in terms of weight and colour used for each job, such as 0.1kg, 0.25kg, 0.5kg and 1kg, depending on the typical class of work and print quantity.

▶ Recovering the cost of ink as part of the general overheads of the business, or recovering the cost of ink in proportion to the value of the substrate. For example, a printer with an annual expenditure of £500,000 on substrates and £50,000 on ink could decide to recover ink costs by adding 10% to the substrate price charged to each job.

Even where ink, or toner in the case of digital printing, is not applied as a separate direct cost, it is still a very important factor in the printing process. Estimators need to have an appreciation of ink and its properties and how it can affect the running speeds of presses and postpress equipment. Examples include waiting time for wet work on short-run work-and-turn sheet-fed offset litho printing, plus varnishing and coating to avoid marking and improve rub resistance on matt coated stocks.

Inks, toners, varnishes and coatings

Inks, toners, varnishes and coatings are manufactured with specific properties and characteristics to suit printing processes, applications and substrates. Printing inks, for example, are specially formulated not just for each printing process such as offset litho, but to suit the different variations within the process, such as sheet-fed offset litho, heatset and coldset. Similarly, inks are made to accommodate the varying requirements of flexography, letterpress, gravure, screen and digital. Additional considerations include the working speed of the printing presses as higher running speeds require thinner inks, along with specialist inks such as ultraviolet (UV), metallic, laser-compatible and inkjet. The substrate has a marked impact on the performance and drying properties of ink. Apart from inks being formulated to print on paper and board, a wide range of non-cellulose substrates are manufactured covering such diverse materials as polythene, polyester, latex and aluminium foil.

The main ingredients of inks are the pigment and the vehicle. The pigment supplies the colour that is dispersed into the vehicle or varnish. The varnish is the medium for carrying the pigment during the printing process and subsequently binding it to the substrate. Most coloured pigments are petrochemical in origin, although naturally occurring pigments are still used. The quality of the pigment and the fineness to which it is ground largely govern the printing qualities of the ink and its effect on the final printed result. In addition to the pigment and vehicle, additives such as thinners, pastes and drying agents are included in the ink formulation to establish the required properties. The better quality inks are more concentrated and achieve a higher density than cheaper inks, consequently a thinner ink film can be used.

Ink drying

There are three main types of conventional ink drying – evaporation, absorption and oxidisation – and depending on the substrate, most inks dry by a combination of these methods. Ink drying based on evaporation relies on the varnish consisting of a resin, dissolved in a volatile liquid, evaporating rapidly into the atmosphere, leaving a dry ink film consisting of the pigment bound to the substrate by the resin. Ink drying based on absorption operates by the ink penetrating or being sufficiently absorbed into the substrate, although the ink itself often remains in a relatively liquid state for some time. Ink drying based on oxidisation works through the oxygen from the air being absorbed by the wet film of ink on the substrate, and through chemical reaction the vehicle becomes solid and dry, binding the pigment to the substrate.

Properties and uses of printing inks

Coldset web offset presses, used extensively for printing newspapers and newspaper-type products, require the printing ink to be absorbed into the paper quickly, but also to be non-drying on the machine. A vehicle is used that easily penetrates the paper and is absorbed but never really dries, staying open and so avoiding the need for washing up. The absorption-based drying process, representative of newspaper inks, produces a dull, flat finish often with poor rub resistance that prevents its use in higher-quality commercial work.

Flexographic and gravure inks dry mainly by evaporation and absorption; screen printing inks dry mainly by oxidisation and evaporation. Most letterpress inks dry by oxidisation and absorption and only to a small extent by evaporation, because only solvents or vehicles of the slowest evaporation rate can be used. However, some means of accelerated drying is now popular in all printing processes.

Generally speaking, offset litho requires stiff viscous ink, with good definition on all kinds of substrate and yet it must not dry rapidly on the rollers. Inks drying by the oxidisation of thickened linseed oil meet these requirements very well, although they have the drawback of taking several hours to dry. However, inks are available for hard-surfaced and similar non-absorbent substrates that dry quickly by oxidisation. Gravure, flexographic and screen inks tend to be either solvent- or water-based.

Properties and uses of toners

Toners, available in dry or liquid form, are the main colouring medium for digital printing systems. The main properties of toners required for digital printing are that the toner particle size must be small enough to achieve sharp definition, and the toner must flow or transport in a controlled manner to ensure uniform application.

Dry toners come in two main types, single- or monocomponent and dual-component. The monocomponent type, as the name implies, is a one-part system that does not require an additional carrier to function. Dual-component toners, on the other hand, consist of toner particles plus a granular or powder carrier, to help transport and bind the toner to the substrate. They generally also have the advantage over monocomponent toner in that their particle size is smaller, yielding higher resolution and brighter printed colours. The fusing of dry toners to produce the final printed result is mainly through radiant heat or heat pressure, whereas liquid toners use hot transfer or hot air to produce a dried printed result.

Liquid toners consist of pigmented toner and carrier that is normally a liquid hydrocarbon or mineral spirit, with the toner being 'liquefied', as it is suspended in the carrier. Liquid toner systems are generally considered to give superior printed results than dry toner systems, through brighter colours and smaller toner particle size. They result in printed work with features more in keeping with conventional printing inks, rather than the glazed appearance that is often associated with dry toner. More highly intensive transparent colours are also possible with liquid toners.

Inkjet is a major inking system used in digital printing where the vehicle or wetting agent is either water or solvent, and the drying process is absorption, evaporation or a mixture of the two. The vast majority of sheet-fed copier/printer systems use dry toners or dry inks, as they are called in some systems; whereas a large quantity of large-format reel and web digital printing systems are inkjet based. In digital printing, the cost of toners and inks is often included in the click rate cost per copy (Chapter 10).

Coatings and finishes

The appearance of finished printed products can be enhanced significantly by the application of a coating or varnish. Apart from looking more attractive, the printed product is also given added protection when the coating is applied overall, such as on a brochure cover or a carton. Another advantage is the improved aesthetic appeal, where spot varnishing, particularly ultraviolet (UV) based, is used to highlight and make certain areas stand out and appear more prominent. Coatings and varnishes can be applied to a wide range of printed products, and the choice of coating is influenced by the cost and overall finish required. In-line coating on a printing machine, or on a separate machine unit, is available in three main types:

▶ Varnishing is applied via the printing press using a print unit. It gives good moisture protection, has similar properties to ink, but can yellow with age and be slow drying.

▶ Aqueous coating consists of a mixture of water and solids; it is most often applied through an in-line coating system, fitted as an additional unit to sheet-fed offset litho presses. Occasionally aqueous coating is also applied through the offset litho damping unit. It gives a good hard surface with high gloss when required, is fast drying with no yellowing of the printed result. There is a risk, however, of sheet stretch or shrinkage, with lower grammage papers, due to the high water content.

▶ UV-dried varnish is cured by radiation and gives the best finish, where the whole coated surface changes into a solid state. The result is an extremely high-gloss finish comparable to gloss laminating. Instant drying with very high abrasion resistance, but requiring special inks, makes this method more expensive than ordinary varnishing or aqueous coating.

All types of overall coating reduce the amount of anti-set-off powder, so diminishing the effect of anti set-off, which can be detrimental to the final result of sheet-fed offset litho printing. Five- and six-colour sheet-fed offset litho presses have been very popular for many years with carton and label printers. This press configuration has also become popular with commercial printers, where one of the print units is regularly used to apply a varnish; alternatively, presses are fitted with an additional in-line coating unit. A further development has seen the fast growth of 8-, 10- and 12-colour sheet-fed offset litho convertible presses. Here are some examples of sheet-fed offset litho multicolour press configurations regularly used for coating and sealing:

▶ 8-colour convertible press in the 4/4 mode, printing four-colour process both sides in one press pass, with additional in-line aqueous coating units.

▶ 10-colour convertible press in the 5/5 mode, printing four-colour process both sides, plus varnish, in one press pass.

▶ 12-colour convertible press in the 6/6 mode, printing four-colour process, plus one special colour process both sides, plus varnish, in one press pass.

▶ 12-colour convertible press in the 6/6 mode, printing four-colour process, plus two special colour process both sides in one press pass, with additional in-line aqueous coating units.

The application of a seal varnish or aqueous coating, with hot-air accelerated drying, will often result in touch-dry printed work that can be handled immediately or at least within 30 minutes.

Ink calculation formulae

There are several formulae for calculating ink consumption. Most computer estimating software uses ink formulae like the ones in this chapter, where the estimator simply expresses the printed image in a range of units or factors, making adjustments for lighter or heavier coverage than average. There main are several ink formulae covered in this chapter.

Quantities of ink required

The amount of ink required for any job depends on five main factors:

▶ the printing process
▶ the nature of the subject image
▶ the paper (or board) stock
▶ the colour and type of ink
▶ the number of copies required.

There are, however, other factors to consider when assessing ink consumption. Temperature, humidity, the condition of the printing equipment and the skill of the operatives, all have an impact. A badly set ink duct, poor rollers or poor roller settings, a worn offset blanket or ink pollution caused by an incorrect water/ink balance, can result in excess wastage and heavy usage, much higher than the figures in this chapter.

Ink film thickness can be assessed by a densitometer, but it is of little use when estimating ink quantities. It is essential that the actual ink used is accurately recorded and transferred correctly to the job costs and subsequently to the estimator's records when required for checking actual versus estimated ink consumption. In some printing companies, however, it is common practice, especially on special ink mixes, for the full or part order of ink to be booked to a specific job or group of jobs. Ink is sold by weight, its ingredients varying from colour to colour and even within colours, which means that volume for weight varies.

Since ink usage can only be calculated on a theoretical basis and even then only approximately, past records should be used to supplement the calculations for the range of jobs and materials used in any organisation. Suppose a company has printed several 16-page sections of a mail-order catalogue or regular magazine publications over a period of time, records will show the average weight and cost of ink per 1000 sheets or 10,000 cut-offs of paper used in the sample jobs. The only alterations required would involve adjustments for changes in ink costs and the different materials used, if and when required.

Printing processes

Tables 8.1 to 8.5 (pages 157–164) provide guidance figures for the consumption of inks when printing by offset litho. It is difficult, however, to make direct comparisons between the different printing processes for ink consumption and related costs, as the composition and properties of the ink vary greatly. A further factor that affects the quantity of ink required is the typical ink film thickness laid down by the different printing processes. The following figures, stating the average thickness in microns, for the full range of conventional printing processes, are included for general guidance only, as so many variables can be involved.

Process	Average ink film thickness (µm)
Offset litho	2
Flexography	2–3
Letterpress	3–4
Gravure	6–8
Screen	8–40

Offset litho prints the thinnest ink film of all the printing processes. Screen lays down by far the thickest, hence it can overprint light colours on dark substrates without affecting the ink colour.

Nature of subject image

The two extremes of subject image are normally type matter, such as light line matter in bookwork, and solid areas. All other kinds of image can be expressed in terms of one or the other. Heavy display lines can be measured in terms of a solid, just as a reversed line subject needs only to have the non-printing areas deducted from the whole to give the equivalent of a solid. Halftone images consist of a series of varying dot sizes, covering solid, midtone and highlight areas and on average can be expressed as approximately one-third of the solid area. Make allowance for very light work or very dark subjects. In four-colour process work, the density of each colour varies, hence Table 8.2 (page 158) gives separate figures. Tint areas consist of a series of dots of the same size within a designated area and are normally available from 5% to 95%, i.e. a 5% tint area would consist of an inked area of 5% and a clear or uninked area of 95%. A 50% tint represents 50% of the solid calculation, hence it requires half the ink allowed for solid coverage.

Paper and board stock

As can be seen from Table 8.1, high-gloss art paper or board holds up ink on the paper or board surface to the highest extent, thereby giving the best ink coverage per given area and is used as the base figure for the calculations. All other paper and board therefore require more ink for the same job than high-gloss art. To simplify matters, as indicated in Table 8.1, the ink required for different paper and board types can be expressed as an additional percentage, or factor, over the base figure of white art.

Colour and type of ink used

On a similar basis to paper and board, different coloured inks have varying ink coverage capabilities. Black has the best ink coverage, with all the other colours requiring an additional allowance. This is confirmed by the ink formula in Table 8.3, i.e. SPANKS.

Number of copies required

The simple and obvious point is that the more copies are printed, the more ink will be required to print them.

Ink wastage

During the printing process, ink is lost in the duct and on the rollers, so make an allowance to cover this. Follow these suggestions:
▶ For runs of up to 5000 add 10%
▶ For runs of 5001 up to 20,000 add 7.5%
▶ For runs of 20,001 and above add 5%.
Some large printing presses may waste approximately 0.5kg when a duct is cleaned, whereas small machines will waste much less. Loose fibres on some fluffy or loosely bonded papers and boards, such as recycled, result in extra wash-ups and this should be reflected in the calculations. Include overs when calculating the total ink required.

The range of colours in Table 8.1 should be used as a basis for all non-process colours, e.g. brown, made up from predominantly red and green would add 27.5% to the basic figures in Table 8.1. This calculation is based on a 50:50 mix of the two colours. In practice this may not be the case, so assess the composition of the required colour. Using Table 8.1 as a reference, it can be established that 1000 impressions of $1m^2$ ($1m^2$ = 10,000cm²) of plain text in black ink will require 0.40kg of ink when printed offset litho on a white general printing.

TABLE 8.1 Formula for monochrome, single-colour offset litho ink coverage based on the amount of standard black ink (kg) for 1000 impressions of 1m²

Type of printed image	High gloss and cast coated	SC machine and matt coated	MF and smooth general printing	Rough, open general printing	Rough, open antique
	(factor 1)	(factor 1.33)	(factor 1.5)	(factor 1.75)	(factor 2)
Solid area (100%)	1.50	2.00	2.25	2.62	3.00
Complete halftones (33.3%)	0.50	0.66	0.75	0.87	1.00
Heavily illustrated (25%)	0.37	0.45	0.56	0.65	0.75
Lightly illustrated (20%)	0.30	0.49	0.45	0.53	0.60
Plain text (15%)	0.23	0.30	0.35	0.40	0.46
Very light coverage (8%)	0.12	1.16	0.18	0.21	0.24
To adjust for coloured inks	Add				
Blue	15%				
Bronze blue	20%				
Red	25%				
Green	30%				
Yellow and its variations	33.3%				

Source: H. M. Speirs

Ink calculations using Table 8.1

$$\text{Ink required} = \frac{\text{area (cm}^2\text{) of subject image} \times \text{no. of copies (incl. covers)}}{1000 \text{ impressions} \times 10,000\text{cm}^2} \times \text{factor figure}$$

Example 8.1 11,500 copies, including overs, of a booklet size A5, 16 pages self-cover, printed black only on smooth general printing paper quality. The printed page area throughout is 140mm × 100mm and ink coverage is assessed as lightly illustrated.

$$\frac{16 \times 14 \times 10 \times 11,500}{1000 \times 10,000} \times 0.45 = 1.16\text{kg ink} + 7.5\% \text{ wastage} = 1.25\text{kg black ink}$$

Example 8.2 48,000 copies, including overs, of an A1 poster, trimmed to bleed, printed one side only in black, green and red on cast-coated paper. Ink coverage is assessed as 60% red, 40% green and 25% black.

$$\frac{60 \times 84.7 \times 48,000}{1000 \times 10,000} \times 1.5 \times 0.60 \times 1.25 = 27.44\text{kg ink} + 5\% \text{ wastage} = 28.8\text{kg red ink}$$

$$\frac{60 \times 84.7 \times 48,000}{1000 \times 10,000} \times 1.5 \times 0.40 \times 1.3 = 19.03\text{kg ink} + 5\% \text{ wastage} = 20\text{kg green ink}$$

$$\frac{60 \times 84.7 \times 48,000}{1000 \times 10,000} \times 1.5 \times 0.25 = 9.15\text{kg ink} + 5\% \text{ wastage} = 9.6\text{kg black ink}$$

Four-colour process inks

Table 8.2 covers printing in four-colour process by offset litho in art, machine or matt coated and smooth general printing papers. Using Table 8.1, we can adjust the figures for different types of stock, so we get 3.94 (2.25 × 1.75) for rough, open general printing paper and 4.50 (2.25 × 2) for rough, open antique paper. If the exact nature of the image being estimated is known, then the required ink quantities should be adjusted accordingly, e.g. an estimate for a holiday brochure consisting of mainly blue sea and skies may call for an increase in the quantities of cyan, possibly yellow, with a corresponding reduction for magenta and black ink. Note that if undercolour removal (UCR) is used in scanning, this will reduce the quantities of colour inks (CMY) needed, depending on the extent of UCR, and increase the quantity of black (K).

TABLE 8.2 Formula for four-colour process offset litho ink coverage based on the amount of four-colour process ink (kg) for 1000 impressions of 1m²

Type of stock	All four colours	Yellow	Magenta	Cyan	Black
	(factor 1)	(factor 1/3)	(factor 1/6)	(factor 1/4)	(factor 1/4)
High-gloss art	2.25	0.75	0.38	0.56	0.56
Machine or matt coated	3.00	1.00	0.50	0.75	0.75
Smooth general printing	3.36	1.12	0.56	0.84	0.84

Source: H. M. Speirs

Ink calculations using Tables 8.1 and 8.2

$$\text{Ink required} = \frac{\text{area (cm}^2\text{) of subject image} \times \text{no. of copies (incl. overs)}}{1000 \text{ impressions} \times 10{,}000\text{cm}^2} \times \text{factor figure}$$

Example 8.3 21,000 copies, including overs, of a brochure size A4 upright, trimmed to bleed, 48 pages self cover, printed sheet-fed offset litho throughout in four-colour process on 115gsm white art.

$$\frac{48 \times 21 \times 30.3 \times 21{,}000}{1000 \times 10{,}000} \times 2.25 = 146.37\text{kg ink} + 5\% \text{ wastage} = 153.7\text{kg ink}$$

$$= 154\text{kg to the nearest kg}$$

Yellow	154 × 0.33 = 51.33kg	= 51kg
Magenta	154 × 0.17 = 26.18kg	= 26kg
Cyan	154 × 0.25 = 38.50kg	= 38.50kg
Black	154 × 0.25 = 38.50kg	= 38.50kg

Example 8.4 288,000 cartons, including overs, overall image size assessed at 620mm × 840mm, 9-up, printed sheet-fed offset litho in four-colour process, plus fifth colour red, on cartonboard with top surface equivalent of machine coated finish. The four colour process area is assessed as 75% coverage and red as 15% solid.

Number of sheets printed = 288,000/9 = 32,000

$$\frac{62 \times 84 \times 32,000}{1000 \times 10,000} \times 3 \times 0.75 = 37.5\text{kg ink} + 5\% \text{ wastage} = 39.4\text{kg ink}$$

$$= 39\text{kg to the nearest kg}$$

Yellow	39 × 0.33	= 13kg
Magenta	39 × 0.17	= 6.5kg
Cyan	39 × 0.25	= 9.75kg
Black	39 × 0.25	= 9.75kg

$$\frac{62 \times 84 \times 32,000}{1000 \times 10,000} \times 2 \times 0.15 \times 1.25 = 6.25\text{kg ink} + 5\% \text{ wastage} = 6.56\text{kg red ink}$$

Metallic inks

To obtain the best results from metallic inks, it is advisable to print a base ink, such as a tint of yellow or cyan depending on the circumstances, before printing the metallic ink. This needs to be included in the calculations. The approximate coverage per kilogram for metallic inks on gloss material works out as follows:

▶ Gold: 1000 impressions of 2000cm^2.

▶ Silver: 1000 impressions of 2700cm^2.

The SPANKS formula in Table 8.3 is often known as the Coates formula, although most ink manufacturers use it, or an adapted version, plus the formulae in Tables 8.1 and 8.2.

TABLE 8.3 Formula for four-colour process offset litho ink coverage using SPANKS

The ink calculation is SPANKS/356 where

S = stock, type of substrate and surface finish, broken down into	
High-gloss art	1.0
Matt and machine coated	1.2
Supercalendered (SC)	1.3
Machine finished (MF) printing	1.4
Smooth cartridge	1.6
Newsprint	1.8
Rough antique	2.0
Cartonboard	2.0
Cover paper or board	2.2
P = printing process	
Offset litho	0.5
Letterpress or flexography	1.0
A = area of printed coverage	
N = number of sides printed	
K = kind of printed area, broken down into	
Solids	1.0
Reverse lettering (assuming 30% white-out)	0.7
Heavily illustrated	0.4
Catalogue work with illustrations (mix of illustrations, tints and type)	0.3
Heavy type	0.2
Light type	0.15

TABLE 8.3 Formula for four-colour process offset litho ink coverage using SPANKS (cont)	
S(g) = specific gravity or relative density of ink, broken down into	
Black	1.1
Transparent colours such as process yellow, magenta and cyan	1.3
Opaque colours	1.5
Opaque white	1.8
Fluorescent colours	1.4
Gold	1.7
Silver	1.5
Overprint varnish	1.0

Source: Pira International Ltd

Ink calculations using Table 8.3

Example 8.5 65,000 sheets, including overs, size 720mm × 1020mm, consisting of folding box cartons 8-up to view, i.e. 520,000 single cartons in total. Printed one side only in sheet-fed offset litho in special brown and orange, four-colour process and overprint varnish. Assessed breakdown of area and type of printed coverage are as follows.

Brown	Solid and 40% of overall area
Orange	Solid and 10% of overall area
Four-colour process	Heavily illustrated and 45% of overall area
Black type – heavy	20% of overall area
Overprint varnish	Solid and 95% of overall area
Fully printed area of B1 sheet	650mm × 950mm

Brown ink

$$\frac{65,000 \times 2.0\,(S) \times 0.5\,(P) \times 0.65 \times 0.95\,(A) \times 1.0\,(N) \times 0.40 \times 1.0\,(K) \times 1.5\,(S)}{356}$$

= 67.65kg + 5% wastage

= 71.03, so allow 71kg

Orange ink

$$\frac{65,000 \times 2.0\,(S) \times 0.5\,(P) \times 0.65 \times 0.95\,(A) \times 1.0\,(N) \times 0.10 \times 1.0\,(K) \times 1.5\,(S)}{356}$$

= 16.91kg + 5% wastage

= 17.76, so allow 18kg

Process colours: yellow, magenta and cyan ink

$$\frac{65,000 \times 2.0 \text{ (S)} \times 0.5 \text{ (P)} \times 0.65 \times 0.95 \text{ (A)} \times 1.0 \text{ (N)} \times 0.45 \times 0.4 \text{ (K)} \times 1.3 \text{ (S)}}{356}$$

= 26.38kg + 5% wastage
= 27.70, so allow 28kg

Process black ink

$$\frac{65,000 \times 2.0 \text{ (S)} \times 0.5 \text{ (P)} \times 0.65 \times 0.95 \text{ (A)} \times 1.0 \text{ (N)} \times 0.45 \times 0.4 \text{ (K)} \times 1.1 \text{ (S)}}{356}$$

= 22.32kg + 5% wastage
= 23.44, so allow 24kg

Black type ink

$$\frac{65,000 \times 2.0 \text{ (S)} \times 0.5 \text{ (P)} \times 0.65 \times 0.95 \text{ (A)} \times 1.0 \text{ (N)} \times 0.20 \times 0.2 \text{ (K)} \times 1.1 \text{ (S)}}{356}$$

= 4.96kg + 5% wastage
= 5.21, so allow 5kg

Varnish

$$\frac{65,000 \times 2.0 \text{ (S)} \times 0.5 \text{ (P)} \times 0.65 \times 0.95 \text{ (A)} \times 1.0 \text{ (N)} \times 0.95 \times 1.0 \text{ (K)} \times 1.0 \text{ (S)}}{356}$$

= 107.11kg + 5% wastage
= 112.5, so allow 113kg

Summary

Brown ink	71kg
Orange ink	18kg
Process ink colours: yellow, magenta and cyan	28kg of each colour
Process black (24kg) and black type ink (5kg)	29kg
Overprint varnish	113kg

Example 8.6 180,000 copies of a leaflet, including overs, size 210mm × 148mm trimmed to bleed, printed both sides in sheet-fed offset litho in overall four-colour process on white gloss art 135gsm.

$$\frac{180,000 \times 1.0 \text{ (S)} \times 0.5 \text{ (P)} \times 0.216 \times 0.154 \text{ (A)} \times 2.0 \text{ (N)} \times 0.4 \text{ (K)} \times 1.3 \text{ (S)}}{356}$$

= 8.75kg + 5% wastage

= 9.19, so allow 9.25kg each of yellow, magenta and cyan ink

$$\frac{180,000 \times 1.0 \text{ (S)} \times 0.5 \text{ (P)} \times 0.216 \times 0.154 \text{ (A)} \times 2.0 \text{ (N)} \times 0.4 \text{ (K)} \times 1.1 \text{ (S)}}{356}$$

= 7.40kg + 5% wastage

= 7.77, so allow 8kg of black ink

Ink prices   The price of ink can vary by as much as 100% from one printer to another, depending on the size and purchasing power of the buyer. A large reel or web company and a sheet-fed company that are members of a print group with a group purchasing policy will be able to buy inks much more cheaply than a smaller, independent printing company. The figures and costs in Table 8.4 are based on printing by offset litho. Average ink usage and price figures can be built up for other printing processes. In Table 8.4, (a) represents ink costs for a printer with large buying power, gaining considerable economies of scale, whereas (b) represents a relatively small printer that orders ink in small quantities and weights. The costs and usage figures for ink, varnish and coating calculations, based on each company's consumption records and prices, need to be checked regularly then adjusted accordingly to keep them accurate.

TABLE 8.4 Average ink costs per 1000 sheets assuming an average coverage of 40%		
	Average ink costs (£)	
	Example (a)	**Example (b)**
Four-colour process		
SRA2/B2 sheet (450mm × 640mm/520mm × 720mm) printed both sides	2.00	4.00
SRA1/B1 sheet (640mm × 900mm/720mm × 1,040mm) printed both sides	4.00	8.00
Per separate four-colour process colour		
SRA2 /B2 sheet (450 × 640mm/520 × 720mm) printed both sides	0.50	1.00
SRA1/B1 sheet (640 × 900mm/720 × 1,040mm) printed both sides	1.00	2.00
Although black is the cheapest of the four process colours, it normally has the largest coverage; this tends to balance the cost equally between the process colours.		
Special colours, PMS and non-process colours		
SRA2 /B2 sheet (450mm × 640mm/520mm × 720mm) printed both sides	1.50	3.00
SRA1/B1 sheet (640mm × 900mm/720mm × 1,040mm) printed both sides	3.00	6.00

Source: H. M. Speirs

Medium to large printing companies buy process colour sets in reasonable bulk. This is not the case with other colours, so non-process colours such as PMS (Pantone Matching System) and/or special mixes can cost three times process colours or even more. Ink manufacturers also gain economies of scale from producing process inks in bulk, whereas non-process colours are usually made in much smaller batches. The pigments for non-process colours also tend to be more expensive. Some print companies adjust the prices in Table 8.4 to include the type of paper and board used. Suppose the Table 8.4 figures are based mainly on gloss art, but the job uses matt coated paper, then the prices may be increased by 33.3%. Other printers using figures similar to those in Table 8.4 apply them as an average covering the main range of stock they use without alteration.

Most sheet-fed offset litho presses are now based on B sizes rather than SRA sizes, which represents an increase of 27.5% over SRA sizes. Although the average sheet size printed by UK printers still tends to be based around SRA sizes or smaller, e.g. 630mm × 880mm, the ink calculations as expressed in Table 8.4 are generally applied in the industry based around B, SRA and slight variations thereof.

Ink calculations using Table 8.4

Example 8.7 110,000 SRA2 sheets, including overs, printed four-colour process both sides on coated stock. Ink charged at £2.00 per 1000 sheets, per four process colours.

110 × £2.00 + 5% wastage = £231.00

Example 8.8 5500 manuals size 297mm × 210mm, 32 pages self-cover, printed two PMS colours both sides on general offset printing, on a B2 press. Ink charged at £1.50 per 1000 sheets per colour.

$$\frac{32 \text{ pages}}{8 \text{ pages out per sheet}} = 4 \text{ SRA2 sheets per copy}$$

5.5 × 4 × £1.50 × 2 + 5% wastage = £70.95

UV inks

The ink prices in Table 8.4 are based on conventional inks, whereas UV inks are on average 2–3 times more expensive. In addition to calculations based on costs per 1000 sheets, some printers use weight-based calculations such as the guidelines in Table 8.5, mainly for bookwork in black only, on general offset printing paper.

TABLE 8.5 Average monochrome black ink usage	
Average ink usage (kg) per 10,000 sheets printed both sides	
Type or line only	
SRA2/B2 sheet (450mm × 640mm/520mm × 720mm)	1.5
SRA1/B1 sheet (640mm × 900mm/720mm × 1,040mm)	3.0
50:50 split between type and halftones	
SRA2/B2 sheet (450mm × 640mm/520mm × 720mm)	2.5
SRA1/B1 sheet (640mm × 900mm/720mm × 1,040mm)	5.0
Overall coverage in halftones	
SRA2/B2 sheet (450mm × 640mm/520mm × 720mm)	3.5
SRA1/B1 sheet (640mm × 900mm/720mm × 1,040mm)	7.0

Source: H. M. Speirs

Ink calculations using Table 8.5

Example 8.9 3750 copies, including overs, of a case-bound book, size 210mm × 210mm, 192 pages text, consisting of an even split between text and illustrations printed black only on white wove paper. Ink usage to be based on 5kg per 10,000 SRA1 sheets printed both sides.

$$\frac{192 \text{ pages}}{24 \text{ pages out of SRA1}} = 8 \text{ sheets per book}$$

0.375 × 8 × 5kg + 10% wastage = 16.5kg

Example 8.10 56,000 copies, including overs, of a manual, size 210mm × 148mm, 72 pages text plus cover, with text printed black only on white general offset printing paper. Ink usage to be based on 1.5kg per 10,000 SRA2 sheets printed both sides.

$$\frac{72 \text{ pages}}{16 \text{ pages out of SRA2}} = 4.5 \text{ sheets per manual}$$

5.6 × 4.5 × 1.5kg + 5% wastage = 39.6kg, so allow 40kg

Most of the previous ink calculations and assumptions have centred on offset litho, although the typical ink film thicknesses laid down by each of the main printing processes are stated on page 155. If the appropriate ratio is applied to the figures for offset litho in Tables 8.1 and 8.2 (pages 157 and 158) then figures for other printing processes can be roughly calculated. Here are some examples of ink calculations used by printers on different printing processes.

Screen Ten times the amount and cost of ink used for offset litho.

Gravure Four-colour process periodical printing on SC type paper at £2.50 per 1000 copies of 16 pages A4 cut-off.

Flexography On high-gloss flexible packaging material in three to six colours at 2.5gsm.

Letterpress Reel-fed self-adhesive labels in four-colour process allowing for 100% coverage: 1kg of each process colour covers 15,000in^2.

Digital The cost of inks and toners in digital printing is often recovered in the inclusive click rate charged by the equipment suppliers. As a guide, on HP Indigo colour presses, 700–1000 SRA3 sheets printed solid coverage, one side only, uses 1kg per colour. In examples where digital printers purchase their ink as separate consumables, printers will build up their specific ink coverage, usage and cost from their ongoing records, which differ from one user to another on the mix of work undertaken.

Seal or overprint varnish and coating

A seal or overprint varnish has become very popular in recent years to ensure quicker and easier handling of printed work, especially solids and heavy coverage on matt and satin coated papers. The following figures give guidance on the possible usage and cost. The average material costs of applying varnish or aqueous coating, based on 100% coverage both sides, per 1000 SRA1 sheets, is from £10.00 to £20.00. The amount of varnish or coating used, and the resultant cost, depends on the thickness of solution applied and the absorbency of the substrate.

Prepress

9

The changing face of prepress

On the one hand, prepress is now very much more streamlined and simplified into predictable digital workflows, culminating in for example computer-to-plate (CTP) and computer-to-print. But there is a confusing plethora of prepress options within the industry, both equipment and personnel, leading to a variable range of outcomes.

Desktop publishing (DTP), introduced in the mid 1980s, to a great extent democratised printing, taking away the dominant role printers had held for so long in preparing printed images for press through the use and control of specialist equipment only available to the printer. Since then the practically universal adoption of DTP has led to print-buying customers, copy writers and authors, creatives and designers, photographers, printers, repro trade houses and service bureau working at least initially from the same, if not similar, digital tools. This has led to closer and closer working relationships between customer and printer, but it has also fragmented the prepress cycle.

Most printing and print-related companies have currently been in business for over 20 years, and therefore they will originally have set up with traditional analogue-based prepress equipment. However, the pace of change and development in printing in the past two decades, especially in prepress, has been nothing short of extraordinary. At its most advanced level, prepress processes that traditionally used a wide range of equipment and different operations can now be carried out in one integrated digital workflow. However, although printing as part of the wider communication industries, is moving more and more towards a fully digital prepress scenario, the reality is that different print companies and print buyers are often at widely differing points in their adoption of prepress technology. Although traditional methods of working are largely dated, they are still in everyday use by many printers and will be for some time, although to a declining extent.

Prepress workflows

One of the main developments of recent times has been the emergence of the term 'prepress workflows' as the way of describing and examining the processes, operations and activities undertaken in prepress. These are systems within the area of prepress consisting of inputs and outputs leading to a designated final outcome such as approved digital artwork from a design brief; alternatively plates, cylinders and stencils passed for press from analogue or digital data. Today's fast-moving environment means that many players are involved in the prepress chain, and one creator's output will be another creator's input.

The measured control and management of workflows has become a major consideration and requirement in prepress as in some ways digital processes are invisible, but unfortunately they cannot be said to be truly seamless, at least not at the moment. The complexity of prepress workflows adds further to the potential for mistakes, errors and omissions, along with problems of incompatibility within one workflow or series of workflows. At each stage of the workflow, many problems and misunderstandings can be eliminated or reduced if preliminary and ongoing discussions take place between all parties involved in the workflow.

Although print creation and preparation are now based predominantly on a common platform of DTP, there are still alternative options used in printing and print-related areas, including dedicated proprietary systems in specialist areas, along with analogue and mixed-media working in the origination and reproduction of printed matter.

Different types of prepress reproduction

Traditional reproduction

Up to the stage of preparing plates for offset litho, flexography and letterpress, plus cylinders for gravure and stencils for screen printing, traditional reproduction, also known as conventional or analogue reproduction, involves a wide range of operations all producing a physical product that is passed on to the next stage for processing, converting and positioning into the required format. Traditional prepress reproduction is predominantly based on a photographic, film-based and light-sensitive series of activities, generally including a selection of bromides, negative and positive films from filmsetters and occasionally graphic arts cameras or other photographic equipment. Following the planning and/or outputting of film, film-based proofs are produced such as bromides, ozalids and colour photomechanicals, e.g. Cromalins and wet proofs, plus press image carriers for the appropriate conventional printing process.

Digital reproduction

The principle of digital reproduction is radically different from traditional reproduction in that the system creates and manipulates digital data. A digital prepress workflow produces physical or mechanical data only as a checking mechanism, such as hard-copy proofs from a laser or inkjet printer. The vast majority of print origination for all printing processes is now done on a DTP platform at least at the creative and initial prepress stages. Several options with different levels of digital working practices have been developed, largely confirming the technological progress made by all printing processes within a relatively short time. Such systems include computer-to-film (CTF), computer-to-plate (CTP), or cylinder and stencil, plus computer-to-press (CTPr) for specialist offset litho presses and computer-to-print or digital printing. See Figures 9.7 to 9.11 (pages 190–197).

Mixed-media reproduction

Most printers would choose to work completely digitally, but still find themselves having to work with mixed media, i.e. a mixture of digital and analogue or film-based media. This is because they operate in markets, such as magazines, journals and newspapers, where they regularly work with publishers, advertising and design agencies, plus general customers who supply at least some film or camera-ready copy for jobs, along with digital data in its many forms. To operate efficiently, printing companies have to find a common working environment, and that increasingly involves a digital workflow.

Apart from the external influences of printers being supplied with print-related material in non-digital form, there is often an immense amount of useful archived material in film form still being held or stored by printers, at least some of which would prove invaluable to the printer if it were available in digital form. A popular solution to this problem lies in the use of a scanner or scanning system that will digitise the analogue media, creating a common digital working environment including computer output systems.

Specialist dot-for-dot scanners and software updates to turn conventional scanners into dot-for-dot scanners have been developed to create digital data from line artwork, continuous tone or colour separated (prescreened) negative and positive film, transparencies and reflection colour prints. The scanner often has the facility to reproduce each single dot or line of a prescreened original. Alternatively, for the occasional film-based standing or reprint job, some printers find it more practical to strip in the film amendments and adopt a traditional working pattern, or simply to contract the job out to another printer whose working practices are still predominantly film-based. In addition, some print sectors of the industry, such as flexo, letterpress and screen, still rely heavily on film-based workflows.

Initial stages of prepress workflows

The following outline relates to Figure 9.1 (page 173). As printing is largely a bespoke industry, the earliest stages of a job rest largely with the customer; stages such as initial idea or need, market research, justification to proceed, budgeting and planning up to the design brief stage. Having decided to create a printed product or print-related product, various options are available.

Design brief: sketch or visual

The design briefing stage will normally begin with the customer or customer's representative briefing the person responsible for preparing the initial sketches and visuals. They will discuss the type of product, its use, house style, corporate image, illustrations, photographs, graphics and materials to be used, as well as the proposed budget and schedule. Preliminary discussions should ideally take place between the person responsible for coordinating the work for the customer, design agency, appropriate intermediaries and printing company staff. This is to ensure the artwork, film or digital data is prepared in the most effective manner and to the correct specification. The creation, manipulation and transfer of digital data are now the main driving force in all current communication media, including print.

Text writing and editing

Writing and editing are predominantly carried out by a member of the customer's staff or handled by someone on their behalf such as a professional copywriter. Text will generally be created in digital form on a PC using a word-processing program such as Microsoft Word, or in certain cases clean hard copy suitable for optical character reading (OCR) may be supplied.

Photography

Amateur photography will vary in quality depending on the skills of the individual plus their equipment, lighting and subject matter. Professional photographers are often commissioned to take a series of shots to a specific brief of subject matter, composition and balance, etc., but they may still need retouching to ensure the required printed result. The conventional photographic products used for printing reproduction fall into the main categories of monochrome or colour photographs, colour negatives or positive transparencies. New technology has led to higher-quality digital imaging through the use of digital cameras and copying or burning of analogue images on to CDs. The quality of digital photography is improving all the time, avoiding a number of intermediary processes and associated problems found in traditional photography, such as a tendency for emulsion fading and colour casts. A further development is the use of digital picture and image libraries.

Production layout
Unless the creative or graphic designer prepares the combined design and image elements on a DTP or computer-aided design (CAD) system up to the final print output stage, a production layout must be prepared for each job to ensure that the desired printed result is expressed in the elements or components necessary to create the printed images required.

Whatever system is adopted, the designer or creative will still need to produce sketches and visuals at the required stages to ensure the customer's approval to proceed and to discuss reproduction aspects with the next party in the reproduction workflow, including the printer. Production layouts are simply the equivalent of what in engineering would be outline drawings or blueprints. Professionally prepared, they can result in high-quality production visuals allowing the customer an ideal, inexpensive preview of the finished job and providing the printer with a preview and guide to work from.

Regular or repeat-format printing jobs such as periodicals, newsletters, common series of labels, cartons, etc., will often be prepared to an agreed template-based format, where either the printing company sets up a job-specific production layout template, accurately incorporating all the required parameters of the job for its own internal use, or it is passed on to the customer or other suppliers working on their behalf, so the work the printers receive is to a highly finished stage, with possibly only minor amendments and adjustments being required.

Graphic design
Graphic design for print is now predominantly produced on Apple Macintosh (Mac) and Windows-based PC computer systems using relatively standard and popular software application programs, along with more specialist systems such as CAD and dedicated high-end design systems, which are aimed mainly at specific areas of printing such as packaging, labels, high-value tickets and vouchers, direct mail and business forms. These systems are capable of generating digital files of text and graphics in colour, colour separated as applicable, retouched and redrawn to suit particular requirements. The designs are mainly stored in digital form and are therefore easily accessible for amendment, once the basic design parameters are prepared.

Typesetting
The creation of text and typesetting is now almost exclusively done on PCs and Macs. Technology has advanced so rapidly with the advent of DTP and WYSIWYG (what you see is what you get) terminals that the customer, or their print creative suppliers, can prepare or interface with a printing company's equipment to produce digital data in finished form.

Proof-reading and checking are increasingly performed by the person or department generating the keystrokes, which today tends not to be the printer.

Traditional reproduction stages

Text creation and typesetting are still undertaken by printers, albeit in a very limited form, if only for carrying out amendments and corrections. Most text creation and typesetting are carried out by customers, or another party on their behalf such as a word-processing office or specialist typesetting bureau. Photographs, transparencies and hard-copy artwork were traditionally reproduced on graphic arts cameras producing paper bromide or film output, although the majority of printers now do this almost exclusively on scanners. Most printers have disposed of their graphic arts cameras, but some have retained them to reproduce the occasional flat artwork they receive from their customers. Some specialist camera systems, historically popular with small offset and instant print shops, are capable of producing paper- or polyester-based offset litho plates as well as bromides, negative and positive film from camera-ready copy (CRC). These systems have been mainly superseded by digital alternatives.

Film make-up is mainly undertaken using negative or positive film on to plate flats or foils. Most printers still using analogue working practices have the equipment and capability to output complete planned one-piece composite film, via a filmsetter, also known as an imagesetter, from downloaded digital data, i.e. computer-to-film (CTF). This avoids the requirement for any manual film make-up or planning, unless some amendment film is stripped on to the existing master film to save outputting the full film area again. In film-based or analogue processes, proofs are produced as dry photomechanical proofs or wet proofs using plates. Platemaking or image carrier production is generated from punch-pin register film, negative, positive or other analogue-based form, as flats or foils contacted on to offset litho, flexographic or letterpress plates, gravure cylinders or screen stencils.

Digital reproduction stages

Text creation and typesetting are mainly generated on PCs or Macs in the form of transferable digital data such as floppy disk, CD, Iomega Zip or Jaz disk media or via telecommunication links. Sometimes text is created using OCR systems to scan hard copy into electronic text files. Photographs, transparencies and conventional artwork are scanned into the system, using a scanner either for colour or black and white reproduction. A further option is the use of digital cameras to supply digital images that are directly downloaded to the receiving DTP system.

Apart from being reproduced via a scanner or digital camera, graphics are also produced and/or adjusted using draw and paint, manipulation and retouching programs, such as Adobe Illustrator and Photoshop. Except for some highly specialised areas, desktop colour systems have overtaken the previously dominant proprietary electronic page composition (EPC) systems for graphic reproduction and manipulation.

During final image or page make-up all the subjects required for a job – text, photographs, graphics and tints, etc. – are normally reviewed and checked before being made up into the final required form. Also, as far as possible, the colour balance and other reproduction parameters are set up at the input stage. Digital proofing takes place at various stages, from black and white page or 1-up laser proofs to high-end inkjet colour proofs. Output can be in the form of CTF or CTP systems; whichever method is chosen, software is used to plan and impose page images or multiple images.

Examples of prepress workflows

Figure 9.1 illustrates the wide range of job-related and prepress operations, processes and routes commonly used in traditional, digital and mixed-media reproduction.

Combined prepress workflows

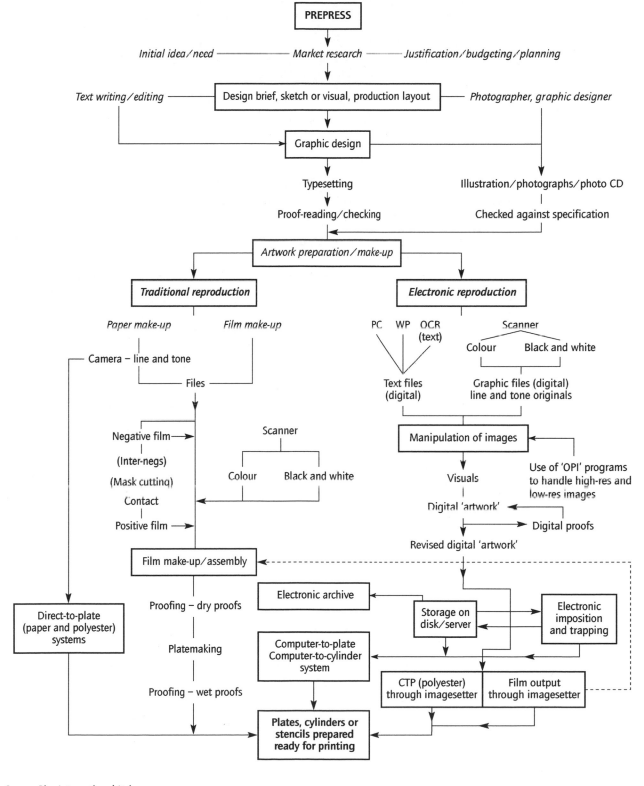

Source: Pira International Ltd

Digital prepress workflow

Figure 9.2 illustrates a modern, mainly digital prepress workflow suitable for a large printing company such as a B1 sheet-fed and/or heatset web offset printer. It indicates the flow of work from receipt of the wide-ranging print-related data that is typically supplied to printers up to final film stage (CTF) and/or CTP. The input elements include hard-copy documents that require converting into digital form using an OCR system that recognises the characters and generates a digital text file for importing into the networked PCs or Macs. Hard-copy originals such as mono (single-colour) or colour originals are scanned to produce graphic digital files suitable for manipulating and retouching.

The floppy disk is included to represent the supply of basic digital data such as text files that require planning and make-up; the Iomega disk represents final digital data in page or 1-up image form. Other digital data is supplied via a digital camera plus digital media as CD, DVD and telecommunications such as email or ISDN, containing either incomplete or final complete data, all of which will be preflighted and checked before being introduced into the host DTP system.

The front-end networked DTP system consists of two PCs and five Macs, supported by a powerful server for storage, archiving, etc. The server also hosts an internet or web connection, to which customers can download their job files, and depending on how the printer's website is set up, it can be used to preflight the files supplied by customers; in addition the system may support online proof checking and progress monitoring. A powerful network hub supports the whole configuration. In addition to the networked PCs and Macs, the workflow contains three high-end workstations to accept, retouch and preflight files and handle raster image processing (RIP); they also act as print servers to the two proofing devices as well as the imagesetter and platesetter.

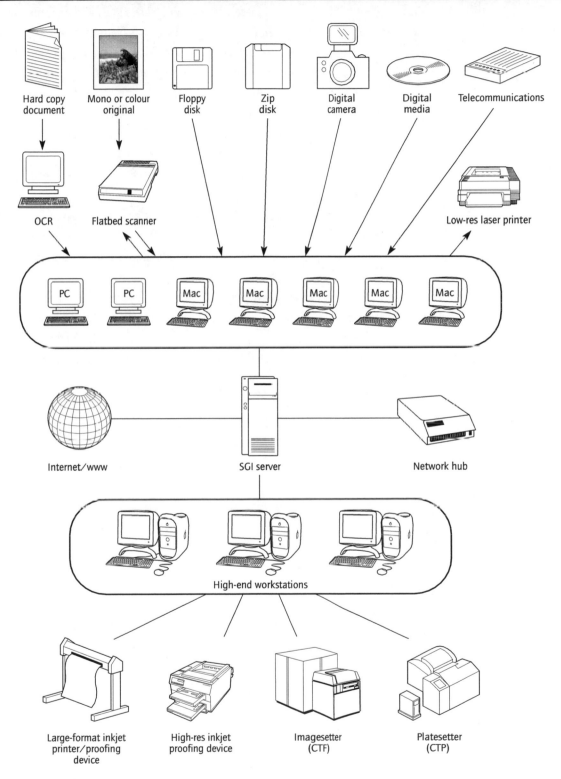

Source: Pira International Ltd

Proprietary integrated workflow

Figure 9.3 illustrates the Creo Synapse workflow system that incorporates the work of designers, print buyers, sales representatives and prepress staff into one integrated prepress-centred workflow. Synapse Prepare software has been designed to help designers, repro companies and prepress bureaux ensure that each file in Portable Document Format (PDF) is created to meet the designated exact intermediary and final output requirements of the users in the specific workflow system. It provides the means for print-related production houses to specify their technical details and requirements to designers. With Synapse Pro, the user creates directives, specifying, for example, the Quark XPress, Adobe Acrobat Distiller and preflight settings that control how Synapse Prepare creates the PDF files. Once a file is complete, the designer selects the press environment and Synapse Prepare software creates the production-ready PDF file.

Synapse InSite is the web portal into the prepress environment. It provides facilities for customers to submit jobs and track job status; it has a remote proof-access facility and it can be used to approve jobs and collaborate with everyone involved in each project using a standard web browser on a secure internet connection. With InSite web collaboration, users can view onscreen data, make annotations and have a virtual conversation online. Synapse Link automates the exchange of data between print production systems and management information systems (MIS). By integrating real-time production and MIS data, invaluable production and management data becomes available for all parties involved in the print chain.

FIGURE 9.3 Schematic of the Creo Synapse proprietary workflow

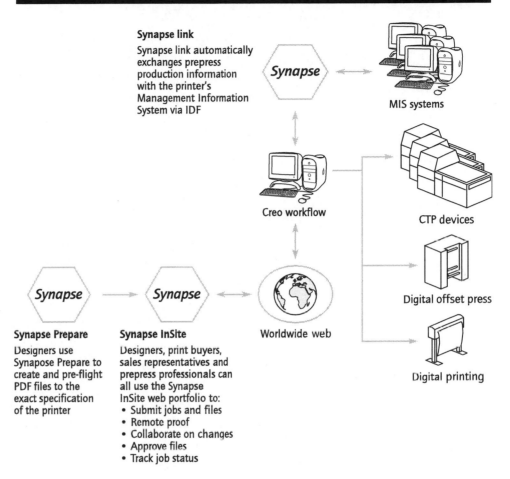

Synapse link

Synapse link automatically exchanges prepress production information with the printer's Management Information System via IDF

MIS systems

Creo workflow

CTP devices

Digital offset press

Worldwide web

Digital printing

Synapse Prepare

Designers use Synapose Prepare to create and pre-flight PDF files to the exact specification of the printer

Synapse InSite

Designers, print buyers, sales representatives and prepress professionals can all use the Synapse InSite web portfolio to:
• Submit jobs and files
• Remote proof
• Collaborate on changes
• Approve files
• Track job status

Source: Creo

Preflighting and workflow management

Due to the fragmentation in the wide range of prepress stages and processes, plus the considerable number of companies supplying prepress equipment and solutions, there is no industry-standard workflow or prepress sequence. Differences in file preparation, platforms, hardware, software, etc., do not entirely preclude a seamless design, create, print cycle but they do present many difficulties. As a result, preflighting and workflow management have become increasingly important in all stages of data creation, transport and receipt.

Preflighting is a simulation exercise that checks for any problems, faults and inconsistencies which may occur in the designated workflow. This is necessary because, in a digital environment, processes are generally automated and hidden, making visual checking impossible or impractical. Time and financial penalties will be incurred if clean and efficient workflows are not established and maintained. Preflighting within workflow management can cover areas such as checking page construction, graphic file formats, trapping, fonts, text matter, output device requirements and software-related problems, along with calibration issues to ensure standards are established, monitored and verified against identified criteria.

Workflow management systems are generally built around a RIP and take the form of an automated checklist system. The capabilities of a workflow system depend on its performance, flexibility and how it is set up to undertake and support the required applications. Due to the fast-moving and changing nature of modern business, many organisations and individuals do not wish to commit themselves to one particular supplier's workflow management system. This can be for a variety of reasons such as not wanting to be too dependent on one vendor or system, the relatively high initial cost of the system plus maintenance and support costs, the need to remain open and flexible in working patterns and the fact that specialist requirements are not met by any one workflow system.

In response to this, one of the options increasingly available to companies and individuals is to develop their own workflow system. Several vendors are now offering an increasing range of products in this area. Enfocus Software has a complete range of products for handling PDF documents: Instant PDF for creation, PitStop Professional for editing and preflighting, and PitStop Server for batch processing. In addition, the Enfocus core technologies Certified PDF and PDF Profile are widely recognised as important contributions to the graphics industry. Certified PDF turns any PDF document into a 'self-aware' file and PDF Profile provides complete PDF creation, preflighting and correction settings. Several international organisations have recognised the capabilities of Enfocus products by recommending them to their members; leading workflow vendors in the graphic arts industry such as Agfa, Creo, Fujifilm, EFI, Heidelberg, Screen Europe and others are integrating Enfocus technology into their core solutions.

Markzware is another major vendor that provides a wide range of quality file-related workflow solutions, including FlightCheck that scans and preflights many file types, including Quark XPress, PageMaker, Illustrator, Freehand, Photoshop, Multi-Ad Creator and PDF, by using a simple drag-and-drop interface to automatically alert the user to over 150 potential problems. Further products include MarkzScout, prepress software that allows users to manage files in their own workflows. MarkzNet is a real-time, web-based solution that checks, collects, compresses and captures job ticket information, and transmits PDF as well as native digital files over the internet to the user's own IP address using standard FTP. It works in conjunction with MarkzScout to provide a smooth workflow operation, routing the received jobs according to output device, colour settings, Mac or PC document types, or any other required destination.

For some time there have been a wide range of national bodies operating in print-related areas that have issued their members with digital production guidelines, which in recent years included recommendations on file preparation, data exchange, preflighting and workflow management. One example is the Swiss Printing Industries Association, which has named Enfocus software and PDF as its official standard for data exchange and workflows. A further example is the UK Periodical Publishers Association (PPA) that launched pass4press, a set of digital advertising standards that aim to eliminate the potential errors in the digital workflow caused by incorrect file formats. The PPA preflighting initiative provides a preflight check solution, where advertising artwork providers and receivers can validate files against elements of the pass4press specification and, once validated, deposit and retrieve the file as appropriate.

Prepress production times and related data

The production times, rates, costs and related details in this section and throughout the book are based on data established from a wide range of printing and print-related organisations. Due to the wide diversity of operational practices, types and levels of equipment and processes, costing systems and pricing policies used throughout the industry, the figures given can only claim to be representative at best of the industry's middle ground. They are intended only as a general guide and should not be taken as a definitive statement on production times and related data. Every organisation will differ in its work mix, equipment and process capability and productivity, operational practices, experience and expertise of its employees. As a result, the production times and related data will inevitably vary from company to company.

Most of the stated prepress times reflect the average time to do a process as a separate one-off operation, including the preparation stages and checking processes required, unless otherwise stated. Faster speeds and higher productivity will be achieved when work is ganged up or worked more than one image at a time, for example in scanning and make-up, so reducing the average time for an individual operation. It is also a relatively common practice for printers to apply a minimum charge per job and process to cover the initial minimum time and costs incurred on all jobs.

Typesetting production times

Although mainly carried out by and/or on behalf of the customer, typesetting is still carried out by most printers at least to undertake corrections, amendments or small takes of copy.

Simple, straightforward text setting, such as bookwork	8000 to 12,000 characters per hour
	1335 to 2000 words per hour
Short takes of mixed copy, such as magazine articles	5000 to 8000 characters per hour
	835 to 1335 words per hour
Complex tabular or mathematical setting, such as examination papers with formulae	2500 to 5000 characters per hour
	420 to 835 words per hour

The production times for foreign language setting depend on the operator's experience of setting each foreign language: 25–75% of normal speeds are experienced on the more common languages such as French, German and Spanish. Here are typical times for general typesetting on a Mac or PC.

	Simple text work	Tabular work
A5 page	15min	30min
A4 page	30min	60min

OCR

The operational time that can be expected using an OCR system to create a digital file from a hard original is 12 × A4 pages per hour. This time, i.e. 5min per A4 page, is based on good, clean typewritten or previously printed copy. Extra time will be required for poor quality originals where operators could misread some areas of copy or certain characters. Tabular work will also normally take much longer to create and/or amend.

Graphic arts camera

Most printers and repro suppliers have disposed of their cameras, but they have been retained in some specialist cases. Most work of this nature tends to be single-colour work or colour-separated hard-copy originals.

Camera	per line shot	5–10min
	per tone shot	10–15min
Contacting negative to positive	per line film	3–5min
	per tone film	5–10min
Retouching films	per film	5–30min
18cm × 24cm to 60cm × 80cm		

Photographic film

When photographing or contacting, it is common practice to use the largest size of film possible or practical for the camera and contacting frame. The major standard film sizes are 18cm × 24cm, 24cm × 30cm, 20cm × 40cm, 35cm × 45cm, 40cm × 50cm, 50cm × 60cm, 50cm × 66cm and 60cm × 80cm. Ideally 2.5cm extra should be allowed on all four film edges for handling.

Scanning

Modern scanners are used with an interface connecting it to a host computer, where scanning operations are controlled by software linking the two. This can take the form of an Adobe Photoshop plug-in or the scanner supplier's proprietary software. There are a wide range of colour scanners available covering high-end drum scanners and vertical or desktop drum scanners, plus entry-level, mid-range and high-quality charge-coupled device (CCD) flatbed scanners. Monochrome, single-colour scanners are available and are used mainly for publications such as newspapers and books which use a large amount of monochrome illustrations. Due to the much faster speed of black and white scanning, the rate is normally at least twice that of equivalent full-colour work.

Minimum scan, A6	12 scans per hour, i.e. 5min each
A5	8 scans per hour, i.e. 7.5min each
A4	6 scans per hour, i.e. 10min each
A3	4 scans per hour, i.e. 15min each
A2	3 scans per hour, i.e. 20min each

Colour retouching

Depending on the quality of the original image and/or scan, there may be the requirement for retouching to correct a flaw or introduce a new feature, by using DTP colour retouching and image editing software such as Adobe Photoshop and/or a proprietary one.

Colour retouching on PC or Mac	5–10min per image, up to 30min and above

Make-up

Make-up into final page form or 1-up image is now mainly carried out on DTP design and layout software programs such as Quark XPress, Adobe InDesign and PageMaker and/or a proprietary one, importing text and continuous tone (CT) files. Some film planning is still carried out, although not very much.

	Time for A5 page	Time for A4 page
DTP	10min	20min
Preparing page template	15min	20–30min
Make-up		
Manual planning		
Preparing layout		5–30min depending on complexity
Planning and assembly		5min per piece of film

Digital file handling, etc.

Customers are increasingly supplying printers with digital files in many different forms, such as text-only files prepared in Microsoft Word; made-up pages and scanned images in Microsoft Word, also in professional DTP programs such as Quark XPress, Adobe InDesign and PageMaker; alternatively in Portable Document Format (PDF) or other designated press-ready format to the printer's exact specifications. In all cases, printers will need to check the files against the customer's instructions and hard-copy proofs when supplied to ensure that all elements are correct and accounted for. Depending on the type and quality of the file and the file construction, printers will use preflighting software and/or manual processes to check the files and report back to the customer on any errors and problems that have been identified. The customer will then normally be given the opportunity to do the required corrective work or give approval for the printer to do it. Additional work to supplied files will be charged extra, but printers and print-related companies handling files from another party will normally also apply an initial file-handling and checking charge for all files supplied.

File handling, preflighting, checking times	
Minimum set-up per job or file	10min to over 1h for complex or large-scale work
File conversion	
From basic file format to press-ready files	minimum 30min up to several hours for complex or large-scale work
From good quality DTP file format to press-ready files	minimum 15min up to over 1h for complex or large-scale work
Planning, imposing composite press-ready files and final check-up to designated output template-based and/or repeat type device, including soft proof to customer, such as CTP, CTPr, digital printing	minimum 10min for simple work up to over 30min for complex work

Proofing

In the initial stages of a printed job, the most common first type of hard-copy proofs generated from a DTP system are laser or inkjet proofs in black and white or colour, size A4, A3 or A3+. These initial proofs and hard-copy reproductions are generally produced by the originators of the files and are mainly used for checking content in the case of a black and white proof, with the colour proof, which is really more of a colour visual, giving the overall general impression of the colour values.

For higher-quality and/or larger proofs, such as for imposed page flats, large single image sizes or multiple laydown planned images, larger-format digital proofing systems are used, either as low-res positional visual colour proofs and high-res target or precontract and contract proofs. Digital proofing devices, such as Iris and Cromalin Digital, are available in sheet form up to at least SRA2+ size and B0+ in large-format reel-fed form. Most sheet-form digital proofs are only available as one-sided proofs, whereas some reel-fed proofs, such as Agfa Sherpa, are available as one-sided and double-sided. There are specialist remote soft proofing software packages and monitor devices.

Besides digital proofs, a reasonably wide range of film-based proofs are still produced by printers and repro companies, although their numbers are fast reducing. These proofs are bromide prints, single- and two-colour ozalid proofs and photomechanical colour proofs, such as Matchprint and Cromalin/DuPont StudioSprint in sizes A3, A2 and A1.

Proofing production times

Monochrome or single colour

The time and cost of producing black and white laser proofs in A4 and A3 size from laser printers and copiers will normally be recovered in the overheads of the prepress department, otherwise a minimum cost or time may be applied, e.g. £1.00 for the first proof, thereafter copies at 5p for A4 and 10p for A3, alternatively 15min for preparing one set of proofs of 16 pages A4.

Ozalid single-colour proof, B1	10–15min
Four-colour process, per proof	
DTP laser or inkjet visual proof, A4 or A3	2–5min
Low-res positional visual colour proofs B1, one side	10min
High-res target or precontract and contract colour proofs B3, one side	10min
High-res target or precontract and contract colour proofs B2, one side	20min
High-res target or precontract and contract colour proofs B1, one side	30min
Photomechanical colour proof, SRA3	20min
Photomechanical colour proof, SRA2	30min
Photomechanical colour proof, SRA1	45min
Wet progressive four-colour proofs, B2 on flatbed proofing press	2h 30min
Wet progressive four-colour proofs, B2 on four-colour production press	1h 15min
Wet progressive four-colour proofs, B1 on flatbed proofing press	3h 30min
Wet progressive four-colour proofs, B1 on four-colour production press	1h 15min

CTF outputting

Imagesetters are available in a range of sizes from B3+ 2-up, B2+ 4-up, B1+ 8-up and very large format (VLF) up to above 2B0. For printers relying on analogue processes, imagesetters are still a popular output device, as well as a back-up for printers that have platesetters.

Outputting film

Up to B3	20 films per hour, i.e. 3min each
SRA2/B2	12 films per hour, i.e. 5min each
SRA1/B1	8 films per hour, i.e. 7.5min each
SRA1/B1+	3–6 films per hour, i.e. 10–20min each

FIGURE 9.4 Creo Lotem 800 Quantum offset litho thermal CTP platesetter

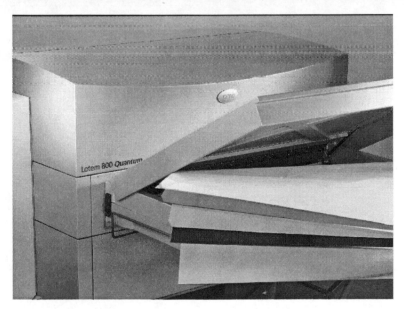

Source: Creo

CTP outputting

Small- to medium-format offset litho plates, using paper and polyester silver-coated plate material are popular for short-run single-, two- and four-colour work with quick printers and inplants, etc. Plates can be produced on some imagesetters or on specialist platesetters designed to output film, paper and polyester plates. Besides the following production figures, paper and plastic plates can be produced on a laser printer up to A3+ size at 2min per plate.

Outputting paper and polyester-based plates

Up to B3	20 films per hour, i.e. 3min each
SRA2/B2	12 films per hour, i.e. 5min each

Offset litho platesetters (Figure 9.4), like imagesetters, are available in a range of sizes covering B3+ 2-up, B2+ 4-up, B1+ 8-up and VLF up to above 2B0. Aluminium CTP plates fall into two main categories, thermal and visible light exposure.

Outputting offset litho metal plates

Up to B3	20 plates per hour, i.e. 3min each
SRA2/B2	12 plates per hour, i.e. 5min each
SRA1/B1	8 plates per hour, i.e. 7.5min each
SRA1/B1+	3–6 plates per hour, i.e. 10–20min each

Platesetters for flexographic plates are now being developed, such as the Creo Thermoflex covering B2+ and B1+ sizes (Figure 9.5).

Outputting flexographic photopolymer plates

B2+	Up to 5 plates per hour, i.e. 12min each
B1+	Up to 3 or more plates per hour, i.e. 19min each

FIGURE 9.5 Creo Thermoflex thermal relief CTP platesetter

Source: Creo

CTPr and DI outputting

CTPr machines are offset litho presses that generate the images to be printed from a front-end computer system direct to the plate material attached to the printing cylinders on the press such as the Heidelberg DI 46-4 using waterless litho, or directly on to the plate in the case of the DicoWeb DI press. Press sizes are available from SRA3/B3+ in four colours, SRA3/B2+ in 4–6 colours and B1+ in 2–8 colours. The DicoWeb has a maximum web width of 520mm and is available in up to six colours.

Outputting or imaging to create DI waterless offset litho plates and images, depending on image resolution and type of imaging system
5–20min or more per set of plates

Film-based step-and-repeat

Step-and-repeat machines are used where multiple-image printing predominates, such as labels and cartons. The step-and-repeat machine operates by the required image film being mounted on to the exposure head and, when in operation, it exposes the image on the exposure head 4, 8 or 16 times, or as many times as required. The image position on the plate is far more accurate with a step-and-repeat machine than with hand film assembly. The use of step-and-repeat machines has declined rapidly in recent years, as digital multiple images are produced on Macs, PCs and powerful Unix-based computers through step-up software programs for outputting on large imagesetters.

Initial set-up	30min, thereafter 0.5min per step

Platemaking and printing surface preparation

Manual offset litho

Offset lithography requires a planographic, i.e. flat, printing plate with ink-accepting image areas and water-accepting non-image areas. Conventional lithographic printing plates may be made from metal, plastic or paper, treated to receive or retain properties that are conducive to the lithographic process. One of the main properties is a photosensitive surface coating, although some paper and plastic plates can be produced on laser printers.

Lithographic plates are available as negative-working or positive-working. Negative-working plates are processed with a photosensitive emulsion which, when exposed to light, hardens; conversely, positive-working plates are processed with a photosensitive emulsion which, when exposed to light, softens. Both types of plate are prepared by placing the presensitised unexposed plate in a printing-down frame with the planned foil consisting of montaged negatives or positives in a predetermined position on top. The plate is then exposed to a high-energy light source and processed manually or on an automatic plate processor. Computer-to-plate systems using platesetters and imagesetters have already been covered in this chapter.

Manual offset litho presensitised aluminium metal platemaking	
SRA3/B3	6 plates per hour, i.e. 10min each
SRA2/B2	4 plates per hour, i.e. 15min each
SRA1/B1	3 plates per hour, i.e. 20min each

The above times allow for exposing the plate in a printing-down frame, online automatic plate processing and checking for any faults or blemishes.

Longevity of offset litho plates

There are a wide range of plates used in offset litho, ranging from paper plates produced on laser printers to CTP aluminium plates. Laser printed paper plates are used for short-run one-colour and spot-colour work; laser printed plastic plates are used for one-colour and spot work with halftones and screen tints up to a maximum of 15,000 impressions. Silver-coated paper and polyester plates are used for medium quality one-, two- and four-colour process work up to 5000 and 25,000 impressions, respectively. Conventional negative-working aluminium plates can produce up to 250,000 impressions and have been known to last for over 1 million impressions when plate baked, i.e. exposed to heat to harden the image emulsion areas. CTP aluminium plates vary widely in longevity from 10,000 impressions to 400,000 impressions before baking, which could then result in over 1 million impressions from one set of plates. Conventional aluminium and CTP aluminium plates give the best quality offset litho printing registration, highest number of impressions, finest screen resolution and greatest likelihood of reusing the plates.

Flexography and letterpress

Flexography and letterpress require a relief printing plate or block with raised image areas, which are inked, and non-image areas, which receive no ink. Photopolymer plates are the most popular printing surfaces for letterpress and flexography. The plates are made from a photosensitive plastic which hardens under the action of ultraviolet light. Photopolymer plates are mounted on the rotary presses by attaching them to a plastic carrier sheet, or they are exposed in the round as one-piece plates. Further examples of relief platemaking are flatbed letterpress plates using double-sided tape or magnetic metal-backed plate mounting.

Apart from photopolymer, flexography uses moulded rubber or hand-cut rubber stereos as plates, where the excess or non-image rubber is cut away with a sharp cutting edge. Laser-engraved rubber plates are also used when high-quality and fine definition flexo plates are required, especially with continuous designs. Here are the procedures and times for making conventional film-based flexo or letterpress photopolymer plates. CTP flexographic platesetters are covered on page 184.

1. The photopolymer plate material is exposed through the back to establish the depth of plate relief required.
2. A dispro (disproportionate) negative is printed down in contact with the photopolymer plate material in a printing-down frame and exposed to UV light.
3. The exposed plate is processed by washing out with solution and post-exposed overall to ensure complete polymerisation.

Time to complete the above platemaking procedures	30–60min per plate
Preparing photopolymer plates for press	
Flatbed letterpress mounted on rigid metal bases	10–15min per plate
Rotary flexo cylinder mounting and positioning multiple-image plates, e.g. with double-sided tape	up to 2h
Ditto using pin bar register system	1h
Ditto using sleeve plate cylinder	30min

Gravure cylinder

The modern gravure process has developed from early hand engraving and etching of flat metal copper plates into a highly sophisticated intaglio, i.e. recessed, printing process. The conventional gravure cylinder consists of recessed minute cavities or cells, forming printing areas of uniform area and shape, but of varying depth, to give tonal variations with the non-printing or background area surrounding each cell remaining at surface level. Further types of gravure cylinder have been developed, such as variable area cylinder, which is an inverted halftone formation where the image areas vary in area but have uniform depth, and gravure conversion, where the recessed cells vary in area and depth. There are two distinct methods of producing gravure cylinders, engraving and etching. As with other printing processes, gravure cylinders can be reproduced by analogue and digital means, i.e. through film-generated engraving and digitally generated engraving, although the great majority of gravure cylinders are now digitally prepared and engraved.

Film-generated (analogue) engraving Film-generated engraving breaks down into three main stages. The first stage is the production of composite continuous tone positive film, right-reading emulsion side down. If film separations are produced or supplied in conventional screened form, they have to be descreened, which can be done through the scanning head of the engraving unit.

In the second stage, the positive film is register punched and exposed in a printing-down contact frame to a correspondingly register-punched white film-based opaline material, which is coated with a direct reversal emulsion processed in a similar way to any photographic material. The opaline material reacts during its exposure and development similar to a positive-working offset litho presensitised plate, leaving a black continuous tone image on a white plastic background.

The third stage, following the exposure and processing of the opaline material, is for the material to be mounted on to the analyse/input drum of the engraving machine. The systems consist of an analyse unit and an output unit. The output unit activates a diamond stylus that engraves copper-plated cylinders in response to the electrical impulses received from the mounted opaline material on the analyse unit. The engraving units can engrave more than 3200 cells per second, with screen rulings varying from around 133lpi (lines per inch) up to 300lpi.

Digitally generated engraving Digital data is created on a prepress host computer system of Macs, PCs and workstations, or is received by the gravure engraving device via telecommunication links, such as ISDN. The digital data is fed into the host system acting as a server direct to the engraving output. Digital data downloads much faster to the engraving device, compared to mounted opaline material; the results have much higher quality.

In the past, the very high cost of producing gravure cylinders has always limited their use to specialist areas such as flexible and semi-flexible packaging and very long-run, highly illustrated publications. However, the adoption of digital engraving has considerably simplified and speeded up the process of gravure cylinder production and improved competitiveness.

Figure 9.6 illustrates the operation of a fully automated digital gravure engraving workflow. The whole operation is controlled by the job ticket that contains all the job parameters, with the overall job details and digital data prepared and planned in TIFF format, then downloaded to the HelioKlischograph 500, where a preloaded cylinder is engraved in response to the data and instructions received.

Digitally engraved large coarse screen cylinder	1h
Digitally engraved large fine screen cylinder	up to 4h

FIGURE 9.6 HelioKlischograph 500 gravure engraving system

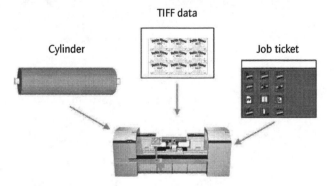

Source: Hell Gravure Systems

Screen stencil   Screen printing requires a stencil-processed frame or cylinder with clear unblocked image areas, through which the ink passes, and non-image areas that are filled in or blocked off. Screen stencils are made from meshes of nylon, polyester or stainless steel. They are better carrying media than silk, the original material from which the process took its name – silk screen printing. Stencils can be produced by hand and electronic cutting, as well as by photomechanical means where a light-sensitive material is exposed to a positive image. The non-image areas harden under light, leaving the unexposed image areas to wash away and creating a stencil area through which the ink will pass.

Flatbed screen photostencil production procedures and times

1. Screen mesh coated with light-sensitive emulsion and dried off.
2. Screen positive right-reading emulsion side up placed into contact with the underside of the coated screen in the printing-down frame, then exposed to UV light.
3. Exposed screen mesh processed by washing off unexposed emulsion with spray jet.
4. Screen mesh dried, inspected, spotted and blocked out, before being passed to the printing section when approved.

Time to prepare a flatbed screen stencil	30–60min

Rotary screen stencil production procedures and times

1. Photosensitive screen mesh material is cut to the exact size of film required. The material used to make rotary screen stencils is in the form of a sensitised microstructure photopolymer material supplied in rolls which are cut into the required lengths using a register system; or a rotary metal screen system is used.
2. The screen mesh material or cylinder is exposed in a printing-down frame to a multi-image positive film (right-reading emulsion side up), or single-image film if only one image will fit on to the printing cylinder
3. The exposed screen mesh material or cylinder is washed out with water jets to leave the printed areas clear and unblocked
4. The photopolymer material is fitted to cylinder end frames to form a rigid screen cylinder ready for printing.

Time to prepare a rotary screen stencil	30min to 1h

Flatbed screen stencils are used in conventional screen printing on a wide range of substrates in sheet form; whereas rotary screen stencils are used mainly for self-adhesive roll-fed printing, also specialist web printing such as wallcoverings and printed textiles.

Prepress 'computer-to' workflow options

CTF with manual film planning

Computer-to-film (CTF) with manual film planning (Figure 9.7, overleaf) is where the printer uses a DTP platform to create and/or import the graphic images required for printing and generally where the printer does not possess the equipment or capability to output full-size planned press-ready film. The process then proceeds with the approval of initial page or 1-up proofs, followed by outputting film via an imagesetter, then manual film planning, imposed proof for final high-resolution target proof checking, and finally manual platemaking to conventional printing process.

FIGURE 9.7 Workflow of computer-to-film (CTF) with manual film planning

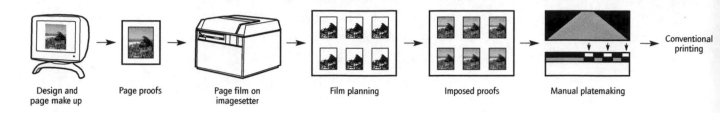

| Design and page make up | Page proofs | Page film on imagesetter | Film planning | Imposed proofs | Manual platemaking | Conventional printing |

Source: Pira International Ltd

Example 9.1 Eight-page booklet, size A4, printed four-colour process on a B1 four-colour sheet-fed offset litho press. Customer to supply Word files with hard-copy proofs, plus 12 min. and three A4 scans with rough layout based on similar previous booklet style. Printer to initially supply a set of colour laser page proofs, then output two sets of four-colour process positive film on B2 imagesetter and supply two sets of SRA2 Cromalin photomechanical proofs (2 × 4 pages) for press approval, followed by manual platemaking.

	Hours	Mins
Work prepared on DTP platform		
Chosen method of working: 1-up work-and-turn on B1 press, requiring four plates		
Scanning		
12 min. scans at 5min each	1	
3 × A4 scans at 10min each		30
Preparing initial page template, allow		15
Make-up: 8 pages at 20min per page	2	40
Planning, imposing composite press-ready files and final check-up to CTF		15
Filmsetting		
Outputting 2 sets of SRA2 film, i.e. 8 films at 5min each		40
Proofing		
Preparing 8 × A4 colour laser proofs at 2min each		16
Preparing 2 × SRA2 Cromalins at 30min each	1	
Manual planning		
Preparing layout – standing, allow		5
Planning 8 pieces of film at 5min each		40
Manual platemaking		
4 × B1 plates at 20min per plate	1	20
Total time	**8**	**41**

Example 9.2 Eight-page booklet, size A4, printed four-colour process on a B1 four-colour sheet-fed offset litho press. Customer to supply complete press-ready files and colour laser proofs for guidance. Printer to initially supply soft proofs, then output two sets of four-colour process positive film on B2 imagesetter and supply two sets of SRA2 Cromalin photomechanical proofs (2 × 4 pages) for press approval, followed by manual platemaking.

	Hours	Mins
Work prepared on DTP platform		
Chosen method of working: 1-up work-and-turn on B1 press, requiring four plates		
Preparing soft proofs, planning, imposing composite press-ready files and check up to CTF		25
Filmsetting		
Outputting 2 sets of SRA2 film, i.e. 8 films at 5min each		40
Proofing		
Preparing 2 × SRA2 Cromalins at 30min each	1	
Manual planning		
Preparing layout – allow		5
Planning 8 pieces of film at 5min each		40
Manual platemaking		
4 × B1 plates at 20min per plate	1	20
Total time	**4**	**10**

Computer-to-film Computer-to-film (Figure 9.8) is where the printer uses an imagesetter large enough to output a composite, one-piece film or set of films, containing all the required planned images in plate-ready form, thereby eliminating any manual planning. CTF is a popular workflow option in the production of relief plates for flexography and letterpress, also in the production of screen stencils.

FIGURE 9.8 Workflow of computer-to-film (CTF)

Design and page make up → Page proofs → Imposed proofs → Page film on imagesetter → Manual platemaking → Conventional printing

Source: Pira International Ltd

Example 9.3 Eight-page booklet, size A4, printed four-colour process on a B1 four-colour sheet-fed offset litho press. Customer to supply Word files with hard-copy proofs, plus 12 min. and three A4 scans with rough layout based on similar previous booklet style. Printer to initially supply a set of colour laser page proofs, then output one set of four-colour process positive film on B1 imagesetter and supply one SRA1 Cromalin photomechanical proof for press approval, followed by CTF platemaking.

	Hours	Mins
Work prepared on DTP platform		
Chosen method of working: 1-up work-and-turn on B1 press, requiring four plates		
Scanning		
12 min. scans at 5min each	1	
3 × A4 scans at 10min each		30
Preparing initial page template, allow		15
Make-up: 8 pages at 20min per page	2	40
Planning, imposing composite press-ready files and final check-up to CTF		15
Filmsetting		
Outputting 1 set of SRA1 film, i.e. 4 films at 7.5min each		30
Proofing		
Preparing 8 × A4 colour laser proofs at 2min each		16
Preparing 1 × SRA1 Cromalin at 45min each		45
Manual platemaking		
4 × B1 plates at 20min per plate	1	20
Total time	**7**	**31**

Example 9.4 Eight-page booklet, size A4, printed four-colour process on a B1 four-colour sheet-fed offset litho press. Customer to supply complete press-ready files and colour laser proofs for guidance. Printer to initially supply soft proofs, then output one set of four-colour process positive film on B1 imagesetter and supply one SRA1 Cromalin photomechanical proof for press approval, followed by CTF platemaking.

	Hours	Mins
Work prepared on DTP platform		
Chosen method of working: 1-up work-and-turn on B1 press, requiring four plates		
Preparing soft proofs, planning, imposing composite press-ready files and check up to CTF		25
Filmsetting		
Outputting 1 set of SRA1 film, i.e. 4 films at 7.5min each		30
Proofing		
Preparing 1 × SRA1 Cromalin at 45min each		45
Manual platemaking		
4 B1 plates at 20min per plate	1	20
Total time	**3**	**00**

Computer-to-plate For most conventional printers in 2004 a computer-to-plate (CTP) cum platesetter system (Figure 9.9) is the ideal way to output from the prepress department as it eliminates manual platemaking. CTP systems are available for relief platemaking for flexo, plus screen stencils, but to a fairly limited degree. Digitally engraved gravure cylinders have become the norm for large-publication web-fed printers.

FIGURE 9.9 Workflow of computer-to-plate (CTP)

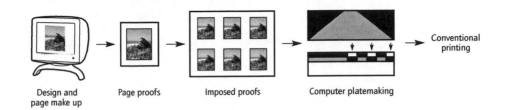

Design and   Page proofs   Imposed proofs   Computer platemaking
page make up

Conventional
printing

Source: Pira International Ltd

Example 9.5 Eight-page booklet, size A4, printed four-colour process on a B1 four-colour sheet-fed offset litho press. Customer to supply Word files with hard-copy proofs, plus 12 min. and three A4 scans with rough layout based on similar previous booklet style. Printer to initially supply a set of colour laser page proofs, then output a high-res digital colour imposed contract proof for press approval, followed by CTP platemaking.

	Hours	Mins
Work prepared on DTP platform		
Chosen method of working: 1-up work-and-turn on B1 press, requiring four plates		
Scanning		
12 min. scans at 5min each	1	
3 × A4 scans at 10min each		30
Preparing initial page template, allow		15
Make-up: 8 pages at 20min per page	2	40
Planning, imposing composite press-ready files and final check-up to CTP		15
Proofing		
Preparing 8 × A4 colour laser proofs at 2min each		16
Preparing 1 × B1 high-res contract proof at 30min each		30
CTP platemaking		
4 × B1 plates at 7.5min per plate		30
Total time	5	56

Example 9.6 Eight-page booklet, size A4, printed four-colour process on a B1 four-colour sheet-fed offset litho press. Customer to supply complete press-ready files and colour laser proofs for guidance. Printer to initially supply soft proofs, then output a high-res digital colour imposed contract proof for press approval, followed by CTP platemaking.

	Hours	Mins
Work prepared on DTP platform		
Chosen method of working: 1-up work-and-turn on B1 press, requiring four plates		
Preparing soft proofs, planning, imposing composite press-ready files and check up to CTP		25
Proofing		
Preparing 1 × B1 high-res contract proof at 30min each		30
CTP platemaking		
4 × B1 plates at 7.5min per plate		30
Total time	1	25

Example 9.7 Four-page cover, size A4, printed four-colour process on a B3 four-colour sheet-fed offset litho press. Customer to supply Word files with hard-copy proofs, plus 4 min. and one A5 scan with rough layout based on similar previous cover style. Printer to initially supply a set of colour laser page proofs, then output a high-res digital colour imposed contract proof for press approval, followed by CTP platemaking.

	Hours	Mins
Work prepared on DTP platform		
Chosen method of working: 1-up sheetwork on a B3 press, requiring eight plates		
Scanning		
4 min. scans at 5min each		20
1 × A4 scan at 7.5min		7.5
Preparing initial page template, allow		10
Make-up: 4 pages at 20min per page	1	20
Planning, imposing composite press-ready files and final check-up to CTP		10
Proofing		
Preparing 2 × A3 colour laser proofs at 5min each		10
Preparing 1 × B3 high-res contract proof at 10min each		10
CTP platemaking		
8 × B3 plates at 3min per plate		24
Total time	2	51.5

Example 9.8 Four-page cover, size A4, printed four-colour process on a B3 four-colour sheet-fed offset litho press. Customer to supply complete press-ready files and colour laser proofs for guidance. Printer to initially supply soft proofs, then output a high-res digital colour imposed contract proof for press approval, followed by CTP platemaking.

	Hours	Mins
Work prepared on DTP platform		
Preparing soft proofs, planning, imposing composite press-ready files and check up to CTP		15
Proofing		
Preparing 1 × B3 high-res contract proof at 10min each		10
CTP platemaking		
8 × B3 plates at 3min per plate		24
Total time		**49**

Computer-to-press

Computer-to-press systems (Figure 9.10) create and process offset lithographic plates directly on-press, i.e. combining prepress and press into one integrated operation. The first CTPr system was introduced in the early 1990s by Heidelberg through development with Presstek in the form of the GTO-DI press that was replaced by the Heidelberg Quickmaster DI 46-4 using Presstek polyester waterless litho plates. Several CTPr systems have now been developed with waterless litho systems using polyester and metal plates. The principle of CTPr is that the presses are fitted with appropriate on-press imaging and processing units that produce plates in perfect register with very little make-ready and set-up. Many of the CTPr systems incorporate thermal plate imaging and processing-free operation. CTPr eliminates mounting and preparing plates for press.

FIGURE 9.10 Workflow of computer-to-press (CTPr)

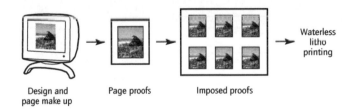

Design and page make up   Page proofs   Imposed proofs   Waterless litho printing

Source: Pira International Ltd

Example 9.9 Four-page cover, size A4, printed four-colour process on an SRA3 four-colour sheet-fed DI offset litho press. Customer to supply Word files with hard-copy proofs, plus 4 min. and one A5 scan with rough layout based on similar previous cover style. Printer to initially supply a set of colour laser page proofs, then output a high-res digital colour imposed contract proof for press approval, followed by preparing plates on the press.

	Hours	Mins
Work prepared on DTP platform		
Chosen method of working: 1-up sheetwork on an SRA3 DI press, requiring eight plates		
Scanning		
4 min. scans at 5min each		20
1 × A4 scan at 7.5min		7.5
Preparing initial page template, allow		10
Make-up: 4 pages at 20min per page	1	20
Planning, imposing composite press-ready files and final check-up to CTPr		10
Proofing		
Preparing 2 × A3 colour laser proofs at 5min each		10
Preparing 1 × B3 high-res contract proof at 10min each		10
Imaging DI plates (includes plates in perfect register on the press)		
4 × SRA3 plates at 15min per set × 2		30
Total time	2	57.5

Example 9.10 Four-page cover, size A4, printed four-colour process on an SRA3 four-colour sheet-fed DI offset litho press. Customer to supply complete press-ready files and colour laser proofs for guidance. Printer to initially supply soft proofs, then output a high-res digital colour imposed contract proof for press approval, followed by preparing plates on the press.

	Hours	Mins
Work prepared on DTP platform		
Chosen method of working: 1-up sheetwork on an SRA3 DI press, requiring eight plates		
Preparing soft proofs, planning, imposing composite press-ready files and check up to CTP		15
Preparing 1 × B3 high-res contract proof at 10min each		10
Imaging DI plates (includes plates in perfect register on the press)		
4 × SRA3 plates at 15min per set × 2		30
Total time		55

Computer-to-print   Computer-to-print is direct to print without the need for any intermediate stages other than soft proofs (monitor screen-based proofs) for checking and approval (Figure 9.11). The digital data is again produced from a computer front-end platform where the data is imported and/or created, approved and planned. Thereafter the data is directly downloaded to a digital printing system using a range of processes including laser, inkjet and electrostatic.

FIGURE 9.11 Workflow of computer-to-print or digital printing

Design and page make up → Soft proof → Imposed soft proofs → Digital printing

Source: Pira International Ltd

Example 9.11 Four-page cover, size A4, printed four-colour process on an SRA3 four-colour digital colour press. Customer to supply Word files with hard-copy proofs, plus 4 min. and one A5 scan with rough layout based on similar previous cover style. Printer to initially supply a set of colour laser page proofs for approval.

	Hours	Mins
Work prepared on DTP platform		
Chosen method of working: 1-up sheetwork/duplexed on an SRA3 digital colour press		
Scanning		
4 min. scans at 5min each		20
1 × A5 scan at 7.5min		7.5
Preparing initial page template, allow		10
Make-up: 4 pages at 20min per page	1	20
Planning, imposing composite press-ready files and final check-up to digital press		10
Proofing		
Preparing 2 × A3 colour laser proofs at 5min each		10
Total time	2	17.5

Example 9.12 Four-page cover, size A4, printed four-colour process on an SRA3 four-colour digital colour press. Customer to supply complete press-ready files. Printer to initially supply soft proofs for approval.

	Hours	Mins
Work prepared on DTP platform		
Chosen method of working: 1-up sheetwork/duplexed on an SRA3 digital colour press		
Preparing soft proofs, planning, imposing composite press-ready files and check up before downloading files to digital press		15
Total time		15

Convergence of prepress workflow systems

Figure 9.12 shows a prepress Creo workflow from concept to converting stage, illustrating the growing convergence of data creation and processing, in that the same workflow is used up to the outputting stage to produce offset litho plates via a CTP Trendsetter system and relief plates via a CTP ThermoFlex system, plus generation of a gravure cylinder.

FIGURE 9.12 Prepress workflow from concept to converting output stages, producing offset litho plates, flexographic plates and gravure cylinders

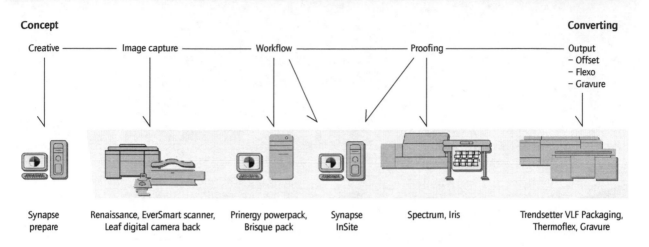

Source: Creo

Different categories of printed work

Jobbing and general commercial

Jobbing and general commercial printing is a multifarious group of printing work, which covers the huge range of general printing requirements from a business card to a large poster, one colour to six colours or more. Estimating for this type of work is marked by a lack of uniformity, and practically every job is treated as a one-off, requiring individual consideration and calculation. Jobbing and general commercial printers represent by far the largest number of companies in the industry. Traditionally the vast majority of this sector was dominated by small to medium-sized jobbing and offset printers handling most of the day-to-day print requirements within their immediate locality and further afield as they expanded into other geographical areas and types of work.

A core area of general commercial printing is often stationery products, such as business cards, letterheadings, compliment slips and leaflets, before moving on to more complex jobs, such as booklets, folders and pamphlets. The print-buying customers are as varied as the work, from totally inexperienced print buyers that order printing very infrequently to experienced print buyers with their own professional prepress facilities, graphic design studios and access to repro bureaux. As a result, jobbing printers have to handle a wide range of hard and soft copy covering laser printed documents, floppy disks and Zip drives with basic text and low-res pictures produced from a wide range of Mac and PC software, photographs, transparencies and some existing film from previous jobs, to press-ready digital files prepared to the printer's specification. During the past decade or so, traditional jobbing and commercial printers have lost a significant amount of their business to high-street quick printers. These organisations are generally set up with a mainly digital base, along with small offset presses for longer-run work, to provide the on-demand sector with a quick turnaround.

The wide variety of prepress inputs and job types means that estimating for prepress processes has to be extremely flexible and wide-ranging.

On-demand   On-demand printing is a relatively new category of work, but it is the fastest-growing print sector, encompassing a wide range of work including short-run, personalised and versioned. At its ultimate, on-demand printing is based on an entirely digital prepress workflow and digital printing, certainly at least with digital prepress and CTP options. Increasingly a wide range of printed work is now transacted online via the internet, intranets and network arrangements, even including online print ordering, proofing, job progressing and billing. It is a fast-developing area covering many print-related sectors. Examples include some of the work that was traditionally undertaken by jobbing and commercial printers such as stationery, leaflets and folders, where either the print buyer prepares their printed work to a set template and price basis accessed on the web, or the print buyer prepares the prepress element internally or through a second party and places the work with a web-based digital printer or print management facility.

Much of the high-volume transactional and personalised printing, such as forms, reports, meeting papers, billings and reports, is handled by inplants, in-house facilities, quick printers and print management facilities. The work is mainly carried out on networked high-volume monochrome laser printers; the prepress element is driven by the requirements of the digital printing system, and in many cases the digital files are downloaded and queued to a network of print engines. Further examples are in short-run high-quality digital colour marketing-driven printing products, plus specialist print areas such as labels, short-run books, cartons, plastic cards and packaging, either for short-run work in its own right or for market testing.

From an estimating viewpoint, the prepress element of on-demand printing is fairly standardised and driven by the digital printing system and, where applicable, by database requirements; in many cases the digital files are automatically downloaded and queued to a network of print engines. However, preflighting, final checking of files and soft proofing will depend on the type and complexity of the work, plus previous file-checking arrangements. Estimating for this type of work is often calculated on an all-inclusive basis, such as cost per copy, batch or per 100,000 documents.

Bookwork   Bookwork contrasts considerably with jobbing work, particularly because it tends to be a much more predictable range of printed products. Bookwork tends to fall into a pattern suited to pricing by scales, e.g. price per 1000 copies of 32-page, 64-page sections, including machine printing per section in one, two, three or four colours, print finishing as softback or hardback, perfect bound, burst or notch binding, thread sewn, etc. Finished sizes are normally within fairly close limits, from metric crown and royal octavo, metric crown quarto, etc. A5 and A4 are becoming more popular, although not as popular as the old imperial sizes. Most publishers, through their own in-house prepress facilities or through a second party, will generally supply press-ready digital files to the printer, often in the form of PDFs. Prepress operations for the printer in bookwork are fairly predictable and standardised.

Magazines and periodicals

In their variety of prepress work, magazines and periodicals tend to fall between jobbing work and bookwork as they can be made up from a variety of sources and prepress elements or they can be supplied as press-ready files to the printer. Short-run specialist and limited readership magazines are often prepared by a wide range of staff, who present articles and associated graphics in a range of formats. This is also true of the advertisers. In contrast, the larger high-volume magazines and periodicals fall into the same category as bookwork, where press-ready prepress files are normally supplied in a very professional form.

Folding box cartons

Folding box cartons differ from most other printed products in that they have three dimensions – length (*a*), width (*b*) and depth (*l* or *c*) – whereas most printing is only two-dimensional, i.e. length and width. Cartons also are available in many different shapes and sizes. The letters in parentheses are used as identifying reference points for cartons. To clarify and standardise carton construction and style, the British Carton Association (BCA) and the European Carton Makers' Association (ECMA) have both published guidance. In addition the BCA has published a glossary of folding carton terms, including descriptions and constructional diagrams of different cartons and their variations. The ECMA publication on folding carton styles divides the different types of carton into groups and the groups are then subdivided. The prepress systems used by carton printers increasingly have access to these reference styles on their software programs. The prepress material supplied for folding box cartons can be from wide and varied sources, such as complete CADCAM digital files supplied in 1-up and multiple-image form with approved contact proofs, analogue film, design brief or mock-up where the different stages need to be prepared on a DTP and/or CADCAM platform.

Labels, tickets and vouchers

The design of labels, tickets and vouchers can be commissioned by the customer through a design agency or graphic designer, or the printer undertakes this type of work in-house on a design-rich DTP system, with ideally the whole operation from initial design being handled digitally up to the creation of multiple-image plates. The laydown of reel-fed and flat sheet cut-to-shape labels, tickets and vouchers is often influenced by the available dies in stock from previous jobs, saving new dies from being made for each new job. The dies can be flatbed or rotary, 1-up or multiple, depending on requirements at the time of printing.

Continuous stationery and business forms

Traditionally, business forms have been printed in one, two or three colours, as black only or as black plus spot colours, but in recent years there has been a move towards more four-colour process work, either to accommodate a more highly specified and wider range of business forms and continuous stationery, or as sheeted commercial work. This four-colour process development has resulted in business forms companies setting up their own prepress system with colour scanning and outputting facilities. Some business forms companies occasionally reproduce from flat camera-ready artwork which they or their customers have generated, but the great majority now operate from a Mac or PC DTP platform, often with specialist software that can generate a wide range of tints, vignettes and security feature backgrounds particularly relevant to cheque, ticket and voucher printing.

Direct response and direct marketing

Direct response and direct marketing cover an extremely wide range of products from web-fed and sheet-fed, one- to four-colour process with additional special colours. Some possible examples are a multicolour complex personalised mailshot consisting of a booklet with a reply form to be detached from the back cover and a single-colour reply-paid mailer generated entirely from computer data on a laser printer.

Careful study

The different categories of printed work would require careful individual study to arrive at the appropriate prepress operational times and costs. In at least some of the categories, the printer could work from conventional, digital or mixed prepress media.

Prepress pricing

The extremely wide range of equipment and processes for producing prepress work, such as scanning, proofs, outputting film and plates, has led to the popularity of prepress matrix pricing. This approach was originally introduced by prepress bureaux undertaking prepress work for printers and print-buying customers. Although most printers and some print-buying customers have increasingly installed their own comprehensive prepress equipment, the use of set or guide prices for particular prepress elements of a job has become popular as a means of simplifying the prepress estimating process.

The prices inevitably vary due to the different circumstances of each job or group of jobs, e.g. the type and quality of prepress elements supplied by the customer, whether the prices are standard unit prices based on average content or on agreed contract prices and the actual volume of work placed. But it is fairly common for a print estimator or a print-buying customer to use predetermined prepress prices to calculate the prepress costs of jobs, especially predictable and regular work such as magazines and journals.

The figures in Table 9.1 (overleaf) have only been included to highlight the principle of prepress pricing and to use in some of this book's examples. There are so many factors which affect such market-related factors that any figures need to be continually checked, amended and agreed as appropriate by all parties concerned.

TABLE 9.1 Illustrative examples of prepress pricing (£) allowing for set-ups and ganging where applicable and possible				
Scanning: price per scan	min.	A5	A4	A3
Four-colour process	10.00	15.00	20.00	30.00
Monochrome scanning (black and white) is 50–60% of the above colour prices				
Cut-outs would add 50–100% to the above prices				
Film output: price per piece of film from clean and approved planned preflighted files				
	min./A5	A4	A3	A2
Single colour	6.00	8.00	12.00	20.00
Reductions would apply for volume and multiple outputting.				
Offset litho platemaking: price per plate or set of plates from press-ready planned preflighted digital files or complete one-piece				
Plate-ready film	SRA3/B3	SRA2/B2	SRA1/B1	
CTP polyester plate	7.50	12.50		
CTP metal plate	15.00	20.00	30.00	
Manual metal plate	15.00	20.00	30.00	
Proofing: price per proof	A4	A3/B3	A2/B2	A1/B1
Black and white laser	1.00			
Colour laser	8.00	12.00		
Ozalid			4.00	6.00
Low-res positional visual colour proof, one side	4.00	5.00	7.00	10.00
High-res target or pre-contract and contract colour proof, one side	15.00	20.00	30.00	50.00
Photomechanical colour proof	30.00	40.00	60.00	100.00
Wet colour proofs, 12 sets, excluding plates			125.00	170.00
Wet colour proofs, 12 sets, including plates			225.00	310.00

Source: H. M. Speirs

Machine printing

10

All printing processes are identified and categorised by the way they create printed images. Printing image carriers have two separate surfaces: image or printing areas and non-image or non-printing areas. In conventional printing, the image or printing areas accept the ink by physical or chemical transfer. Digital printing processes create printed images in a variety of ways, including heat and electricity, covering laser, inkjet, dye sublimation, thermal wax and thermal transfer, plus electrostatic. Non-image areas do not retain ink or toner.

Conventional printing processes work from fixed image surface carriers, such as plates, blocks, cylinders and stencils. As a result, certain relatively expensive fixed costs have to be incurred before the first printed copy can be produced. These costs include all the expenditure covering the prepress stages plus the make-ready and set-up of the printing presses in preparation required for each individual job. Such preparatory costs will be basically the same whether the run is 100 or 1 million copies.

Offset lithography, with its extremely wide range of available press types, both sheet-fed and web-fed, varies considerably in the cost of plates used and the time required to set up a machine for printing, but it is still considered relatively quick and inexpensive on preparation and make-ready. Offset plate material is available in paper, plastic and metal; the plates can be made in a matter of minutes and are relatively inexpensive. The printed work suited to paper plates is limited short-run, line and coarse screen. Conventional and CTP aluminium metal plates, although much more expensive to produce, are capable of over 1 million impressions and fine screen work up to 157 lines per centimetre (400 lines per inch) and beyond.

Flexography has benefited greatly in recent years from improvements in photopolymer plates, UV inks and press design. The set-up costs of plates and machine make-ready are generally reasonable, although normally not as low as offset litho. Letterpress has lost ground to the other printing processes over the past 30 years, having been the dominant process until the late 1960s. It now operates only in a very limited way through niche markets such as reel-fed self-adhesive labels, tickets and vouchers. Its plate and press preparation are very similar to flexography, another relief printing process. Gravure has heavily embraced new digital technology for cylinder preparation and press sophistication, but it still has the highest set-up costs of all the printing processes, through expensive cylinders and make-ready procedures. Screen has generally low preparatory costs with simple screen stencils being produced inexpensively and quickly. Make-ready and set-up are also quick and relatively inexpensive.

In contrast to conventional printing, digital processes do not use a fixed medium to reproduce the same printing image time after time; they can create a different image with each printing cycle from a completely digital and flexible computer-based platform. As a result, the prepress and press set-up costs are minimal compared to conventional printing (Table 10.14, page 248). Table 10.1 (overleaf) illustrates the projected market share of the different printing processes over the decade 2000 to 2010.

TABLE 10.1 Projected market share change of printing processes over time			
Printing processes		**Year**	
	2000	**2005**	**2010**
Offset litho	62%	60%	57%
Gravure	22%	21%	19%
Digital	9%	13%	20%
Flexography, screen, letterpress	7%	6%	4%

Source: Pira International Ltd

Conventional printing processes

Offset lithographic presses

Offset litho presses are designed to print sheet-fed or reel-fed and web-fed on a wide range of substrates. Sheet-fed presses are more flexible and more numerous than web-fed but both types are popular, depending on a company's targeted print market area. Offset litho presses come in a far greater range than for any other process, with presses covering many different configurations such as straight, convertible and perfecting plus coldset and heatset web offset, business forms and continuous presses with fixed and variable cylinder presses. The different types of press also vary in their sophistication from basic or standard to highly advanced (Table 10.3, page 211).

Sheet-fed offset litho presses

Sheet-fed offset litho presses are made in a variety of sizes, which typically equate to just above ISO range B. Some presses, however, are still manufactured to suit just above the SRA sizes, and rounding up and down produces a wide range of press sizes (Table 10.2).

TABLE 10.2 Range of sheet-fed offset litho press sizes	
Maximum sheet size (mm)	**Equivalent stock size**
340 × 450	SRA3+
370 × 520	B3+
508 × 686	SRA2+
530 × 740	B2+
720 × 1,020	B1+
820 × 1,120	
890 × 1,260	
920 × 1,300	SRA0+
1,020 × 1,420	B0
1,200 × 1,620	

Source: Pira International Ltd

Presses based around SRA3, B3 and smaller are often known as small offset presses. They are available in up to at least six print units and as portrait or landscape presses. With a portrait press, the short edge of the sheet is fed into the front lays; with a landscape press, it is the long edge. Feeding a sheet in by the long edge, i.e. landscape, gives greater sheet control and is used in sheet-fed presses SRA2, B2 and above. Small offset presses are used to print relatively small-format, small-quantity and fast-turnaround work, including stationery work such as letterheads, compliment slips, business cards and leaflets.

Medium-format presses based around SRA2 and B2 are available in up to at least 12 colours and are used for a wide range of commercial printing, mainly of larger-format size to small offset presses and/or typically longer print runs. Large-format presses based around B1 are available in up to 14 colours and are used for a wide range of commercial printing, including short- to medium-range, relatively high-pagination work such as magazines, journals and brochures plus specialist work such as cartons and wet gummed labels. Extra large format presses based around B1+ up to B0 and above are available in up to at least 14 colours; fewer presses are sold in this size. They tend to be used for more specialised work, including large-format posters of medium to longer runs, also by book printers producing large pagination signatures (folded sections) and/or large-format publications, plus carton printers producing large print runs and/or large-format cartons.

With print runs in general getting smaller, there has been a move towards smaller press sizes, at least in number of presses sold, but all these press sizes are still supported in the different sectors of sheet-fed offset litho.

Sheet-fed offset litho press configurations

Sheet-fed presses are available in a wide range of configurations, including single-, two-, four-, five- and six-colour, up to at least 14 colours. All printing presses are constructed of basically three main parts: a feed unit that feeds the substrate into the press, a print unit or series of print units depending on the number of printheads on the press, and a delivery unit that delivers the printed sheets into the delivery mechanism.

Most offset litho presses are constructed in modular units. The sheet travels between each unit on transfer cylinders or chain grippers, and each printing unit consists of impression, blanket and plate cylinders plus the necessary inking and damping rollers. Figure 10.1 (overleaf) is a diagram of a single-colour B3 press showing the three elements of the sheet-feed unit, one printing unit and the delivery unit.

FIGURE 10.1 Schematic of a one-colour Heidelberg Printmaster GTO 52-1, B3 small offset press (1/0)

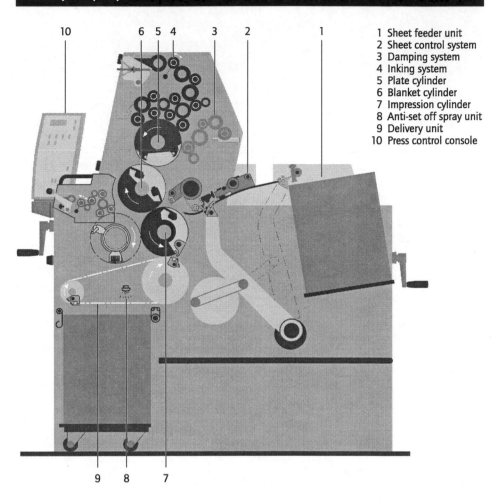

1	Sheet feeder unit
2	Sheet control system
3	Damping system
4	Inking system
5	Plate cylinder
6	Blanket cylinder
7	Impression cylinder
8	Anti-set off spray unit
9	Delivery unit
10	Press control console

Source: Heidelberg

Standard multicolour presses print one side only in one press pass and are known as straight printing presses. Other multicolour presses can convert from printing one side only to both sides and are called convertible printing presses. On convertible presses, a conversion unit is fitted between the selected printing units so that the printed sheet is turned over by the conversion mechanism that changes the direction the sheet is travelling, resulting in the sheet being presented tail end and opposite side first to complete printing on the non-printed side of the sheet. An example of a convertible press is the two-colour press in Figure 10.2. This can either print two colours on one side of the sheet, or it can be changed over to a perfecting mode that prints one colour on both sides, depicted as 2/0 and 1/1. Impression cylinders on convertible presses that are either side of the conversion unit normally have a grained surface or are coated with a material to prevent them taking up ink from newly printed sheets.

FIGURE 10.2 Schematic of a two-colour Heidelberg Printmaster PM74-2P, B2 offset press with conversion option (2/0 and 1/1)

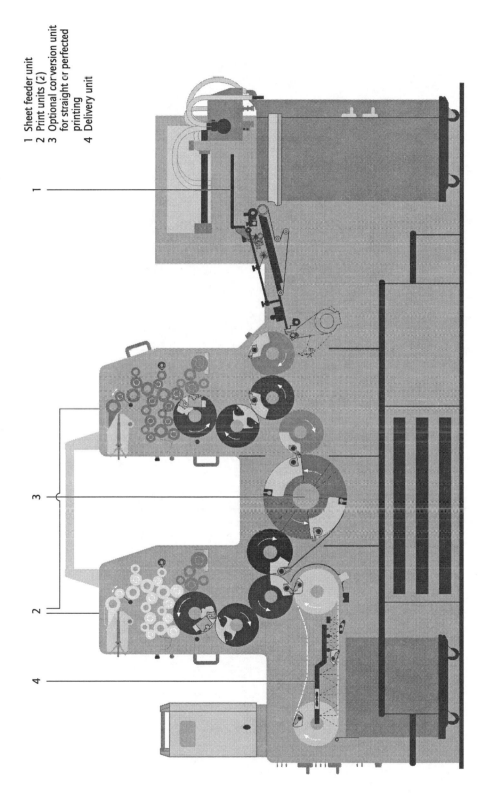

1 Sheet feeder unit
2 Print units (2)
3 Optional conversion unit for straight or perfected printing
4 Delivery unit

Source: Heidelberg

FIGURE 10.3 Komori Lithrone 440SP four-over-four B1 perfector offset press

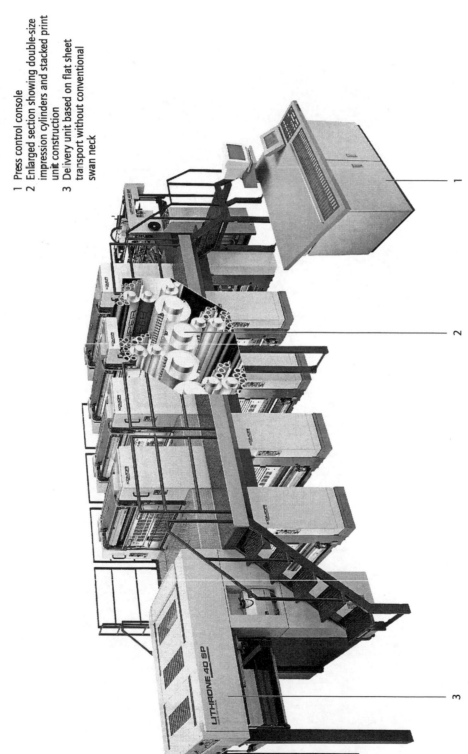

1 Press control console
2 Enlarged section showing double-size impression cylinders and stacked print unit construction
3 Delivery unit based on flat sheet transport without conventional swan neck

Source: Komori

Most sheet-fed presses are built on the blanket-to-impression principle, but dedicated perfectors, i.e. presses that are designed exclusively to print both sides of the sheet in one pass, are ideally suited to printed work that always has to be printed both sides. Heatset perfector presses are built on the blanket-to-blanket principle (Figures 10.5 and 10.6 on page 216). On perfectors built in this manner, the top blanket cylinder also acts as the impression cylinder, the bottom blanket cylinder printing on the reverse of the sheet. Due to the success of convertible presses, which give the printer the option of straight and perfected printing on a wide range of multicolour presses, sheet-fed perfector presses are now very much a small niche market, such as for some book and journal printers specialising in monochrome (single-colour) publications. An interesting innovation and development in perfected printing is the Komori Super Perfector (SP) range of multicolour two-sided sheet-fed presses. The 440SP model is built on a four-over-four basis rather than the four-back-four used by other eight-colour convertible presses (Figure 10.3). A feature of the SP presses is that the same grip edge of the sheet is used throughout the printing operation, whereas convertible perfecting presses grip on different sheet edges.

Lithographic make-ready and printing

The time taken for making ready and setting up a sheet-fed press depends on the type of work being printed, the standard of production required and the degree to which the press is automated. The main press make-ready operations include the setting up of the feed and delivery units, along with the path of the substrate through the press. The inking system has to be set to supply more ink to areas of heavy image coverage than to areas of light image coverage, plus the damping system has to be set to deliver the correct amount of damp for each job. Printing plates also have to be correctly positioned, with the cylinder pressures set to suit the stock being printed and to give the correct print length. Sheet-fed offset litho presses have average net output speeds that vary from just under 3000 sheets per hour for short-run work up to just under 10,000 sheets per hour, depending on the length of the run, the type of material being printed and the sophistication of the press, with overall maximum press speeds of up to at least 18,000 sheets per hour. It can take over two hours to make ready a four-colour standard press. On a highly automated press, this can be reduced to less than one hour.

Remote control and press management systems

Most of the sheet-fed offset litho printing press control panels and indicator gauges are located at the delivery end of the press, with some controls duplicated at the feed end of the press. Also, on a wide range of automated modern machines the presses are controlled by an off-press networked control console that involves considerable automation apart from the mere centralisation of controls. These controls allow the operators to monitor the whole printing process from the initial make-ready and set-up through to press sheet comparison with approved proof and press okay. Along with the use of a proof and press pull viewing booth, they allow constant monitoring of the press settings while examining the sheets being printed.

Operation of the press from a central console linked to the press is now a common feature on multicolour presses. Functions such as light-emitting diode (LED) displays provide data on all aspects of the press, including running speeds, maintenance data and press faults, and where available, they link up to the machine manufacturer's production and information system and/or the printing company's own MIS.

Press sophistication and automation

The degrees of sophistication and automation on sheet-fed offset litho presses vary considerably across the wide range of models available. Two main types are outlined here, but there is a large middle ground between the two:

▶ A standard press range covers the basic model of a press with few additional attachments or facilities; it relies heavily on the operator to set up the press manually.

▶ A highly-advanced press range is fitted with labour-saving features and high levels of sophistication, such as semi-automatic or automatic plate change; presets of ink ducts, font solution, blanket, impression cylinder and register; semi-automatic conversion from straight to convertible printing; plate and plate cylinder cocking; feed, print units and delivery settings, plus links to MIS and CIP4 compatibility.

Table 10.3 illustrates the impact of these features on press make-ready and set-up as well as the average net output in impressions per hour.

TABLE 10.3 Sheet-fed offset litho: average make-ready times and press running speeds

| | Make-ready and set-up | | | Average net output in impressions per hour | | | | | | | | | | | |
| | First/ initial MR | Follow-on MR | Wash-up per unit | Lightweight materials 45gsm to less than 90gsm | | | | Middle range materials 90gsm to less than 150gsm | | | | Heavyweight materials 150gsm and above | | | |
	hrs: min	hrs: min	hrs: min	up to 3,000	3,001– 10,000	10,001– 20,000	above 20,000	up to 3,000	3,001– 10,000	10,001– 20,000	above 20,000	up to 3,000	3,001– 10,000	10,001– 20,000	above 20,000
Standard press: small offset up to B3															
One-colour (1/0)	:25	:10	:20	2,650	3,500	4,750	5,150	3,350	4,450	5,950	6,500	2,650	3,500	4,750	5,150
Two-colour (2/0,1/1)	:40	:30	:20	2,650	3,500	4,750	5,150	3,350	4,450	5,950	6,500	2,650	3,500	4,750	5,150
Four-colour (4/0, 2/2)	1:00	:40	:20	2,650	3,500	4,750	5,150	3,350	4,450	5,950	6,500	2,650	3,500	4,750	5,150
Highly advanced press: small offset up to B3															
Four-colour (4/0, 2/2)	:40	:25	:10	3,550	4,750	6,350	6,950	4,500	6,000	8,000	8,750	3,550	4,750	6,350	6,950
Six-colour (6/0, 4/2)	:50	:35	:10	3,550	4,750	6,350	6,950	4,500	6,000	8,000	8,750	3,550	4,750	6,350	6,950

Small offset presses are currently available in up to six colours, with maximum running speed up to 15,000 sheets per hour

	First/ initial MR	Follow-on MR	Wash-up per unit	up to 3,000	3,001– 10,000	10,001– 20,000	above 20,000	up to 3,000	3,001– 10,000	10,001– 20,000	above 20,000	up to 3,000	3,001– 10,000	10,001– 20,000	above 20,000
Standard press: SRA2/B2															
One-colour (1/0)	:30	:15	:30	2,900	3,750	5,000	5,400	3,600	4,700	6,200	6,750	2,900	3,750	5,000	5,400
Two-colour (2/0,1/1)	:50	:30	:30	2,900	3,750	5,000	5,400	3,600	4,700	6,200	6,750	2,900	3,750	5,000	5,400
Four-colour (4/0, 2/2)	1:20	:45	:30	2,900	3,750	5,000	5,400	3,600	4,700	6,200	6,750	2,900	3,750	5,000	5,400
Highly advanced press: SRA2/B2															
Four-colour (4/0,2/2)	:45	:30	:15	3,800	5,000	6,600	7,200	4,750	6,250	8,250	9,000	3,800	5,000	6,600	7,200
Six-colour (6/0, 4/2)	1:00	:45	:15	3,800	5,000	6,600	7,200	4,750	6,250	8,250	9,000	3,800	5,000	6,600	7,200
Eight-colour (8/0, 4/4)	1:15	1:00	:15	3,800	5,000	6,600	7,200	4,750	6,250	8,250	9,000	3,800	5,000	6,600	7,200

B2 presses are currently available in up to 12 colours, with maximum running speed up to 18,000 sheets per hour

TABLE 10.3 Sheet-fed offset litho: average make-ready times and press running speeds (continued)

| | Make-ready and set-up | | | Average net output in impressions per hour | | | | | | | | | | | |
| | First/ initial MR | Follow-on MR | Wash-up per unit | Lightweight materials 45gsm to less than 90gsm | | | | Middle range materials 90gsm to less than 150gsm | | | | Heavyweight materials 150gsm and above | | | |
	hrs: min	hrs: min	hrs: min	up to 3,000	3,001–10,000	10,001–20,000	above 20,000	up to 3,000	3,001–10,000	10,001–20,000	above 20,000	up to 3,000	3,001–10,000	10,001–20,000	above 20,000
Standard press: B1															
One-colour (1/0)	:40	:25	:35	2,900	3,750	5,000	5,400	3,600	4,700	6,200	6,750	2,900	3,750	5,000	5,400
Two-colour (2/0,1/1)	1:10	:40	:35	2,900	3,750	5,000	5,400	3,600	4,700	6,200	6,750	2,900	3,750	5,000	5,400
Four-colour (4/0, 2/2)	1:50	:55	:35	2,900	3,750	5,000	5,400	3,600	4,700	6,200	6,750	2,900	3,750	5,000	5,400
Highly advanced press: B1															
Four-colour (4/0, 2/2)	:50	:35	:15	3,800	5,000	6,600	7,200	4,750	6,250	8,250	9,000	3,800	5,000	6,600	7,200
Six-colour (6/0, 5/1)	1:10	:50	:15	3,800	5,000	6,600	7,200	4,750	6,250	8,250	9,000	3,800	5,000	6,600	7,200
Ten-colour (10/0, 5/5)	1:30	1:10	:15	3,800	5,000	6,600	7,200	4,750	6,250	8,250	9,000	3,800	5,000	6,600	7,200

B1 presses are currently available in up to 14 colours, with maximum running speed up to 16,000 sheets per hour

	First/ initial MR	Follow-on MR	Wash-up per unit	up to 3,000	3,001–10,000	10,001–20,000	above 20,000	up to 3,000	3,001–10,000	10,001–20,000	above 20,000	up to 3,000	3,001–10,000	10,001–20,000	above 20,000
Standard press: B0															
One-colour (1/0)	1:00	:40	:45	2,400	3,250	4,500	4,900	3,100	4,200	5,700	6,250	2,400	3,250	4,500	4,900
Two-colour (2/0,1/1)	1:40	1:00	:45	2,400	3,250	4,500	4,900	3,100	4,200	5,700	6,250	2,400	3,250	4,500	4,900
Four-colour (4/0, 2/2)	2:30	1:30	:45	2,400	3,250	4,500	4,900	3,100	4,200	5,700	6,250	2,400	3,250	4,500	4,900
Highly advanced press: B0															
Four-colour (4/0, 2/2)	1:30	1:00	:20	3,300	4,500	6,100	6,700	4,250	5,750	7,750	8,500	3,300	4,500	6,100	6,700
Six-colour (6/0, 5/1)	2:00	1:20	:20	3,300	4,500	6,100	6,700	4,250	5,750	7,750	8,500	3,300	4,500	6,100	6,700
Eight-colour (8/0, 4/4)	2:30	1:45	:20	3,300	4,500	6,100	6,700	4,250	5,750	7,750	8,500	3,300	4,500	6,100	6,700

B0 presses are currently available in up to 12 colours, with maximum running speed up to 15,000 sheets per hour

Note: the press running speeds are based on net impressions per hour, i.e. they represent the average number of good copies obtained per hour allowing for stoppages to clean blankets and general minor problems. The actual running speeds of the presses will exceed the figures by 10% or more. Changing from straight printing to converting or perfecting, where applicable, adds an extra 10–30min depending on the press sophistication

Source: H. M. Speirs

Waterless litho

Waterless litho is offset litho printing without the use of water or damping solution. It has been in regular use for over two decades, although only becoming established as a niche sector outside mainstream. However, it possesses many advantages over conventional offset litho. There is no need to achieve ink and water balance, and other advantages are faster make-readies, more vibrant colours and consistent colour balance; less waste makes it a more environmentally friendly process. Waterless litho continues to be a relatively small sector of offset litho printing, especially in the UK, although in Japan it has a much higher market share. In the past few years, companies have released an increasing number of computer-to-press systems using waterless litho, so the process looks set to claim a higher profile and market share of the offset litho printing sector in short- to medium-run work.

Waterless offset litho printing presses

Waterless computer-to-press systems are currently available in SRA3+/B3+ and SRA2+/B2+ formats. They work using on-press plate imaging or digital imaging (DI) where the plates are imaged directly on the press from a computer platform. Additional developments in DI presses are the DicoWeb in up to six colours with a maximum web width of 520mm and the Komori Lithrone S40D, two- to eight-colour B1 sheet-fed press.

An example of a CTPr waterless offset litho press is the Heidelberg Quickmaster DI 46-4 (Figure 10.4, overleaf). The press has a satellite construction with a quadruple-sized central impression cylinder, allowing four-colour printing in one gripper closure, enhancing its high standards of registration. It is a four-colour press printing from direct-imaged Presstek polyester plate material, with a maximum sheet size of 340mm × 460mm and maximum printing speed of 10,000 sheets per hour. The Quickmaster DI is aimed at short-run colour work positioned between digital colour toner print systems and traditional offset litho printing, retaining high-quality offset litho printing combined with short set-up times and directly linked to digital prepress.

In producing the DI plates, the Quickmaster's RIP takes PostScript data from the digital front-end system and converts it into screen data, which is then converted into control signals for 64 infrared laser diodes (16 × 4 colours). The laser beams created by the laser diodes are then bundled into precise rays of controlled light that are focused on to the Presstek multilayer polyester-based plate, ablating or removing material to leave small depressions in the image areas. It is these depressions that accept and form the inked image areas, leaving the untouched silicon layer to form the waterless non-image areas. Two different resolutions are available, 1270dpi and 2540dpi, creating up to 150lpi screen resolution.

The machine operates a plate-spooling system that automatically renews the printing plates in all four units on-press after the previous job was completed. Each job is prepared through the RIP and held in a page buffer unit on the press and is controlled by the operator, who selects and controls the print sequence of jobs. Ink profiles on the four printing units are preset from the digital data file and register is 'automatic'; the plates are exposed directly on the press, with the operator overriding the settings manually as required.

FIGURE 10.4 Schematic of a Heidelberg Quickmaster DI 46-4, waterless SRA3+ four-colour satellite computer-to-press machine

1   Sheet feeder unit
2   Blanket washup system
3   Plate cylinder cleaning system
4   Plate cylinder
5   Temperature controlled inking system for waterless litho
6   Imaging unit
7   Remote controlled ink fountain
8   Blanket cylinder
9   Common quadruple-diameter impression cylinder
10 Delivery unit

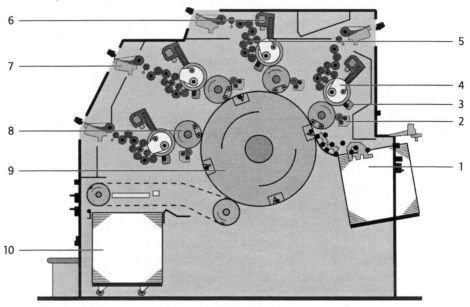

Source: Heidelberg

Waterless sheet-fed DI press production times

The press range includes four-, five- and six-colour presses with a maximum press speed of 13,000 sheets per hour. Automatic imaging of all four printing plates along with cleaning and processing takes 10–20min for B3 plates and 20–30min for B2 plates, depending on image resolution. Average net output in impressions per hour is 3000 up to a 5000 print, 4250 for 5001 to 20,000, and 5000 above 20,000.

Web offset

Web offset printing is printing by presses on to a web or reel, i.e. a continuous roll of substrate. The terms 'web' and 'reel' in this context are synonymous and largely interchangeable when referring to the physical form of the substrate or press. There are a wide range of web offset presses configured and designed to cover product requirements from small-format cheques and forms to very high pagination, large-format magazines and newspapers. Web presses, unlike sheet-fed presses, are largely designed with inline finishing. This allows the press to deliver finished products, or at least partly finished elements of a job such as folded sections and business forms that require further final finishing. Web presses are also built with fixed or variable cylinder circumferences.

Most large-format web presses, such as heatset for commercial products and coldset for newspapers, have a fixed cylinder circumference, hence they have fixed cut-offs that are established by the cylinder circumference used on a particular press. Many heatset presses are built to produce 630mm or 620mm cut-offs, which means that any product they produce is limited to derivations of that cylinder circumference size less allowance for bleed, etc., such as 297mm and 148mm. The exception to this would be where the printed reel is sheeted off, as the flat sheet can then be cut and finished to a non-standard cut-off size. As well as large-format presses, narrow-width continuous business form presses are mainly built to accommodate a range of variable cylinder circumferences, from which size derivations can then be produced. For example, 18in cylinders can be used to produce 18in, 9in and 6in deep jobs, or 24in cylinders to produce 24in, 12in, 8in and 6in deep jobs. The web or reel width of the material to be printed can vary up to the maximum width the press will accommodate, e.g. the printed web could be the equivalent of full width, three-quarter width or half-width.

On a web offset press, reels of paper are fed from reel stands into the printing units, followed by in-line finishing and finally to the delivery end of the press where, depending on the design of the press, the reel is finished in one of three ways. The final products from the press may be delivered as complete or semi-processed finished products, sheeted off in predetermined lengths as finished products, or for further off-line finishing when they may be re-reeled for further finishing. Web presses are available with printing cylinders up to several metres in width and circumference, with maximum running speeds of over 900m/min and over 80,000 cut-offs per hour. Once the presses are set up to run, they are generally controlled by an electronically linked off-press control console or series of consoles.

Heatset and coldset presses

Most of the large web offset presses are classified as coldset or heatset. Heatset presses allow a wider range of papers to be used than coldset presses and produce a much higher quality of work, covering an extensive selection of commercial work, including magazines, journals and catalogues, plus specialist work such as direct mail. As with larger-format web presses, the quantities printed are generally fairly long run, typically in the tens and hundreds of thousands rather than the low thousands. The work also tends to be mainly in four-colour process, but it can be in single-colour and five-colour, normally as four-colour process plus special colour. The most popular cut-off in heatset web offset presses for the UK print market is 630mm. However, in a drive to reduce waste and material cost, press manufacturers are offering cut-offs at 625mm, 620mm and lower.

Coldset presses are used mainly for printing newspapers and relatively long-run newspaper-quality products such as a range of comics, large-format promotional news advertising and sales bulletins; also mainly text-based monochrome magazines and books. The paper needs to be fairly absorbent and the inks formulated to set by a combination of absorption and oxidisation so that the finished sections may be handled after folding without undue marking and setting off. On a satellite press, the web passes through the dryer twice, once after the first unit and again after the second unit and before folding.

Heatset web offset presses

Heatset presses are dedicated perfector presses, i.e. printing both sides of the web in one direct press pass, built on the blanket-to-blanket principle, with printing units arranged in-line and one web or more webs passing between the selected print units. The presses are built in a specific sequence of units, from raw material in web form to finished or semi-processed product, comprising infeed, splicer, printing units, heatset dryer, chill rolls, folder and delivery. Figure 10.5 illustrates a single-web four-unit heatset press showing the reel infeed, single web path through the press, four print units, dryer and chill unit, plus folder. Figure 10.6 illustrates a twin-web eight-unit heatset press showing two reel infeeds, double web path through the press, eight print units, two dryer and chill units, plus folder.

FIGURE 10.5 Schematic of a single-web four-unit heatset web press

Source: Heidelberg

FIGURE 10.6 Schematic of a twin-web eight-unit heatset web press

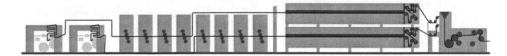

Source: Heidelberg

Folders

The vast majority of the output from heatset web offset presses is folded sections or signatures. Folds are either applied in the direction of the web, i.e. with the grain direction, or across it, i.e. with the cross direction. For off-line finishing, sheeters are popular on the 8-page presses for sheeted commercial work such as covers, pamphlets, direct mail finishing off-line, etc. The range of stock weights used when folding in-line is around 30gsm to 135gsm and up to 200gsm for sheeted work.

Press sizes

Heatset press size descriptions, such as 8-page and 16-page, are mainly based on the maximum number of A4 page sizes, or in some cases undersize and oversize A4 page sizes that can be obtained from each cylinder circumference or cut-off. The range varies from an 8-page press, often known as a mini-web, up to a 64-page press. Sizes other than A4 can be obtained from the presses, such as 32 pages A5 from a 16-page A4 heatset web press. Table 10.4 covers a representative range of press permutations, confirming that the presses are available in single- and twin-web. So a 32-page press can be a single-web 32-

page press or a twin-web 16-page press. There are a wide range of maximum web widths and cylinder circumferences, confirming that not all heatset presses are designed for the A-size markets. Nevertheless, the main cylinder circumference or cut-off is still 630mm, along with 625mm and 620mm, plus a wide range of non-A-size cut-offs for specialist size presses. Double-circumference heatset web offset presses such as 1260mm and 1240mm are popular for large-format presses as full-size 32-page single- and twin-web presses.

TABLE 10.4 Representative range of available heatset web offset press sizes			
Press type	**No. of webs**	**Range of web widths (mm)**	**Range of circumference/cut-off (mm)**
8 pages	1	508 to 673	452 to 630
16 pages	1	895 to 1,020	546 to 700
32 pages	1	980 to 1,448	578.5 to 1,260
32 pages as 2 × 16pp	2	895 to 1,020	546 to 700
48 pages	1	1,450 to 1,905	445 to 620
64 pages	1	1,905 to 1,980	1,092 to 1,260
64 pages as 2 × 32pp	2	980 to 1,448	578.5 to 1,260

Source: Pira International Ltd

Long- and short-grain presses

Traditionally most heatset web presses are long-grain, where the press has a cylinder circumference greater than its width; in short-grain presses the press has a cylinder width greater than its circumference. Long-grain presses derive their name from the fact that the grain of the finished product is typically parallel to the spine; in short-grain presses it is typically at right angles to the spine. As a short-grain press has a smaller cylinder circumference than its cylinder width, it completes more cylinder circumference revolutions per set period of time than the equivalent long-grain press running at the same speed. This makes the short-grain press faster overall. Short-grain presses also offer the possibility of greater output variety in pagination by using ribbon folding.

Figure 10.7 (overleaf) illustrates a 32-page long-grain heatset web press cylinder configuration. It accommodates four 210mm wide pages with allowances such as bleed across the cylinder and four 297mm deep pages with allowances such as bleed around the cylinder circumference. Figure 10.8 (overleaf) illustrates a 32-page short-grain heatset web press cylinder configuration, accommodating four 297mm deep pages with allowances such as bleed across the cylinder. Plus there are four 210mm deep pages with allowances such as bleed around the cylinder circumference. In both cases the finished product is A4 upright or portrait. Table 10.5 (overleaf) gives average make-ready times and press running speeds.

FIGURE 10.7 Schematic of a 32-page long-grain heatset web press cylinder configuration

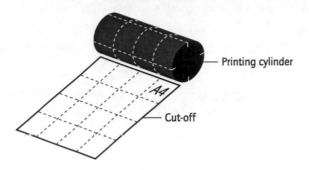

Source: Pira International Ltd

FIGURE 10.8 Schematic of a 32-page short-grain heatset web press cylinder configuration

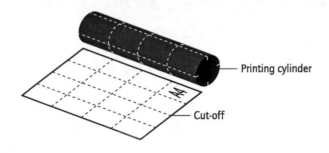

Source: Pira International Ltd

TABLE 10.5 Heatset web offset: average make-ready times and press running speeds

16-page 4-unit (4/4) press	
Make-ready and set-up	
Initial press set-up	30min
All four printing units	45min
Single plate change	10min
Four-colour plate change	45min
Changing folder configurations	10–30min
Setting up rotary trimmer, if available	30–45min
Setting up spine gluing, if available	30–45min
Average net output in cylinder cut-offs per hour	
25,000 copies and below	25,000
25,001–40,000 copies	30,000
40,001–100,000 copies	38,000
100,001–500,000 copies	40,000
500,001 copies and above	42,000

Source: H. M. Speirs

Coldset web offset presses

Coldset web offset presses are mainly associated with newspapers and newspaper-type products; they come in two different configurations: common impression or satellite and blanket-to-blanket, with the printing units arranged horizontally. The presses tend to be multiple-web as they are generally built to produce a relatively high pagination and/or large-format finished product in one press pass. The need to produce a wide product range means the presses are often custom-built to suit specific requirements, with a wide range of print unit configurations and web paths. Coldset is a printing process where, to all intents and purposes, there is no accelerated drying of the ink. Coldset presses are built with several reel infeeds having splicer facilities, plus print units, folder options and delivery system. The blanket-to-blanket coldset presses are generally built in a modular fashion to a distinctive pattern or shape, including U, Y and H.

With combination coldset web presses, satellite print units are normally the preferred option for colour work and blanket-to-blanket for single-colour work. Coldset press cut-offs vary from 470mm to 630mm, normally with double circumference cylinders from 940mm to 1260mm and web widths up to 2m and beyond. Presses are available in up to ten-cylinder satellite modules, with blanket-to-blanket modules mainly in groups of two and four print units. Overall pagination from one press line can be up to, and in excess of 160 broadsheet pages and beyond. The maximum speed of coldset web presses exceeds 800m/min.

Production times The average make-ready and press running speeds of coldset web offset presses are generally commensurate with those given for heatset. However, the press configuration is often bespoke and this can affect make-ready and set-up times as well as net output speeds.

Narrow-width web- or reel-fed offset presses

A wide range of printed products, including continuous, business forms, direct mail and general commercial, are printed on narrow-width web offset presses in some form or other. These presses are mainly designed on the blanket-to-impression principle and generally with the option of variable cylinder sizes. They have comprehensive finishing facilities. Most narrow-width web offset presses are single-web. However, there are a few twin-web presses used for specialist work such as receipts, duplicate forms and sets. There are a wide range of cylinder widths and circumferences and the three cylinder inserts of plate, blanket and impression are easily removed from the press when changing from one cylinder size to another. As well as changing the printing units, the operator needs to reset the press to suit the size and type of product to be printed.

Continuous basic business forms presses are typically available in one-, two- and three-colours. Four-colour presses and above are often used for a wider range of work than just business forms. Printing speeds are in excess of 650ft/min (Table 10.6, overleaf). With comprehensive finishing the net output is much lower. A stock range of 40gsm to 240gsm can be printed on these presses. A typical press configuration consists of a reel unwind system, printing units – consisting of a plate cylinder, inking and damping system – plus blanket and impression units. There is also in-line finishing equipment such as sprocket hole punching, perforating, folding and sheeting.

TABLE 10.6 Continuous narrow-width web offset: average make-ready times and press running speeds	
Make-ready and set-up	
First print unit	30min
Per subsequent print units	20min
Cylinder size change	10min
Wash-up per colour	15–20min
Set-up per separate in-line finishing unit	5–30min
Average net output	
Reel-to-reel	152–198m/min (500–650ft/min)
Reel-to-pack/fold	107–122m/min (350–400ft/min)
Pack-to-pack	61–91m/min (200–300ft/min)
Reel-to-sheet	91–107m/min (300–350ft/min)

Source: H. M. Speirs

Due to the relative decline of the business forms industry, which started in the 1990s, a growing trend with reel-fed continuous machines is in the development of higher-specification presses, up to at least ten colours, offering a range of web printing configurations such as five-back-five (5/5), six-back-four (6/4), etc. Additional facilities include interdeck UV drying and in-line finishing, e.g. additional varnishing, die-cutting, remoist glue, scratch-off application, file and line hole punching; cross, running and skip perforation units, plus reel-to-reel, reel-to-fold and reel-to-sheet in-line finishing. The result is a highly productive press aimed at direct mail and direct response marketing, security printing, continuous and multiple-set forms, plus promotional and general commercial printing.

Figure 10.9 illustrates a high-specification four-unit press, available in up to ten units. It is suitable for direct mail and commercial applications. The main drawing shows the sequence of operations from the reel unwind unit. This includes a web cleaning device to remove paper fluff and loose fibre, plus a web guiding mechanism to ensure control of the reel as it is fed into the press. The patterned line as it passes through the machine indicates the path of the reel. Next come four print units, fitted with UV dryers after each unit and turn bars between print units 1 and 2, 2 and 3. The in-line finishing section illustrates the reel path as it first passes through options of skip perforating, followed by die-cutting, embossing, file hole and line hole punching, cross perforating, in-line perforating, crush and scissor/slit. This is followed by the options of finishing as reel-to-sheet (sheeter), reel-to-reel (rewinder) and reel-to-fold (zigzag and signature folder).

The diagram at the bottom left shows the printing reel path between the blanket and impression cylinder and the maximum and minimum web path for the two presses on which the main drawing is based, i.e. the Müller Martini A52 and A68. It also shows the range of in-line finishing operations it can carry out. Presses of the type illustrated in Figure 10.9 have running speeds up to at least 450m/min; the A52 has a maximum web width of 520mm and the A68 has a maximum web width of 686mm. Depending on the

FIGURE 10.9 Schematic of an A68/A52 high-specification four-unit narrow-width web offset press showing web paper specifications and inline finishing operations

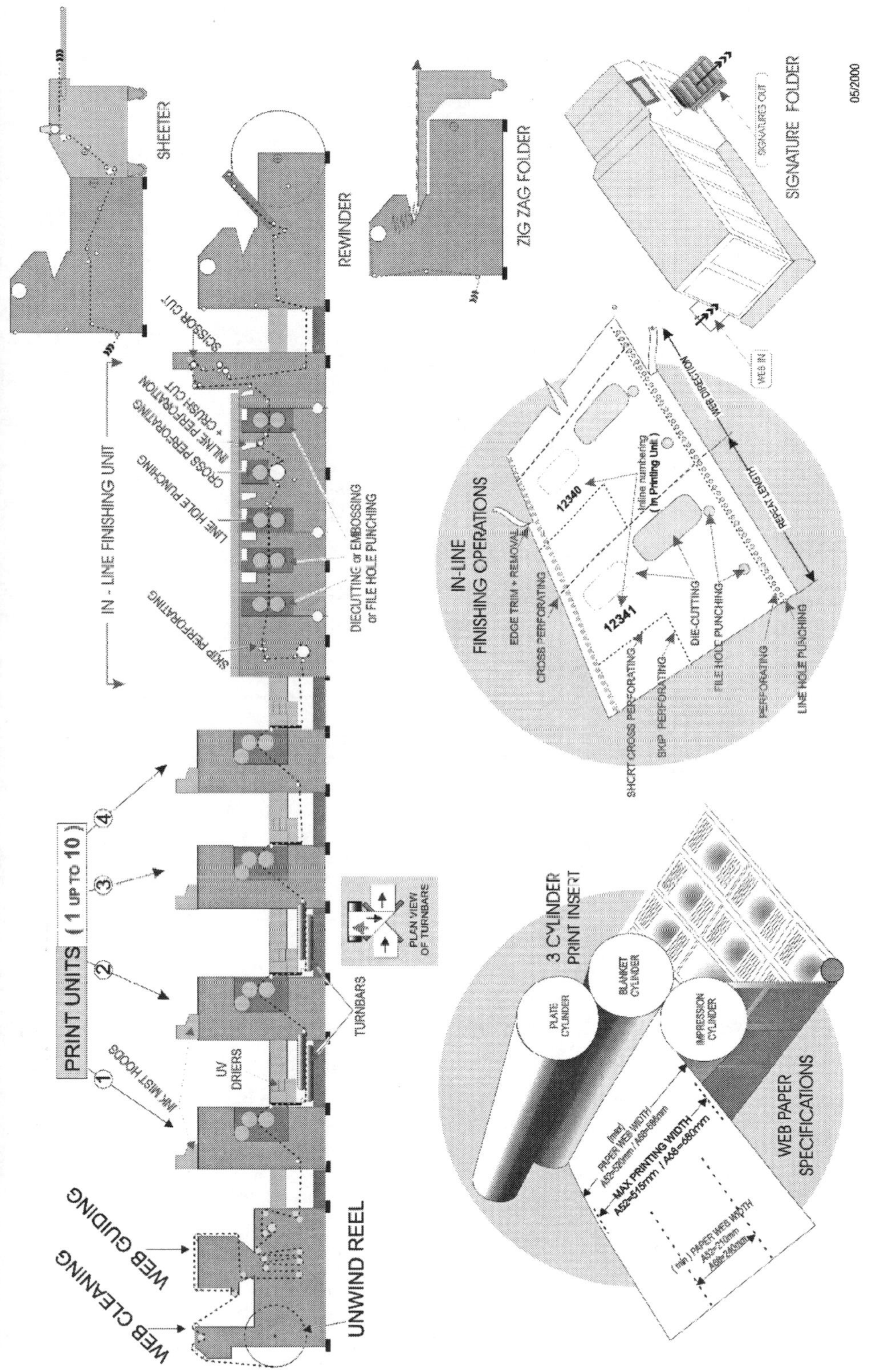

Source: Peter Kearns, Müller Martini Ltd

in-line finishing, the make-ready times and net running speeds will be similar to those in Table 10.6 (page 220) However, complex direct mail work will result in high make-ready times and lower running speeds.

Book web offset presses

Book web offset presses are specialist presses based on blanket-to-blanket configurations; they are designed specifically to print and fold sections or signatures in-line for books, diaries, technical publications and manuals, mainly in one and two colours. Often these presses are built to a customer's specific requirements from relatively standard components. Heatset and coldset web offset presses are used generally for four-colour work where relatively high print quantities justify printing by web rather than by sheet.

Book presses tend to have a fixed printing circumference. They come in one- and two-colour print units and in single- and twin-web options. This is either as a single-web option printed two colours both sides, or a twin-web option printed one colour both sides. Printing cylinder sizes are varied to cater for the different page formats of books. Circumference sizes vary from 647mm to over 2m, and web widths of over 1m. Press speeds go up to 300m/min and beyond, and the range of stock that can be printed and folded in-line ranges from lightweight stock at 28gsm up to 120gsm.

The typical press configuration of a book web press consists of a reel infeed and web guide system, followed by print units and folding system. This is often based on slitting the web into superimposed ribbons before folding into signatures. Infrared or hot-air dryers are often fitted as accelerated ink-drying systems. A typical specialist book web offset press is the Timson T32. Table 10.7 is based on this press configured in twin-web mode running paper with an 880mm web width, a fixed cut-off of 1282mm and capable of delivering the following A-sized products in one press pass:

▶ 64 pages A4 single-colour
▶ 32 pages A4 two-colour
▶ 64 pages A5 single-colour (joined pairs)
▶ 32 pages A5 two-colour (joined pairs)
▶ 64 pages A6 single- or two-colour (joined pairs).

When running over 40gsm and below 60gsm paper, the running speeds in Table 10.7 would be reduced by 15%. The maximum press speed of the T32 is rated at up to 360m/min or 1180ft/min depending on press and folder configuration.

TABLE 10.7 Book web offset: average make-ready times and press running speeds based on a 32-page A4 two-colour configuration	
Initial make-ready and set-up	
Includes plating up (two or four plates), obtaining position and final colour adjustment	
Single-web	75min
Twin-web	120min
Follow-on make-ready	
Two plates	15min
Four plates	30min
Average net output in copies per hour using 60–100gsm paper	
A4 collect 4 configuration	
One copy per cylinder cut-off, e.g. 32pp single-web, 64pp twin-web	
10,000 copies and below	13,000
10,001 copies and above	17,000
A4 collect 2 configuration	
Two copies per cylinder cut-off, e.g. 2 × 16pp single-web, 2 × 32pp twin-web	
10,000 copies and below	18,000 (9,000 per cut-off)
10,001 copies and above	24,000 (12,000 per cut-off)

Source: H. M. Speirs

Commercial web offset presses

Commercial web offset presses aim to offer a competitive advantage and alternative to sheet-fed offset litho printing due to their faster running speeds. Web-fed presses will run at more than 3–4 times the speed of sheet-fed presses. By their very nature these presses are relatively general-purpose and address a wide range of printed products up to an overall cut-off or flat size of around 685mm × 520mm wide. Cylinder circumferences are 356–660mm and cut-offs are 178–660mm. The paper stocks that can be printed on commercial web offset presses typically range from under 40gsm to 180gsm, at speeds up to 300m/min and beyond.

Presses are available in blanket-to-impression configuration with interchangeable three-cylinder print cylinder inserts and turn bars to perfect the web. They are also available with dedicated blanket-to-blanket perfectors on a reel-to-sheet basis, sheeting off work mainly for off-line finishing. Unlike narrow-width web offset presses, in-line finishing is limited, at least on basic models. Apart from the basic presses, there are a range of popular upgrade facilities. These include plough folder, pattern gluers and perforators, UV and heatset drying units and die-cutting, making the high-specification presses suitable for direct mail work in up to ten colours.

As this category of press overlaps with the continuous narrow-width web offset presses, the make-ready times and press running speeds are similar to those of Table 10.6 (page 220) in the reel-to-reel and reel-to-sheet categories.

Flexography

Flexography is the dominant relief printing process. It boasts machine printing speeds and improving quality to match and even overtake offset litho in certain areas. This is especially true since the introduction of flexo UV inks and heavy investment in the development of flexographic presses. Flexography is a direct rotary printing process using photopolymer or resilient rubber relief plates, mounted, cut or exposed on to variable repeat image plate cylinders. Engraved anilox rollers ink the plates with fast-drying solvent-based inks, and increasingly water-based inks, on to virtually any type of material. Flexographic presses are available in unit and satellite or common impression construction.

Narrow-width presses

Narrow-width presses are often multi-process configurations with flexo, letterpress, screen, wet or dry offset printing units on the same machine that are designed to print in six or more colours. Further processes typically include die-cutting, hole punching, waste stripping, sheeting, slitting or rewinding, plus additional options, including hot-foil blocking, embossing, laminating and varnishing. Figure 10.10 illustrates the Edale eight-colour Beta narrow-width combination press. It is available in flexo and rotary screen printing units in either 250mm or 330mm reel widths. Typical applications for this type of press include peel-and-read labels, technical labels, lottery tickets, scratch-off inks, promotional labels, and gift vouchers. Narrow-width reel-fed presses, used for self-adhesive label printing, are available from starting at width 125mm, with repeat lengths ranging from 100 to 600mm, plus speeds of up to around 175m/min (Table 10.8). The larger narrow-width presses, used for labels and cartons, etc., are available in widths up to 500mm and beyond, with repeat lengths ranging from 200 to 610mm. They boast speeds of up to 175m/min and 12 print units, with optional reverse printing.

FIGURE 10.10 Edale eight-colour beta flexographic and combination press

Source: Edale

TABLE 10.8 Narrow-width reel-fed flexographic presses: average make-ready times and press running speeds	
Make-ready and set-up	
First print unit	25min
Per subsequent print units	15min
Wash-up per colour	10–15min
Set-up per separate in-line finishing unit	5–30min
Average net output	
Straightforward printing and die-cutting	70m/min (230ft/min)
More complex printing and die-cutting	50m/min (164ft/min)
Highly complex finishing and printing on more difficult substrates	40m/min (131ft/min)

Source: H. M. Speirs

Medium-width presses

Medium-width presses cover web widths up to 1300mm and repeat lengths or cylinder circumferences of up to 800mm. They are used mainly for specialist products such as flexible packaging and laminating, e.g. food wrappers, decorative wrapping paper and butter or spread wrappers with gold foil lamination. Presses of this type are often up to 12 units and are available with combination gravure units. Maximum print speeds vary from 100m/min to over 600m/min.

Large-width presses

Large-width presses have web widths up to 3000mm, with up to 12 printing units. They have an autowind, unwind, rewind mechanism, with repeat images from 480mm up to 1250mm from one cylinder revolution. Presses are used for a wide range of flexible packaging and folding cartonboard. The main applications for web-fed or reel-fed flexography are flexible packaging, newspapers, paperback books, reel-fed labels, tickets and vouchers, plastic bags, cartons and wallcoverings such as vinyls and flocks. Maximum print speeds vary from under 100m/min to 600m/min.

Sheet-fed presses

Sheet-fed flexographic presses, although considerably more limited than web-fed or reel-fed presses, are available and mainly used for corrugated cartons and plastics. Press sizes are generally large format, covering from above B1 to well over B0. The presses are either hand fed or mechanically fed, printing from a rubber or photopolymer plate. The print area can be adjusted to print in any position on the sheet, and ink is applied via an anilox roller and doctor roller system. The presses are available in one, two, three and four colours, with additional drying options for printing on plastics and other non-absorbent materials. As the presses generally have a modular construction, they can be upgraded with automatic feeders and extra colour units as required. Maximum press speeds are up to 5000 sheets per hour and 350m/min. Due to the widely differing range of press configurations, productivity and sophistication, plus in-line finishing options on medium-width, large-width and sheet-fed presses, it is not possible or practical to state meaningful average make-ready times and press running speeds.

Letterpress Flatbed letterpress, using platen and cylinder presses, is still used in a very limited way for printing mainly short-run general jobbing work such as business cards and letterheadings, as well as overprinting on envelopes. This type of printed work is in black only, or black and spot colour. Flatbed letterpress printing machinery has been given an extended lease of life, not so much for conventional printing, but for other related finishing processes, including perforating, slitting, cutting-and-creasing, numbering, embossing and foil blocking. Rotary letterpress printing has been superseded by flexography and/or offset litho, although reel-fed letterpress is still very popular for printing self-adhesive labels, tickets and vouchers. The presses are similar to flexo presses in their construction, size and printing speeds; in fact, they occur most commonly in combination letterpress and flexo presses. The average make-ready times and press running speeds for reel-fed letterpress are similar to the figures in Table 10.8 (page 225).

Some cutting-and-creasing formes are still hand-made, but most are machine-prepared. The most advanced and sophisticated are laser generated. When making a simple cutting-and-creasing forme for a folder or cover with gussets and fold-in glued flap, it takes 15–30min to do a precise drawing of the outline. Preparation of the forme itself, with the rule set into wood frame and rubber strips to eject the board, would take 30–90min, depending on the size and shape of the forme. Fitting the folding-box cutting-and-creasing rule to the profile-cut wood takes approximately 30–60min per image. Table 10.9 gives some typical times for finishing operations and Table 10.10 gives some examples of make-ready times and press running speeds.

TABLE 10.9 Finishing operations, such as cutting-and-creasing on adapted sheet-fed letterpress presses: average make-ready times and press running speeds	
Make-ready and set-up	
Small platen (260mm × 380mm)	
– Simple work	20–30min
– Complex work, such as multiple images, resetting press for embossing	30–60min
SBB size cylinder (570mm × 820mm)	
– Simple work	30–45min
– Complex work, such as multiple images, resetting press for embossing	45–60min
Net impressions per hour	
Small platen (260mm × 380mm)	2,000–3,000
SBB cylinder	1,500–2,500

Source: H. M. Speirs

TABLE 10.10 Reel-fed letterpress flatbed and rotary presses, used for labels, tickets and vouchers: average make-ready times and press running speeds	
Make-ready and set-up	
Flatbed	
Initial press make-ready	45min
First print unit/plate change	10–20min
Wash-up per colour	10–15min
Cutter change	30min
Rotary	
Initial press make-ready	60min
First print unit/plate change	20–30min
Wash-up per colour	10–15min
Cutter change	45min
Average net output	
Flatbed	
Straightforward printing	95m/min (312ft/min)
More complex printing and die-cutting	50m/min (164ft/min)
Complex finishing and printing	30m/min (98ft/min)
Rotary	
Straightforward printing one side only	80m/min (262ft/min)
Printing one side with rotary die-cutters	30m/min (98ft/min)
Printing both sides with rotary die-cutters	20m/min (66ft/min)

Source: H. M. Speirs

Gravure

Gravure printing is an intaglio printing process capable of producing very high-quality colour printing at high running speeds. The process is best suited for publication work such as long-run magazines, periodicals, colour supplements and mail-order catalogues, plus flexible and rigid packaging along with labels, postage stamps and security work. Gravure presses have either fixed or variable cylinder circumferences to suit the page or repeat length required. Although a great variety of printed matter is produced by gravure, it is more specialised than lithography because it is costly to make the gravure cylinders. But chromium-plated gravure cylinders have considerable durability, so run lengths of several million copies can be obtained from one set of cylinders.

Rotogravure (rotary gravure) has been developed mainly for printing in four-colour process on web-fed presses. Examples are publications such as magazines and other pictorial matter for which the customer requires a fast level of output and good quality reproduction of illustrations on relatively inexpensive grades of uncoated paper, such as a supercalendered newsprint. This is used extensively in high-volume, high-pagination colour supplements, and direct mail catalogues.

Gravure presses used for publication work are available with cylinder circumferences up to 1900mm and beyond and web widths up to 3600mm. The maximum printing speeds are up to 900m/min and beyond, with up to 16 print units and twin-reel stands, although most presses used for periodicals are single-reel or single-web. Gravure presses used for packaging are available with cylinder circumferences up to 1000mm and beyond and web widths of over 1800mm. The maximum printing speed is 650m/min and the number of printing colours goes up to 12. Here are the main types of gravure press.

Sheet-fed presses

A very limited range of sheet-fed gravure presses, sizes B2 and B1, with hot-air dryers are still used in specialist markets requiring high-quality, decorative effects using gold, silver and brilliant fluorescent colours on metallised papers and vinyls. Sheet-fed presses have a maximum running speed of around 10,000 sheets per hour, with an average make-ready of 30–60min per colour and 5000 net impressions per hour.

Narrow- and medium-width web presses

There are a range of gravure and flexo presses aimed at flexible packaging and foil laminating. There are also a specialist range of gravure and flexo presses developed for cigarette cartons, folding box cartons and packaging. The presses can be configured to print and finish completely in-line, such as those manufactured by Bobst Lemanic. Narrow- and medium-width presses vary in their configurations and capability, with average make-ready times ranging from an initial press set-up of one hour to several hours, plus 15min to over an hour per print unit and net output of 150–300m/min.

Large-width web presses

Large-width web presses are mainly used for publications, such as magazines and catalogues, and are assessed in terms of ribbons and etchings. A ribbon is the number of images or pages running parallel to the printed web; an etching is the number of images or pages running around the cylinder circumference. Figure 10.11 shows a schematic drawing of the KBA eight-unit rotogravure TR 10 B/352 press with two folder units. The press is 3520mm wide and can produce up to 256 pages as eight etchings and 16 ribbons in one press pass. The press supports a wide variety of product formats through the double folder units with combination superstructures for former production and magazine production. Further flexibility is offered by two flexo-imprinting units, with the result that flying imprints can be applied to both sides of the web. Table 10.11 gives examples of make-ready times and running speeds. Here are a selection of KBA TR machines:

▶ The TR4 has a maximum web width of around 1600mm
▶ The TR5 has a maximum web width of around 2150mm
▶ The TR6 has a maximum web width of around 2750mm
▶ The TR8 has a maximum web width of around 3280mm
▶ The TR10 has a maximum web width of around 3680mm.

FIGURE 10.11 Schematic of a KBA eight-unit rotogravure TR 10 B/352 press

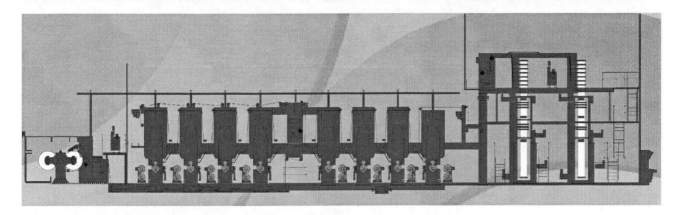

Source: KBA

TABLE 10.11 Large-width gravure presses: average make-ready times and press running speeds

Example 1

TR4S with a web width of 1,300mm, eight-unit press, resulting in

48 pages	With 6 etchings and 4 ribbons, i.e. 6 pages running around the cylinder circumference and 4 pages running parallel to the web, printed both sides
24 pages	With 4 etchings and 3 ribbons, i.e. 4 pages running around the cylinder circumference and 3 pages running parallel to the web, printed both sides

Make-ready and set-up

Eight print units	Up to 3 hours
	Up to 2 hours follow-on make-ready

Average net output in copies per hour

	6 etchings: up to 26,000
	4 etchings: up to 40,000 (1-up), up to 75,000 (2-up)

The maximum cylinder circumference for 6 etchings is 1,560mm; for 4 etchings it is 1,160mm

Example 2

TR5B with a web width of 2,144mm, eight-unit press, resulting in

84 pages	With 6 etchings and 7 ribbons, i.e. 6 pages running around the cylinder circumference and 7 pages running parallel to the web, printed both sides
64 pages	With 4 etchings and 8 ribbons, i.e. 4 pages running around the cylinder circumference and 8 pages running parallel to the web, printed both sides

Make-ready and set-up

Eight print units	Up to 4 hours
	Up to 3 hours follow-on make-ready

Average net output in copies per hour

	6 etchings: up to 30,000
	4 etchings: up to 50,000 (1-up), up to 80,000 (2-up)

The maximum cylinder circumference for 6 etchings is 1,560mm; for 4 etchings it is 1,140mm

Source: H. M. Speirs

Screen printing

Screen printing is a stencilling process where the ink is forced through the clear or porous elements of the stencil on to the substrate to be printed. It is a very versatile printing process capable of printing on all the usual printing materials and substrates, as well as many others, including metal, wood, plastic, glass, cork and fabric. In recent years, screen machine printing has changed considerably from being a slow-speed, mainly hand-fed process to a highly technical printing process, capable of sheet-fed speeds of 5000 impressions per hour and 60m/min. It has also developed as a rotary process through the use of narrow-width rotary screen printing presses. They are often combined with other processes to provide a range of presses that print and finish in-line products, predominantly for the self-adhesive reel-fed label market. Wallcoverings and fabric printing are other major markets for rotary screen printing.

The screen printing process has always been mainly suited to short-run work due to its low set-up costs and relatively slow running speeds, but the increased automation and improvements to the process mean it can be more competitive across a wider range of work, although it is under tremendous pressure from large- and wide-format digital presses that continue to take work previously printed by screen. Figure 10.12 illustrates a fully automatic five-colour screen press with LCD touch control panels covering large-format sizes up to 1650mm × 3350mm. This type of press can be upgraded to seven printing units, and UV flash curing eliminates ozone emission. Here are the main types of screen press.

FIGURE 10.12 Svecia five-colour SAMX fully automatic flatbed screen printing press

Source: Registerprint Machinery Ltd

| Flatbed platen presses | Flatbed platen presses are available in a variety of types. Hand-fed presses operate with hand feeding, printing and take-off. Semi-automatic presses operate with hand feeding but with auto printing and hand take-off. Three-quarter automatic presses again operate as hand feeding, auto printing and take-off, but they can be fully automatic. Press speeds are up to 1500 impressions per hour. |

Cylinder presses

In cylinder presses, the squeegee remains stationary while the vacuum cylinder retains the substrate to be printed as it moves under the reciprocating screen mesh. Press speeds are up to 5000 impressions per hour.

Rotary presses

Rotary presses are based on a rotary screen cylinder. The squeegee is fixed inside the rotary printing cylinder, pressing the ink through the open screen wall on to the substrate. An ink pump system ensures a constant supply of ink to the inside of the printing cylinder. A narrow-width rotary screen machine is primarily used for self-adhesive labels, scratch cards and packaging products, whereas the larger and wider rotary screen machines are used for printing wallcoverings, vinyls and floor coverings. Figure 10.10 (page 224) shows the Edale eight-colour Beta flexographic press, which can be fitted with a rotary screen unit. The rotary screen unit is popular for producing labels with high added value, especially for the pharmaceutical industries. Press speeds are up to 60m/min, recording average net output below 50% of flexographic presses (Table 10.8, page 225).

Specialty presses

Besides the other press types, there are two specialty screen presses: the carousel is primarily used for printing textile garments such as T-shirts, and the container is used for printing on bottles, drums and other containers.

Versatility

The versatility of the printing process is shown in the very wide variety of products produced by screen printing. These include large posters, cover overprints, point-of-sale (POS) display work, printed circuit boards, banners, fabric printing, instrument facia, heavy-gauge metal, glass and rigid plastic. Table 10.12 (overleaf) gives some average make-ready and set-up times.

TABLE 10.12 Screen presses: average make-ready times and press running speeds		
	Small format	**Large format**
Flatbed platens		
Make-ready and set-up time (min): single colour		
Press make-ready	15	40
Wash-up	15	30
Average net output (sheets per hour)		
Hand-fed	150	100
Semi-automatic	250	200
Three-quarter automatic	600	400
Fully automatic	900	650
Fully automatic cylinders		
Make-ready and set-up time (min)		
Press make-ready – single colour	20	40
Per additional print unit	10	20
Wash-up	15	30
Average net output (sheets per hour)		
Fully automatic	3,000	2,200

Source: H. M. Speirs

Digital printing

Over the centuries, conventional printing processes have taken a production-centred approach, concentrating on economies of scale. They produce the exact same printed product, time after time, at increasing production speeds as further developments are introduced. Whereas up to now, digital printing has established itself particularly in the following areas:

▶ Short-run batch printing that allows inexpensive set-up and reprint costs. Versioned, customised or regionalised brochure-type printed products, allowing specific targeting to an identified market, rather than a composite, general, all-embracing brochure.

▶ On-demand reproduction of specialist manuals.

▶ Reproductions of out-of-print publications, even down to one copy.

▶ Distribute-and-print instead of conventional printing's print-and-distribute.

Printers are well aware that print-buying patterns are changing and in response they need to be sufficiently flexible and adaptable to embrace the new customer demands and opportunities. Digital printing is at the forefront of this challenge.

Although starting from a relatively low base, digital printing is becoming a major printing process; its market share is growing at a faster rate than any other (Table 10.1, page 204). To confirm this trend, there are increasing examples of printed work previously produced on a high-volume basis by conventional printing processes, such as computer and instruction manuals, that have changed to a digital print-on-demand basis. A further example is in the increasing use of large- or wide-format digital colour printing systems in place of screen printing for short-run poster work. Fast turnaround is increasingly being recognised as one of the major assets of digital printing systems.

Digital printing has created the reality of on-demand printing, due to the absence of extensive make-ready and set-up associated with conventional printing processes. Up until now, digital printing systems have generally created new market opportunities and niches, instead of replacing conventional printing processes such as offset lithography. The exception has been the short-run market of up to 500 or 1500 copies, depending on the type of job and equipment used, where digital printing has become increasingly competitive. However, direct substitution by digital printing is set to gain momentum and increasingly affect all areas of printing in the future, as digital workflows and the experiences of printers and print buyers mature in a growing multimedia arena.

The images to be digitally printed are generated and manipulated in a digital form on a Mac, PC or other host computer system. They are then downloaded on to the host printing system via a raster image processor (RIP) and digital link. This can be part of an online networked system, or the data can be transferred offline by storage media such as a disk or tape. The print unit is then set up for the required number of copies, and if a finishing unit is included or required, the job can be collated and bound completely online or in-line. There are a wide range of printing processes, or technologies, that fall under the generic term 'digital printing'. They can be categorised in so many different ways that a definitive list would be difficult to create, perhaps impossible. Table 10.13 illustrates the main types of digital printing, excluding computer-to-press (CTPr) systems, covered earlier in this chapter under waterless litho. CTPr is a form of digital imaging (DI), on-press printing where the plates are directly imaged on the press before offset litho conventional fixed-image printing.

TABLE 10.13 Main types of digital printing

Laser			
Inkjet			
	Liquid		
		Continuous flow	
		Drop-on-demand	Piezo and thermal
	Solid or phase change		
Dye sublimation			
Thermal wax/thermal transfer			
Electrostatic			
	Xerography		
	Electrophotography		
	Electron beam		
	Ion deposition		
	Electrocoagulation		
	Magnetography		

Source: Pira International Ltd

Digital processes

Laser

A laser creates a printed image using a controlled light source. Laser light shines on a charged photoconductive drum or belt. The light selectively dissipates the charge in the non-image areas. The latent image is created point by point on the imaging device, i.e. the drum, to match the bitmapped RIP data. Toners are then attracted on to the drum or belt in the charged image areas, and the toners are transferred and fused on to the substrate carrier. Laser printers use the same printing technology as most copiers. A RIP interface allows the machines to produce digital prints, rather than copies of a hard-copy original, receiving instructions from a local computer or a workstation on a network.

Liquid inkjet

There are a wide range of liquid inkjet applications, including continuous flow and drop-on-demand. In continuous flow, the printing head continuously directs ink droplets towards the substrate to be printed. During the printing cycle, the ink droplets are given an electric charge so that the image-forming droplets can be directed on to the substrate. The unwanted, non-image droplets are then deflected into a recycling reservoir. Continuous flow was the first type of inkjet printing to be introduced and retains a significant share of the inkjet printing market. It is used in a diverse range of applications such as sheet-fed and web-fed printing or overprinting of documents in black, spot colour and four-colour process, plus personalised billings, direct mailshots, high-end contract proofs and wide-format posters, displays, barcoding and marking, etc. It is generally acknowledged that continuous flow systems produce the best quality results of all the inkjet technologies.

Drop-on-demand is subdivided into piezo and thermal. Piezo devices have a pump action to force droplets of ink on to the substrate. The inkjet head is an array of minute nozzles fitted with a piezoelectric crystal. When an electrical charge is applied to each crystal, it expands and pushes out the liquid ink in a controlled manner to form different sized dots. Piezo inkjet systems are very versatile because they can use a wide range of inks, including UV, oil-based, solvent-based and water-based. Thermal inkjet systems use swift alternate heating and cooling to create a gas bubble that forces directed droplets of ink on to the required substrate. It is a form of bubblejet, a term introduced by Canon.

In thermal inkjet systems the printing heads, or nozzles, include ink and a heating element. When activated, these nozzles heat up the ink, vaporising it and turning it into a gaseous state. As the ink vapour expands with the heat, it forms a bubble and forces its way out of the nozzle. The printing cycle continues as the heating element cools down and new ink is sucked into the vacuum created by the expelled ink. By controlling the heat applied during the process, the ink droplet size and speed of expulsion can be controlled. Thermal inkjet systems are limited to water-based inks, so they require special coated papers for higher-quality reproduction. However, heavy ink coverage can cause problems due to the amount of water-based ink that has to be applied.

Solid inkjet

Solid inkjet printers, also known as phase change printers, use solid ink sticks of yellow, magenta, cyan and black for four-colour process work. These ink sticks change from a solid state to a liquid state when heated. The heated liquid inkjets are then directed on to the substrate. As the liquid ink comes into contact with the substrate, it returns to its original solid state. This type of inkjet system has generally been superseded by liquid systems.

Dye sublimation

Dye sublimation produces a high-sheen, continuous tone, photographic type of print. Heat is generated in a thermal printhead consisting of thousands of minute heated heads. The heat acts on yellow, magenta, cyan and black coloured laminates. As the laminates are heated, the coloured dye sublimates or vaporises on to the substrate carrier to form the printed result.

Thermal wax and thermal transfer

Thermal wax and thermal transfer create the printed image by heating coloured wax panels and forming them into minute wax dots that fuse on to the substrate. Four passes, one each for yellow, magenta, cyan and black, are required to produce the four-colour process print.

Electrostatic

Electrostatic printing systems include devices such as photocopiers and lasers and incorporate different processes such as xerography, electron beam (e-beam) deposition and ion deposition, based largely on the principle that unlike charges attract whereas like charges repel. Unlike charges are positive and negative; like charges are negative and negative or positive and positive. There are exceptions, such as the Xeikon digital printing system, where a negative charge is used in the image and non-image areas. Here it is the charge differential that produces the image.

An electrostatic system has a rotating drum, often with a selenium coating, that can hold an electrical photoconductive charge, e.g. a positive charge. The image areas are created on the drum by exposure to an intense light source. The light dissipates the electrical charge wherever it shines on the drum. Oppositely charged toner, here negative, is then applied to the drum, adhering only to the image areas. The toner is then transferred from the charged drum on to the substrate, where it is fused to complete the process. Photocopiers conventionally reflect the original copy through a lens system on to the charged drum. Laser devices use laser light to generate a stream of negative ions, which form the charged image on the drum.

Electrostatic printing systems use either solid or liquid toners. Liquid toner generally produces finer quality and faster running, although it is highly influenced by the overall quality of the system, including front end, software, consumables, print engine and associated equipment. Electrophotography is a form of electrostatic printing used in a large proportion of digital printing systems and extensively in sheet-fed and web-fed digital colour printing systems. The HP Indigo systems use ElectroInk, a liquid-based toner system, whereas the Xeikon systems use a solid-based toner. The term 'xerography' comes from the Greek for 'dry writing'; it was first used commercially by Xerox. A photoreceptor is uniformly charged, and an optical image of the original is projected on to the photoreceptor, leaving a 'copy' of the original in the form of latent charges. Charged toner is attracted to the latent image then heated to form a permanent image when transferred to the substrate.

E-beam devices charge the substrate in the required image areas and toner is crushed on to the substrate as it passes through the printer; toner ink adheres to the charged areas but not the uncharged areas. To complete the process, the substrate is sealed and cured. In ion deposition the image carrier, called a dielectric cylinder, is charged with an ion beam controlled by a series of electrodes. Dry toner is then applied to the dielectric cylinder, which transfers it to the substrate to form the printed image. Electrocoagulation works by applying very short electric impulses to a colloidal ink solution sandwiched between a cathode electrode array and a passivated rotary electrode. The ink adheres to the positive electrode areas and is then transferred after removal of surplus ink on to the substrate. Magnetography is the oldest of the non-impact printing processes; it creates a latent image on a magnetic metal surface by applying a magnetic field. The toner, made of pigmented fine particles, is attracted to the magnetised areas and then transferred to the substrate and fused.

Digital systems

In just over a decade, an extensive range of digital printers and presses have been developed and launched on a regular basis, with increasingly higher specifications and capabilities. A wide range of sheet-fed and web-fed digital printing systems are now available to print one or both sides in one press pass or cycle. Here are the main categories and their specifications.

Sheet-fed digital monochrome

The latest generation of digital monochrome copier/printer systems use technology that offers much higher resolution than before, and scanning-in has improved quality, especially on photographs. The more advanced digital copiers are changed into a printer through a RIP/server linked to digital data from a Mac or PC. A further option is where RIPs are built into the machines. Whether or not they are linked to a system, some photocopiers can produce spot colours by simply using coloured toner powder. In 2004 Xerox remains the top manufacturer in this sector, a position it has held since the sector was established, with the introduction of the DocuTech range of high-volume copier/printers.

The DocuTech range now extends to the 2000 series 75 and 90, representing a top speed of 75 and 90 A4 single-sided sheets per minute. The main group of machines covers the DocuTech 6100, 6115, 6135, 6155 and 6180, representing 96, 115, 135, 155 and 180 A4 single-sided A4 sheets per minute. Besides the DocuTech range, Xerox also offers the DocuPrint series (Figure 10.13). This covers a wide range of machines, from the DocuPrint 65 production printer to the DocuPrint 180; here too the numbers represent the top speed in A4 single-sided sheets per minute. The DocuPrint machines have extra functionality over the DocuTech machines in that the DocuPrint can handle variable data. DocuPrint machines can also split monochrome and colour documents between different printers. The DocuTech and DocuPrint machines use laser imaging technology.

Source: Xerox

Other major players are Heidelberg with its DigiMaster 9110 and 9150 at 110 and 150 A4 single-sided sheets per minute, plus Océ with its DemandStream, PageStream and VarioPrint series, capable of variable data production at up to 162 A4 single-sided sheets per minute. Canon and Minolta are also well established in this sector with similarly competitive machines. Many of these sheet-fed digital monochrome copier/printer systems have the following capabilities and facilities:

▶ automatic two-sided copying and printing, i.e. duplexing;
▶ hard-copy originals scanned in then electronic cut-and-paste;
▶ automatic download of job details, plus generation of job data and progress;
▶ digital data download from a range of options, including local area network (LAN), wide area network (WAN) and email;
▶ a wide range of in-line finishing and binding equipment, including stitching, bookletmakers, thermal and perfect binding;
▶ application of job and imposition templates;
▶ integral or add-on facility to create variable data and/or versioning options.

The main specifications of sheet-fed digital monochrome copier/printer systems include size range from A3 to B3+, substrate substance up to 300gsm, printing speeds of up to 12,000 A4 single-sided pages in black only, resolution range of 300–2400dpi (dots per inch) and imaging technologies including laser, LED, electrophotography and electron beam.

Production times Based on a planned queue of downloaded and rasterised files that are press-ready and compatible, monochrome copier/printer systems will generally run at 90–95% of full rated speeds. For average straightforward work, allowing for on-the-fly proofing and monitor check, intelligent job loading and stock replenishment during the run, 5–10min would normally be sufficient for make-ready and set-up on each reasonable-sized job. Overall average running speeds will be reduced by changes to stock type on a regular basis, which cannot be achieved through available paper trays, as well as the use of lightweight and heavyweight stocks. In addition, delays will be experienced through problems with files and proofs that require amendments, plus lack of forward planning and readily available work.

Sheet-fed and web-fed colour

Digital colour printing, aimed at the general commercial jobbing market, as well as specialist areas, has established a growing reputation for improved quality standards and reliability. Some early colour digital systems never got past the development stage, and a lot of lessons have been learnt along the way. Most of the problems have been overcome to create open and flexible workflows. Improvements are being developed all the time, including more competitive consumables and running costs as well as new, exciting presses and systems with high productivity and innovative features, and better methods of digital finishing. However, the full potential of digital colour printing has not yet been capitalised and people are still working to achieve this.

The supply element of digital printing is certainly better able to take up the challenge of providing an effective vehicle for dynamic quality communications. However, the demand side lags some way behind. Early on, digital press manufacturers recognised the need to boost the demand side and support press users in marketing the benefits of digital printing. This is now being stepped up to establish digital colour printing and significantly boost its market share. Marketing applications and promotion are the largest sector for colour printing and increasingly they are focusing on personalised printing to achieve a quick response and high added value, something digital colour is well placed to offer.

Companies such as Canon, Xerox, Hewlett-Packard and Océ, long established in colour copier/printers, have been developing this market. But the most significant event of recent years has seen long-established players in conventional printing, such as MAN Roland, Heidelberg, KBA and Komori, develop digital colour options. Alongside this, major digital printer companies, such as Xerox and Hewlett-Packard, have invested heavily in new presses and continued developing their existing digital colour production presses.

Sheet-fed colour copier/printers

As with monochrome sheet-fed digital copier/printer systems, Xerox holds a significant share of the colour sector through its DocuColor 2000 series and other digital printing solutions. The series covers the DocuColor 12 copier/printer, at up to 12 A4 single-sided sheets per hour, suitable for colour proofing and commercial colour production work. The main DocuColor series includes the DocuColor 2045 and 2060, at 45 and 60 A4 colour single-sided sheets per hour. In addition there are the DocuColor 1632 and 2240 at 16 and 22 A4 single-sided sheets per hour. All the DocuColor printers have a maximum resolution of 800dpi. They use laser imaging technology.

In addition to the medium- to long-run DocuColor copier/printers, Xerox produces the 2101 and the 6060, at 101 and 60 A4 colour pages per hour. The 6060 has a resolution of 600dpi and the imaging technology is low-oil fusing using a digital blanket. This takes the form of a wide thin belt that runs underneath the four printing units, with no pressure applied to form the image on the sheet. The 6060 can add on a wide range of finishing equipment, including bookletmaker, document binder and stapler.

Canon produces the CLC range of colour copier/printers that include the CLC5100 at 50 A4 colour pages per hour. Océ's CPS700 (Figure 10.14) is a digital colour copier/printer with seven-colour capability of CMYK and RGB. It has a speed of 25 A4 colour pages per hour with a resolution of 400dpi × 1600dpi. Due to its straight paper path around one large common imaging drum, where each of the colour toners is applied using low-oil fusing technology, the printing result is much closer to offset litho than the normal glazed colour copy finish.

The main specifications of sheet-fed digital colour copier/printer systems include format size range from A4 to A3+, substrate substance range up to 350gsm, printing speeds of over 6000 A4 single-sided pages in four-colour process, resolution range of 400–800dpi and imaging technologies including laser, LED and electrophotography.

FIGURE 10.14 Océ CPS700 seven-colour colour copier/printer showing the straight paper path around one common imaging drum

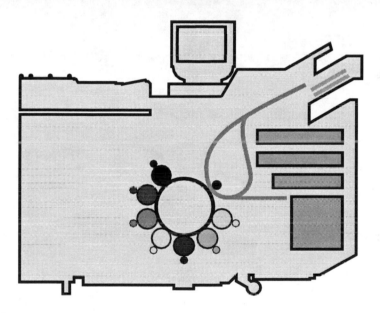

Source: Océ

Sheet-fed and web-fed production colour presses

In addition to the digital colour copier/printer systems, recent developments have seen the introduction of more robust and higher-specification production digital colour presses that take digital colour printing to higher levels of quality and productivity. This sector includes the sheet-fed colour production presses introduced by Xerox and Heidelberg, plus the sheet-fed and web-fed HP Indigo and Xeikon web presses. Xerox has introduced the DocuColor iGen3, which prints in a straight paper path at 6000 A4 four colour single-sided sheets per hour or, for example, 1500 A3 four colour double-sided sheets per hour up to a maximum sheet size of 364mm × 521mm, i.e. oversize B3. The printed stock range covers 60gsm to 280gsm, with line screen options of 150lpi, 175lpi and 200lpi, stochastic.

The press is controlled by SmartPress technology that includes SmartPress Imaging to control all the elements of imaging and printing, SmartPress Paper Handling and SmartPress Sentry. This monitors every printed sheet and provides constant diagnostic data on the press. The initial target area for the press is still relatively short-run, although it has a much higher break-even point with offset litho than was the case with earlier copier/printer and digital systems. The iGen3 is targeted to be competitive up to around 5000 copies, going head-to-head with offset litho, with the additional advantages of variable data and online applications such as books-on-demand. Figure 10.15, from left to right, shows the four paper trays, straight paper path, CMYK imaging and dry ink toner containers, image carrier belt, single-point image transfer, fusing unit, wheeled stacker carts used for unloading while running, and top tray for press proofs.

FIGURE 10.15 Schematic of the DocuColor iGen3 digital colour production press

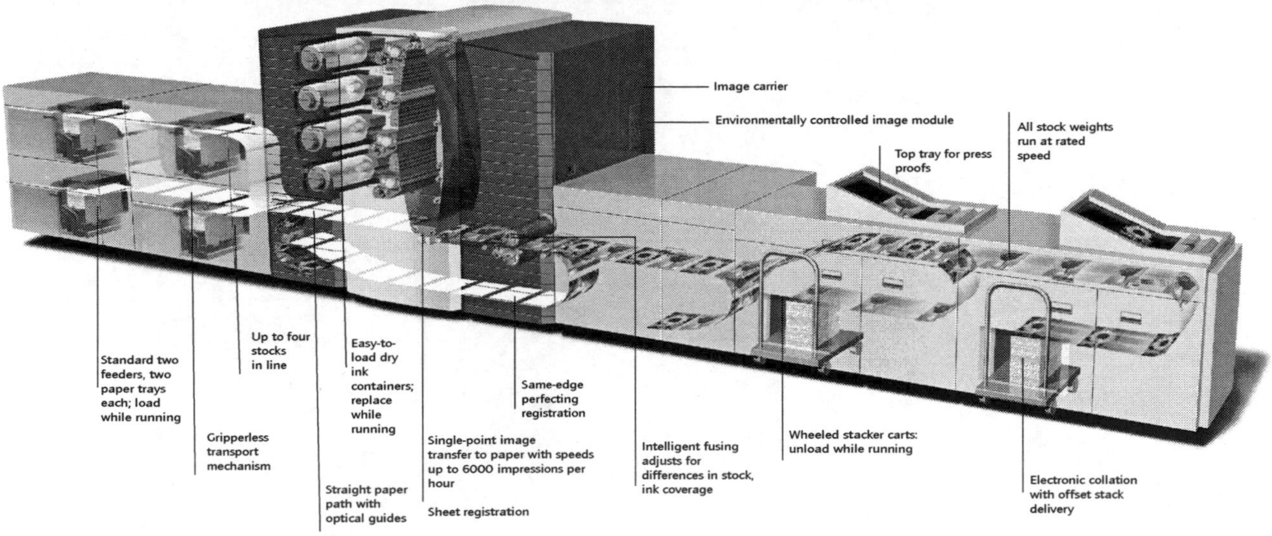

Image carrier

Environmentally controlled image module

All stock weights run at rated speed

Top tray for press proofs

Standard two feeders, two paper trays each; load while running

Up to four stocks in line

Easy-to-load dry ink containers; replace while running

Same-edge perfecting registration

Gripperless transport mechanism

Single-point image transfer to paper with speeds up to 6000 impressions per hour

Intelligent fusing adjusts for differences in stock, ink coverage

Wheeled stacker carts: unload while running

Straight paper path with optical guides

Sheet registration

Electronic collation with offset stack delivery

Source: Xerox

Like the iGen3, the Heidelberg NexPress 2100 press has been designed as a production printing press, rather than the less sturdy office digital printers. The applications identified by Heidelberg for the NexPress 2100 are quick turnaround, short-run colour, print-on-demand full colour, web-based marketing, e-commerce, personalisation, versioning, customisation, full variable data printing and proofing. Its suitability for variable data is confirmed by the fact that it can allow up to 6000 variable fields in one job.

The NexPress uses an offset process where the image is transferred to the substrate using a blanket (NexBlanket), allowing it to print on a variety of paper and board stocks, 80gsm to 300gsm, including coated, uncoated and textured, plus foils. As with offset litho presses, the NexBlanket is formed on a cylinder, resulting in good colour register and a high print quality close to offset litho. The intermediate blanket also extends the life of the imaging cylinders by protecting them from direct contact with abrasive substrates. The press uses dry toner and electrophotography to give a dry finished result straight off the press.

The 2100 press has a multifeeder system consisting of three feeder units allowing three different papers to be used on one printing job at any time. The maximum format size is 350mm × 470mm, i.e. SRA3+. The printing speeds result in output options of 2100 double-sided four-colour A4 sheets per hour, 1050 double-sided four-colour A3 sheets per hour, 4200 single-sided four-colour A4 sheets per hour and 2100 single-sided four-colour A3 sheets per hour. The press has been designed to produce up to 1,000,000 pages per month, with space to accommodate a fifth unit that could be used for a fifth colour, overall or spot varnish.

Figure 10.16, from right to left, shows the paper conditioner unit, same edge perfector system, the multifeeder's four paper trays, straight paper path, CMYK imaging and dry ink toner containers, image carrier belt, single-point image transfer, fusing unit, wheeled stacker carts used for unloading while running, and top tray for press proofs.

FIGURE 10.16 Schematic of the NexPress digital colour production press

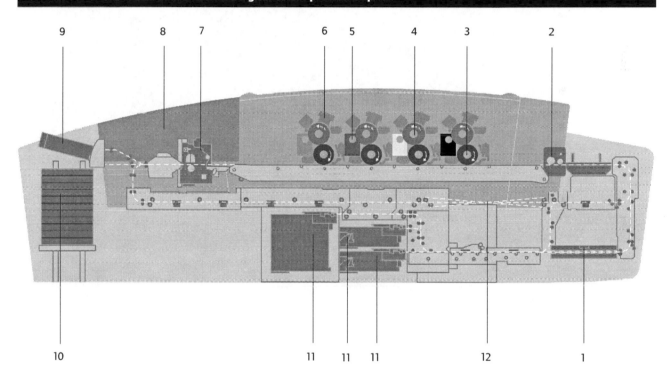

1	Paper conditioner	7	Fuser
2	Automatic sheet positioner (ASP)	8	Environmental control system (ECS)
3	Blanket cylinder	9	Proof delivery
4	Imaging cylinder	10	Main delivery
5	DryInk station	11	Multi-feeder system: 1 x 450mm feeder, 2 x 100mm feeder
6	Imaging unit	12	Same edge perfector (SEP)

Source: Heidelberg

HP Indigo has introduced a wide range of sheet-fed and web-fed digital colour presses to this sector, including the 1000 and 3000 sheet-fed presses producing 2000 and 4000 four-colour A4 single-sided sheets per hour, respectively. Several web-fed presses are available aimed at the general commercial colour market or specialist sectors, such as labels and photo products. Xeikon International's web-fed digital colour presses are the DCP 320 D (Figure 10.17), which has a 320mm web width and can produce 3900 double-sided A4 sheets per hour, and the DCP 500 D, which has a 500mm web width and can print B2 products with unlimited lengths.

FIGURE 10.17 Xeikon DCP 320 D digital colour web-fed production press showing the one-pass duplex printing operation

Source: Xeikon International

The main specifications of sheet-fed digital colour copier/printers and presses include format size range from A3 to B2, substrates up to 350gsm, printing speed of 8000 A4 single-sided pages in four-colour process, resolution range of 400–800dpi and imaging technologies including laser, LED and electrophotography. The main specifications of web-fed digital colour presses include format widths up to 650mm and beyond, substrates up to 300gsm, printing speed of 24m/min, resolution range of 300–800dpi and imaging technologies including electrophotography and electrocoagulation.

Production times Based on a planned queue of downloaded and rasterised files that are press-ready and compatible, sheet-fed and web-fed production digital colour presses will generally run at 75–85% of full rated speeds. For average straightforward work, allowing for on-the-fly proofing and monitor check, intelligent job loading and stock replenishment during the run, then 5–20min would normally be sufficient for make-ready and set-up per reasonable-sized job, depending on its complexity. Overall average running speeds will be reduced by regular changes to stock type, which cannot be achieved through available paper trays, as well as the use of lightweight, heavyweight and high-gloss stocks. In addition, delays will be experienced through problems with files and proofs that require amendments, plus lack of forward planning and readily available work.

Web-fed systems
Most digital printing systems can be adapted to reproduce at least partial variable data by using software that creates flexible field areas in the document where personalised or variable data can be dropped in. This section highlights systems used mainly in document management, print-on-demand systems, mainly for overprinting or personalising statements, flyers, tickets, vouchers and forms, as well as short-run and one-off work such as posters, and also proofs. Alternatively, they can produce entire products from plain paper in sheet or reel form. The range of online and offline finishing equipment is also wide and varied.

High-speed inkjets are now being used on web offset presses in excess of 50,000 personalised copies per hour, with several field changes, including name, address and other variable data. The more nozzles and printheads on an inkjet unit, the greater the overall area that can be covered. Variable information and data systems go from limited personalisation to print-on-demand, often known as bespoke document production. Improving data storage, manipulation and handling linked to faster and more productive printers have driven this rapidly developing area.

Although printing inks have been developed that withstand the tremendous heat generated by laser printers, printing companies still need to be careful when overprinting previously printed stock. The Nipson VaryPress range uses cold-fusing magnetography, allowing a much wider range of substrate such as pre-glued mailers, plastic and cellophane-type products to be manufactured that would otherwise melt with conventional hot inkjet fusion or laser. Here are some examples of web-fed digital monochrome, spot-colour and four-colour printing systems grouped under their main suppliers.

Nipson A wide range of monochrome options are produced by Nipson, including the 7000-200, 7000-300 and 7000-400 with maximum speeds of 30, 45 and 60m/min at 480dpi resolution and maximum image area of 457mm × 812mm. Further equipment includes the VaryPress series, with the T550, T700 and T800 at speeds of 80, 105 and 120m/min, having the same maximum image area as the 7000 series. Imaging technology on the Nipson equipment is magnetography or electrophotography.

Océ Océ is another major supplier in this monochrome sector, with the DemandStream and PageStream series, plus the later VarioPrint 7000 series that prints over 1200 A4 pages per minute, or 72,000 per hour. The VarioPrint 7000 series covers over 20 different models configured to offer a wide range of flexibility, including MICR and spot-colour facility. The DemandStream speed varies from 200 to 1000 A4 pages per minute, with the

PageStream speed from 145 to 500 pages per minute. Imaging technology on the Océ equipment is LED.

Xerox Xerox makes the monochrome DocuPrint continuous feed (CF) series, targeted particularly at transactional and publishing documents. The series consists of the DocuPrint 350CF and 500CF, with maximum speeds of 350 and 500 impressions per minute. In addition the DocuPrint 700CFD and 1000CFD produce simplex or one-sided work and duplex or two-sided work. The imaging technology on this equipment is laser.

IBM IBM produces the monochrome Infoprint series of continuous form printers, including the 3000, 4000 and 4100 advanced function printing systems. The 3000 prints at speeds of up to 344 2-up A4 pages simplex per minute or 324 2-up A4 pages duplex per minute, at either 480 or 600dpi. The 4000 prints at speeds from 229 2-up A4 pages simplex per minute up to 994 2-up A4 pages duplex per minute, at 240, 300, 480 or 600dpi. The 4100 is a continuous pin-fed option with maximum print width of 469mm and pinless at 482mm suitable for printing or overprinting plain or boxed fanfold forms and roll-fed paper in simplex or duplex mode. Printing speeds are up to 1148 2-up A4 pages duplex per minute, at 240, 300, 480 or 600dpi. The extra-paper width format of 495mm allows 2-up A4 and 3-up A5, ideal for books, manuals and loose-leaf documents. The imaging technology on this equipment is LED or electrophotography.

Scitex Scitex Digital Printing is recognised as a world leader and innovator in ultra high-speed digital printing solutions, with over 5000 system installations worldwide and in a variety of applications ranging from addressing, personalisation and variable messaging through to direct mail and short-run book printing, billing and statements. The range of presses cover monochrome, spot colour and full colour. The company's products include the Dijit narrow-format printers, 3700 printing system and VersaMark high-resolution page printing systems.

The Dijit 5122 printing system is designed to address the increasing demand for customer relationship management through one-to-one customised mailing, personalised business forms, bar coding and numbering, etc. The system prints at speeds of up to 300m/min at 120dpi resolution. The 5122 printing system and printer integrate with mailboxes, web-fed and sheet-fed presses, plus collators for use as an in-line or offline printing operation.

The Scitex 3700 printing system is a modular digital printing system designed to give commercial printers the flexibility of a wide range of work from monochrome and spot colour to four-colour process. Suggested work includes personalised direct mail with variable text and graphics, billing statements with personalised messaging, book publishing, business forms, lottery and gaming tickets, plus general mailings with colour messaging. The printing system features multiple rail configurations supporting multiple rows of Scitex printheads, full page, part page or a combination of both. This allows for printing anywhere across a wide web with 100% variable text and four-colour process image data at speeds over 300m/min.

The VersaMark Advantage printing system (Figure 10.18) is targeted at users who require high-quality digital printing and 100% variable data, covering commercial work, one-to-one direct mailing, personalised applications and on-demand printing for books or catalogues. Besides its high-quality printing, Scitex claims the VersaMark Advantage has the fastest printing speeds and lowest imaging costs of any digital colour system available.

The printing system will produce 100% variable image data in black, spot colour or four-colour process depending on the configuration. It can run at speeds up to 100m/min, 20,000 A4 pages one-wide per hour and 40,000 A4 pages two-wide per hour. Resolution is 300dpi × 300dpi and 300dpi × 600dpi with print modes of 1-up simplex or duplex, 2-up simplex and colour options of 2/2, 3/1, 4/0, 3/2 and 4/1. The maximum print width is 227.6mm and the maximum web width is 508mm, covering paper weights of 60gsm to 160gsm and finishing options of roll-to-roll, roll-to-sheet and roll-to-fanfold. The imaging technology on this equipment is inkjet.

FIGURE 10.18 VersaMark printing system

Source: Scitex Digital Printing

Wide-format colour systems Wide-format colour systems have seen significant growth in recent years, partly through the partial replacement of conventional screen printing with wide-format digital colour printing systems in short-run poster, promotional backdrops and banner printing, as well as creating significant new markets. Many wide-format printers have been developed and targeted at general or specific market sectors and applications, supported by specialist software and inks resistant to fading. The vast majority are based on inkjet. They often have six printing units, using a six-colour set of inks, either as Hexachrome with enhanced CMYK plus highly pigmented green and orange, or extended CMYK with additional light cyan and magenta. The number of printheads can total over 100.

Machine speeds vary greatly up to 200m²/h. Resolution varies from below 100dpi to over 2000dpi, with the speed of the presses being reduced to below 2m/min at the highest resolution. The substrates that can be printed across the range of machines include paper, cloth, canvas, backlit film, rigid board and vinyl, with a maximum substrate thickness of around 40mm. The most popular imaging process for this group of digital printing systems is inkjet. Electrostatics and LED are also used, often for mono or spot-colour large-format digital printers. Here are a selection of wide-format digital colour printing systems.

Agfa Grand Sherpa The Agfa Grand Sherpa printers are available up to 1620mm and can print a maximum substrate thickness of 1.7mm at a maximum printing speed of 39.5m²/h. The imaging system uses piezo inkjet with water-based ink at resolutions from 360 to 1440dpi in two, four or six colours. Apart from medium- to wide-format printing, Sherpa printers are also popular for producing imposed digital colour proofs.

Inca Digital Printers Eagle 44 The Inca Digital Printers Eagle 44 (Figure 10.19) is at the relatively smaller width range of 1600mm, but it can print a maximum substrate thickness of 40mm at variable printing speeds of up to 75m²/h. The imaging system also uses piezo inkjet with UV-curable ink at resolutions from 360 to 720dpi in four colours. It can print on a very wide range of substrates, including acrylic, coated metal, corrugated, display board, paper, wood and polystyrene.

The Eagle 44 was launched as the 'first ever flatbed inkjet digital press designed for screen printers'. The link with screen printing is confirmed by Inca's partnership with Sericol, a company well established in the screen printing sector, which now acts as agent to market the machine and supply the UV ink. The Eagle is targeted as a general-purpose machine capable of handling a 2400mm × 1600mm format. The flatbed printer operates through a sliding vacuum table, fitted with register pins for accurate positioning on single-sided or double-sided printing. To complete the printing operation, the table base travels under the printheads as they apply ink to the substrate.

Full edge-to-edge printing is possible, saving on trimming and cut-off waste material. A higher-specification version of the Eagle, the Eagle H, can print up to 800dpi with a printing speed of up to 100m²/h, targeting the machine at the photo lab and backlit

FIGURE 10.19 Inca Eagle 44

Source: Inca Digital Printers

display markets. Besides the Eagle printers, Inca produces the larger-format Columbia flatbed printer at 3200mm × 1600mm.

Scitex XLjet 5 The Scitex XLjet 5 is in the superwidth range of 5000mm, capable of printing a maximum substrate thickness of 10mm at a maximum printing speed of 86m²/h. The imaging system uses piezo inkjet with solvent-based ink at resolutions from five to 370dpi in four to six colours. Due to its extra width and flexibility, the XLjet 5 can print on a very wide range of materials, including canvas, mesh, Tyvek, flex-face banner, vinyl, fabrics, carpet and paper. Typical work includes backlit applications, point-of-sale, exhibition graphics, truck-side curtains, theatre and TV backdrops, and vehicle wrap.

Main specifications The main specifications of web-fed digital monochrome printing systems include width up to 643mm and beyond, substrate substance up to 305gsm, printing speed of 120m/min, resolution range of 240–600dpi and imaging technologies including laser, LED, electrophotography, magnetography and inkjet. The main specifications of wide-format digital colour printing systems include format size range up to 5m wide and beyond, substrate thickness up to 40mm, printing speed of 800m²/h, resolution range of 5–2400dpi and imaging technologies including inkjet, thermal transfer and electrostatic.

Production times This group of presses come in a wide range of sizes and types, including single- and multicolour, sheet-fed and web-fed, fixed and variable data; they also have a wide range of resolutions and run many different materials. All of these factors combine to create vastly different make-ready and set-up times and printing speeds. Use actual experience to establish job- and machine-specific make-ready and set-up times and running speeds. The printing speed ranges in this section are included for general guidance; actual printing speeds may vary by 10% to 100% of the rated speeds. Online make-ready and set-up times will vary from 15min or under for straightforward repetitive work to well over 60min for complex work. Most of the make-ready and set-up times on digital printing equipment involve the offline operations of data and file preparation.

Comparative costs of digital and conventional offset litho printing

The calculations in Table 10.14 (overleaf) establish the cost per copy by dividing the weekly cost of operating each of the three presses by the number of copies produced. Taken in isolation, they can be very misleading when trying to establish the overall costs for individual jobs. By simply considering the projected press running costs to produce one sheet from each of the three presses, the following figures are established.

The comparative cost per A3 sheet works out on the SRA3 sheet-fed offset litho press at 1.9p. On the B2 reel-fed digital press, run as 2-up one-sided, it works out at 6p per sheet. And on the B3 sheet-fed digital press it is 8p per sheet. However, conventional printing processes, including offset litho, have generally much more expensive fixed preparatory costs than digital printing. To illustrate this, I have calculated the cost per copy including prepress and press set-up fixed costs and press running costs. The least expensive total cost and resultant cost per copy are underlined.

TABLE 10.14 Comparative estimates of digital and conventional offset litho printing

The following illustration consists of enquiries for two separate jobs in three different quantities, 500, 1,500 and 2,500 copies. Three four-colour printing presses are available, two digital and one conventional offset litho, with the calculations per copy outlined below, based on press operations only. To demonstrate the process, hourly cost rates have been applied to the presses, from which the cost per copy has been calculated. This has been arrived at by establishing the weekly cost of each machine, based on full-recovery hourly cost rates divided by the projected number of copies to be produced in a week on the machine. To complete the picture, prepress costs and press make-ready/set-up costs need to be added to give a more accurate illustration of overall costs per copy, apart from ink or toner, paper, print finishing, etc. To simplify the calculations, overs and spoilage have been excluded

1. Four-colour sheet-fed SRA3 digital press for printing one side only, rated at an average speed of 750 one-sided SRA3 sheets per hour

Machine hourly cost rate	£60
Machine run on a single-shift basis at five direct hours per day, i.e. 25 hours per week	

Cost calculation per copy

£60 per hour × 25 hours per week	= £1,500
25 hours × 750 sheets per hour	= 18,750 sheets
£1,500 /18,750 = £0.08	= 8p per A3 sheet printed one-side only

2. Four-colour reel-fed B2 digital press for printing one or both sides, rated at an average speed of 1,500 B2 sheets/cut-offs per hour

Machine hourly cost rate	£180
Machine run on a double-shift basis at 10 direct hours per day, i.e. 50 hours per week	

Cost calculation per copy

£180 per hour × 50 hours per week	= £9,000
50 hours × 1,500 sheets/cut-offs per hour	= 75,000 sheets
£9,000/5,000 = £0.12	= 12p per A2 sheet printed one- or two-sided

3. Four-colour sheet-fed SRA3 offset litho press for printing one side only, rated at an average speed of 4,000 B3 sheets per hour

Machine hourly cost rate	£76
Machine run on a double-shift basis at 12 direct hours per day, i.e. 60 hours per week	

Cost calculation per copy

£76 per hour × 60 hours per week	= £4,560
60 hours × 4,000 sheets per hour	= 240,000 sheets
£4,560/240,000 = £0.019	= 1.9p per A3 sheet one-side only

Estimate enquiry details

Job 1: 500, 1,500 and 2,500 copies size A3, of 'Print Seminar' notice, printed four-colour process one side only, from press-ready digital files supplied

Job 2: 500, 1,500 and 2,500 copies size A4, eight pages self-cover, of 'Print for Today' booklet, printed four-colour process throughout, from press-ready digital files supplied

To more accurately reflect the inclusive cost per copy, prepress and press make-ready/set-up costs are included. No cost for proofs has been included. If proofs were included, this would increase the prepress fixed conventional printing set-up costs in comparison to digital

TABLE 10.14 Comparative estimates of digital and conventional offset litho printing (continued)

Prepress times and costs

Prepress preparation charge from compatible data supplied per two pages A4, four-colour process for digital and conventional printing	15min @ £40h⁻¹*
Offset litho computer-to-plate (CTP) for a set of C, M, Y and K SRA3 plates of two pages A4	20min @ £72h⁻¹
Material cost for SRA3 CTP per plate	£5

Press make-ready and set-up times

Four-colour digital press: sheet-fed	5min
Four-colour digital press: reel-fed	20min
Subsequent and follow-on make-readies: reel-fed	10min

Four-colour offset litho press: sheet-fed

First make-ready	40min
Subsequent and follow-on make-readies	30min

Job 1

A3 'Print Seminar' notice, printed four-colour process one side only

		Quantities		
		500	1,500	2,500
Digital printing				
Four-colour sheet-fed SRA3 press				
Digital prepress preparation	15min @ £40h⁻¹	£10	£10	£10
Press/printing make-ready and set-up	5min @ £60h⁻¹	£5	£5	£5
Prepress and press set-up fixed costs		£15	£15	£15
Press running costs @ 750 A3+ sheets/hr	40min, 2h, 3h 20min @ £60h⁻¹	£40	£120	£200
Total cost		£55	£135	£215
Cost per copy		11p	9p	8.6p
Four-colour reel-fed B2 press				
Digital prepress preparation	15min @ £40h⁻¹	£10	£10	£10
Press/printing make-ready and set-up	20min @ £180h⁻¹	£60	£60	£60
Prepress and press set-up fixed costs		£70	£70	£70
Press running costs @ 1,500 A2+ sheets/hr	10min, 30min, 50min @ £180h⁻¹	£30	£90	£150
Total cost		£100	£160	£220
Cost per copy		20p	10.7p	8.8p
Conventional offset litho printing				
Four-colour sheet-fed B3 press				
Conventional prepress preparation	15min @ £40h⁻¹	£10	£10	£10
CTP	20min @ £72h⁻¹	£24	£24	£24
Plate costs	4 plates @ £5 per plate	£20	£20	£20
Press/printing make-ready and set-up	40min @ £76h⁻¹	£50.67	£50.67	£50.67
Prepress and press set-up fixed costs		£104.67	£104.67	£104.67
Press running costs @ 4,000 A3+ sheets/hr	7.5min, 22.5min. 37.5min @ £76h⁻¹			
		£9.50	£28.50	£47.50
Total cost		£114.17	£133.17	£152.17
Cost per copy		22.8p	8.9p	6.1p

* ⁻¹ = per hour

TABLE 10.14 Comparative estimates of digital and conventional offset litho printing (continued)

Job 2

A4, eight-page 'Print for Today' booklet, printed four-colour process throughout

		Quantities		
		500	1,500	2,500
Digital printing				
Four-colour sheet-fed SRA3 press				
Digital prepress preparation	4 × 15min @ £40h⁻¹	£40	£40	£40
Press/printing make-ready and set-up	4 × 5min @ £60h⁻¹	£20	£20	£20
Prepress and press set-up fixed costs		£60	£60	£60
Press running costs @ 750 A3+ sheets/hr	2h 40min, 8h, 13h 20min @ £60h⁻¹			
		£160	£480	£800
Total cost		£220	£540	£860
Cost per copy		44p	36p	34.4p
Four-colour reel-fed B2 press				
Digital prepress preparation	4 × 15min @ £40h⁻¹	£40	£40	£40
Press/printing make-ready and set-up	20 + 10min @ £180h⁻¹	£90	£90	£90
Prepress and press set-up fixed costs		£130	£130	£130
Press running costs @ 1,500 A2+ sheets/hr	20min, 1h, 1h 40min @ £180h⁻¹			
		£60	£180	£300
Total cost		£190	£310	£430
Cost per copy		38p	20.7p	17.2p
Conventional offset litho printing				
Four-colour sheet-fed B3 press				
Conventional prepress preparation	4 × 15min @ £40h⁻¹	£40	£40	£40
CTP	4 × 20min @ £72h⁻¹	£96	£96	£96
Plate costs	4 plates @ £5 per plate	£80	£80	£80
Press/printing make-ready and set-up	40min + 3 × 30min = 2h 10min @ £76h⁻¹			
		£164.67	£164.67	£164.67
Prepress and press set-up fixed costs		£380.67	£380.67	£380.67
Press running costs @ 4,000 A3+ sheets/hur	30min, 1h 30min, 2h 30min @ £76h⁻¹			
		£38	£114	£190
Total cost		£418.67	£494.67	£570.67
Cost per copy		83.7p	33p	22.8p

Source: H. M. Speirs

In job 1, for the 500 quantity, the sheet-fed digital press has the lowest cost per copy at 11p, followed by the digital reel-fed press at 20p and the offset press at 22.8p. For the 1500 quantity, the offset press works out at the lowest cost per copy at 8.9p, followed by the digital sheet-fed press at 9p and the digital reel-fed press at 10.7p. For the 2500 quantity, the offset press again works out at the lowest cost per copy at 6.1p, followed by the digital sheet-fed press at 8.6p and the digital reel-fed press at 8.8p. Notice that up to 500 copies the two digital presses are more cost-effective than offset litho. Furthermore, the break-even point between the offset litho press and the sheet-fed digital press is just below the 1500 quantity at 8.9p and 9p, respectively.

In job 2, due to the B2 reel-fed press being able to produce one 8-page A4 cut-off in one press pass against four press passes for the sheet-fed presses, it works out the least expensive at all three print quantities. However, the very high unit cost of the offset litho press for 500 copies at 83.7p drops to 22.8p at the 2500 quantity. The actual break-even point where the offset press starts to work out less expensive per copy compared to the digital sheet-fed press is just above 1300 copies; and compared with the reel-fed press, it is just below 5700 copies.

I have included these calculations mainly to illustrate how comparative conventional and digital estimating examples can be constructed and also to show the effect of different quantities on the overall cost per copy. Digital printing has a low set-up and fixed cost base compared to conventional printing processes, but generally lower and fixed printing speeds. This results in competitive costs per copy at low quantities, say up to 500 copies, but thereafter the cost does not significantly reduce to any great extent. By contrast, conventional printing processes have a high set-up and fixed cost base, but much faster running speeds, which gain from economies of scale in the sense that the average running speed increases with the quantity printed, up to a maximum level. This leads to high unit costs for small quantities; the burden is carried by only a few copies, but when it is spread over much larger quantities, the impact is significantly reduced.

Due to the vast range and variety of presses and configurations available on offset litho presses and increasing productivity on digital presses, it is generally found that the break-even point between digital and offset litho printing falls in the region of 500–1500 single copies or sheets; that is, any quantity above these figures, depending on the individual circumstances, would generally be more competitive when printed by offset litho.

Table 10.15 (overleaf) taken from the publication *What Digital Press*, illustrates an example of comparable costs covering sheet-fed offset litho, DI and digital presses, in run lengths from one to 25,000. For this example the prepress and press make-ready costs are put at £75 for sheet-fed offset litho, £25 for the DI press and £5 for the digital press. Additional costs per copy are set at 1p for conventional offset litho, 2.2p for DI and 10p for digital. The table shows that the digital press is the most cost-effective up to at least 100 copies; the break-even or crossover point between the two presses occurs at around 250 copies. Thereafter, the DI press is the most cost-effective press up to just above 5000 copies. Above this total, offset litho is the most cost-effective.

In all similar comparative examples of digital, DI and conventional offset litho presses, the same type of ratio would occur, with digital being the most cost-effective in the low 100s. An overlap then occurs between digital presses, covering the lower-end copier/printer up to the higher-end digital production models, and the DI presses, over as wide a range as 250–5000 copies. Offset litho's cost-effectiveness overlaps with these presses, particularly the DI presses, through the wide range from 1500 copies to 5000. Above 5000 copies, offset litho generally tends to become more competitive than the DI press, although the break-even or crossover point can be much greater, depending on individual job configurations, press types, etc.

TABLE 10.15 Unit costs of varying quantities of a colour print job (four-page colour leaflet, £)

Run length	Conventional	DI	Digital
1	75.01	25.02	5.10
10	7.51	2.52	0.60
100	0.76	0.27	0.15
500	0.16	0.07	0.11
2,500	0.04	0.03	0.10
5,000	0.025	0.024	0.101
7,500	0.020	0.022	0.101
10,000	0.018	0.022	0.101
15,000	0.015	0.021	0.100
20,000	0.014	0.020	0.100
25,000	0.013	0.020	0.100

Source: Pira International Ltd

Print finishing

11

Processes and operations

Print finishing covers a wide range of processes and operations for getting a printed product into its required finished state, but it is most commonly associated with general commercial printed work, such as booklets, brochures, leaflets, folders, posters, wallcharts and reports. Binding is more directly associated with more durable publications such as books, instruction manuals, telephone directories and catalogues. The term 'converting' is used extensively in specific market sectors, especially rigid and flexible packing, including folding box cartons, corrugated boxes and self-adhesive labels, plastic bags and flexible food wrappers. In this chapter the term 'print finishing' will be used to cover all forms of finishing, binding or converting semi-processed items into finished products. Inevitably, there is considerable overlap between the different terms. This often happens more by tradition and/or general custom and practice than because there is any fundamental difference.

Print finishing covers a wide range of operations carried out entirely by hand, i.e. manually, by automated systems, or most popularly a combination of manual and automated systems. Each can be conveniently divided into three main groups:

▶ Handwork-only operations include gathering, inserting, counting, tipping in, sorting and inspecting, hand folding, making up folders or wallets, banding, packing and hand-mailing operations.

▶ Single machine operations include guillotining, machine folding, separate stitching or perfect binding units, punching and drilling.

▶ Multiple-flowline operations include saddle stitching, perfect binding, case-making, inserting, addressing and mailing lines.

Print finishing can also be broken down into in-line finishing, online or nearline finishing, and offline finishing.

In-line finishing

In-line finishing is where the finishing occurs at the same time as the printing. It is particularly associated with reel-fed and web-fed operations. The main advantage of in-line finishing is the potential to print and finish the complete printed product in one continuous flow of operations. The major drawback is that the press running speed can be considerably slowed by on-press finishing operations, such as the folder. Set-up times can also be considerable. For example, on a complex direct mail job it can take over ten hours to set up the complete operation before printing begins.

However, taking everything into consideration, it is still often cheaper and faster to finish in-line if possible, especially for long-run work where the proportion of make-ready to high added value machine running becomes less significant. In the move towards automation in print finishing and bindery operations, there has also been significant growth in automated binding lines, where several operations are linked together in an in-line configuration. Examples are available for saddle stitching, perfect, burst or notch binding and thread sewing.

Online or nearline finishing

Online or nearline finishing is something of a halfway house between in-line and offline finishing where, depending on the particular circumstances of the job, finishing components are brought together to complete a set of operations and then disengaged and reconfigured later for other jobs as required.

An example of online or nearline finishing is the temporary linking up of a sheet collator and padding/finishing unit to the delivery end of a small offset press producing finished multi-part sets. Another example is the growing range of finishing, personalising and mailing equipment targeted at new web-fed and sheet-fed digital printing systems. They can reconfigure quickly and efficiently from job to job with a wide range of requirements. This trend has become well established and is likely to accelerate as finishing operations become more modular and under greater computer control.

Online finishing displays the advantages of in-line and offline finishing. It allows for a streamlined, combined operation in a predetermined configuration when there is an economic or time advantage, but it also allows each unit to be run separately to its full independent capacity when required.

Offline finishing

Offline finishing is where finishing is done separately after the printing operation. This is the main type of print finishing used in sheet-fed printing. This chapter will generally concentrate on each operation separately, although some printing equipment is designed to be used in stand-alone mode as well as in a combined production line to suit specific circumstances.

Other processes

Few sheet-fed printed jobs are complete when they come off the printing machine; most have to pass through another process or department for further finishing, such as cutting to size and packing. In some printing companies, many finishing operations are performed in the warehouse, where they are regarded as part of warehousing, whereas in other companies there is a separate bindery or finishing department. Bookbinding has become highly mechanised and specialised, particularly where large quantities of books are required. However, hand binding of books is still done for very small quantities or where quality editions are required.

The term 'warehousing' is also used in connection with plain, unprocessed paper and board storage, where the substrate is stored and cut to size as required before being issued for printing. The term 'printed paper and board warehouse' refers to the area and/or operation where printed sheets and folded sections are held and stored while awaiting finishing. In book printing, for example, a number of the printed sheets may be left unbound or semi-bound to avoid the additional expense of binding if the publisher does not initially require the full quantity. A further example of warehousing would be the storage and/or stock management of printed and related items held by the printer for call-off by the customer.

All printers have some form of finishing equipment such as a guillotine for sheet-fed printers, and sheeter facilities for reel-fed and web-fed printers. Many printers are self-contained in their finishing equipment, apart from highly specialist areas, but some printers rely on trade finishers for most of their finishing requirements.

Common finishing operations

Here are some common print finishing operations that are carried out with varying degrees of automation. General commercial binding includes the two main types of saddle stitching and perfect binding, including slot, notch and binding, plus side-wire, thread stitching, plastic comb and spiral wire.

► counting and knocking up
► guillotining
► three- and five-knife trimming
► folding
► gathering, collating, insetting and inserting
► general commercial binding
► padding, strip gumming, wrappering and covering
► numbering, scoring, perforating
► laminating, varnishing and encapsulating
► bookbinding, including softback and hardback
► mailing, packing and dispatching
► miscellaneous operations
► operations associated with different types of work and products.

Counting and knocking-up

Counting is particularly necessary if you need to be very accurate about the quantity delivered. Examples include security documents, numbered sets, leaflets and brochures to be packed in specified quantities. Knocking up, or jogging, is always necessary if the material to be processed has undergone a previous process such as printing or sheeting, to be followed by a further operation such as guillotining. The cost of this work is normally regarded as an indirect expense and knocking up is often included in the hourly cost rates of the guillotine and/or any other equipment involved. The operational figures below provide a guide where these operations are treated as chargeable items.

Counting sheets by hand

Output varies from 2500 to 6000 sheets per hour depending on the size and type of stock being counted, as well as on the experience and skill of the individual. The larger the sheet and the more difficult the stock to handle, e.g. lightweight and flimsy or thick and rigid, the lower the output speeds.

Counting, batching and tabbing machines

Sheet-counting machines normally operate on a corner of a stack of paper or the edge of boards and place tags at predetermined intervals, such as every 250, 500 or 1000 sheets. They can be fully mobile to be set up in situ for counting sheets of paper or board for different operations or requirements. Alternatively, fully automatic tab-inserting machines can be fitted to sheet-fed or web-fed presses. Speeds vary from 50,000 to 120,000 sheets counted per hour, depending on the type of stock and machine used.

Knocking-up by hand

Output varies from 20,000 to 30,000 sheets per hour, perhaps more, for small sheet sizes such as A4, and 10,000 to 20,000 for B1 sizes and above. If the paper is very thin or thick, gummed or varnished, output will be about 20% lower. When a machine jogger is available, output will increase by 50–100%.

Guillotining

Guillotines are essential for all sheet-fed printers preparing materials for printing and/or final finishing operations. The term 'cutting' or 'pre-cutting' is used when sheets are cut on a guillotine to enable other finishing operations to be carried out. For example, a sheet printed work-and-turn has to be cut or slit in half before it can be folded. Slitting, which has the same effect as cutting, although is generally not as accurate or as high quality, can be carried out on the printing press or after the first fold on some folders. Careful setting up and supervision are needed since, if the position of the slit wanders during a run, the inaccuracy will affect all subsequent operations. The term 'trimming' is used when a job is guillotined to its finished size, such as a magazine or trimmed-flush softback book. Cutting and trimming operations are carried out on a guillotine. Guillotine machines used for cutting and trimming are available in a wide range of sizes to suit the press sizes used by printers, e.g. B1, B2 and B3.

Guillotine operations

To ensure accurate cutting and trimming, the pile or batch of printed sheets to be cut are knocked up square manually or by using a jogger unit, so that all edges lie flat against the back gauge. A powerful clamp ensures the sheets do not move during the cutting operation. The actual cutting operation is rapid, but knocking up, building up the pile and subsequent offcut and waste removal may take a considerable time. This is especially true if the sheets are large and the substrate being cut is heavy or very thin and difficult to handle, and there is no power-assisted handling or automatic waste removal.

Most guillotines are now programmable in some form or other, where the position of the back gauge and the operation of the clamp and knife are controlled electronically and the machine operated automatically or semi-automatically, depending on the complexity of the work being cut. In practice the operator plans the cutting procedure and measurements before programming the machine. Programming is normally achieved by moving the back gauge to the correct position and activating the procedure that records this position on one of the electronic channels of the guillotine. The operator repeats this operation for all the movements and measurements that have been planned. Some automatic guillotines now come with an unlimited number of programs that can be held in their online memory.

Where a considerable amount of cutting and trimming is carried out on a regular basis, such as by a sheet-fed label printer, then the guillotine forms the central part of a workflow system. The operation is streamlined by additional materials-handling equipment such as stacklifting and sheet-turning systems, additional air tables, automatic joggers, loading and unloading, plus packing facilities. They also considerably increase the productivity of guillotining and related finishing operations.

Figure 11.1 illustrates a typical comprehensive guillotine-based workflow system consisting of an automatic guillotine and a stacklift to lift and lower the printed work to working height. Also shown are a jogger and loader for edge-precise alignment of the sheets before cutting and a piling shelf system used for handling and unloading cut sheets. There is a gripper loading system that receives and transfers the cut sheets away from the guillotine, and an automatic unloading device on to pallets.

In addition to single-knife trimming guillotine systems, as described above, there are also three-knife trimmers. These trim all three edges – or in some cases five edges of 2-up work – of single copies or batches of magazines and books in one operation. They are designed for trimming only and cannot be used for cutting flat sheets. The machines can be free-standing for three-or five-knife trimming as a separate operation, or part of a larger binding line, such as an integrated gather, stitcher and trimmer machine. Guillotine production times and speeds are influenced by the following factors.

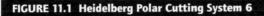

FIGURE 11.1 Heidelberg Polar Cutting System 6

Source: Heidelberg

Pile height capacity of the guillotine Although the maximum pile height capacity of guillotines is up to 170mm and beyond, the average operating flat height capacity of a pile of sheets in a guillotine is 75mm. Thus, if a pile of 1000 sheets of 0.075mm can be cut at one descent of the knife, it would be possible to cut 500 sheets of 0.15mm, or 250 boards calipering 0.30mm. The caliper or thickness of the paper and board can vary widely between different makes and types of stock, as illustrated by the following examples, for illustration only, of material having the same grammage that can be accommodated in a 75mm pile height.

Substrate type	Thickness per sheet (mm)	Number of sheets in a 75mm pile
100gsm white art	0.075	1,000
100gsm white printing	0.12	625
115gsm white art	0.09	833
115gsm white printing	0.12	625
240gsm pulpboard	0.32	234
240gsm silk-coated boxboard	0.37	202

It is possible to accommodate far more flat sheets in a pile than folded or stitched sections, as allowance must be made for the swell in the folds and backs. Therefore it is essential to reduce the equivalent number of sheets when trimming folded or stitched products. The reduction equates to approximately one-third of the allowance for flat sheets, e.g. the above figures indicate that 1000 sheets of white art 100gsm could be accommodated in a 75mm guillotine pile height. If trimming of a folded product on this substrate were to be considered, the number of folded sheets or leaves would be reduced to 666 per 75mm pile height.

Width capacity of the guillotine The width capacity of the guillotine varies from under 500mm to over 4000mm, although for commercial printing the maximum width is around 1370mm. In considering the length capacity of a guillotine, allowance must be made for handling space, hence the working capacities of guillotines should be adjusted accordingly. For example, a 920mm guillotine has a working capacity of approximately 775mm, i.e. B2+. The size 1040mm is often taken as the industry norm for guillotines around 1370mm, coinciding with the B1+ format.

Time to load and unload the guillotine This allowance will depend on the size and weight of stock used, also the automatic handling equipment available to the guillotine operator.

Operational times

Printers often allow a guillotine set-up time for loading and unloading of 1–5min per pile and/or 5–15min minimum time for each job to allow for job set-up and program setting. The average number of cuts per hour allowed by printers ranges from 30 to over 100, but 60 cuts per hour is increasingly being adopted by printers in general commercial work with programmatic guillotines, and up to 150 cuts per hour for repetitive multi-image work such as leaflets and labels, requiring a high number of cuts per sheet. Further examples of guillotine operational times applied by printers are 12–20 piles per hour, allowing for loading and unloading, plus single cuts or splitting in two as with work-and-turn, etc. Here is another guillotine example used by printers, based on the number of sheets of one cut per hour. By checking past production guillotine records, estimators can accurately establish the average number of cuts or piles per hour within their own organisation.

Up to 135gsm	30,000 sheets one cut per hour
Up to 170gsm	20,000 sheets one cut per hour
Above 170gsm	15,000 sheets one cut per hour.

Three-knife trimmer

Three-knife trimmers are used as offline stand-alone equipment or as part of in-line automatic binding equipment, such as on an adhesive or saddle-stitch binding line. The maximum thickness that can be handled on stand-alone three-knife trimmers varies from under 10mm to over 100mm and speeds from under 1000 to over 10,000 per hour. Using a pile height of 75mm, hand-fed machines give an average output of around 250–500 piles per hour, with automatic three-knife trimmers at 1200–2500 piles per hour. A make-ready and set-up allowance of 30min is common for stand-alone three-knife trimmers.

Folding

Hand folding

Today most folding is carried out on machines, but for very short-run work, complex folding configurations and specialist areas such as prescored folders, hand folding is still common. A skilled benchwork individual can fold at the speed of 1000 folds per hour for straightforward work to 360 or less with more complex work.

Machine folding

Folding is mostly carried out on combination folders, which can produce knife and buckle folds. The knife operation will create a cross or right-angle fold, whereas the buckle operation will create a parallel fold. Folding speeds are affected by these factors:
- Size of sheet to be folded: generally speaking, the smaller the sheet, the faster the sheet will fold.
- Number and complexity of folds required: the greater the number of folds and the greater the complexity, the slower the folding machine will operate.
- Type of feeder on the folding machine: a high-pile continuous-stream feeder will run much faster than a low-pile single-sheet feeder.

Sheet fed folding machines can handle sheet sizes from A3 to over B0. Folding machines are also available up to 30,000sph (sheets per hour) and 230m/min. Note that folding machines are increasingly being used by printers for much more than just folding. Certain specialised types of folding machine can now be fitted with attachments to perform a range of additional tasks online.

The TechniFold TriCreaser attachment, or its equivalent, is a major innovation in creasing. When fitted to folding machines, it eliminates fibre cracking, covering substrates mainly from 150 to 350gsm. This is a particularly serious problem that has afflicted digital printing for many years – when folded and/or scored in the normal way, unsightly and uneven white fibres show through down the fold, particularly on solid printed areas.

Certain specialised types of folding machine can now be fitted with attachments to perform a range of additional tasks online. They include continuous and stop-and-start perforations, numbering, slitting, spine gluing, production of reply cards through doubling paper thickness and gluing down, application of remoistenable gum strips and envelopes with fold-over gummed edging. Specialist highly sophisticated folding machines have been developed for the direct mail market. Examples are Stahl mailers and Hunkeler mailers. Specific speeds of operation can only be established by checking the output on a range of work over a period of time.

Table 11.1 reflects the average output of folding operations on conventional folding machines based on using a standard range of paper from 60 to 115gsm. For lightweight, difficult or heavier stock, output would be reduced accordingly. Output speeds need to be reduced for short-run work.

TABLE 11.1 Folding machines: average make-ready times and running speeds		
Make-ready		
1 fold	20min	
2 folds	30min	
3 folds	45min	
4 folds	60min	
Output speeds		
250mm	4 pages	16,000 sheets per hour
500mm	6 or 8 pages	8,000 sheets per hour
750mm	12 or 16 pages	6,000 sheets per hour
1,000mm	24 or 32 pages	4,000 sheets per hour
Small-format folders running A5 jobs and smaller will achieve an increase of 50% or more on these figures for 4-, 6- and 8-page folded products		

Source: H. M. Speirs

Scoring and creasing

Paper and board 150gsm and above will normally need to be pre-scored or creased to avoid cracking the substrate where folded. This can be carried out on a printing machine (pages 226 and 274) or a folding machine if it is fitted with a pre-scoring or creasing unit (see my previous comments on the TechniFold TriCreaser attachment). A pre-scoring facility is also a feature with the cover feed on a saddle-stitching or perfect binding line. A specialist scoring machine such as a Rollem is also popular; here are some average production times.

Make-ready	15–30min
Output speeds	
Hand feed	500 sheets per hour
Automatic feed	2,500 sheets per hour

Gathering, collating, insetting and inserting

Gathering is the process of placing sheets or sections in the correct order to make up a booklet, book, sets or pads of sets of forms. Gathering by hand with experienced personnel will give an output of between 1000 and 1500 sections or sheets per hour.

Gathering

Collating   Strictly speaking, collating is checking through the printed sheets to ensure they are complete and in the correct sequence for binding. But the term 'collating' is now usually synonymous with collecting sheets into a predetermined order. When back-step collating marks are used, checking the sequence of gathered sections or sheets can be done at 1500 sections per hour. Without collating marks, the speed drops to around 1000 sections per hour. Collating is often dispensed with on machine-gathered work.

Collators, i.e. collating machines, have become much more popular in recent years, because they are relatively cheap and easy to use. Working arrangements take the form of collating bins in horizontal, vertical or circular configurations. Sheets or sections are drawn from each section or bin and dropped on to a collecting area as precollated sets. Stand-alone collators are available in small-format size with approximately 16 bins or stations handling from A5+ to A4+ size in speeds up to 8000 sets of 15 × A4 leaves per hour, with up to 80 bin machines. Large-format collators are available in up to B1 at 2500 sets and up to 15 bins. The output speed of sets per hour depends on

▶ the type of stock being collated

▶ the number of sheets per set

▶ the type of machine in use.

Although the higher-capacity bin machines are designed to run at higher speeds, the increased number per set brings down the overall output per set. Laminated or varnished sheets will reduce output as slower running speeds are necessary to ensure accurate pick-up and separation of sheets during the collating process. Depending on the technology and sophistication of the collating machine, jobs are run to get the maximum benefit of the machine capabilities by using as many of the bins as practical to produce multiple copies of a job. The following example illustrates an eight-bin collator with an average fixed running speed of 2500 SRA3 sheets per hour.

Example 11.1 10,000 two-part NCR (no carbon required) sets size A4 printed 2-up on SRA3 sheet, where the collator is set to pick up four sheets, 2-up of the duplicate sets from the eight bins

Set up stations and bins	15min
Output speed and resultant time, 10,000 A4 duplicate sets at 20,000 sets per hour*	30min

* Made up from 2,500 SRA3 sheets per hour, four duplicate sets × two bins

Example 11.2 10,000 four-part NCR sets size A4 printed 2-up on SRA3 sheet, where the collator is set to pick up two sheets, 2-up of the quadruplicate sets from the eight bins.

Set up stations and bins	15min
Output speed and resultant time, 10,000 A4 quadruplicate sets at 10,000 sets per hour*	60min

* Made up from 2,500 SRA3 sheets per hour, two duplicate sets × two bins

Establish average speeds per collated set, based on the types of machine used within a specific company and the class of work involved. In small offset and digital printing it is becoming a common feature to link collators with bookletmakers (page 264).

Insetting

Insetting is the process of placing one section inside another for subsequent binding. It is necessary when there are two or more sections in a booklet or magazine which is to be saddle stitched. Most insetting is now carried out in-line on an automatic continuous gatherer, stitcher, three-knife trimmer (page 259). For short-run work, hand insetting is still practised in a limited way. Two sections produce one inset, three sections produce two insets, and so on. If a cover is included, it counts as one section. Landscape booklets tend to reduce output by up to 20%. Here are some average speeds for insetting by hand.

Number of sections	Insets	Average insetting speed (units)	
		Up to A5	Up to A4
2	1	1,500	1,200
3	2	750	600
4	3	500	400
5	4	375	300
6	5	300	240

Inserting

Inserting is the process of placing a loose insert, such as an order form or piece of advertising material, between the leaves of a booklet or magazine without binding to the main printed product. The output for hand inserting in a random set position is approximately 1000 inserts per hour. When inserting between two particular leaves is required, 50% should be added to the time required for random inserting, reducing output to around 650 inserts per hour. For each additional insert at the same time in the same position, use 75% of the time allowed for the first random insert. For long-run work, such as magazines, catalogues and mailshots, the inserting is built into the full in-line finishing process, such as on a saddle-stitch, adhesive binding and/or mailing line.

Binding

Binding includes a wide range of finishing operations that culminate in holding together different elements of a job, such as single leaves or folded sections, into a single unit. There are many types of binding, from simple side-stitched chequebooks to hard-case thread-sewn library books.

Saddle-wire stitching

The cheapest and fastest method of binding single sections, or insetted material, for work such as magazines and booklets is saddle-wire stitching. In the operation of a saddle-stitching machine, a copy of the insetted job is opened at its centre and placed astride the saddle of the machine. Wire, fed from a reel, is automatically cut to the correct length for the stitch and driven by the stitching head through the back fold, being clenched beneath at the centre to form a staple that holds the sections firmly together. A looped wire is used, when required, to provide a wire stitch and a loop suitable for a ring binder in one operation; these loops are normally 80mm apart and equidistant from the centre of the spine. Saddle-wire stitching allows the leaves of the book to open flat, but the thickness that may be bound in this way does not usually exceed 10mm. This is because a greater thickness in the back fold would prevent the book from lying flat when closed. It would also give uneven margins, unless due allowance had been made when planning the page positions.

Insetter stitchers are machines having an endless chain-feed, saddle-shaped device on which the separate sections are placed, either by hand or from automatic feeders, before being carried under one or more stitching heads. They allow insetting of sections to be carried out at the same time as stitching and greatly increase output, as the operation of the stitching heads is automatic. The section capacity of the machine can be increased by running part of the job through first, using a single stitch, and treating the result as a single insetted section. This then forms the centre part of the booklet when the other sections are fed on to it.

Adding a three-knife trimmer so that stitched copies can be trimmed ready for packing and dispatch can further increase output. A machine so equipped is usually known as a gather/inset, stitcher, trimmer (GST). Figure 11.2. illustrates a GST binding line. A further method of saddle-wire stitching, often called a bookletmaker, is a machine where flat 4-page sections are gathered and fed to a multiple stitching head and stitched,

FIGURE 11.2 Müller Martini Bravo Plus gather/inset, saddle stitch, trim machine

Source: Müller Martini

after which the complete booklet is folded and trimmed, often just on the foredge. The head and tail margins are then trimmed to size on a guillotine to finish the job. These booklet folder/stitchers eliminate the need for a separate folding operation and are more common in organisations where small offset size presses are used.

Handfed saddle-stitching machines Handfed saddle-stitching machines are used for short-run work. Operating from pre-insetted sections, the average make-ready and set-up time is 15–30min with speeds of 800 copies per hour, one section, size A5 one stitch, one section, to 450 copies per hour, size A5 two stitches, four sections. If the machine works from an endless chain-feed combining insetting and wire stitching, the make-ready time is 15–45min, depending on the number of feed stations or hoppers, and average running speeds are 2500 for one section and 1500 for up to eight sections.

Bookletmakers In-line folding, stitching and foredge trimming operations are available in average speeds up to 4000 booklets per hour and make-ready times of 10–15min for a high-speed bookletmaker saddle-stitching machine.

Side-wire stitching

As an alternative to saddle-stitching, gathered work consisting of separate sections may be stitched through the side near the binding edge from front to back. This is known as side-wire stitching or flat-wire stitching and it has the advantage of being able to stitch thicker jobs. The most powerful machines take work up to 50mm thick. Side-wire stitched work requires a wider binding margin than saddle-stitched work and has the disadvantage that the book will not open easily and the opened leaves will not lie flat. As no fold is required in the back, loose leaves may be side-stitched or inset into or gathered with folded sections that are to be side-stitched. Round wire is generally used for saddle stitching and flat wire for side stitching.

Hand-fed side-wire stitching machines The production times and speeds for hand-fed side-wire stitching machines are commensurate with those for the equivalent saddle-stitching machines. Many of these types of machine are dual-purpose in that they can be easily adjusted to side-wire stitching and saddle-stitching. Desktop stitching machines and electronic staplers have become popular, offering flat side-wire, saddle-wire and sometimes loop-wire stitching.

Thread sewing and stitching

Sewing is mainly used in better quality binding, but is also used for some jobbing and magazine work. It may be done by hand, but is more usually carried out on a sewing machine. Hand sewing is rare except on specialist work that cannot be machine sewn. In machine sewing, the sections are opened at the centre and sewn from the folded edge through to the centre as sections are placed on the feed arm of the machine one by one, by hand or from an automatic feeder. Side stitching with thread is an alternative to side-wire stitching for binding gathered sections and loose leaves, but is not often used. It differs from thread sewing in that the stitches are made through the side along the binding edge. Machines with a single needle are used and the stitches are similar to those made by a domestic sewing machine. Machines are made to stitch thickness of up to nearly 40mm and to give stitches as much as 25mm in length. Thread sewing is popular for children's picture books, schoolbooks, theses, dissertations and bank or building society passbooks.

Hand-fed thread sewing and stitching machines Hand-fed thread sewing and stitching machine are again suited to short-run work, with average make-ready and set-up times of 15–30min and speeds of 500 copies per hour.

Perfect or adhesive binding

Perfect or adhesive binding, also known as unsewn, is the preferred method for binding thick publications. It is used where saddle stitching cannot cope, thread sewing is too slow and costly, and side-wire stitching is impractical due to the bound copy not opening and lying flat. It is accepted as the most practical method of binding thicker pagination magazines, directories and paperback books where economy is a prime consideration. It can also be used to produce book blocks for case-bound books. The gathered sections are fed to the adhesive binder unit, where the individual sections are clamped securely and the folded part of the spine is removed. The binding edge is milled, or roughened off, to allow the adhesive to penetrate the individual sheets. The adhesive is then worked into the edges of the spine and a suitable lining, or cover, is attached to the back, where applicable.

Many adhesive binding machines operate as part of a complete binding line, where sections are gathered automatically and conveyed to the binder. They may include a one- or two-shot adhesive system. The first adhesive shot may be cold polyvinyl acetate (PVA) that is dried as the backs of the books pass over a heating system, or it may be the hot-melt system. Hot-melt adhesives are not glues in the conventional sense but resemble the plastics in a hot glue gun. When melted they penetrate the book's back and dry quickly. PVA is water-based and will penetrate the binding block better than a hot melt, but requires hot-air or radiation drying for relatively quick setting. Unlike PVA, hot melt has a very short open time, perhaps only a few seconds before setting. After the first shot, the block is ready to be glued a second time, with a hot melt, before the cover is applied and pressed firmly on to the second gluing. Hot-melt systems were initially preferred because they dried quickly, and now a new generation of flexible hot melts have been developed that combine fast drying with the flexible properties of PVA.

Hand-fed perfect binding machines Hand-fed perfect binding machines are also suited to short-run work. Operating from pre-insetted sections, the make-ready and set-up time is 15–45min with average speeds of 250–1250 copies per hour, depending on the type and size of the machine.

Burst, slot or notch binding

Burst, slot or notch binding produces a stronger spine than the standard perfect or adhesive binding. It differs from perfect or adhesive binding in that the back folds of the sections are not entirely removed, but are slit or slotted through in parts, rather like a long wide perforation. This operation takes place at the last fold on the sheet or web folder. On binding, the adhesive then penetrates through the perforations, or slots, to hold the pages together. Together with the retained folded parts of the section, this creates a much stronger bound unit than adhesive alone. With notch binding, the normal grinding wheels, as used on the perfect or adhesive binder, are replaced with a set that cut a series of slots, or notches, across the spine of the book block to a depth of around 3mm.

Automated binding lines

Many of the major binding methods have been streamlined or combined into automated binding lines. Integrated binding lines have been developed for many systems, including saddle stitching, perfect or adhesive binding in its many forms, and thread sewing.

Gather/inset, saddle stitch, trim

Gather/inset, saddle stitch, trim (GST) machines are the most popular binding machine used by sheet-fed and web-fed commercial printers to produce brochures, booklets, magazines and catalogues up to around 72 pages, plus cover, on relatively heavy stock and around 96 pages, self-cover, on more lightweight stock. Here is the typical production sequence:

▶ Folded sections, or signatures, are fed into hoppers or stations by hand, singly or in batches, long blocks or logs, used by web printers after the printed and folded sections have been ram- or block-bundled.

▶ The signatures are insetted into sequence by a continuous moving-belt system to form complete copies. They are then knocked up to the head or tail and stitched with wire through the back into the centre fold. The wire is then closed into a staple.

▶ A three-knife trimmer (or five-knife trimmer for 2-up copies) trims the bound copies to final size.

▶ Additional facilities that can be included on an automated binding line are cover feed, obviating the need to score and fold cover boards; inserters to feed loose inserts into the publication; and card gluers to feed and tip cards and other items on to the bound publication. Other facilities include a shrink-wrap tunnel for packaging, and a strapper for improved handing of bundles and palletising.

Figure 11.2 (page 263) shows an example of a modern high-speed automatic GST machine that is fully compatible with CIP4 and JDF. The machine is also fitted with Müller Martini's Automatic Make-Ready System (AMRYS) where data is fed into the machine via a touch screen or via a JDF file, resulting in the feeders, stitching heads, trimmer and compensating stacker being set up automatically for each job.

Staffing levels The staffing levels and running speeds for high-volume medium- and high-speed saddle-stitching machines – in fact, any finishing operations or other series of operations – can vary considerably between one company and another. Staffing levels will also vary within the same company, depending on the circumstances of the work; on certain types of work an assistant could handle feeding three stations or hoppers, whereas on more bulky stock they could only feed two stations or hoppers.

It is also extremely important that the estimator is fully aware of the correct hourly cost rates to apply on multi-operation areas such as binding lines. Most printing companies use two-tier hourly cost rates. One rate covers the fully absorbed capital and other related costs of the equipment, including the main operator, who will set up and run the operation. A separate labour-based rate times the number of assistants required for the circumstances in question. High-speed GST machines are available in up to SRA3+ and speeds of 15,000 trimmed and finished books per hour. Table 11.2 illustrates typical production data for a modern high-speed GST with cover feed, including required staffing levels per number of sections.

TABLE 11.2 Gather, stitch, trim machine: average make-ready times and running speeds

No. of sections, incl. cover feed	No. of assistants				
Up to 3	1				
From 4 to 6	2				
Over 6	3				
Time taken (min)					
Make-ready					
General machine set-up per pass	30–45				
Set-up per each section or hopper	5				
				Average net copies per hour	
Run length	4,000	7,000	10,000	15,000	20,000
Run speed					
1 section	5,000	5,500	6,000	7,000	8,000
2 sections	4,500	5,000	6,000	7,000	8,000
3 sections	4,000	4,500	5,000	5,500	6,500
4 sections	3,500	4,000	4,500	5,000	6,000
5 and 6 sections	2,500	3,000	3,500	4,000	5,000
Loop wire and landscape format would each reduce the above speeds by 500–1,000 net copies per hour					

Source: H. M. Speirs

Gather, adhesive, trim
Gather, adhesive, trim machines (Figure 11.3, overleaf) handle much thicker items than saddle-stitched publications, such as high-pagination catalogues and directories, telephone directories and paperback books. The range of operations are generally the same as for saddle-stitch binding lines, but the sections are gathered, often having been burst or slot-treated on the folder. This is then followed by adhesive binding, as described earlier, including notch treatment as appropriate. All the other operations and additional facilities also follow the same lines. Medium- to high-speed gather, adhesive, trim machines are available in up to SRA3+ and speeds of 7000 trimmed and finished books per hour. Table 11.3 (page 269) illustrates typical production data for a modern high-speed adhesive binding line with cover feed, including required staffing levels per number of sections.

Source: Müller Martini

TABLE 11.3 Gather, adhesive, trim machine: average make-ready times and running speeds				
No. of sections, incl. cover feed	**No. of assistants**			
Up to 3	1			
4 to 6	2			
6 to 9	3			
10 to 12	4			
13 to 14	5			
	Time taken (min)			
Make-ready				
General machine set-up per pass	30–45			
Set-up per each section or hopper	5			
		Average net copies per hour		
Run length	7,000	10,000	15,000	20,000
Run speed				
– 1 to 12 sections	2,500	3,000	3,250	3,750
– 13 sections and over	1,500	2,000	2,500	3.000

Source: H. M. Speirs

Gather, thread sew, trim

Various binding lines carry out high-quality thread sewing (Figure 11.4, overleaf) for a wide range of work, including commercial bound products, softback and hardback books. The workflow sequence is largely as before. Additional processes are included when required, such as pasting on endpapers to the first and last signature, rounding and backing, case-making, and blind or foil blocking for hardback publications. Due to the complexity of the work, particularly on hardback and case-bound items, there are often at least two separate binding lines rather than one integrated line. For example, one line could produce the book blocks and one could produce the cases. Table 11.4 (overleaf) gives average book production make-ready times and running speeds.

FIGURE 11.4 Müller Martini Ventura book sewing machine

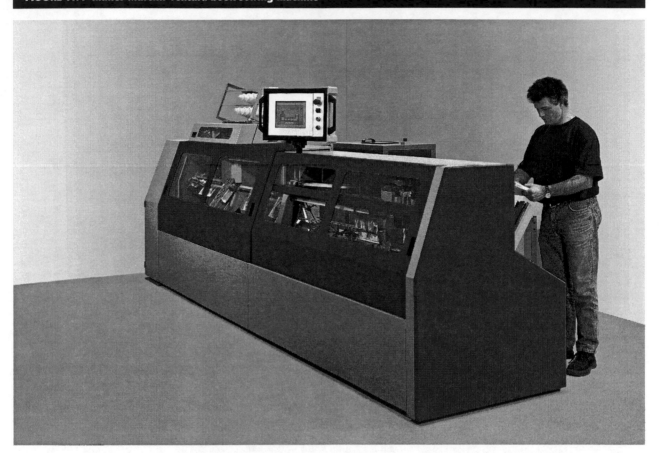

Source: Müller Martini

TABLE 11.4 Average book production make-ready times and running speeds

Make-ready: from 15min to several hours depending on the complexity and degree of changes
required from one job to the next

Glued or perfect binding lines for brochure and book block manufacture

1	Endpaper gluing machine at 2,000 per hour
2	Section gathering machine at 5,000 per hour
3	Perfect binding machine similar to general commercial binding, producing up to 3,750 book blocks per hour
4	Three-knife trimmer specialist high-capacity machine developed for book blocks at 4,000 cycles per hour

Thread-sewn case-bound manufacture

1	High-speed thread-sewing machine designed to produce sewn book blocks awaiting casing-in at 6,000 sections per hour
2	Book rounding and backing machine at 2,500 per hour
3	Bookmark inserting machine at 2,500 per hour
4	Backlining and headbanding machine at 2,500 per hour
5	High-speed case-making machine at 3,000 cases per hour
6	Automatic embossing press at 2,500 per hour
7	High-speed casing-in machine at 1,500 per hour
8	Book jacketing machine at 2,500 per hour

Source: H. M. Speirs

Additional methods of binding

Several methods of binding are based on retaining or binding mainly loose leaves into some form of binding system. Most of these systems gather loose leaves or folded sections and make them into a complete bound copy. If in folded sections, the backs of the books or copies to be bound may be trimmed before binding. Allow at least 3mm for trimming off single back margins where appropriate, plus marginal space taken up the comb or ring mechanism, for example. Binding then takes place using a variety of methods and systems with output speeds that depend on the amount of hand make-up or mechanisation. The simplest handwork-based systems include loose-leaf binders, securing bound edges with plastic comb and spiral wire binding, and thermal binding.

Loose-leaf

Gathered leaves for loose-leaf binding are predrilled at around 100, 40mm piles per hour depending on the number of drilling heads available at a time and/or the number of holes to be drilled. The average rate of inserting the drilled and gathered leaves into binders works out at approximately 60–200 sets per hour, depending on the complexity of the job.

Plastic comb and spiral wire

Plastic comb binding The material to be bound is placed in a punching machine where a multi-head punch makes a series of slots on the binding edge. The comb-binding machine is loaded with the correct length of preformed plastic comb, then the comb is opened with the teeth locating in the punched slots and, as the comb closes, the punched sheets are secured. Covers can simply be a sheet of clear acetate, a printed board or a plastic welded front and back sheet. Binding speeds, including punching and comb binding, depend on the thickness of the material to be bound and vary from 3 to 10 copies per hour for hand to semi-automatic systems.

Spiral wire binding Spiral wire binding is similar to plastic comb binding, except that the leaves are punched on a special multi-headed punching machine. A continuous reel of wire is fed into a former to spiral the wire and space the loops the same distance apart as the pitch or punched holes. Work bound in this way is often used for calendars and notebooks. This system does not allow for the contents to be changed. Output speeds for plastic comb binding and spiral wire binding vary considerably depending on the mechanisation of the system. Entirely manual systems have output speeds of approximately 50 per hour; automated systems such as Rilekart or Womako, used on calendar and similar products, have a make-ready time of 60min and speeds from 500 per hour to in excess of 2000 per hour. Automated comb-binding machines have running speeds from 750 to 2500 per hour.

Thermal binding Thermal binding is often used as an alternative to plastic comb binding. It is simpler and quicker as the sheets to be bound do not need to be pre-punched. The collated sheets are bound by thermoplastic adhesive producing a very strong bond. Thermal binding systems will bind up to a spine width of 50mm or 500 sheets at 80gsm. Some systems have an editing facility where sheets can be added, removed or changed after binding. They have virtually no set-up time and average running speeds are from 50 to 100 copies per hour.

Padding, strip gumming, wrappering and covering

Padding Padding involves securing sheets of paper with glue as a convenient method of handling forms and documents and creating notepads that can easily be detached into single leaves. The pads may consist of 50, 100, 200 or 250 leaves, according to specification, and may be with or without a thin strawboard at the back. Also they may have a protective flap cover. If the forms are made into sets having different forms, e.g. duplicate sets of first copy printed and perforated, second copy plain and fast, then gathering into sets would have to take place. The leaves are bound together and padded with a polyvinyl adhesive.

The procedure after printing is firstly counting the sheets as printed. A waste sheet of a distinctive colour, or a tag, is normally inserted after every 50, 100, 200 or 250 sheets, according to the number of leaves required per pad. This is followed by gathering into sets if required, cutting and trimming to finished size, padding and packing. Pads can be made up in multiples, glued at head, then cut into single pads. Here are some expected average operational outputs for the actual padding process, including knocking up, gluing and stripping before packing.

Pads up to A5 pads	100 per hour
Up to A4 pads	80–90 per hour
Above A4 pads	50–80 per hour

Strip gumming Strip gumming will occasionally be required, especially for receipt books. On very small orders the gum can be applied by hand with a brush, but a much cleaner and better result is obtained using a strip-gumming machine. Operational times are outlined below.

Hand-fed strip-gumming machine	
Make-ready and set-up	15min
	Average output in sheets per hour
Strip 125mm long	350–400
Strip 200mm long	300–350
Strip 250mm long	250–300

For gumming edges of postal wrappers on a hand-gumming machine, the output is approximately 800–1000 per hour. For large quantities of postal wrappers gummed on a power-driven gumming machine with drying attachment, the output is approximately 3000–4000 per hour. Gum strips can be produced as an add-on feature on some folding machines. Strip gumming, however, tends to cause curling of the paper and thus reduces output on processes that come after gumming, such as perforating.

Wrappering Also known as drawing-on, wrappering is gluing on a paper or board cover using a strip of glue at the spine or back of the book only. The cover may afterwards be trimmed flush by cutting the complete book, or the inside may be trimmed at the edges before binding, and the cover left with overlapping edges. On a side-stitched book or magazine in this style, the wire stitches will be visible when the cover is opened. Where this is considered undesirable, the cover may have to be creased to form side hinges and sufficient of the cover must be glued at the side to hide the wires. This is the same process as carried out in adhesive binding.

Hand-fed wrappering machine

Make-ready and set-up	15min		
Thickness	Average output in books per hour		
	Up to A5	Up to A4	Over A4
6mm and below	225	190	140
6mm to 18mm	190	160	125
18mm and over	150	125	100

Outputs are reduced by 20% on overlapping covers. Additional time needs to be allowed for gluing down at the side (back wrapping) to the extent of the score marks to hide wire stitches and to improve the quality of binding.

Numbering It is not always practical or desirable to number at press, even if the equipment is available, such as comprehensive numbering boxes. Consultation and cooperation with the printing and binding departments are always advisable to ensure the most presentable and cost-effective method of numbering. For example, if the number is to appear at the top right-hand corner of the page, the numbering may be done by hand or treadle-operated paging machine after binding, but if it is to appear in an awkward position on the page, the operation may have to be done before sewing or stitching.

Double-numbered books, e.g. receipt books, in which the two numbers appear side by side, are often done on a double-headed machine. The wheels in the numbering heads can be adjusted to number consecutively, or in duplicate, triplicate or quadruplicate. When accuracy is of prime importance, as in chequebooks, the numbering must be examined very carefully. Average numbering output times are outlined overleaf, covering a range of options. Modern microprocessor monitoring and verifying equipment is now available to check numbers automatically, so a random check by operators may be all that is needed.

Conventional numbering	
Make-ready and set-up	5–10min per box
	Average output
Straightforward simple numbering by treadle or hand machine in a convenient place	1,500–2,000 books per hour
At the foot of the page or near the spine	900 books per hour
In an awkward or difficult position	500 books per hour
Examination and certification of numbers	2,000–3,000 books per hour
Double numbering with two-headed machine	1,000–1,250 books per hour
Specialist numbering	
Make-ready and set-up	5–10min per number, set or batch
Crash numbering on collator or numbering machine	2,000 numbered sets per hour
Inkjet numbering, serial numbers only	4,250 numbers per hour
Inkjet numbering, number and related letters such as ticket numbering with block or row	2,500 numbers or letters per hour
Cheque numbering ion deposition based on four-to-view numbering	
500 and below	2,000 sheets per hour
501 to 2,000	2,500 sheets per hour
2,001 and above	2,000 sheets per hour

Numbering at press

Numbering at press on small offset presses is a popular process, especially for printed products such as numbered NCR sets, sheet-fed printed tickets and vouchers. Using a printing press for printing and numbering in one press pass is time-saving and price competitive. Numbering at press will involve additional set-up and make-ready of 15–30min, depending on how many numbering wheels are used and their complexity. Average net press running speeds are 2500–4000 sheets per hour.

Electronic numbering systems

There are a wide range of highly productive and versatile electronic numbering systems that can number at high speeds, plus perforate, score and slit, all in one operation. For greater flexibility, the machines can often be upgraded to increase their running speed and in-line features. Sheet sizes vary from around A6 to over SRA3, covering running speeds from 3000 to 12,000 A4 sheets per hour. The most advanced machines are fully programmable with features such as up to four numbering heads and online job memory, plus the ability to automatically feed open- or side-glued sets up to SRA3. They can also handle coated and uncoated stock, single sheets and multi-part sets, with the ability to crash number up to ten-part NCR sets.

Scoring and creasing

If covers printed on heavyweight material have to be folded, it is normally necessary to score or crease at the actual position of the fold to prevent the surface from cracking. This scoring is sometimes done on a converted flatbed letterpress machine or on a specially constructed cutting-and-creasing machine using a forme containing blunt brass or steel rules made specifically for the purpose. Make-ready is from one hour for a simple 1-up image forme to several hours for a complex or multiple-image forme. Running speeds are approximately 1500–2500 sheets per hour for old letterpress machines and 2250–6000 on specialist cutting-and-creasing machines.

Besides using converted letterpress machines for cutting-and-creasing, a relatively new innovation is to use the last printing unit on compatible B3 and B2 sheet-fed offset litho presses to in-line finish slit/cut, cut-and-crease and perforate online. An example is the CITO system. This works by fitting the blanket cylinder with a protective base plate, followed by a Mylar grid on to which self-adhesive cutting, creasing, slitting or perforating pieces are fitted. The impression cylinder is then fitted with a self-adhesive protective cylinder jacket. The press runs slower than for straightforward printing, by about 500–1000 copies per hour. Specialist rotary dies for labels, cartons, envelopes, etc., can also be prepared for in-line printing and finishing to shape.

Perforating

Perforating is now increasingly carried out with other processes such as folding, printing, cutting-and-creasing and electronic systems. Relevant production details can be found under those headings.

Laminating, encapsulating, varnishing

The surface of printed matter may be protected by laminating, varnishing or encapsulation; encapsulation is very similar to laminating but with a thicker and more rigid plastic. An estimator is often asked to include these operations when submitting a quotation.

Sheet-fed offset litho printers are capable of printing a machine varnish instead of ink, and applying spot varnish or overall varnish as a normal printing operation. A special in-line coater unit can be fitted to printing machines in addition to printing units, or in some cases the damping system can be adapted to run a protective varnish. The fitting of an IR or UV drying unit and the use of an appropriate UV varnish will produce a very hard glossy finish comparable to gloss lamination. When applying a varnish on a printing press, the cost will often be calculated on the basis of cost or consumption per 1000 sheets.

Traditionally most printers have relied on trade houses to supply their laminating requirements, but in the past few years there has been a definite upturn in printers installing laminating facilities in-house. A wide range of laminating machines are now available, mainly sheet-fed from B3 size up to B1 and beyond. Some machines can laminate one or both sides in one pass. They can handle a maximum stock weight of 950gsm. Average set-up and make-ready from job to job is 5–10min; printing speed is 4000–6000 sheets per hour or 50–100m/min. Reel-fed and reel-to-reel machines are available at up to 75m/min.

Apart from the laminating systems already covered, there are also a wide range of combined desktop systems for single- and double-sided laminating and encapsulating. Sizes are available up to A0 with speeds up to 500 A1 sheets per hour.

Varnishing

Varnishing as a protective and/or enhancing feature in solid or spot coverage can be applied on specialist varnishing machines or more likely on standard printing presses. Printers, particularly sheet-fed offset litho printers, will regularly use one of the printing units in a final process to apply a varnish or seal to the finished sheet (Chapter 10).

Alternatively, sheet-fed offset litho printers can have specialist in-line aqueous coating units fitted to their presses to apply a protective coating to the printed sheet. Estimates for varnishing and in-line aqueous coating are covered under the time and cost charges for machine printing. The average make-ready and set-up of a dedicated varnishing machine is 15–30min and the average net output is 1500–3500 sheets per hour.

Mailing, packing and dispatch

Automatic wrapping and mailing lines

Automatic wrapping and mailing lines have been developed in response to the growth of magazine distribution and direct mail products. Specialist magazine printers often install their own mailing lines to satisfy publishers' demands for a complete printing and mailing service, whereas general printers will tend to use specialist trade mailing houses. Automated mailing systems come in two distinct types: those that fold up the printed product and wrap round an address paper, and those that wrap in sealed polythene. Sealed polythene is the more popular method.

Most polythene- and paper-wrapping in-line systems automatically feed copies on to a travelling conveyor belt. Inserts and address carriers are then dropped on or glued on if required. Printed copies are then wrapped in polythene, normally pre-printed with the details of the magazine or publisher, sealed longways, sealed crossways and slit or perforated into separate copies. With sophisticated automated systems such as these, you can expect outputs of 5000–8000 copies per hour and above. Similar hand-fed polythene-wrapping machines operate at 500–2000 copies per hour, depending on the system employed.

Packing and dispatch

In many small printing companies, costs related to packing the finished job for delivery to the customer are treated as materials expenses and are included in the job cost per unit weight. However, when operational times for packing can be recorded accurately, it is better to treat these costs as a directly chargeable item. The type of packing depends mainly on the requirements of the customer. The method of delivery depends on the time and distance involved, and on the nature and weight of the goods to be packed.

Parcels

If printed goods are to be delivered directly, by hand or van, it will probably suffice to wrap them as parcels in a single sheet of kraft paper or good quality imitation kraft paper, sealing the parcels with gummed tape or in shrink-wrapped parcels. The number of parcels for any job depends on how many items can be contained in a 10–12kg parcel. If the substance of the cover is much heavier than that of the text, the number of copies per parcel will be somewhat less. The time taken by experienced packers to wrap the goods into parcels is approximately as follows. Magazines and other printed matter for delivery to wholesale distributors are usually shrink-wrapped and bundled with string or plastic strapping. Shrink-wrapping normally works out at 50–100 parcels per hour.

Capacity of 12kg parcels (based on a paper substance of 80gsm)

Trimmed size	Number of copies including cover in 12kg parcels at pagination p							
	p = 2	p = 4	p = 8	p = 16	p = 32	p = 48	p = 96	p = 128
A6	8,000	4,000	2,000	1,000	500	320	160	120
A5	4,000	2,000	1,000	500	250	160	80	60
A4	2,000	1,000	500	250	125	80	40	30

Packing parcels	Number per hour
Standard parcels of size 10–12kg each	20
Smaller parcels, say 6–8kg each	24
Packets of 1,000 A4 sheets with specimen pasted outside	28
Packets of 500 A4 sheets with specimen pasted outside	34
Packets of 1,000 A5 sheets with specimen pasted outside	34
Packets of 500 A5 sheets with specimen pasted outside	50

Cartons and boxes

When packaging on longer runs, it is more economical and practical to use special cartons and boxes that can be filled directly from the end of the machine. Cartoning normally works out at 20–40 boxes per hour, depending on the size of the box and the number of items packed in a box. The time taken will depend on whether the packing is online or offline.

Shrink-wrapping

Depending on the sophistication of the equipment, plus the size and bulk of the material to be shrink-wrapped, the number of wraps works out at 120–240 per hour.

Palletised work

In preparation for transport, printed work is often placed on a pallet in an orderly fashion then wrapped in special protective paper or spin-wrapped in plastic film. The load is often topped with a piece of wood or another pallet and plastic or steel bands placed around the load to hold the work firmly. A total weight of 750–1000kg is the most common, as this is suitable for the majority of mechanical-handling equipment. Palletising normally works out at approximately six pallets per hour, including bulk packing, strapping and shrink-wrapping.

Baling

Goods for conveyance by rail or other outside carrier will need additional protection such as baling in substantial thickness of strong brown paper and, possibly, shrink-wrapping tied securely with stout banding or rope. This baling will be in addition to the ordinary parcelling, not instead of it. Bales may weigh up to 40kg. Anything much heavier will render the loading inconvenient, and the risk of damage will be greater. Manual outputs are 4–5 bales per hour.

Export

After initial parcelling, if goods are to be exported in bulk, the time of the packers for packing goods into the case, nailing down cases, stencilling shipping marks, weights, etc., must be recovered. On average it takes about 30min to prepare the destination and other identifying details and pack each case.

Door-to-door containers

Door-to-door containers are frequently used to dispatch large quantities of printed goods in lots of 1 tonne and upwards. As the containers are completely watertight and weatherproof, the original parcels can be loaded into the containers without further external baling. Companies having to deliver goods within a limited radius only will probably include the expense of transport and delivery as part of the materials expenses. Quotations should state clearly whether the quoted price includes delivery to the customer's address as one drop or several part deliveries to possibly different addresses, or whether carriage will be charged ad valorem, i.e. according to the value.

If the order involves the dispatch by post of a large number of envelopes or other forms of postal packet, it is normal to ask the customer for a special payment, on a prompt basis, for the actual value of the postage. Publishers or printers involved in dispatching publications regularly in the post qualify for postal discounts, plus additional discounts for pre-sorting the mailing items into preferred postal areas. Details of special rates, discounts and conditions for dispatching newspapers, magazines and periodicals can be obtained from the Royal Mail.

Miscellaneous print finishing, packing and dispatch operations

	Per hour
Postal operations	
Banding	100
Sealing envelopes	800
Franking envelopes	900
Inserting	
One piece in envelope and tucking in flap	350
One piece in envelope and sealing flap	250
For each additional piece inserted	750
Inserting leaflets in clasps or string-fastener envelopes and fastening flaps	200
Wrappering booklets in postal wrapper, rolled	200
Inserting posters or charts into cardboard tubes	75
Pasting addressed labels on to a small package	250
Inserting an item or parcel into a rigid carton and sealing	100
Round cornering	
Paper, caliper 0.08mm, approx. 100–115gsm, per corner	20,000
Paper, caliper 0.08mm, approx. 100–115gsm, four corners	8,000
Board, caliper 0.25mm, approx. 240gsm, per corner	7,000
Board, caliper 0.25mm, approx. 240gsm, four corners	3,000
32-page booklets, two corners	800
Punching round or slotted hole	
Paper, caliper 0.08mm, approx. 100–115gsm	3,500
Board, caliper 0.25mm, approx. 240gsm	1,000
Hole drilling	
Piles of 40mm high drilled, single drillhead	100
Piles of 40mm high drilled, multiple drillhead (up to six heads)	30–50

Finishing for different sectors

General commercial or jobbing work

General commercial or jobbing work is the largest and most comprehensive group of all printers, where the vast majority of print finishing operations carried out by small- to medium-sized printers are offline, including equipment such as guillotines, folding machines and wire stitching, plus a wide range of miscellaneous often bench-linked operations, such as drilling, numbering, scoring, perforating and padding. At smaller-sized printers, gathering, collating, insetting and inserting are mainly manual operations.

Print finishing equipment used by medium-to larger-sized printers producing sizeable quantities of collated sets, booklets, brochures and magazines is likely to be at least partially automated either online or in-line. Examples are a collating machine linked to a padding unit, automated saddle-stitching or perfect binding line consisting of section feeding, binding and a three-knife trimming unit. This chapter has covered the vast majority of print finishing equipment and operations that would be undertaken by general or jobbing printers.

Periodical printers

Periodical printers usually have a more restricted range of print finishing equipment than general printers and tend to use a more specialised and automated range. Sheet-fed periodical printers use guillotines, folding machines and in-line automated saddle-stitching and perfect binding lines with cover feed and insert feeders, plus mailing and packing lines often linked to postal sorting systems. Web-fed periodical printers do not normally have the requirement for folding machines as the printing presses produce folded sections. The use of a guillotine is often only restricted to cutting covers down to size, otherwise the equipment is as for sheet-fed periodical printers, apart from additional handling equipment due to the bulk produced by the web machines.

Newspapers are produced on dedicated in-line presses which print, fold and finish, resulting in a broadsheet or tabloid newspaper. Depending on the capacity of the press, there may be a requirement for a section inserter if the pagination cannot be produced in one web pass. This chapter has already covered the vast majority of print finishing equipment and operations undertaken by most sheet-fed, web-fed heatset and coldset periodical printers. Web-fed operations include a high degree of in-line finishing. This is especially true of newspapers, which are commonly printed and finished in one press pass on a multi-web press.

Bookwork

Books undertaken by specialist book printers and finishers are mostly produced on specialist equipment, often adapted to individual company needs. It can either be in the form of free-standing batch processing lines or as integrated mass production flow lines. Glued or perfect binding lines for thick publications, softback and book block manufacturers use the following equipment: endpaper gluing, section gathering, perfect binding and three-knife trimmer. And here are the machines for thread-sewn, case-bound manufacture: high-speed thread sewing, book rounding and backing, bookmark inserting, backlining and headlining, high-speed case-making, automatic foil blocking or embossing, high-speed casing-in and book jacketing.

Continuous stationery and business forms

Continuous stationery and business forms produced on multi-web presses can be printed and finished in-line. With the right facilities, the printed webs can be numbered as required, file or sprocket hole punched, perforated, slit, glued, crimped, collated, bar coded and block-out decarbonised to deliver the product in finished reel-to-pack form. The items are used for offline finishing of continuous business forms.

Converter and paper processor A converter and paper processor is a simple machine which processes reel stock, normally into pack form, for further processing, or for producing plain paper stock. Operations will include producing fan-folded or pack products, which can be sprocket hole punched, perforated and also numbered. Make-ready and set-up usually take 15–30min and 1 hour maximum; average output speed is 250–350ft/min.

Pack-to-pack collator A pack-to-pack collator collates pack sets, normally with up to seven loading tables, therefore producing up to seven-part sets. Its facilities include crimping, tab fastening, gluing, numbering and perforating. Make-ready and set-up usually take 15–30min and 1 hour maximum; average output speed is 200–300ft/min.

Reel-to-reel collator A reel-to-reel collator is used where there is a predominance of long runs and multi-set work, either cut or continuous. Collators can be up to eight stations with sets being glued, crimped, crash or conventional numbered as required. Make-ready and set-up usually take 15–30min and 2 hours maximum; average output speeds are 450–650ft/min. The make-ready and set-up times depend heavily on the number of reels and stations to be processed.

Direct marketing, etc.

Direct marketing, direct mail and special products cover a wide range of items produced by web-fed in-line printing and finishing or by sheet-fed printing and offline finishing before being mailed and distributed through the post or by other means such as inserting into magazines. If sheet-fed, the central finishing unit takes the form of a folding machine with a wide range of additional finishing attachments capable of producing a one-piece mailer. Whether web-fed or sheet-fed, the principal finishing applications are folding, impact glue, remoist glue, perforations, personalisation plus additional applications such as die-cutting, window patching, rub-off and aromatic inks, also enclosing additional inserts.

The most popular machines for sheet-fed finishing in direct mail products are the Hunkeler mailers and Stahl flexo mailers, although many folding machines are now being fitted with glue lines, perforating, slitting attachments, etc. The finishing facilities on these machines include

▶ scoring, cutting and perforating, continuous and/or spaced, as well as slitting;
▶ remoistenable and heat-activated hot-melt glue application, continuous and/or spaced, for gluing flaps, stamp gumming and lateral closures suitable for posting;
▶ spaced application of cold glue for card doubling and lateral envelope closures.

Make-ready is from 1 hour on a simple job to as much as 7 hours on a very complex one, with an average of 2 to 2$^1/_2$ hours; 45min is often allowed per unit or section with up to 15min per gluehead. Depending on the number of units, output is from 2000 to 10,000 per hour.

Personalisation from a variable database is common with direct mail products, along with envelope making, which covers many applications such as itemised billing or statements and mailshots, in sheet and continuous form. For long runs on direct marketing products, 8-page and 16-page heatset web offset presses with a wide range of in-line finishing facilities are popular. Depending on the complexity of the in-line finishing processes and the web direction changes, the press speeds will be considerably less, 25–75% of straight printing, as outlined in Chapter 10.

Cartons

Cartons and packaging products are printed mainly on sheet-fed offset litho presses with offline finishing. Very long-run work such as cigarette and liquid food cartons are often printed on web-fed gravure presses with in-line finishing. Sheet-fed presses used for carton printing tend to be five, six or more colours with in-line coating, plus hot-air, UV or IR drying to enhance the aesthetic appearance and finish of the carton. Cartons are generally made up from groups or sets of multiple images printed on a large sheet, therefore requiring die-cutting, creasing and waste stripping after printing on a large die-cutter and creaser (Figure 11.5, overleaf). The machines used for this work can often do embossing as well, plus foil blocking and windowing or window patching (Figure 11.6, overleaf). A Bobst automatic platen is the most popular example of this type of specialist machine. The cartons are then finished on specialist folder/gluer machines, which fold and glue the cartons before packing in suitable batches.

Folding box cartons can be finished on separate stand-alone offline equipment which could involve five or more different operations as indicated below. Here are the finishing operations used to produce folding box cartons:

▶ forme making
▶ die-cutting, embossing and hot-foil stamping
▶ waste stripping, automatically or manually
▶ folding and gluing.

FIGURE 11.5 SP104-E Autoplaten die-cutter/cutting-and-creasing press

Source: Bobst Group

FIGURE 11.6 SP102-BMA Foilmaster foil-stamping press

Source: Bobst Group

Forme making Forme making can be done by hand or by an automated system using laser cutting and mechanised fitting of the rules. The time to prepare a carton forme, either manually or automatically, will depend on the intricacy of the carton shape and construction, as well as the number of multiple images. The following times are given as a general guide for producing a tuck end (style 1) carton.

Setting up CADCAM system	for new job	up to 7h 30min
	for existing job	up to 2h 30min
Producing Astrafoil tracing for 1-up profile of carton		up to 1h 30min
Laser cut carton profiles	first one	up to 1h 15min
	per subsequent one	20min
Rubbering and ruling	first one	up to 5h 30min
	per subsequent one	1h 45min
Preparing stripping board	4-on and below	up to 2h
	5-on and above	2h 30min and above

Cutting-and-creasing, die-cutting, embossing and hot-foil blocking on specialist machines The lower running speeds will be for short runs and also where embossing and/or hot-foil blocking are carried out as well as die-cutting. The highest speed would be achieved on long-run straight die-cutting work.

Pre make-ready		40min per carton
Make-ready and set-up		up to 3h
	per subsequent one	1h 45min
Average net output in sheets per hour		3,000–8,000

Hand-fed die-cutting Hand-fed die-cutting platens are mainly used for short-run single- or multicolour work.

| Make-ready | 1–2h |
| Average output in sheets per hour | 1,000 |

Manual waste stripping The overall output will depend on the number of cartons up on a full sheet. Fully automatic waste stripping will be carried out in-line on the press.

| Average output in cartons per hour | 7,000–20,000 |

Folding and gluing The output speed achieved will depend on the length of the carton being glued and folded and its construction. As a general guide, a 300mm long carton, straight line type, will run at around 25,000 per hour.

Make-ready and set-up	straight line	30min
	double wall, etc.	up to 2h
Average net output in single cartons per hour	straight line	20,000–80,000
	double wall, etc.	5,000–8,000

Other processes Windowing and window patching, including cutting out the window aperture, carton lining and punching out the profile film membranes are often carried out on specialist equipment such as the Kohmann 1350, working out at around 10,000–12,000 cartons per hour. Foil blocking and embossing can be carried out as separate operations.

If so, make-ready for each example would be 2–4 hours or more, depending on the number of multiple images on the sheet. Average net output speed would be 1000–5000 sheets per hour. In-line web-fed flexo and gravure presses are available for printing and finishing cartons. Machines can run at 300m/min with rotary die-cutters and at 210m/min with flatbed cutters.

Labels

Labels can be either sheet-fed or reel-fed printed on plain, ungummed paper or self-adhesive material. Sheet-fed labels can be printed on any substrate, although most high-volume work is printed on plain, ungummed paper around 75gsm. Nearly all reel-fed labels are printed on self-adhesive material covering a very wide range of paper and plastic substrates.

Sheet-fed labels Sheet-fed labels having a straight-edged rectangular shape are trimmed to size on a guillotine, followed by banding and packaging in batches as required (Figure 11.7). Here are the finishing operations for bulk quantities of irregularly shaped labels:

1. Before finishing, labels are printed in groups or sets of multiple images on a suitable sheet size.
2. Printed sheets of labels are cut up on the guillotine into single blocks of labels or long logs or strips of labels.
3. Labels are then ram punched to their final shape and size, with operational times as set out below.
4. Banding and packing are performed as required.

Hand-fed ram-punched labels in single blocks	
Make-ready and set-up	1h
Average net output in single labels per hour	150,000–200,000
Automated ram-punched system in multiple strips	
Make-ready and set-up	1h
Average net output in single labels per hour based on 14 strokes × 1,000 sheets per min	840,000

FIGURE 11.7 Atlas 110 label production system

Source: Blumer

Reel-fed labels Reel-fed self-adhesive labels are finished on an in-line basis, mainly on a flexographic or letterpress machine, as covered in Chapter 10. The finishing processes include die-cutting and waste stripping, through to re-reeling and/or slitting and sheeting units, plus optional hot-foil and laminating units.

Digital

Digital printing With the almost exponential growth in launching and development of digital systems, both sheet-fed and web-fed, print finishing suppliers have introduced a wide range of equipment to meet this relatively new market sector. It covers offline, online and in-line options allowing flexible configurations to suit the nature of this highly variable work.

Suppliers have introduced a range of mainly sheet-fed finishing options that can be fully integrated with a high-speed digital printing system or alternatively operated on an online, nearline or offline basis, as required. This type of equipment typically includes saddle-stitch bookletmakers consisting of collating unit, jogger and stitcher, folding system, foredge trimmer, delivery and pack. Perfect binding lines generally consist of sheet section feed, clamping section, milling, gluing, cover feeder, ripping unit, delivery and pack. Figure 11.8 (overleaf) shows the Horizon BQ-340-SPF-9 Hybrid digital print-and-bind solution that can switch between perfect bound and saddle-stitched books.

FIGURE 11.8 Horizon online binding system linked to a sheet-fed digital printing system

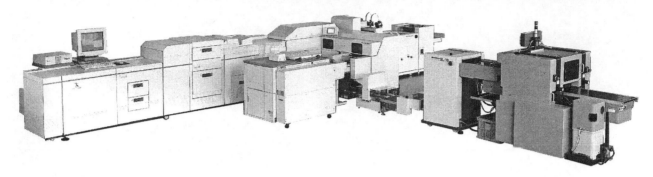

Source: GAE and Horizon

In-line finishing equipment has been developed to allow the digital printing engine to run as near as possible to full capacity while finishing. Hunkeler, for example, has introduced a 'paper online paper processing' range of equipment specifically targeted at high-speed laser printer equipment through print-on-demand and electronic data processing. The equipment range includes reel buffer units to assist continuous running of reel-fed printing and processing as far as possible, reel-to-sheeter unit and continuous folding unit. Figure 11.9 illustrates a continuous in-line print-and-finish process incorporating the HP Indigo w3200 webpress delivering printed webs cut by the Hunkeler CS4-Wide cutter system and folded by a Matthias Bäuerle folder. The press is designed to run up to a maximum 8000 A4 colour pages per hour (2-up).

FIGURE 11.9 HP Indigo web-fed digital press with printed product being cut and folded in-line

Source: Hunkeler

The Roll Systems DocuSheeter LS (Figure 11.10) is an example of a web sheeting and feed device developed to work with digital printing systems. It can run for 18 hours non-stop, feeding paper to the Canon ImageRunner 110, Heidelberg Digimaster 9110, 9150 or IBM Infoprint 2000 printers. The sheeter device sits next to the input side of the printer and comes with a quick-change unwind unit and precision cutter. Up to 60,000 sheets can be obtained from one roll or web of paper, running all the form sizes and paper weights the printer can handle. The system allows switching between A3 and A4, for example, without changing rolls.

FIGURE 11.10 A Roll Systems DocuSheeter LS connected to a Heidelberg DigiMaster 9110 digital printing system

Source: Roll Systems

Worked examples

12

This chapter sets out a comprehensive selection of worked estimates that cover the wide range of printed products and services offered by general and specialist printing companies, as well as work completed by all the main conventional and digital processes. Each estimate has been laid out in a similar format to aid comparison. Wherever possible, I have illustrated the different approaches adopted by printing companies.

Box 12.1
Box 12.1 covers an enquiry for 5000 copies of a multisection saddle-stitched booklet printed by sheet-fed offset litho. The format of the job is A4, consisting of 16 pages plus cover, with the cover and an 8-page section in four-colour process. In addition there are two 4-page sections printed black and one common PMS colour. The customer is to supply press-ready PDF files and the printer is to submit contract digital colour proofs to the customer for approval before proceeding to print. Ten-colour and four-colour convertible B2 and SRA2 presses plus CTP prepress are used in the estimate calculations. Sheetwork is chosen as the most economical method of working to take the maximum benefit of the available equipment and facilities. Once the material and outwork costs have been calculated and operational times extended at the appropriate hourly cost rates, a final 10% mark-up has been applied, resulting in a total figure of £3842.19. Company records and the MIS predict a price of £3720 and it is decided to quote £3795, which represents an overall 8.6% mark-up and a healthy 73.5% value added.

Box 12.2
Box 12.2 covers an enquiry for 300,000 labels on ungummed paper printed by sheet-fed offset litho. Due to the large quantity required, multi-image working is the obvious choice. Most sheet-fed offset litho label printers have B1 multicolour presses and in this instance the most economic method of working is chosen as 20-up on a B1 sheet. A six-colour press with in-line aqueous coating allows the job to be completed in one press pass. As high-quality wet proofs have been requested by the customer, they will be produced using the production press on which this estimate is based. Wet proofs produced on a proofing press cannot match the quality and integrity of production press proofs. A final 5% mark-up results in an estimated total of £3341.70. The price quoted is £3395, reflecting an overall 6.7% mark-up, but a relatively poor value added of 52.5%, due to nearly 50% of the job costs being material costs.

Box 12.3
Box 12.3 does not take the form of a typical estimate, but has been prepared as a worked example to illustrate one-colour digital versus conventional offset litho price per copy based on the assumptions listed in the table. One digital A3+ press and two conventional B3 and B2 offset litho presses have been included for comparison. Due to the low prepress and press set-up fixed costs for the digital press, it is the least expensive at the 500 quantity. However, as the print run increases, the faster running speeds of the conventional offset litho presses balances these fixed preparatory costs against the fixed cost per copy of digital printing. This is illustrated in the following summary.

	Description	Price per copy (pence)
500 copies		
Digital press	Cheapest at	4.17
B3 offset press	Next cheapest at	4.79
B2 offset press	Most expensive at	6.93
700 copies		
Digital press	Relative break-even point	3.64
B3 offset press	Relative break-even point	3.60
B2 offset press	Most expensive	5.08
1,500 copies		
B3 offset press	Cheapest at	2.01
B2 offset press	Next cheapest	2.63
Digital press	Most expensive	2.94

It is not until the 7500 quantity that the B2 and B3 offset presses break even at 0.90p per copy, therefore any quantities above 7500 would be cheaper by the B2 offset litho press. A further point to note between digital and conventional offset litho is the fact that although digital starts at the lowest cost per copy, it reduces more slowly than offset litho for additional copies. The digital example reduces by 12.7% per copy from 500 to 700 copies and by 29.5% from 500 to 1500 copies. The B3 offset litho example reduces by 24.8% from 500 to 700 copies and by 58% from 500 to 1500 copies. The B2 offset litho example reduces by 26.7% from 500 to 700 copies and by 62% from 500 to 1500 copies.

Box 12.4 Box 12.4 covers an enquiry for stationery consisting of three different products printed in common colours and quantities. The combination presents an ideal scenario for all three jobs to be run together on an RA2 sheet in one press pass, without any subsequent extra waste. This combination of different products using common inks and substrates occurs most frequently in label, carton and stationery work. A final 15% mark-up results in an estimated total of £873.05. The price quoted is £875.00, reflecting an overall 15% mark-up and value added of only 57.4% due to a high proportion of material costs.

Box 12.5 Box 12.5 covers an enquiry for 10,000 copies of a small-format pamphlet printed sheet-fed offset litho in four-colour process. The customer is to supply a Microsoft Word file and mock-up, plus 12 colour pictures for scanning. To suit the small format means, a small offset SRA3 press has been chosen, with 1-up work-and-turn as the method of working. With a 20% mark-up the estimated total is £821.22. The price quoted is £825.00, resulting in a high added value of 82.3%.

Box 12.6 Box 12.6 covers an enquiry for 1 million copies of a 64-page self-cover magazine. The very high print run makes this job ideally suited to periodical web-fed gravure printing. The press chosen for the enquiry can print the publication in one press, finishing in-line including folding, stitching, trimming, plus online strapping and shrink-wrapping. A final 10% mark-up results in an estimated total of £121,886.49. The price quoted is £122,000, reflecting an overall 10% mark-up, but a value added of only 38.3% due to the high material costs, including paper, ink and gravure cylinders.

Box 12.7

Box 12.7 covers an enquiry for 30,000 copies of a multisection adhesive notch bound catalogue printed by sheet-fed offset litho. The job, finished size A4, consists of 80 pages plus cover printed throughout in four-colour process. The most suitable sheet-fed press available to run this job is an eight-colour convertible (4/4). Sheetwork is chosen as the most economical method of working to take the maximum benefit of the available equipment and facilities. This results in the cover being printed 4-up and the text as 5 × 16-page sections. The material costs, including 10% handling, are £9,920.13 and labour costs at £10,374.09, which with a final 10% mark-up results in an estimated total of £23,323.64. Company records and the MIS predict a price of £23,490 and it is decided to quote £23,325, which represents an overall 10% mark-up and 62.2% value added.

Box 12.8

Box 12.8 represents the same enquiry as Box 12.7, except the estimate is based on printing the job by heatset web offset on a 16-page four-unit press. The job is again estimated as sheetwork with the cover printed 4-up and the text as 5 × 16-page sections. This time the material costs, including 10% handling, work out at £8693.81 and the labour costs at £7328.26. A final 10% mark-up results in an estimated total of £17,624.28. The quoted price is £17,625 giving an added value of 56.3%.

The material costs with handling charge work out at 87.6% of the costs in Box 12.7 and the labour costs work out at 73.9%. The main savings result from web paper being cheaper than sheet and the web press delivering folded sections direct off the press. Web printing speeds are also much faster than sheet. If the quoted figure in Box 12.7 was used, i.e. £23,325.00, the mark-up would rise to 31.3% and the added value to 67%.

But do not assume that the same proportions always exist between sheet and web printing. On shorter print runs, sheet-fed would progressively narrow the cost difference due to the lower set-up costs compared to the web option. If the print quantity, for example, were only 10,000 copies, the 4/4 sheet-fed B1 press would work out less expensive.

Box 12.9

Box 12.9 covers an enquiry for 300 copies of a 16-page self-cover brochure printed by sheet-fed digital colour. Digital colour has been chosen due to the short print run on the basis of a duplexed A3 click rate or price per copy. The job is run as double-page spreads and produced as four 4-page sections. Soft proofing has been applied, with a four-colour SRA3 digital copier/printer system and a bookletmaker that in-line folds, stitches and trims the foredge. The total estimated cost works out at £661.24, and a final 20% mark-up gives a total figure of £793.49. The quoted figure of £795.00 represents a 21% mark-up with a high value added of 90.6%.

Box 12.10

Box 12.10 is another short-run enquiry suited to digital printing. The job specification and details are for 500 copies of an 80-page A4 report printed in black only with front and back cover. The equipment chosen to quote on is a high-volume monochrome digital copier/printer with online thermal binding facility. Microsoft Word files are to be supplied by the customer, with the printer supplying soft proofs and the customer downloading any amendments through the printer's web-based workflow. Files will be prepared to deliver finished copies off the press, made up with front and back cover leaves. The total estimated cost works out at £927.12 and a final 20% mark-up gives a total figure of £1112.54. The quoted figure of £1115.00 results in a value added of 81.2%.

Box 12.11   Box 12.11 covers an enquiry for a counter display dispenser printed by sheet-fed screen. The material to be used is 1000µm display board, which makes it most suited to sheet-fed screen printing. The flat overall size is relatively small and the quantity is 5000 copies, so it is decided to print sheetwork 3-up on a B2+ sheet. Cutting-and-creasing is required and the dispensers are to be delivered flat for the customer to assemble at source. The customer is to supply press-ready Quark XPress files and the printer press-ready film for stencil processing. The total estimated cost works out at £1452.06, which with a final 10% mark-up results in a total figure of £1597.27. The quoted figure of £1595.00 gives a value added of 55.1%.

Box 12.12   Box 12.12 covers an enquiry for 500,000 copies of a direct mail leaflet printed throughout in four-colour process plus a fifth colour. It requires complex finishing, including inkjet numbering and remoist glue application. To meet the very high print run, the company has selected a ten-colour highly advanced reel-fed offset litho continuous press with in-line capabilities and high productivity. The chosen method of working is 2-up sheetwork, with reels being sheeted for offline finishing consisting of the overall sheet being trimmed outside four edges before being folded 2-up, slit into singles, packed and shrink-wrapped online. A final 10% mark-up results in an estimated total of £14,634.59. The price quoted is £14,995.00, representing an overall 11.3% mark-up and a value added of 62.7%.

Box 12.13   Box 12.13 covers an enquiry for a self-adhesive label printed by reel-fed flexography. The print quantity is 20,000 copies printed four-colour process plus two special colours and die-cut to shape. The chosen method of working is two-wide by two-around labels on a 13.625in cylinder × 192mm reel width. The estimate is based on using a highly automated six-colour press with flatbed in-line cutting. A final 20% mark-up gives an estimated total of £1499.22. The quoted price quoted is £1495.00, giving a value added of 62.7%.

Box 12.14   Box 12.14 covers an enquiry for a two-part continuous business form printed by reel-fed offset litho. The customer has requested quotes for multiple quantities: 10,000, 20,000, 30,000, 40,000 and 50,000. The selected press is a two-colour twin-web press and the chosen method of working is one-wide on a 12in cylinder. Existing digital artwork is to be used apart from updating the job reference number. Printing and finishing are completed in-line, including packing in boxes off the press. For the five print quantities the quoted prices per 1000 copies work out at £126.00, £105.00, £100.00, £97.50 and £95.00, in ascending order from 10,000.

Box 12.15   Box 12.15 covers an enquiry for a folding box carton printed by sheet-fed offset litho. The quantity required is 100,000 with 1000 run-on. A B1 six-colour highly advanced press is available and it is calculated that the most economical number out is 9-up on a sheet size 675mm × 975mm. The press is run with four-colour process, special colour and UV varnish in the six printing units. Finishing includes cutting-and-creasing, waste stripping, folder/gluer, packed and delivered flat to the customer. The 100,000 copies are quoted at £54.95 per 1000, 44.7% added value, and the 1000 run-on at £49.00, 48.8% added value, per 1000 copies.

Box 12.16   Box 12.16 covers an enquiry for a hard case-bound thread-sewn book printed by sheet-fed offset litho. The quantity required is 2000 copies. A B0 two-colour (1/1) press is available and it is calculated that the most economical method of working is 5 × 64-page sections and 1 × 32-page section 2-up on a sheet size 960mm × 1272mm. Folding is to be carried out as 11 × 32-page sections. A final 10% mark-up results in an estimated total of £9595.51. The price quoted is £9830, giving a value added of 65.4%.

BOX 12.1 A multisection saddle-stitched booklet printed by sheet-fed offset litho

Customer	Print Arena		Customer code PA 335
Address	Caxton House		
	Bedford Row		Date	1 June 2004
	London WC1		Estimate no.	6548
Attn. of	R. Williamson		Contact	L. Reilly
Job title	The Future of Printing MIS booklets		Quantities	5000

5000 copies 'The Future of printing MIS' booklets, size 297mm × 210mm, 16 pages plus cover, printed sheet-fed offset litho. Cover printed four-colour process throughout on two-sided matt coated board 250gsm, overall seal coated and gloss laminated on outside spread only. 8 pages of text printed throughout in four-colour process on matt coated paper 115gsm, plus overall seal coated. 2 kinds of 4 pages of text printed Black and one common PMS colour on different coloured uncoated general printing paper 80gsm, with light text and tint-based ink coverage. Product folded, insetted, saddle-stitched and trimmed two wires. Customer to supply press-ready PDF files to the printer's specifications with colour laser visual proofs. Printer to submit contract digital colour proofs to the customer for approval before proceeding to print. Packed in boxes in 250s and delivered to one address in London.

Printed as	*Cover – 2-up sheetwork, plus 8-page section sheetwork*	
	and 2 of 4-page sections 2-up sheetwork on an SRA2 sheet (450mm × 640mm)	
Materials		**Total**
Paper	*Cover* – SRA2 250gsm matt coated board, overs allowance – 300 + 300 sheets set-up	
	+ 10% running waste = 2500 + 850 = 3350 sheets @ £60.00 per 1000 sheets	£201.00
	8-page – SRA2 115gsm matt coated paper, overs allowance – 300 + 300 sheets set-up	
	+ 8% running waste = 5000 + 1000 = 6000 sheets @ £25.00 per 1000 sheets	£150.00
	2 × 4-page – SRA2 80gsm coloured paper, overs allowance – 150 + 150 sheets set-up	
	+ 5% running waste = 2500 + 250 = 2925 × 2 sheets @ £30.00 per 1000 sheets	£175.50
Inks	*Cover* – Four-colour process 3.35 @ £3.00 per 1000 sheets	£10.05
	8-page – Four-colour process 6.0 @ £3.00 per 1000 sheets	£18.00
	2 × 4-page – Black plus one PMS 5.85 @ £3.00 (£0.75 + £2.25) per 1000 sheets	£17.55
Varnish coating	Seal varnish 9.35 (3350 + 6000) @ £7.50 per 1000 sheets	£70.12
Proofing	4 SRA2 high-res four-colour (1 – cover, 2 – 8-page) @ £30.00	£120.00
	4 SRA2 positional two-colour (2 × 4-page) @ £7.00	£28.00
	(Cost of proofs split 50:50 when calculating value added)	
CTP plates	24 (cover – 8, 8-page – 8, 2 × 4-page – 8) SRA2 plates @ £3.00	£72.00
	(no direct charge for standing solid plates for overall seal varnish)	
Packing boxes	20 @ 20p	£4.00
		£866.22
Outwork	Laminating 3350 SRA2 sheets @ £60.00 per 1000 sheets	£201.00

BOX 12.1 A multisection saddle-stitched booklet printed by sheet-fed offset litho (continued)

Cost centres	quantity	speed /hour	hrs mins	HCR	Total
Prepress					
Press-ready PDF file supplied with colour laser visual proofs					
File handling, preflighting check – 4 files			0:30	40.00	£20.00
Planning and final check – 4 files			0:40	40.00	£26.67
Computer-to-plate (CTP)	24 SRA2 plates	12	2:00	95.00	£190.00
Printing					
Ten-colour B2 convertible highly advanced press (in 5/5 mode)					
Make-ready – cover 1h 30min, wash-up two units	30min		2:00	190:00	£380.00
Running – cover	3350	5000	0:40	190.00	£126.67
Make-ready – 8-page 1h 30min, no wash-up allowed			1:30	190:00	£285.00
Running – 8-page	6000	6250	0:58	190.00	£183.67
Four-colour SRA2 convertible basic press (in 2/2 mode)					
Make-ready – 2 × 4-page 1h 20min + 45min, wash-up two units 1h					
changing to converting 20min			3:25	90.00	£307.50
Running – 2 × 4-page	(2925 × 2) 5850	2900	2:00	90.00	£180.00
Finishing					
Cutting – using programmatic guillotine					
3350 sheets SRA2 250gsm in half – assuming 200 sheets per pile					
3350 ÷ 200 = 17 piles	17	60	0:17	30.00	£8.50
5500 sheets SRA2 80gsm in half – assuming 1000 sheets per pile					
5500 ÷ 1000 = 6 piles, allow minimum 15min	6	60	0:15	30.00	£7.50
Folding					
Make-ready – 2 × 4-page			0:20	33.00	£11.00
Running – 2 × 4-page	5500 × 2	16,000	0:41	33.00	£22.55
Make-ready – 1 × 8-page			0:30	33.00	£16.50
Running – 1 × 8-page	6700	8000	0:50	33.00	£27.50
Gather, stitch, trim with cover scorer and feed unit – allowing for finishing 5000 copies + 10% overs					
Make-ready – 4 sections 30min + 20min			0.50	60.00	£50.00
Running – with three assistants,	5500	3750	1:30	114.00	£162.00
two assistants feeding hoppers, one packing online					
Carriage Delivery to customer					£100.00
Carriage allowance to laminators					£30.00
(Cost of carriage split 50/50 when calculating value added)					
Summary Materials					£866.22
10% handling					£86.62
Outwork					£180.00
10% handling					£18.00
Labour, inclusive of carriage					£2342.06
Total					£3492.90
plus 10% mark-up					£349.29
Predicted price – £3720					£3842.19
Quoted price – £3795 (8.6% mark-up) – value added £2789.88 (73.5%)					

Source: H. M. Speirs

BOX 12.2 A multi-image label printed by sheet-fed offset litho

Customer	Print Arena		Customer code PA 336
Address	Caxton House		
	Bedford Row		Date	1 June 2004
	London WC1		Estimate no.	6549
Attn. of	R. Williamson		Contact	L. Reilly
Job title	Celebrate Print labels		Quantities	300,000

300,000 'Celebrate Print' labels, size 164mm × 190mm (long grain), printed sheet-fed offset litho one side only in four-colour process and two special colours, plus spot gloss seal coating on 90gsm one-sided label paper. Customer to supply press ready PDF file of 1-up label to the printer's specifications with single-image high-quality digital colour proof. Printer to submit multiple-image wet proofs produced from proposed press plates on job stock to the customer for approval before proceeding to print. Shrink-wrapped in 1000s and delivered to one address in London.

Printed as	20-up on a B1 sheet (720mm × 1020mm)	

Materials		Total
Paper	B1 90gsm one-sided label paper, overs allowance – 550 sheets set-up	
	+ 7% running waste = 15,000 + 1600 = 16,600 sheets @ £66.10 per 1000 sheets	£1,097.26
Inks	Four-colour process + two special colours 16.6 @ £10.00 per 1000 sheets	£166.00
Aqueous coating	Seal coating 16.6 @ £14.25 per 1000 sheets	£236.55
Proofing	1 minimum high-res. four-colour – for guide only @ £20.00	£20.00
	(Cost of proofs split 50/50 when calculating value added)	
CTP plates	7 B1 plates @ £6.00	£42.00
Packing boards	allowance	£10.00
		£1,571.81

Cost centres		quantity	speed /hour	hrs mins	HCR	
Prepress						
Press-ready PDF file supplied with high quality digital proof						
File handling, preflighting check – 1 file, minimum allowance				0:15	40.00	£10.00
Planning and final check – 20-up image				0:30	40.00	£20.00
Computer-to-plate (CTP)		7 B1 plates	8	0:53	130:00	£114.83
Printing						
Six-colour B1 highly advanced press with in-line aqueous coating unit						
Production press proofs	Make-ready 1h 10min, wash-up two units 30min, run proofs 10min					
	Total			1:50	175.00	£320.83
Production run	Make-ready 1h 10min, wash-up two units 30min			1:40	175.00	£291.67
Running		16,600	8250	2:00	175.00	£350.00

BOX 12.2 A multi-image label printed by sheet-fed offset litho (continued)					
Cost centres	quantity	speed /hour	hrs mins	HCR	
Finishing					
Cutting – using programmatic guillotine					
Set-up programme			0:10	45.00	£7.50
– assuming 1000 sheets per pile					
16,600 sheets × 0.1mm ÷ 75mm pile					
= 17 piles × 22 cuts (double cuts)	374 cuts	100	3:45	45.00	£168.75
Cutting packing boards			0:15	40.00	£10.00
Packing, shrink-wrapping – in 1000s	300	150	2:00	30.00	£60.00
Carriage (Cost of carriage split 50:50 when calculating value added)					£100.00
Summary Materials					£1571.81
10% handling					£157.18
Outwork					–
Labour, inclusive of carriage					£1453.58
Total					£3182.57
plus 5% mark-up					£159.13
Predicted price – £3450					£3341.70
Quoted price – £3395 (6.7% mark-up) – value added £1783.19 (52.5%)					
Source: H. M. Speirs					

BOX 12.3 One-colour digital versus conventional offset litho price per copy		500	700	1,500
Digital printing				
One-colour sheet-fed A3+ press				
Prepress preparation	5min @ £40.00h⁻¹	£3.33	£3.33	£3.33
Press/printing make-ready and setup	5min @ £70.00h⁻¹	£5.83	£5.83	£5.83
Prepress and press set-up fixed costs		£9.16	£9.16	£9.16
Printing @ 3,000 A3 sheets per hour	10min, 14min, 30min @ 70.00h⁻¹	£11.67	£16.33	£35.00
Total cost		£20.83	£25.49	£44.16
Cost per copy		4.17p	3.64p	2.94p
Conventional offset litho printing				
One-colour sheet-fed B3 press				
Prepress preparation	5min @ £40.00h⁻¹	£3.33	£3.33	£3.33
CTP	5min @ £72.00h⁻¹	£6.00	£6.00	£6.00
Plate costs	1 @ £4.00 per plate	£4.00	£4.00	£4.00
Press/printing make-ready and setup	15min @ £30.00h⁻¹	£7.50	£7.50	£7.50
Prepress and press set-up fixed costs		£20.83	£20.83	£20.83
Printing @ 5,000 A3+ sheets per hour	6min, 8.4min, 18min @ £30.00h⁻¹	£3.00	£4.20	£9.00
Ink cost	500, 700 and 1,500 @ 25p per 1,000	£0.13	£0.18	£0.38
Total cost		£23.96	£25.21	£30.21
Cost per copy		4.79p	3.60p	2.01p
One-colour sheet-fed B2 press				
Prepress preparation	5min @ £40.00h⁻¹	£3.33	£3.33	£3.33
CTP	5min @ £95.00h⁻¹	£7.92	£7.92	£7.92
Plate costs	1 @ £6.00 per plate	£6.00	£6.00	£6.00
Press/printing make-ready and setup	20min @ £45.00h⁻¹	£15.00	£15.00	£15.00
Prepress and press set-up fixed costs		£32.25	£32.25	£32.25
Printing @ 10,000 A3+ sheets per hour	3min, 4.2min, 9min @ £45.00h⁻¹	£2.25	£3.15	£6.75
Ink cost	500, 700 and 1,500 @ 25p per 1,000	£0.13	£0.18	£0.38
Total cost		£34.63	£35.58	£39.38
Cost per copy		6.93p	5.08p	2.63p

Source: H. M. Speirs

BOX 12.4 A combined stationery order printed by sheet-fed offset litho

Customer	Print Arena		Customer code PA 337
Address	Caxton House		
	Bedford Row		Date	1 June 2004
	London WC1		Estimate no.	6550
Attn. of	R. Williamson		Contact	L. Reilly
Job title	New Stationery		Quantities	5000 each of 3 kinds

5000, each of three kinds, 'Print Arena', A4 Letterheadings, 2/3 and 1/3 compliment slips, printed sheet-fed offset litho one side only in four-colour process on 90gsm bond paper. Customer to supply press-ready Quark XPress file with colour laser proof. Printer to submit soft-copy proofs online for approval before proceeding to print. Packed and delivered to one address in London.

Printed as	1-up letterheading, $^2/_3$ compliment slip and $^1/_3$ compliment slip printed together on an RA2 sheet

Materials		Total
Paper	RA2 90gsm white bond paper, overs allowance – 200 sheets set-up (simple work) + 8% running waste = 5000 + 600 = 5600 sheets @ £60.00 per 1000 sheets	£336.00
Inks	Four-colour process – low ink coverage, allow minimum cost	£10.00
CTP plates	4 SRA2 plates @ £3.00	£12.00
Packing boxes	10 @ 20p	£2.00
		£360.00

Cost centres	quantity	speed /hour	hrs mins	HCR	
Prepress					
Quark XPress files supplied with colour laser visual proof					
File handling, preflighting check – minimum allowance			0:15	40.00	£10.00
Planning and final check – 3-up image, plus soft proofs			0:15	40.00	£10.00
Computer-to-plate (CTP) '	4 SRA2 plates	12	0:20	95.00	£31.67
Printing					
Four-colour SRA2 basic press					
Make-ready			1:20	90.00	£120.00
Running	5600	3600	1:35	90.00	£142.50

BOX 12.4 A combined stationery order printed by sheet-fed offset litho (continued)

Finishing

Cutting

6 piles × 6 cuts (double cuts)	36 cuts	60	0:36	30.00	£18.00
Packing in boxes	10	30	0:20	18.00	£6.00

Carriage	(Cost of carriage split 50:50 when calculating value added)	£25.00

Summary	Materials	£360.00
	10% handling	£36.00
	Outwork	–
	Labour, inclusive of carriage	£363.17
	Total	£759.17
	plus 15% mark-up	£113.88
	Predicted price – £840.00	£873.05
	Quoted price – £875.00 (15% mark-up) – value added £502.50 (57.4%)	

Source: H. M. Speirs

BOX 12.5 A pamphlet printed by sheet-fed offset litho

Customer	Print Arena	Customer code PA 338	
Address	Caxton House		
	Bedford Row	Date	1 June 2004
	London WC1	Estimate no.	6551
Attn. of	R. Williamson	Contact	L. Reilly
Job title	Print Extravaganza Series 2 pamphlets	Quantities	10,000

10,000 copies 'Print Extravaganza Series 2' pamphlets, size 1/3 A4, 12 pages, printed sheet-fed offset litho in four-colour process on 115gsm gloss art paper. Customer to supply Microsoft Word file and mock-up, 12 minimum colour pictures for scanning and B&W laser proof. Existing artwork from previous 'Print Extravaganza Series 2' pamphlet, such as background tints, etc., to be used. Printer to submit contract digital colour proofs to the customer for approval before proceeding to print. Packed and delivered to one address in London.

Printed as	1-up work-and-turn on an SRA3 sheet

Materials		*Total*
Paper	SRA3 115gsm gloss art paper, overs allowance − 400 + 200 sheets set-up + 5% running waste = 5000 + 1100 = 6100 sheets @ £15.75 per 1000 sheets	£96.07
Inks	Four-colour process 6.1 @ £2.00 per 1000 sheets	£12.20
Proofing	SRA3 high-res four-colour @ £20.00 (Cost of proofs split 50:50 when calculating value added)	£20.00
CTP plates	4 SRA3 plates @ £2.00	£8.00
Packing boxes	10 @ 20p	£2.00
		£138.27

Cost centres	quantity	speed/hour	hrs mins	HCR	
Prepress					
Microsoft Word files supplied with B&W proof					
File check − minimum allowance			0:15	40.00	£10.00
Scanning	12	12	1:00	50.00	£50.00
Make-up into press-ready files			1:00	40.00	£40.00
Planning and preflighting check			0:15	40.00	£10.00
Computer-to-plate (CTP)	4 SRA3 plates	20	0:15	95.00	£23.75
Printing					
Four-colour SRA3 basic press					
Make-ready			1:00	75.00	£75.00
Running	6100 × 2	4450	2:45	75:00	£206.25

BOX 12.5 A pamphlet printed by sheet-fed offset litho

Finishing

Folding

Make-ready – 1 × 12-page				0:45	33.00	£24.75
Running – 1 × 12-page	5000 + 10% overs = 5500	6000	0:50	33.00	£27.50

Cutting – using programmatic guillotine

8 piles × 6 cuts (double cuts)	48 cuts	60	0:48	30.00	£24.00
Packing in boxes	10	30	0:20	18.00	£6.00

Carriage	(Cost of carriage split 50:50 when calculating value added)	£35.00

Summary	Materials	£138.27
	10% handling	£13.83
	Outwork	–
	Labour, inclusive of carriage	£532.25
	Total	£684.35
	plus 20% mark-up	£136.87
	Predicted price – £870.00	£821.22

Quoted price – £825.00 (20.5% mark-up) – value added £679.22 (82.3%)

Source: H. M. Speirs

BOX 12.6 A magazine printed by web-fed gravure

Customer	World Geographical Association	Customer code WGA 44423	
Address	Planet House		
	110 Northern Street	Date	1 June 2004
	London	Estimate no.	3156
Attn. of	J. Intaglio	Contact	J. Spencer
Job title	World Geographical magazine	Quantity	1,000,000

1,000,000 copies 'World Geographical' magazine, size 260mm deep × 220mm wide, 64 pages self-cover,
printed web-fed gravure in four-colour process on LWC 60gsm. Finished in-line on press, i.e. folded, in-line stitched two
wires and trimmed to size. Publisher or customer to supply complete PDF press-ready files, from which gravure cylinders
are to be digitally engraved. Digital colour proofs supplied by customer for press guide. Bulk packed on pallets; customer to arrange for
carriers or distributors to pick up from printer's factory as per agreed schedule.

Printed as	1 × 64pp web-fed section, 2144mm cylinder width or face × 920mm cylinder circumference or cut-off

Materials		*Total*
Paper	LWC 60gsm, 2128mm × 900mm cut-off	
	260 × 220	
	6 × 5	
	266 × 225	
	8 × 4	
	web width 2128mm × 900mm cylinder cut-off	

$$\frac{900 \times 2{,}128}{1000 \times 1000} \times \frac{60}{1} \times \frac{1{,}000{,}000}{1000} \times \frac{1}{1000}$$

= 114.91 tonnes + 9% waste = 125.25 tonnes @ £495 per tonne	£61,998.75
Inks Four-colour process 1090 × 64pp @ £2.35 per 1000 16pp	£10,246.00
Cylinder production 8 cylinders @ £750 per cylinder	£6,000.00
(Cost of cylinder split as 50:50 when calculating value added)	

Cost centres	quantity	speed /hour	hrs	HCR	
Printing and finishing					
KBA TR5B eight-unit web-fed gravure press, with in-line stitching, trimming, strapping and shrink-wrapping facilities					
Make-ready		8 units	4:00	750.00	£3,000.00
Printing and in-line finishing	1,090,000	45,000	24.22	750.00	£18,166.67
Bulk packed on pallets 119 tonnes @ £30.00 per tonne					£3,570.00

Summary	Materials, including cylinders	£78,244.75
	10% handling	£7,824.48
	Outwork	–
	Labour	£24,736.67
	Total	£110,805.90
	10% mark-up	£11,080.59
		£121,886.49
	Predicted price – £126,000.00	
	Quoted price – £122,000.00 (10% mark-up) – value added £46,755.25 (38.3%)	

Source: H. M. Speirs

BOX 12.7 A multisection adhesive notch bound catalogue printed by sheet-fed offset litho

Customer	More+More Stores		Customer code MMS A	
Address	Shopping House			
	Bakers Row		Date	8 June 2004
	London EC1		Estimate no.	5633
Attn. of	D. Law		Contact	G. Smith
Job title	More+More Stores 2005 catalogues		Quantities	30,000

30,000 copies 'More+More Stores 2005' catalogues, size 297mm × 210mm, 80 pages plus cover, printed sheet-fed offset litho. Cover printed four-colour process on gloss coated board 250gsm. Text printed throughout in four-colour process on mechanical coated 90gsm. Folded, gathered, adhesive notch bound and trimmed to size. Customer to supply press-ready PDF files to the printer's specifications with colour laser visual proofs. Printer to submit contract digital colour proofs to the customer for approval before proceeding to print. Delivered bulk packed on pallets to one address in London.

Printed as	Cover – 4-up sheetwork on an SRA1 sheet
	Text – 5 × 16-page sections sheetwork on a 630mm × 880mm sheet

Materials		Total
Paper	Cover – SRA1 250gsm gloss coated board, overs allowance – 600 sheets set-up	
	+ 8% running waste = 7500 + 1200 = 8700 sheets @ £115.00 per 1000 sheets	£1,000.50
	Text – 630mm × 880mm 90gsm mechanical coated paper, overs allowance	
	– 600 sheets set-up + 8% running waste = 30,000 + 3000	
	= 33,000 × 5 sheets @ £39.00 per 1000 sheets	£6,435.00
Inks	Cover – Four-colour process 8.7 @ £4.00 per 1000 sheets	£34.80
	16-page × 5 – Four-colour process 165 @ £4.00 per 1000 sheets	£660.00
Proofing	Cover – 2 × SRA1 high-res four-colour @ £50.00	£100.00
	Text – 10 × SRA1 high-res four-colour @ £50.00	£500.00
	(Cost of proofs split 50:50 when calculating value added)	
CTP plates	48 B1 plates @ £6.00	£288.00
		£9,018.30

Cost centres	quantity	speed /hour	hrs mins	HCR	
Prepress					
Press-ready PDF file supplied with colour laser visual proofs					
File handling, preflighting check			1:00	40.00	£40.00
Planning and final check – 4-up cover plus 5x16-page			2:00	40.00	£80.00
Computer-to-plate (CTP)	48 B1 plates	8	6:00	130.00	£780.00

BOX 12.7 A multisection adhesive notch bound catalogue printed by sheet-fed offset litho (continued)

Cost centres		Quantity	Speed/hr	Hrs mins	HCR	
Printing						
Fight-colour B1 convertible highly advanced press (in 4/4 mode)						
Make-ready – cover 1h 20min + 1h				2:20	235:00	£548.33
Running – cover		8700	5000	1:45	235.00	£411.25
Make-ready – 5 × 16-page sections						
	1h 20min + 4h			5:20	235:00	£1,253.33
Running – 5 × 16-page sections		33,000 × 5	9000	18:20	235.00	£4,308.33
Finishing						
Cutting – using programmatic guillotine						
8700 sheets SRA1 250gsm – assuming 200 sheets per pile						
8700 ÷ 200 = 44 piles × 4 cuts		176	60	3:00	45.00	£135.00
Folding						
Make-ready – 5 × 16-page				0:45	40.00	£30.00
Running – 5 × 16-page		33,000 × 5	6000	27:50	40.00	£1,100.00
Gather, perfect bind, trim with cover scorer and feed unit						
Make-ready – 6 sections 45min + 30min				1:15	85.00	£106.25
Running – with four assistants,						
three assistants feeding hoppers, one palletising online		33,000	3750	0:48	157.00	£1,381.60
Carriage	(Cost of carriage split 50:50 when calculating value added)					£200.00
Summary	Materials					£9,018.30
	10% handling					£901.83
	Outwork					–
	Labour, inclusive of carriage					£10,374.09
	Total					£20,294.22
	plus 10% mark-up					£2,029.42
	Predicted price – £23,490.00					£23,323.04
	Quoted price – £23,325.00 (10% mark-up) – value added £14,506.70 (62.2%)					

Source: H. M. Speirs

BOX 12.8 A multisection adhesive notch bound catalogue printed by sheet-fed offset litho and heatset web offset

Customer	More+More Stores	Customer code MMS A	
Address	Shopping House		
	Bakers Row	Date	8 June 2004
	London EC1	Estimate no.	5634
Attn. of	D. Law	Contact	G. Smith
Job title	More+More Stores 2005 catalogues	Quantities	30,000

30,000 copies 'More+More Stores 2005' catalogues, size 297mm × 210mm, 80 pages plus cover. Cover printed sheet-fed offset four-colour process on gloss coated board 250gsm. Text printed heatset web offset throughout in four-colour process on mechanical coated 90gsm. Folded, gathered, adhesive notch bound and trimmed to size. Customer to supply press-ready PDF files to the printer's specifications with colour laser visual proofs. Printer to submit contract digital colour proofs to the customer for approval before proceeding to print. Delivered bulk packed on pallets to one address in London.

Printed as	Cover − 4-up sheetwork on an SRA1 sheet
	Text − 5 × 16-page sections sheetwork on a 625mm × 872mm cut-off

Materials		*Total*
Paper	Cover − SRA1 250gsm gloss coated board, overs allowance − 600 sheets set-up	
	+ 8% running waste = 7500 + 1200 = 8700 sheets @ £115.00 per 1000 sheets	£1,000.50
	Text − 625mm × 872mm 90gsm mechanical coated paper, overs allowance	
	− 4000 cut-offs + 10% running waste = 7000 cut-offs × 5	
	= 150,000 + 35,000 = 185,000 cut-offs × 0.625 × 0.872 × 90 ÷ 1000 = 9.074 tonnes	
	9.704 tonnes @ £540 per tonne	£5,240.16
Inks	Cover − Four-colour process 8.7 @ £4.00 per 1000 sheets	£34.80
	16-page × 5 − Four-colour process 185 @ £4.00 per 1000 sheets	£740.00
Proofing	Cover − 2 × SRA1 high-res four-colour @ £50.00	£100.00
	Text − 10 × SRA1 high-res four-colour @ £50.00	£500.00
	(Cost of proofs split 50:50 when calculating value added)	
CTP plates	48 B1 plates @ £6.00	£288.00
		£7,903.46

Cost centres	quantity	speed /hour	hrs mins	HCR	
Prepress					
Press-ready PDF file supplied with colour laser visual proofs					
File handling, preflighting check			1:00	40.00	£40.00
Planning and final check − 4-up cover plus 5 × 16-page			2:00	40.00	£80.00
Computer-to-plate (CTP)	48 B1 plates	8	6:00	130.00	£780.00

BOX 12.8 A multisection adhesive notch bound catalogue printed by sheet-fed offset litho and heatset web offset (cont)					
Cost centres	Quantity	Speed/hr	Hrs mins	HCR	
Printing					
Eight-colour B1 convertible highly advanced press (in 4/4 mode)					
Make-ready – cover 1h 20min + 1h			2:20	235:00	£548.33
Running – cover	8700	5000	1:45	235.00	£411.25
16-page four unit heatset web offset press					
Make-ready – 5 × 16-page sections					
1h 15min + 4 × 45min			4:15	350:00	£1,487.50
Running – 5 × 16-page sections	185,000 cut-offs	30,000	6:10	350.00	£2,158.33
Finishing					
Cutting – using programmatic guillotine					
8700 sheets SRA1 250gsm – assuming 200 sheets per pile					
8700 ÷ 200 = 44 piles × 4 cuts	176	60	3:00	45.00	£135.00
Gather, perfect bind, trim with cover scorer and feed unit					
Make-ready – 6 sections 45min + 30min			1:15	85.00	£106.25
Running – with four assistants,					
three assistants feeding hoppers, one palletising online	33,000	3750	8:48	157.00	£1,381.60
Carriage (Cost of carriage split 50:50 when calculating value added)					£200.00
Summary	Materials				£7,903.46
	10% handling				£790.35
	Outwork				–
	Labour, inclusive of carriage				£7,328.26
	Total				£16,022.07
	plus 10% mark-up				£1,602.21
	Predicted price – £18,250.00				£17,624.28
	Quoted price – £17,625.00 (10% mark-up) – value added £9,921.54 (56.3%)				
	Alternative quote – £23,325.00 (31.3% mark-up) – value added £15,621.54 (67%)				

Source: H. M. Speirs

BOX 12.9 A brochure printed by sheet-fed digital colour

Customer	Print Arena	Customer code	PA 338
Address	Caxton House		
	Bedford Row	Date	1 June 2004
	London WC1	Estimate no.	6552
Attn. of	R. Williamson	Contact	L. Reilly
Job title	Printing Case Studies brochures	Quantities	300

300 copies 'Printing Case Studies' brochures, size A4, 16 pages self-cover, printed sheet-fed digital in four-colour process on 135gsm gloss art laser quality paper. Customer to supply press-ready Quark XPress file with colour laser proof. Printer to submit online soft proofs to the customer for approval before proceeding to print. Packed and delivered to one address in London.

Printed as	4 × A4 pages on SRA3 duplexed sheet × 4

Materials		*Total*
Paper	SRA3 135gsm gloss art paper, overs allowance	
	− 300 + 15% running waste, inclusive of duplexing and binding offline	
	= 300 + 45 × 4 = 1380 sheets @ £16.50 per 1000 sheets	£66.00
Toner	Cost included in click rate or cost per copy	−
Packing boxes	2 @ 20p	£0.40
		£66.40

Cost centres	quantity speed/hour	hrs mins	HCR	
Prepress				
Quark XPress files supplied with colour laser visual proof				
File handling, preflighting check		1:00	40.00	£40.00
Planning and final check − plus soft proof service		0:30	40.00	£20.00
Printing				
Four-colour SRA3 digital copier/printer				
Click rate/copy per A3 duplex	1380 @ 34p per copy			£469.20
Finishing				
Cutting				
Post trim head and tail one cut − minimum		0:15	30.00	£7.50
Bookletmaker − in-line folding, stitching and foredge trimming, online packing				
Make-ready − 4 × 4-pages		0:15	44.00	£11.00
Running − 4 × 4-pages − minimum	300 + overs	0.15	44.00	£11.00
Packing in boxes		0:15	18.00	£4.50

BOX 12.9 A brochure printed by sheet-fed digital colour (continued)

Carriage	(Cost of carriage split 50:50 when calculating value added)	£25.00
Summary	Materials	£66.40
	10% handling	£6.64
	Outwork	–
	Labour, inclusive of carriage	£588.20
	Total	£661.24
	plus 20% mark-up	£132.25
	Predicted price – £820.00	£793.49
	Quoted price – £795.00 (21% mark-up) – value added £716.10 (90.6%)	
	Cost per copy – £2.65	

Source: H. M. Speirs

BOX 12.10 A report printed by sheet-fed digital B&W and finished online

Customer	Print Arena	Customer code PA 338	
Address	Caxton House		
	Bedford Row	Date	1 June 2004
	London WC1	Estimate no.	6553
Attn. of	R. Williamson	Contact	L. Reilly
Job title	New Stationery	Quantities	500

500 copies 'Printing Statistics' report, size A4, 80 pages, plus cover. Cover front leaf printed black one side only, back cover leaf blank, both on tinted stock 100gsm. Text pages duplex printed and finished online on a monochrome sheet-fed digital printer/copier on 80gsm white bond. Printed, collated and online thermal bound. Customer to supply press-ready Microsoft Word files to our specification with B&W laser proofs. Printer to submit online soft proofs to the customer for approval before proceeding to print. Packed and delivered to one address in London.

Printed as	Single A4 pages – front cover page 1, plus 80 duplexed text pages

Materials		**Total**
Paper	Cover – 100gsm tinted, overs allowance	
	– 500 + 5% running waste, inclusive of binding online	
	= 500 + 25 × 2 = 1050 A4 sheets @ £10.00 per 1000 sheets	£10.50
	Text – 80gsm white bond, overs allowance	
	– 500 × 40 + 5% running waste, inclusive of duplexing and binding online	
	= 20,000 + 1000 A4 sheets = 21,000 A4 sheets @ £4.00 per 1000 sheets	£84.00
Toner	Cost included in click rate or cost per copy	–
Thermal binding tape 500 + 5% overs = 525 @ £70 per roll with 400 A4 lengths		£91.88
Packing boxes	5 @ 20p	£1.00
		£187.38

Cost centres		quantity	speed /hour	hrs mins	HCR	
Prepress						
Microsoft Word files supplied with B&W laser proof						
File handling, preflighting check – good quality files				0:30	40.00	£20.00
Planning and final check – plus soft proof service				0:30	40.00	£20.00

BOX 12.10 A report printed by sheet-fed digital B&W and finished online (continued)

Cost centres		quantity	speed /hour	hrs mins	HCR	
Printing						
Monochrome SRA3 digital copier/printer						
Click rate/copy per A4	21,050 @ 3p per copy					£631.50
duplex, including online thermal binding						
Finishing						
Packing in boxes				0:15	18.00	£4.50
Carriage	(Cost of carriage split 50:50 when calculating value added)					£45.00
Summary	Materials					£187.38
	10% handling					£18.74
	Outwork					–
	Labour, inclusive of carriage					£721.00
	Total					£927.12
	plus 20% mark-up					£185.42
	Predicted price – £1260.00					£1,112.54
	Quoted price – £1115.00 (20% mark-up) – value added £905.12 (81.2%)					
	Cost per copy – £2.23					

Source: H. M. Speirs

BOX 12.11 A counter display dispenser printed by sheet-fed screen

Customer	More+More Stores		Customer code MMS A	
Address	Shopping House			
	Bakers Row		Date	8 June 2004
	London EC1		Estimate no.	5635
Attn. of	D. Law		Contact	G. Smith
Job title	More+More Stores counter display dispensers		Quantities	5000

5000 'More+More Stores' counter display dispensers, finished size 220mm × 230mm, flat overall size 240mm × 500mm, printed sheet-fed screen one side only in red on white display board 1000 microns. Cut-and-creased to shape, delivered flat. Customer to supply press-ready Quark XPress file with colour laser proof. Printer to submit digital colour proof to the customer for approval before proceeding to print. Packed and delivered to one address in London.

Printed as	3-up sheetwork on a 520mm × 760mm sheet

Materials		*Total*
Paper	520mm × 760mm white display board 1000 microns, overs allowance	
	+ 10% running waste = 1667 + 167 = 1834 sheets,	
	allow 1900 sheets, inclusive of cut-and-creasing @ £195.00 per 1000 sheets	£370.50
Inks	UV screen ink	£80.00
Proofing	B2	£15.00
	(Cost of proof split 50:50 when calculating value added)	
Stencil	Stencil preparation	£15.00
	(Cost of stencil split 50:50 when calculating value added)	
Packing boxes	20 @ £1.00	£20.00
		£500.50
Outwork	Cutting-and-creasing forme	£190.00

Cost centres	quantity	speed /hour	hrs mins	HCR	
Prepress					
Quark XPress file supplied with colour laser visual proof					
File handling, preflighting check – minimum allowance			0:15	40.00	£10.00
Planning and final check – 3-up image			0:15	40.00	£10.00
Computer-to-film (CTF)	1 B2	min.	0:15	60.00	£15.00
Processing stencil	1	3	0:20	40.00	£13.34

BOX 12.11 A counter display dispenser printed by sheet-fed screen (continued)

Cost centres		quantity	speed /hour	hrs mins	HCR	
Printing						
One-colour screen three-quarter automatic sheet-fed press						
Make-ready	30min, wash-up 20min			0:50	50.00	£41.67
Running		1900	400	4:45	50.00	£237.50
Finishing						
Cutting-and-creasing press						
Make-ready				1:00	50:00	£50.00
Running		1900	500	3:48	50.00	£190.00
Waste strip and packing in boxes				2:30	18:00	£45.00
Carriage	(Cost of carriage split 50:50 when calculating value added)					£80.00
Summary	Materials					£500.50
	10% handling					£50.05
	Outwork					£190.00
	10% handling					£19.00
	Labour, inclusive of carriage					£692.51
	Total					£1,452.06
				plus 10% mark-up		£145.21
	Predicted price – £1630.00					£1,597.27
	Quoted price – £1595.00 (10% mark-up) – value added £879.50 (55.1%)					

Source: H. M. Speirs

BOX 12.12 A direct mail leaflet printed by reel-fed offset litho

Customer	More+More Stores		Customer code MMS A	
Address	Shopping House			
	Bakers Row		Date	22 June 2004
	London EC1		Estimate no.	5636
Attn. of	D. Law		Contact	G. Smith
Job title	More+More Stores direct mail leaflets		Quantities	500,000

500,000 copies 'More+More Stores' direct mail leaflets, flat size 210mm × 610mm, finished size 210mm × 148mm 6 pages with nested 2 pages. Printed reel-fed offset litho four-colour process and one fifth colour both sides, plus on-press inkjet numbering on inset with unique number and horseshoe remoist gum applied on one side of inset on part-mechanical matt coated 90gsm. Trimmed, folded 2-up, waste slit off and slit to final single size. Customer to supply press-ready Quark XPress files with colour laser proof. Printer to submit digital colour proofs to the customer for approval before proceeding to print. Packed and delivered to one address in London.

Printed as	2-up on 520mm × 24in (610mm) cylinder

Materials		Total
Paper	Part mechanical matt coated 90gsm, 432mm reel width	
	= 5.925 tonnes +12% overs = 6.636 tonnes @ £650 per tonne	£4,313.40
Inks	Four-colour process plus PMS special 280 @ £2.30 per 1000 cut-offs	£644.00
Proofing	2 B2 high-res five-colour @ £40.00	£80.00
	(Cost of proofs split 50:50 when calculating value added)	
CTP plates	2 sets of 10 B2 plates @ £3.00	£60.00
Hot-melt glue	280 @ £1.40 per 1000	£392.00
		£5,489.40

Cost centres	quantity	speed /hour	hrs mins	HCR	
Prepress					
Quark XPress file supplied with colour laser visual proof					
File handling, preflighting check			1:00	40.00	£40.00
Planning and final check – 2-up image, perfected			1:00	40.00	£40.00
Computer-to-plate (CTP)	20	12	1:40	95.00	£158.33

BOX 12.12 A direct mail leaflet printed by reel-fed offset litho (continued)

Cost centres		quantity	speed /hour	hrs mins	HCR	
Printing						
Highly automated ten-colour press (5/5 mode), inkjet and remoist gum application in-line						
Make-ready	2h 30min, wash-up and clean press 1h			3:30	240.00	£840.00
Running		280,000	24,000	11:40	240.00	£2,800.00
Finishing						
Cutting – using programmatic guillotine						
280,000 sheets, 70 microns = 262 × 4 cuts		1048	100	10:30	35.00	£367.50
Folding – folded 2-up and slit online						
Make-ready				1:30	40.00	£60.00
Running – with two assistants,						
packing and shrink-wrapping online						
250,000, 2-up + 5%		262,500	7500	35:00	76.00	£2,660.00
Carriage	(Cost of carriage split 50:50 when calculating value added)					£300.00
Summary	Materials					£5,489.40
	10% handling					£548.94
	Outwork					–
	Labour, inclusive of carriage					£7,265.83
	Total					£13,304.17
	plus 10% mark-up					£1,330.42
	Predicted price – £15,200.00					£14,634.59
	Quoted price – £14,995.00 (11.3% mark-up) – value added £9395.60 (62.7%)					

Source: H. M. Speirs

BOX 12.13 A self-adhesive label printed by reel-fed flexography

Customer	More+More Stores	Customer code MMS A	
Address	Shopping House		
	Bakers Row	Date	22 June 2004
	London EC1	Estimate no.	5637
Attn. of	D. Law	Contact	G. Smith
Job title	'More+More Stores Own Brand' self-adhesive labels	Quantities	20,000

20,000 copies 'More+More Stores Own Brand' self-adhesive labels, finished size 169mm × 85mm die cut to shape. Printed reel-fed flexography in six colours on machine-coated permanent 90gsm self-adhesive material. Customer to supply press-ready Quark XPress files with colour laser proof. Printer to submit digital colour proofs to the customer for approval before proceeding to print. Packed and delivered to one address in London.

Printed as	Two-wide, two-around on a 13.625in (346.08mm) cylinder × 192mm reel width	

Materials		*Total*
Paper	Machine-coated 90gsm permanent self-adhesive material	
	169mm + 3mm trim = 172mm × 2 out of 346.08mm cylinder circumference	
	85mm + 19mm allowance (covering registration marks, selvage and bearers)	
	= 104 × one-wide, plus 85mm + 3mm trim = 88 + 104mm + 192mm for two-wide	
	1000mm ÷ 173.04 = 5.77 per linear metre × two labels = 11.55 labels per linear metre	
	20,000 ÷ 11.55 = 1732 + overs of 473 linear metres (50 metres per colour, plus 10%	
	running waste) = 2205 linear metres × 200mm wide @ £10.00 per 100 linear metres	£220.50
Inks	Four-colour process plus 2 specials @ £3.50 per colour	£21.00
Proofing	1 minimum size six-colour	£25.00
	(Cost of proofs split 50:50 when calculating value added)	
Photopolymer plates	346.08mm × 192mm = 0.066m^2 × 6 = 0.396m2 @ £130.00m^{-2}	£51.48
Packing materials	21 cores @ 15p each	£3.15
	11 boxes @ 25p each	£2.75
		£323.88
Outwork	Flatbed cutter	£100.00

BOX 12.13 A self-adhesive label printed by reel-fed flexography

Cost centres		quantity	speed /hour	hrs mins	HCR	
Prepress						
Quark XPress file supplied with colour laser visual proof						
File handling, preflighting check				0:15	40.00	£10.00
Planning and final check – 2-up image				0:15	40.00	£10.00
Computer-to-film (CTF)		6	20	0:18	60.00	£16.00
Processing plates		6	2	3:00	40.00	£120.00
Mounting plates onto cylinders		6	4	1:30	30.00	£45.00
Printing						
Highly automated six-colour reel-fed flexo press, using flatbed cutter in-line on press						
Make-ready	1 × 1h, 5 × 30min, wash-up 2 × 20min			4:10	95.00	£395.83
Running		2205	2100	1:03	95.00	£99.75
Finishing						
Slit and rewind						
Make-ready				0:15	30.00	£7.50
Running		2205	2000	1:06	30.00	£33.00
Packing				0:20	18.00	£6.00
Carriage	(Cost of carriage split 50:50 when calculating value added)					£40.00
Summary	Materials					£323.88
	10% handling					£32.39
	Outwork					£100.00
	10% handling					£10.00
	Labour, inclusive of carriage					£783.08
	Total					£1,249.35
	plus 20% mark-up					£249.87
	Predicted price – £1570.00					£1,499.22
	Quoted price – £1495.00 (20% mark-up) – value added £1063.62 (62.7%)					

Source: H. M. Speirs

BOX 12.14 A two-part continuous business form printed by reel-fed offset litho

Customer	More+More Stores	Customer code MMS A	
Address	Shopping House		
	Bakers Row	Date	22 June 2004
	London EC1	Estimate no.	5638
Attn. of	D. Law	Contact	G. Smith
Job title	'More+More Stores Home Shopping' two-part invoice sets	Quantities	10,000, 20,000, 30,000, 40,000 and 50,000

'More+More Stores Home Shopping' two-part invoice sets, finished size 12in deep × 310mm wide, printed reel-fed offset litho in two colours – top sheet on carbonless CB61 white and bottom sheet on carbonless CF58 white, fan-folded and boxed in 1000s. Printer to use existing digital artwork, but with new updated job reference and submit soft proof to the customer for approval before proceeding to print. Packed and delivered to one address in London.

Printed as	One-wide on a 12in cylinder

Paper	Carbonless top sheet – CB61 white 316mm reel width @ 32.50p/m²,
	wastage allowances – 10,000 10%, 20,000 8%, 30,000 8%, 40,000 8%, 50,000 7%
	Carbonless bottom sheet – CF58 white 316mm reel width @ 32.00p/m²,
	Wastage allowances – 10,000 10%, 20,000 8%, 30,000 8%, 40,000 8%, 50,000 7%

Inks	£1.50 per colour per 10,000 forms

Prepress	Amendments to ref. no.	15min @ £40.00	£10.00
	Artwork archive – min charge and set-up	30min @ £40.00	£20.00
	Computer-to-plate (CTP)	4 plates × 5min @ £60.00	£20.00
			£50.00

Printing	– includes in-line finishing and packing in boxes off press

Two-colour twin-web continuous business forms press

Make-ready – 2.5h made up of initial machine set-up 1h, marginal perfs. 30min,

wash-up of two ink units 30min, set file holes and folder 30min

Running – net speed in copies per hour 10,000 – 12,000, 20,000 – 18,000, 30,000 – 19,000, 40,000 – 19,000, 50,000 – 19,000

BOX 12.14 A two-part continuous business form printed by reel-fed offset litho (continued)

		10,000	20,000	30,000	40,000	50,000
				quantities		
Prepress		£50.00	£50.00	£50.00	£50.00	£50.00
Press make-ready 2.5 + running 0.83,1.11, 1.58, 2.11, 2.50 @ £90h⁻¹		299.70	324.90	367.20	414.90	450.00
	Total	349.70	374.90	417.20	464.90	500.00
Paper − 1059.48, 2080.44, 3120.56, 4160.89, 5152.95 @ 32.5p/m²		344.33	676.14	1014.18	1352.29	1674.71
1059.48, 2080.44, 3120.56, 4160.89, 5152.95 @ 32p/m²		339.03	665.74	998.58	1331.49	1648.94
	10% handling	68.34	134.19	201.28	268.38	332.36
	Total	£751.70	£1,476.07	£2,214.04	£2,952.16	£3,656.01
Ink		£6.00	£12.00	£18.00	£24.00	£30.00
Boxes − 50p per box		£5.00	£10.00	£15.00	£20.00	£25.00
Carriage		£30.00	£40.00	£60.00	£80.00	£100.00
	Total	£1,142.40	£1,912.97	£2,724.24	£3,541.06	£4,311.01
	10% handling	£114.24	£191.30	£272.42	£354.11	£431.10
Estimated price per quantity		£1,256.64	£2,104.27	£2,996.66	£3,895.17	£4,742.11
Quoted price per quantity		£1,260.00	£2,100.00	£3,000.00	£3,900.00	£4,750.00
Quoted price per 1000		£126.00	£105.00	£100.00	£97.50	£95.00

Source: H. M. Speirs

BOX 12.15 A folding box carton printed by sheet-fed offset litho

Customer	More+More Stores	Customer code MMS A	
Address	Shopping House		
	Bakers Row	Date	22 June 2004
	London EC1	Estimate no.	5639
Attn. of	D. Law	Contact	G. Smith
Job title	'More+More Stores Own Brand' cosmetics cartons	Size	100mm × 50mm × 120mm
Style no. 9	R. tuck, top tuck on 4th panel	Open size	264mm × 315mm
		Quantity	100,000 and 1000 run-on

'More+More Stores Own Brand' cosmetics cartons, finished overall size 264mm × 315mm printed sheet-fed offset litho one side only in four-colour process colours plus one special and UV varnish, 95% coverage, on coated white-lined chipboard 600 microns (400gsm). Customer to supply press-ready PDF files to the printer's specifications with colour laser visual proofs. Printer to submit contract digital colour proofs to the customer for approval before proceeding to print. Delivered in bulk to one address in London.

Printed as	9-up on a sheet size 675mm × 975mm	
Materials		***Total***
Cartonboard	675mm × 975mm 600 microns, coated WLC 11,112 sheets + 9.5% overs	
	= 12,167 sheets @ £650 per tonne	£2,060.58
Inks	Four-colour process + one special colour 12.167 @ £8.00 per 1000 sheets	£97.34
UV varnish	12.167 @ £25.00 per 1000 sheets	£304.17
Proofing	1 B1 high-res five-colour	£70.00
	(Cost of proofs split 50:50 when calculating value added)	
CTP plates	5 B1 plates @ £6.00	£30.00
	Relief photopolymer plate material, including film	£45.00
		£2,607.09
Outwork	Cutting forme	£400.00

BOX 12.15 A folding box carton printed by sheet-fed offset litho (continued)

Cost centres	quantity	speed /hour	hours mins		HCR
Prepress					
Press-ready PDF file supplied with colour laser proof					
File handling, preflighting check – 1 file, minimum allowance			0:15	40.00	£10.00
Planning and final check – 9-up image			1:30	40.00	£60.00
Computer-to-plate (CTP)	5 B1	8	0:38	130:00	£81.25
UV varnish photopolymer plate	1		1:30	40:00	£60.00
Printing and finishing					
Six-colour B1 highly-advanced press					
Make-ready 1h 10min, wash-up two units 30min			1.40	160.00	£266.67
Running	12,167	5000	2.26	160.00	£389.33
Cutting-and-creasing					
Make-ready			3.30	80.00	£280.00
Running	12,167	4000	3.05	80.00	£246.67
Waste stripping	100,000 + 5% overs	10000	10.30	18.00	£189.00
Folder/gluer					
Make-ready			0.40	54.00	£36.00
Running	100,000 + 5% overs	22,000	4.45	54.00	£256.50
Packing			4.45	36.00	£171.00

				100,000	per 1000 r/o
Outwork	£400.00 + 10% handling			£440.00	
Materials	£2,607.09 + handling			£2,867.80	£28.68
Carriage				£150.00	£1.50
Labour				£2,046.42	£20.46
Total				£5,504.22	£50.64
Quoted price				£5,495.00	£49.00
Added value				£2,458.91	£23.89
				(44.7%)	(48.8%)

Source: H. M. Speirs

BOX 12.16 A hard case-bound thread-sewn book printed by sheet-fed offset litho

Customer	Print Arena		Customer code PA 338	
Address	Caxton House			
	Bedford Row		Date	17 June 2004
	London WC1		Estimate no.	6554
Attn. of	R. Williamson		Contact	L. Reilly
Job title	Printing developments – 2005 and beyond books		Quantities	2000

2000 copies 'Printing Developments – 2005 and Beyond', hard case-bound books, size 234mm × 156mm wide, 352 pages plus hard case-bound cover. Text printed black only on 90gsm matt coated, section-sewn cased binding with plain paper endpapers, cases made in full library buckram over 2500 micron chipboard, head and tail bands, gold-blocked on front and spine, jacketed and individually shrink-wrapped and packed in bulk. Publisher or customer to supply press-ready PDF files to the printer's specifications with B&W laser proofs. Printer to submit low-res imposed positional B&W backed-up proofs to the customer for approval before proceeding to print. Ex works – books held in stock for call-offs as instructed.

Printed as	5 × 64pp sheet work on sheet size 960mm × 1272mm	
	1 × 32pp 2-up sheet work on sheet size 960mm × 1272mm	

Materials		Total
Paper	960mm × 1272mm 90gsm matt coated (64pp out), 5 × 64pp, 1 × 32pp	
	= 11,930 sheets inclusive of overs @ £120 per 1000 sheets	£1,431.60
Inks	Black only – 11.93 @ £3.00 per 1000 sheets	£35.79
Proofing	11 × 32pp @ £6.00	£66.00
CTP plates	11 × 32pp @ £15.00	£165.00
Cover cloth	Library buckram	£1,300.00
Endpapers	Plain white printing 120gsm	£70.00
Cover boards	2500 microns chipboard	£175.00
Head/tail bands		£33.00
Materials total		*£3,276.39*
Outwork	Binding blocks	£150.00

Cost centres	quantity	speed /hour	hrs mins	HCR	
Prepress					
Press-ready PDF file supplied with B&W laser proofs					
File handling, preflighting check – 11 × 30min			5:30	40.00	£220.00
Planning, imposing and final check – 11 × 30min			5:30	40.00	£220.00
Computer-to-plate (CTP)	11	4	2:45	180.00	£495.00

BOX 12.16 A hard case-bound thread-sewn book printed by sheet-fed offset litho (continued)

Cost centres (continued)	quantity	speed /hour	hrs mins	HCR	
Printing					
Two-colour standard B0 convertible press (in 1/1 mode)					
5 × 32pp, plus 1 × 32pp 2-up					
Make-ready 1 × 1h 40min, 4 × 1h, 1 × 1h					
change to converting mode, 2 × 30min			7:40	115.00	£881.67
Running	11,930	3100	3:51	115:00	£442.27
Finishing					
Cutting 2-up sheetwork section in half and 64 pages into 32 pages			1:00	45.00	£45.00
Folding					
Make-ready – 32pp, allow two make-readies 1h × 2			2:00	40.00	£80.00
Running – 11 × 32pp 2000 + 7.5% × 11		4000	5:46	58.00	£334.47
Section gatherer					
Make-ready – 32pp			0:45	30.00	£22.50
Running	2000 + 7.5% × 11	4000	5:46	30.00	£173.00
Section sewing					
Make-ready			0:45	30.00	£22.50
Running	2000 + 7.5% × 11	2250	10:30	30.00	£315.00
Prepress, printing and finishing total					£3,251.41

BOX 12.16 A hard case-bound thread-sewn book printed by sheet-fed offset litho (continued)

Cost centres	quantity	speed /hour	hrs mins	HCR	
Binding					
Nipping sections					
Make-ready			0:15	30.00	£7.50
Running			4:30	48.00	£216.00
Binding sections					
Make-ready			1:00	40.00	£40.00
Running			2:00	40.00	£80.00
Three-knife trim bound sections					
Make-ready			0:30	45.00	£22.50
Running			1:15	63.00	£78.75
Cutting cloth to size for cases			1:30	45.00	£67.50
Cutting board to size for cases			1:15	45.00	£56.25
Casemaking					
Make-ready			1:30	60.00	£90.00
Running			1:45	98.00	£171.50
Casing-in					
Make-ready			1:45	55.00	£96.25
Running			2:00	91.00	£182.00
Gold blocking cases					
Make-ready			1:15	45.00	£56.25
Running			3:00	45.00	£135.00
Endpapering			1:00	35.00	£35.00
Jacketing, using existing printed book jackets from stock					
Trimming to size			0:20	45.00	£15.00
Folding			0:45	35.00	£26.25
Wrappering			5:30	18.00	£99.00
Packing – shrink-wrap individual copies			6:00	20.00	£120.00
Bulk packed – in 10s			6:00	18.00	£108.00
Binding total					**£1,702.75**

Summary	*Materials*		£3,276.39
	10% handling		£327.64
	Outwork		£150.00
	10% handling		£15.00
	Prepress, printing and finishing		£3,251.41
	Binding		£1,702.75
	Total		£8,723.19
	plus 10% mark-up		£872.32
			£9,595.51
	Predicted price – £9830.00		
	Quoted price – £9795.00 (10.9% mark-up) – value added £6401.61 (65.4%)		

Source: H. M. Speirs

Estimating standards

13

The printing industry has a tremendous range of printing equipment and working practices that result in widely varying productivity, operational costs and methods of cost recovery. Consequently, each organisation needs to establish its own estimating standards using the operational times and speeds that result from its unique combination of operations, workflows, printing tasks and services. Regularly check actual versus estimated production data and related areas to ensure the operational targets are going as planned. Maintain a complete and comprehensive model of the company's activities in a MIS or a manual database.

Data will normally be split up into cost centres or work centres with estimating standards in the form of speed tables for machinery-based areas, such as machine printing and print finishing. These are further broken down into set-up and make-ready times and machine running times starting from a low base figure, through a series of quantity steps or breakpoints up to a maximum speed. Additional variables affecting the figures include difficulty factors and deviations from the norm by type of substrate, quality, ink coverage and size, etc. In labour-based areas, such as predominate in prepress, estimating standards are often expressed as times to execute certain predetermined operations, e.g. preflighting and checking files, make-up of press-ready files from different file components, CTP and digital proofing. Material allowances and associated calculations for paper, board and other types of substrate, along with other direct materials such as ink, film, plates, cylinders and stencils, need to be included in the estimating standards used by a printing company, supplier, bureau or trade house.

Boxes 13.1 to 13.5 (pages 326 to 344) take the estimating standards from earlier chapters and collect them in one place for convenient reference. The data reflects a comprehensive range of estimating standards used by a very wide cross section of printers throughout the UK, and as such reflects an overview rather than any specific approach. The standards reflect average overall feeds and speeds, so some companies will use and record lower or higher values. Target performance figures for production planning and control will often exceed those quoted, as production figures are often set as a target to aim at, not an expected outcome averaged over a given time.

BOX 13.1 Paper and board allowances

Working allowances

Sheet-fed offset litho printing
Gripper allowance: 6–15mm, average 10–12mm
Double gripper allowance is often required on convertible presses when perfecting
Colour control strip: 10mm
Auto register control strip (where applicable), e.g. 5mm on both short edges of the sheet on a Heidelberg system
Side and leave margins: 6mm back leaf, 6mm for each of the side leaves
Print finishing and binding allowances
Trimming and die-cutting: single cuts 3mm, double cuts 6mm
Binding lap: 9mm
Lamination and varnishing: up to 12mm
Perfect binding: 6mm in the backs, 3mm for each leaf
Web offset printing: finishing and binding allowances
Saddle-stitched, insetted work: 25mm on web width
Perfect bound, gathered work: 32mm on web width

Spoilage allowances, including press and general finishing and binding operations

Due to the very wide range of press and postpress equipment, printers apply a wide range of wastage and overs allowances. The figures quoted reflect the middle ground.

Sheet-fed offset litho: straight or convertible presses

Number of colours or print units	1	2	4	5	6	8
Make-ready and set-up waste per press pass (no. of sheets); second side of work-and-turn charged at 50% of first side						
	100	150	400	500	550	600
Running waste (%)	3	4	5	6	7	8

Web offset: perfector press

Number of colours or print units	1	2	4
Make-ready and cut-off set-up waste per press pass (no. of sheets)	2,000	3,500	4,000

Running waste up to 9,999 copies 30%, 10,000–19,999 copies 20%, 20,000–29,999 copies 15%, 30,000 copies and above 10%

Narrow reel-fed presses: used for self-adhesive labels, roll tickets and continuous business forms, direct mail, etc.

Number of colours or print units	1	2	4	5	6
Make-ready and set-up waste per press pass (m)	200	300	500	600	850
Running waste (%)	5	6	8	9	10

Web-fed gravure: perfector presses

Number of copies in (000s)	< 500	501–750	751–1,500	1,501–2,500	> 2,500
Combined make-ready and running waste (%)	> 10	10	9	8	7

Sheet-fed screen

Average make-ready, set-up and running waste (%)	10

Digital printing: monochrome

Make-ready and set-up waste per press pass (no. of sheets/cut-offs)	minimal
Running waste (%)	1–2

Digital printing: colour

Make-ready and set-up waste per press pass (no. of sheets/cut-offs)	5–10
Running waste (%)	up to 10

Additional binding and finishing allowances

Each additional finishing, binding, converting process applied to a printed sheet or reel will increase the total overs required, so that the correct quantity will be delivered to the customer. Additional finishing processes, such as varnishing, laminating, cutting-and-creasing and foil blocking will each add a further 1–5% to the wastage figures above. When outwork is involved, allow sufficient wastage to cover the work involved. Advice on spoilage allowances should always be sought from the suppliers.

Source: H. M. Speirs

BOX 13.2 Ink calculations and allowances

Ink formula for monochrome, single-colour offset litho ink coverage based on the amount of standard black ink (kg) for 1000 impressions of 1m²

Type of printed image	High gloss and cast coated (factor 1)	SC machine and matt coated (factor 1.33)	MF and smooth general printing (factor 1.5)	Rough, open general printing (factor 1.75)	Rough, open antique (factor 2)
Solid area (100%)	1.50	2.00	2.25	2.62	3.00
Complete halftones (33.3%)	0.50	0.66	0.75	0.87	1.00
Heavily illustrated (25%)	0.37	0.45	0.56	0.65	0.75
Lightly illustrated (20%)	0.30	0.49	0.45	0.53	0.60
Plain text (15%)	0.23	0.30	0.35	0.40	0.46
Very light coverage (8%)	0.12	1.16	0.18	0.21	0.24
To adjust for coloured inks	Add				
Blue	15%				
Bronze blue	20%				
Red	25%				
Green	30%				
Yellow and its variations	33.3%				

Ink formula for four-colour process offset litho ink coverage based on the amount of four-colour process ink (kg) for 1,000 impressions of 1m²

Type of stock	All four colours (factor 1)	Yellow (factor 1/3)	Magenta (factor 1/6)	Cyan (factor 1/4)	Black (factor 1/4)
High-gloss art	2.25	0.75	0.38	0.56	0.56
Machine or matt coated	3.00	1.00	0.50	0.75	0.75
Smooth general printing	3.36	1.12	0.56	0.84	0.84

Average monochrome black ink usage

	Average ink usage (kg) per 10,000 sheets printed both sides
Type or line only	
SRA2/B2 sheet (450mm × 640mm/520mm × 720mm)	1.5
SRA1/B1sheet (640mm × 900mm/720mm × 1,040mm)	3.0
50:50 split between type and halftones	
SRA2/B2 sheet (450mm × 640mm/520mm× 720mm)	2.5
SRA1/B1sheet (640mm × 900mm/720mm × 1,040mm)	5.0
Overall coverage in halftones	
SRA2/B2 sheet (450mm × 640mm/520mm × 720mm)	3.5
SRA1/B1sheet (640mm × 900mm/720mm × 1,040mm)	7.0

BOX 13.2 Ink calculations and allowances (continued)

Average ink costs per 1000 sheets assuming average coverage is 40%

	Average ink costs (£)	
	Example (a)	Example (b)
Four-colour process		
SRA2/B2 sheet (450mm × 640mm/520mm × 720mm) printed both sides	2.00	4.00
SRA1/B1 sheet (640mm × 900mm/720mm × 1,040mm) printed both sides	4.00	8.00
Per separate four-colour process colour		
SRA2 /B2 sheet (450 × 640mm/520 × 720mm) printed both sides	0.50	1.00
SRA1/B1 sheet (640 × 900mm/720 × 1,040mm) printed both sides	1.00	2.00
Although black is the cheapest of the four process colours, it normally has the largest coverage; this tends to balance the cost equally between the process colours.		
Special colours, PMS and non-process colours		
SRA2 /B2 sheet (450mm × 640mm/520mm × 720mm) printed both sides	1.50	3.00
SRA1/B1 sheet (640mm × 900mm/720mm × 1,040mm) printed both sides	3.00	6.00

Seal or overprint varnish and coating

A seal or overprint varnish has become very popular in recent years to ensure quicker and easier handling of printed work, especially solids and heavy coverage on matt and satin coated papers. The following figures give guidance on the possible usage and cost. The average material costs of applying varnish or aqueous coating, based on 100% coverage both sides, per 1000 SRA1 sheets, is from £10.00 to £20.00. The amount of varnish or coating used, and resultant cost, varies depending on the thickness of solution applied and the absorbency of the substrate.

Ink and toner calculations for processes besides offset litho

All the previous formulae and calculations are based on offset litho. Here is a general guide to ink consumption and/or costs for other printing processes.

Screen

Ten times the amount and cost of ink used for offset litho.

Gravure

Four-colour process periodical printing on SC type paper at £2.50 per 1000 copies of 16 pages A4 cut-off.

Flexography

On high-gloss flexible packaging material in three to six colours at 2.5gsm.

Letterpress

Reel-fed self-adhesive labels in four-colour process allowing for 100% coverage: 1kg of each process colour covers 15,000in2.

Digital

The cost of inks and toners in digital printing is often recovered in the inclusive click rate charged by the equipment suppliers. As a guide, on HP Indigo colour presses, 700–1000 SRA3 sheets printed solid coverage, one side only, uses 1kg per colour. In examples where digital printers purchase their ink as separate consumables, printers will build up their specific ink coverage, usage and cost from their ongoing records, which differ from one user to another on the mix of work undertaken.

BOX 13.2 Ink calculations and allowances (continued)

Ink coverage of different printing processes

It is difficult to make direct comparisons between the different printing processes for ink consumption and related costs, as the composition and properties of the ink vary greatly. A further factor that affects the quantity of ink required is the typical ink film thickness laid down by the different printing processes. The following figures, stating the average thickness in microns, for the full range of conventional printing processes, are included for general guidance only, as so many variables can be involved.

Process	Average ink film thickness (μm)
Offset litho	2
Flexography	2–3
Letterpress	3–4
Gravure	6–8
Screen	8–40

Ink wastage

During the printing process, ink is lost in the duct and on the rollers, so make an allowance to cover this. Follow these suggestions:
► For runs of up to 5000 add 10%
► For runs of 5001 up to 20,000 add 7.5%
► For runs of 20,001 and above add 5%.

Some large printing presses may waste approximately 0.5kg when a duct is cleaned, whereas small machines will waste much less. Loose fibres on some fluffy or loosely bonded papers and boards, such as recycled, result in extra wash-ups and this should be reflected in the calculations. Include overs when calculating the total ink required.

Source: H. M. Speirs

BOX 13.3 Prepress		
Typesetting and keyboarding		
Simple straightforward text setting		8,000–12,000 characters per hour
Mac and PC setting	Simple text	Tabular
A5 page	15min	30min
A4 page	30min	60min
OCR and camera work		
OCR production times on good quality hard copy		12 × A4 pages per hour
Camera	per shot	5–15min
Contacting negative to positive	per film	3–10min
Scanning		
Minimum scan/A6		12 scans per hour, i.e. 5min each
A5		8 scans per hour, i.e. 7.5min each
A4		6 scans per hour, i.e. 10min each
A3		4 scans per hour, i.e. 15min each
A2		3 scans per hour, i.e. 20min each
Colour retouching on PC or Mac		5–10min per image, up to 30min and above
Make-up and planning	**A5 page**	**A4 page**
DTP		
Preparing page template	10min	20min
Make-up	15min	20–30min
Manual planning		
Preparing layout (time depends on complexity)	5–30min	
Planning and assembly	5min per piece of film	
Digital file handling, preflighting, checking, converting, planning and imposing production times		
File handling, preflighting, checking times		
Minimum set-up per job/file	10min to over 1h for complex or large-scale work	
File conversion		
From basic file format to press-ready files	minimum 30min up to several hours for complex or large-scale work	
From good quality DTP file format to press-ready files	minimum 15min up to over 1h for complex or large-scale work	
Planning, imposing composite press-ready files and final check-up to designated output template-based and/or repeat type device, including soft proof to customer, such as CTP, CTPr, digital printing	minimum 10min for simple work up to over 30min for complex work	
Proofing		
Ozalid single-colour proof, B1	10–15min	
DTP laser or inkjet visual proof, A4 or A3	2–5min	
Low-res positional visual colour proofs B1, one side	10min	
High-res target or precontract and contract colour proofs B3, one side	10min	
High-res target or precontract and contract colour proofs B2, one side	20min	
High-res target or precontract and contract colour proofs B1, one side	30min	
Photomechanical colour proof, SRA3	20min	
Photomechanical colour proof, SRA2	30min	
Photomechanical colour proof, SRA1	45min	
Wet progressive four-colour proofs, B2 on flatbed proofing press	2h 30min	
Wet progressive four-colour proofs, B2 on four-colour production press	1h 15min	
Wet progressive four-colour proofs, B1 on flatbed proofing press	3h 30min	
Wet progressive four-colour proofs, B1 on four-colour production press	1h 15min	

BOX 13.3 Prepress (continued)

CTF and CTP: offset litho plates

Up to B3	20 films per hour, i.e. 3min each
SRA2/B2	12 films per hour, i.e. 5min each
SRA1/B1	8 films per hour, i.e. 7.5min each
SRA1/B1+	3–6 films per hour, i.e. 10–20min each

CTP: flexographic polymer plates

Up to B2+	up to 5 plates per hour, i.e. 12min each
B1+	5–20min or more per set of plates
CTP/DI plates	5–20min or more per set of plates

Film-based step and repeat

Initial set-up	30min, thereafter 0.5min per step

Manual offset litho platemaking: presensitised aluminium metal platemaking

SRA3/B3	6 plates per hour, i.e. 10min each
SRA2/B2	4 plates per hour, i.e. 15min each
SRA1/B1	3 plates per hour, i.e. 20min each

Manual flexography and letterpress platemaking: from negative film

Exposing and processing	30–60min per plate

Preparing photopolymer plates for press

Flatbed letterpress mounted on rigid metal bases	10–15min per plate
Rotary flexo cylinder mounting and positioning multiple-image plates, e.g. with double sided tape	2h
Ditto using pin bar register system	1h
Ditto using sleeve plate cylinder	30min

Gravure cylinder preparation

Digitally engraved large coarse screen cylinder	1h
Digitally engraved large fine screen cylinder	up to 4h

Screen stencil preparation

Exposing and processing	30–60min per stencil
Prepress pricing	See Table 9.1 (page 202)

Source: H. M. Speirs

BOX 13.4 Machine printing

Sheet-fed offset litho: average make-ready times and press running speeds

| | Make-ready and set-up | | | Average net output in impressions per hour | | | | | | | | | | | | |
| | First/ initial MR | Follow-on MR | Wash-up per unit | Lightweight materials 45gsm to less than 90gsm | | | | Middle range materials 90gsm to less than 150gsm | | | | Heavyweight materials 150gsm and above | | | |
	hrs: min	hrs: min	hrs: min	up to 3,000	3,001– 10,000	10,001– 20,000	above 20,000	up to 3,000	3,001– 10,000	10,001– 20,000	above 20,000	up to 3,000	3,001– 10,000	10,001– 20,000	above 20,000
Standard press: small offset up to B3															
One-colour (1/0)	:25	:10	:20	2,650	3,500	4,750	5,150	3,350	4,450	5,950	6,500	2,650	3,500	4,750	5,150
Two-colour (2/0,1/1)	:40	:30	:20	2,650	3,500	4,750	5,150	3,350	4,450	5,950	6,500	2,650	3,500	4,750	5,150
Four-colour (4/0, 2/2)	1:00	:40	:20	2,650	3,500	4,750	5,150	3,350	4,450	5,950	6,500	2,650	3,500	4,750	5,150
Highly advanced press: small offset up to B3															
Four-colour (4/0, 2/2)	:40	:25	:10	3,550	4,750	6,350	6,950	4,500	6,000	8,000	8,750	3,550	4,750	6,350	6,950
Six-colour (6/0, 4/2)	:50	:35	:10	3,550	4,750	6,350	6,950	4,500	6,000	8,000	8,750	3,550	4,750	6,350	6,950

Small offset presses are currently available in up to six colours, with maximum running speed up to 15,000 sheets per hour

	First/ initial MR	Follow-on MR	Wash-up per unit	up to 3,000	3,001– 10,000	10,001– 20,000	above 20,000	up to 3,000	3,001– 10,000	10,001– 20,000	above 20,000	up to 3,000	3,001– 10,000	10,001– 20,000	above 20,000
Standard press: SRA2/B2															
One-colour (1/0)	:30	:15	:30	2,900	3,750	5,000	5,400	3,600	4,700	6,200	6,750	2,900	3,750	5,000	5,400
Two-colour (2/0,1/1)	:50	:30	:30	2,900	3,750	5,000	5,400	3,600	4,700	6,200	6,750	2,900	3,750	5,000	5,400
Four-colour (4/0, 2/2)	1:20	:45	:30	2,900	3,750	5,000	5,400	3,600	4,700	6,200	6,750	2,900	3,750	5,000	5,400
Highly advanced press: SRA2/B2															
Four-colour (4/0,2/2)	:45	:30	:15	3,800	5,000	6,600	7,200	4,750	6,250	8,250	9,000	3,800	5,000	6,600	7,200
Six-colour (6/0, 4/2)	1:00	:45	:15	3,800	5,000	6,600	7,200	4,750	6,250	8,250	9,000	3,800	5,000	6,600	7,200
Eight-colour (8/0, 4/4)	1:15	1:00	:15	3,800	5,000	6,600	7,200	4,750	6,250	8,250	9,000	3,800	5,000	6,600	7,200

B2 presses are currently available in up to 12 colours, with maximum running speed up to 18,000 sheets per hour

BOX 13.4 Machine printing (continued)

Sheet-fed offset litho: average make-ready times and press running speeds (continued)

| | Make-ready and set-up | | | Average net output in impressions per hour | | | | | | | | | | | |
| | First/ initial MR | Follow-on MR | Wash-up per unit | Lightweight materials 45gsm to less than 90gsm | | | | Middle range materials 90gsm to less than 150gsm | | | | Heavyweight materials 150gsm and above | | | |
	hrs: min	hrs: min	hrs: min	up to 3,000	3,001– 10,000	10,001– 20,000	above 20,000	up to 3,000	3,001– 10,000	10,001– 20,000	above 20,000	up to 3,000	3,001– 10,000	10,001– 20,000	above 20,000
Standard press: B1															
One-colour (1/0)	:40	:25	:35	2,900	3,750	5,000	5,400	3,500	4,700	6,200	6,750	2,900	3,750	5,000	5,400
Two-colour (2/0,1/1)	1:10	:40	:35	2,900	3,750	5,000	5,400	3,500	4,700	6,200	6,750	2,900	3,750	5,000	5,400
Four-colour (4/0, 2/2)	1:50	:55	:35	2,900	3,750	5,000	5,400	3,500	4,700	6,200	6,750	2,900	3,750	5,000	5,400
Highly advanced press: B1															
Four-colour (4/0, 2/2)	:50	:35	:15	3,800	5,000	6,600	7,200	4,750	6,250	8,250	9,000	3,800	5,000	6,600	7,200
Six-colour (6/0, 5/1)	1:10	:50	:15	3,800	5,000	6,600	7,200	4,750	6,250	8,250	9,000	3,800	5,000	6,600	7,200
Ten-colour (10/0, 5/5)	1:30	1:10	:15	3,800	5,000	6,600	7,200	4,750	6,250	8,250	9,000	3,800	5,000	6,600	7,200

B1 presses are currently available in up to 14 colours, with maximum running speed up to 16,000 sheets per hour

	First/ initial MR	Follow-on MR	Wash-up per unit	up to 3,000	3,001– 10,000	10,001– 20,000	above 20,000	up to 3,000	3,001– 10,000	10,001– 20,000	above 20,000	up to 3,000	3,001– 10,000	10,001– 20,000	above 20,000
Standard press: B0															
One-colour (1/0)	1:00	:40	:45	2,400	3,250	4,500	4,900	3,100	4,200	5,700	6,250	2,400	3,250	4,500	4,900
Two-colour (2/0,1/1)	1:40	1:00	:45	2,400	3,250	4,500	4,900	3,100	4,200	5,700	6,250	2,400	3,250	4,500	4,900
Four-colour (4/0, 2/2)	2:30	1:30	:45	2,400	3,250	4,500	4,900	3,100	4,200	5,700	6,250	2,400	3,250	4,500	4,900
Highly advanced press: B0															
Four-colour (4/0, 2/2)	1:30	1:00	:20	3,300	4,500	6,100	6,700	4,250	5,750	7,750	8,500	3,300	4,500	6,100	6,700
Six-colour (6/0, 5/1)	2:00	1:20	:20	3,300	4,500	6,100	6,700	4,250	5,750	7,750	8,500	3,300	4,500	6,100	6,700
Eight-colour (8/0, 4/4)	2:30	1:45	:20	3,300	4,500	6,100	6,700	4,250	5,750	7,750	8,500	3,300	4,500	6,100	6,700

B0 presses are currently available in up to 12 colours, with maximum running speed up to 15,000 sheets per hour

Note: the press running speeds are based on net impressions per hour, i.e. they represent the average number of good copies obtained per hour allowing for stoppages to clean blankets and general minor problems. The actual running speeds of the presses will exceed the figures by 10% or more. Changing from straight printing to converting or perfecting, where applicable, adds an extra 10–30min depending on the press sophistication

BOX 13.4 Machine printing (continued)	
Waterless sheet-fed DI	
Make-ready: imaging of all four printing plates, including processing the plates, depending on image resolution	B3 10–20min B2 20–30min
Running: average net output in impressions per hour	
5,000 copies and below	3,000
5,001 to 20,000 copies	4,250
20,001 copies and over	5,000
Heatset web offset based on a 16-page 4-unit (4/4) press	
Make-ready and set-up	
Initial press set-up	30min
All four printing units	45min
Single plate change	10min
Four-colour plate change	45min
Changing folder configurations	10–30min
Setting up rotary trimmer, if available	30–45min
Setting up spine gluing, if available	30–45min
Average net output in cylinder cut-offs per hour	
25,000 copies and below	25,000
25,001 to 40,000 copies	30,000
40,001 to 100,000 copies	38,000
100,001 to 500,000 copies	40,000
500,001 copies and over	42,000
Continuous narrow-width web offset presses	
Make-ready and set-up	
First print unit	30min
Per subsequent print units	20min
Cylinder size change	10min
Wash-up per colour	15–20min
Set-up per separate in-line finishing unit	5–30min
Average net output	
Reel-to-reel	52–198m/min (500–650ft/min)
Reel-to-pack/fold	107–122m/min (350–400ft/min)
Pack-to-pack	61–91m/min (200–300ft/min)
Reel-to-sheet	91–107m/min (300–350ft/min)
Book web offset presses based on a 32-page A4 two-colour configuration	
Initial make-ready and set-up	
Includes plating up (two or four plates), obtaining position and final colour adjustment	
Single-web	75min
Twin-web	120min
Follow-on make-ready	
Two plates	15min
Four plates	30min

BOX 13.4 Machine printing (continued)

Average net output in copies per hour using 60–100gsm paper

A4 collect 4 configuration

One copy per cylinder cut-off, e.g. 32pp single-web, 64pp twin-web

10,000 copies and below	13,000
10,001 copies and above	17,000

A4 collect 2 configuration

Two copies per cylinder cut-off, e.g. 2 × 16pp single-web, 2 × 32pp twin-web

10,000 copies and below	18,000 (9,000 per cut-off)
10,001 copies and above	24,000 (12,000 per cut-off)

Narrow-width reel-fed flexographic presses

Make-ready and set-up

First print unit	25min
Per subsequent print units	15min
Wash-up per colour	10–15min
Set-up per separate in-line finishing unit	5–30min

Average net output

Straightforward, printing and die-cutting	70m/min (230ft/min)
More complex printing and die-cutting	50m/min (164ft/min)
Highly complex finishing and printing on more difficult substrates	40m/min (131ft/min)

Finishing operations, such as cutting-and-creasing on adapted sheet-fed letterpress presses

Make-ready and set-up

Small platen (260mm × 380mm)

Simple work	20–30min
Complex work, such as multiple images, resetting press for embossing	30–60min

SBB size cylinder (570mm × 820mm)

Simple work	30–45min
Complex work, such as multiple images, resetting press for embossing	45–60min

Net impressions per hour

Small platen (260mm × 380mm)	2,000–3,000
SBB cylinder	1,500–2,500

Reel-fed letterpress flatbed and rotary presses

Make-ready and set-up

Flatbed

Initial press make-ready	45min
First print unit/plate change	10–20min
Wash-up per colour	10–15min
Cutter change	30min

Rotary

Initial press make-ready	60min
First print unit/plate change	20–30min
Wash-up per colour	10–15min
Cutter change	45min

Average net output

Flatbed

Straightforward printing	95m/min (312ft/min)
More complex printing and die-cutting	50m/min (164ft/min)
Complex finishing and printing	30m/min (98ft/min)

Rotary

Straightforward printing one side only	80m/min (262ft/min)
Printing one side with rotary die-cutters	30m/min (98ft/min)
Printing both sides with rotary die-cutters	20m/min (66ft/min)

BOX 13.4 Machine printing (continued)		
Large-width web-fed gravure presses		
Make-ready and set-up		
Eight print units	Up to 3h	
	Up to 2h follow-on make-ready	
Average net output in copies per hour		
	6 etchings: up to 26,000 or 30,000	
	4 etchings: up to 40,000 or 50,000 (1-up)	
	4 etchings: up to 75,000 or 80,000 (2-up)	

Screen presses	Small format	Large format
Flatbed platens		
Make-ready and set-up time (min): single colour		
Press make-ready	15	40
Wash-up	15	30
Average net output (sheets per hour)		
Handfed	150	100
Semi-automatic	250	200
Three-quarter automatic	600	400
Fully automatic	900	650
Fully automatic cylinders		
Make-ready and set-up time (min)		
Press make-ready – single colour	20	40
Per additional print unit	10	20
Wash-up	15	30
Average net output (sheets per hour)		
Fully automatic	3,000	2,200

Digital printing

Digital presses come in a wide range of sizes and types, including single- and multicolour, sheet-fed and web-fed, fixed and variable data; they also have a wide range of resolutions and run many different materials. All of these factors combine to create vastly different make-ready and set-up times and printing speeds. Use actual experience to establish job- and machine-specific make-ready and set-up times and running speeds. The printing speed ranges in this section are included for general guidance; actual printing speeds may vary by 10% to 100% of the rated speeds. Online make-ready and set-up times will vary from 15min or under for straightforward repetitive work to well over 60min for complex work. Most of the make-ready and set-up times on digital printing equipment involve the off-line operations of data and file preparation.

Sheet-fed digital monochrome copier/printer systems

Format sizes of up to A3+ and printing speeds up to 12,000 A4 single-sided pages in black only.

Sheet-fed digital colour copier/printer systems

Format sizes of up to A3+ and printing speeds up to over 6000 A4 single-sided pages in four-colour process.

Sheet-fed and web-fed production digital colour presses

Format sizes from A3 to B2 and printing speeds up to 8000 A4 single-sided pages in four-colour process sheet-fed, plus web-fed 3900 double-sided A4 sheets per hour and B2 products of unlimited lengths.

BOX 13.4 Machine printing (continued)

Web-fed digital monochrome, spot colour and multicolour printing systems

Web widths above 500mm. They include high-speed inkjet systems in excess of 50,000 personalised copies per hour and 40,000 A4 pages two-wide per hour.

Wide-format digital colour printing systems

The vast majority of wide-format web-fed digital printing systems are based on inkjet. They often have six printing units, using a six-colour set of inks, either as Hexachrome with enhanced CMYK plus highly pigmented green and orange, or extended CMYK with additional light cyan and magenta. The number of printheads can total over 100. Machine speeds vary greatly up to over $200m^2/h$ and beyond. Resolution varies from below 100dpi to over 2000dpi, with the speed of the presses being reduced to below 2m/min at the highest resolution. At the lower end of the range are printing systems up to 1620mm that can print a maximum substrate thickness of 1.7mm using speeds up to $39.5m^2/h$. At the other extreme, there are superwidth presses up to 5000mm that can print a maximum substrate thickness of 10mm using speeds up to $86m^2/h$. Large-format sheet-fed systems may go up to 2400mm × 1600mm with a printing speed of up to $100m^2/h$, plus the larger 3200mm × 1600mm size.

Source: H. M. Speirs

BOX 13.5 Print finishing

Guillotine

Normal pile height working capacity of 75mm

Single-knife

General cutting or trimming on basic guillotine	30 cuts per hour
General cutting or trimming on programmatic guillotine	60 cuts per hour
Repetitive cutting on programmatic guillotine or workflow unit	100 cuts per hour
Cutting into two, i.e. one cut	10–12 piles per hour

Three-knife trimmer

Make-ready and set-up	30min
Hand-fed	250–500 piles per hour
Automatic	1,200–2,500 piles per hour

Folding

Make-ready

1 fold	20min
2 folds	30min
3 folds	45min
4 folds	60min

Output speeds

250mm	4 pages	16,000 sheets per hour
500mm	6 or 8 pages	8,000 sheets per hour
750mm	12 or 16 pages	6,000 sheets per hour
1,000mm	24 or 32 pages	4,000 sheets per hour

Small-format folders running A5 jobs and smaller will achieve an increase of 50% or more on these figures for 4-, 6- and 8-page folded products

Machine collating

Make-ready and set-up of stations and bins	15–60min

Output speeds

Stand-alone collators are available in small-format size with approximately 16 bins or stations handling from A5+ to A4+ in speeds up to 8,000 sets of 15 × A4 leaves per hour, with up to 80 bins. Large-format collators are available in up to B1 at 2,500 sets per hour and up to 15 bins

Insetting by hand	1,200 A4 items per hour
Inserting by hand	1,000 inserts per hour

BOX 13.5 Print finishing (continued)

Handfed wire stitching with pre-insetted booklets

Make-ready				15–30min			
Number of							

Number of sections	Average output speed per hour for given number of stitches S						
	Up to A5			Up to A4		Over A4	
	S = 1	S = 2	S = 4	S = 2	S = 4	S = 2	S = 4
1	800	650	550	600	500	500	400
2 to 3	700	525	450	500	400	400	300
4 to 6	600	450	400	400	300	300	250

Bookletmaker

Finishing 4-page sections with in-line folding, stitching and foredge trimming

Make-ready	15–30min
Output speed	2,500–4,000 per hour

Side-wire stitching

Make-ready				15–30min			

Number of sections	Average output speed per hour for given number of stitches S						
	Up to A5		Up to A4		Over A4		
	S = 2	S = 3/4	S = 2	S = 3/4	S = 2	S = 3/4	
2 to 5	525	450	500	400	400	300	
6 to 9	450	400	450	300	300	250	
10 and over	400	375	400	275	275	200	

Thread stitching

Make-ready	15–30min
Output speed	500 copies per hour

Gather, stitch, trim: automated high-speed systems

No. of sections, incl. cover feed	No. of assistants
Up to 3	1
From 4 to 6	2
Over 6	3

	Time taken (min)
Make-ready	
General machine set-up per pass	30–45
Set-up per each section or hopper	5

	Average net copies per hour				
Run length	4,000	7,000	10,000	15,000	20,000
Run speed					
1 section	5,000	5,500	6,000	7,000	8,000
2 sections	4,500	5,000	6,000	7,000	8,000
3 sections	4,000	4,500	5,000	5,500	6,500
4 sections	3,500	4,000	4,500	5,000	6,000
5 and 6 sections	2,500	3,000	3,500	4,000	5,000

Loop wire and landscape format would each reduce the above speeds by 500–1,000 net copies per hour

BOX 13.5 Print finishing (continued)

Gather, adhesive, trim: automated high-speed systems

No. of sections, incl. cover feed	No. of assistants
Up to 3	1
4 to 6	2
6 to 9	3
10 to 12	4
13 to 14	5

Time taken (min)	
Make-ready	
General machine set-up per pass	30–45
Set-up per each section or hopper	5

		Average net copies per hour		
Run length	7,000	10,000	15,000	20,000
Run speed				
1 to 12 sections	2,500	3,000	3,250	3,750
13 sections and over	1,500	2,000	2,500	3.000

Book production: sequence of operations

Make-ready: from 15min to several hours depending on the complexity and degree of changes required from one job to the next

Glued or perfect binding lines for brochure and book block manufacture

1	Endpaper gluing machine at 2,000 per hour
2	Section gathering machine at 5,000 per hour
3	Perfect binding machine similar to general commercial binding, producing up to 3,750 book blocks per hour
4	Three-knife trimmer specialist high-capacity machine developed for book blocks at 4,000 cycles per hour

Thread-sewn case-bound manufacture

1	High-speed thread-sewing machine designed to produce sewn book blocks awaiting casing-in at 6,000 sections per hour
2	Book rounding and backing machine at 2,500 per hour
3	Bookmark inserting machine at 2,500 per hour
4	Backlining and headbanding machine at 2,500 per hour
5	High-speed case-making machine at 3,000 cases per hour
6	Automatic embossing press at 2,500 per hour
7	High-speed casing-in machine at 1,500 per hour
8	Book jacketing machine at 2,500 per hour

Loose-leaf binding

Predrilling, 40mm piles	100 per hour
Inserting drilled and gathered leaves into binders	60–200 sets per hour

Plastic comb binding

Manual system	
Pre-punching each copy from pre-collated leaves	30–60 sets per hour
Inserting gathered leaves in sets into binders	30 sets per hour
Automated system	
Make-ready	30–60min
Output speed	750–2,500 per hour

Spiral wire binding

Automated system	
Make-ready	30–60min
Output speed	500–2,000 per hour

BOX 13.5 Print finishing (continued)

Padding by hand

Pads up to A5	100 per hour
Pads above A5 and up to A4	80–90 per hour
Pads above A4	50–80 per hour

Numbering

Conventional numbering

Make-ready and set-up	5–10min per box

	Average output
Straightforward simple numbering by treadle or hand machine in a convenient place	1,500–2,000 books per hour
At the foot of the page or near the spine	900 books per hour
In an awkward or difficult position	500 books per hour
Examination and certification of numbers	2,000–3,000 books per hour
Double numbering with two-headed machine	1,000–1,250 books per hour

Specialist numbering	
Make-ready and set-up	5–10min per number, set or batch
Crash numbering on collator or numbering machine	2,000 numbered sets per hour
Inkjet numbering, serial numbers only	4,250 numbers per hour
Inkjet numbering, number and related letters such as ticket numbering with block or row	2,500 numbers or letters per hour

Cheque numbering ion deposition based on four-to-view numbering	
500 and below	2,000 sheets per hour
501 to 2,000	2,500 sheets per hour
2,001 and above	2,000 sheets per hour

Electronic numbering systems

There are a wide range of highly productive and versatile electronic numbering systems that can number at high speeds, plus perforate, score and slit, all in one operation. For greater flexibility, the machines can often be upgraded to increase their running speed and in-line features. Sheet sizes vary from around A6 to over SRA3, covering running speeds from 3000 to 12,000 A4 sheets per hour. The most advanced machines are fully programmable with features such as up to four numbering heads and online job memory, plus the ability to automatically feed open- or side-glued sets up to SRA3. They can also handle coated and uncoated stock, single sheets and multi-part sets, with the ability to crash number up to ten-part NCR sets.

Make-ready	15–30min
Average output	2,000–8,000 sheets per hour

Scoring and creasing

Specialist scoring and creasing machines	
Make-ready	15–30min
Hand feed	500 sheets per hour
Automatic feed	2,500 sheets per hour

Scoring at press on flatbed letterpress machines	
Make-ready	30min to 1h
Average output	2,500–4,000 sheets per hour

Specialist heavy-duty cutting-and creasing machines, often multi-image finishing	
Make-ready	30min to 2h
Average output	2,250 to 6,000 sheets per hour

Cutting-and-creasing jacket fitted to offset litho presses	
Make-ready	30–90min to fit sleeve
Average output	500–1,000 sheets per hour slower than straight printing

BOX 13.5 Print finishing (continued)

Mailing, packing and dispatch

Mailing lines: polythene wrapping

Hand feed	500–2,000 per hour
Make-ready	15–60min
Automatic feed	5,000–8,000 per hour

Packing parcels

Standard parcels of size 10–12kg each	20 per hour
Smaller parcels, say 6–8kg each	24 per hour
Packets of 1,000 A4 sheets with specimen pasted outside	28 per hour
Packets of 500 A4 sheets with specimen pasted outside	34 per hour
Packets of 1,000 A5 sheets with specimen pasted outside	34 per hour
Packets of 500 A5 sheets with specimen pasted outside	50 per hour
Cartons and boxes	20–40 boxes per hour

Shrink-wrapping

Shrink-wrapping parcels	50–100 per hour
Shrink-wrapping small items such as batches of labels or leaflets	120–240 per hour
Palletising, 750–1,000kg per pallet	6 pallets per hour
Baling, up to 40kg	4–5 bales per hour

Miscellaneous print finishing, packing and dispatch operations

	Per hour
Postal operations	
Banding	100
Sealing envelopes	800
Franking envelopes	900
Inserting	
One piece in envelope and tucking in flap	350
One piece in envelope and sealing flap	250
For each additional piece inserted	750
Inserting leaflets in clasps or string-fastener envelopes and fastening flaps	200
Wrappering booklets in postal wrapper, rolled	200
Inserting posters or charts into cardboard tubes	75
Pasting addressed labels on to a small package	250
Inserting an item or parcel into a rigid carton and sealing	100
Round cornering	
Paper, caliper 0.08mm, approx. 100–115gsm, per corner	20,000
Paper, caliper 0.08mm, approx. 100–115gsm, four corners	8,000
Board, caliper 0.25mm, approx. 240gsm, per corner	7,000
Board, caliper 0.25mm, approx. 240gsm, four corners	3,000
32-page booklets, two corners	800
Punching round or slotted hole	
Paper, caliper 0.08mm, approx. 100–115gsm	3,500
Board, caliper 0.25mm, approx. 240gsm	1,000
Hole drilling	
Piles of 40mm high drilled, single drillhead	100
Piles of 40mm high drilled, multiple drillhead (up to six heads)	30–50

BOX 13.5 Print finishing (continued)

Continuous stationery and business

Converter or paper processor

Make-ready	15min to 1h
Average output	250–350ft/min

Pack-to-pack collator

Make-ready	15min to 1h
Average output	200–300ft/min

Reel-to-reel collator

Make-ready	15min to 2h
Average output	450–650ft/min

These make-ready and set-up times vary with the number of reels or stations being processed

Direct marketing, direct mail and special products

Sheet-fed finishing on Hunkeler or Stahl flexo mailer type of machine

Make-ready	From 1h on a simple job to as much as 7h on a very complex job, with an average of 2h to 2h 30min; 45min is often allowed per unit or section with up to 15min per gluehead
Average output speeds	From 2,000 to 10,000 per hour, depending on the number of units or sections used

Folding box cartons

Forme making

Setting up CADCAM system	for new job	up to 7h 30min
	for existing job	up to 2h 30min
Producing Astrafoil tracing for 1-up profile of carton		up to 1h 30min
Laser cut carton profiles	first one	up to 1h 15min
	per subsequent one	20min
Rubbering and ruling	first one	up to 5h 30min
	per subsequent one	1h 45min
Preparing stripping board	4-on and below	up to 2h
	5-on and above	2h 30min and above

Cutting-and-creasing or die-cutting, embossing and hot-foil blocking on specialist machines

Pre make-ready		40min per carton
Make-ready and set-up		up to 3h
	per subsequent one	1h 45min
Average net output in sheets per hour		3,000–6,000

Hand-fed die-cutting platens

Make-ready	1–2h
Average output in sheets per hour	1,000

Waste stripping: manual operation

Average output in cartons per hour	7,000–20,000

Folder/gluer

Make-ready	straight line	30min
	double wall, etc.	up to 2h
Average output in single cartons per hour	straight line	20,000–80,000
	double wall, etc.	5,000–8,000

BOX 13.5 Print finishing (continued)	
Windowing and window patching	
Including cutting out window aperture, carton lining and punching out the profile film membranes; these are often carried out on a specialist machine such as the Kohmann 1350 working out at around 10,000–12,000 cartons per hour	
Foil blocking and embossing as separate or stand-alone operations	
Make-ready	2–4h or more
Average output in sheets per hour	3,000–6,000
Sheet-fed labels	
Hand-fed ram-punched labels in single blocks	
Make-ready	1h
Average output in single labels per hour	150,000–200,000
Automated ram-punched system in multiple strips	
Make-ready	1h
Average output in single labels per hour based on 14 strokes × 1,000 sheets per min	840,000
Source: H. M. Speirs	

Glossary

A sizes Main series of finished printing trimmed sizes in the ISO international paper size range.

access To retrieve data from a computer storage area.

achromatic printing Method of colour printing in which any hue is created from two colours plus black, rather than three. An extension of undercolour removal (UCR).

additive primaries Coloured lights in red, green and blue, (R, G, B) that when combined with each other in equal proportions produce white light; other colours may be produced by mixing different proportions of each light source. Video monitors use this principle to produce colour television images. Input scanner detectors sense red, green and blue components of the scanned image before electronic conversion to the printing colours cyan, magenta, yellow and black (C, M, Y, K).

adhesive binding Style of threadless binding in which the leaves of a book are held together at the binding edge by glue or synthetic adhesive. See also burst binding.

air-dried paper Paper dried by a current of warm air after tub sizing.

American Standard Code for Information Interchange (ASCII) A standard coding system used within the computer industry to convert keyboard input into digital information. It covers all the printable characters in normal use and control characters such as carriage return and line feed. The full table contains 127 elements. Variations and extensions of the basic code can be found in special applications.

antique finish A rough, uncalendered finish applied to paper used for book printing, when bulk and light weight are required.

application A software program to do tasks such as word processing and desktop publishing.

archiving Offline storage of completed or partial work, which is stored and retained for future use.

art Substrate that has received a coating to the base material. It has a very smooth surface, which may be gloss, matt, satin or vellum.

artwork Text, graphic and illustrations arranged individually or in any combination for subsequent printing. Artwork will normally be computer originated and supplied in electronic form, or it may be produced conventionally on suitable paper or board. Artwork may be prepared in black and white or full colour; full colour will require colour separation.

asymmetric digital subscriber line (ADSL) Fast means of transferring digital data on a permanent connection using the same wiring as a standard telephone line.

author's corrections Corrections made by the author or customer on proofs that alter the original copy. The cost of making these alterations is charged for. Printer's errors or house corrections are not charged for.

B sizes ISO sizes intended primarily for posters, wallcharts and similar items where the difference in size of the larger sheets in the A series represents too large a gap.

back The back of a book is the binding edge. To back a book is to shape the back of a previously rounded book, so as to make a shoulder on either side against which the front and back covers fit closely.

back up To print the reverse side of a sheet.

bandwidth The rate at which data is sent over a network. The difference between the lowest and highest frequencies, measured in hertz (Hz).

bank A fine writing or typewriting paper, white or tinted, made in a range of weights from 45gsm to under 63gsm. Heavier weights of otherwise similar material are called bonds.

bit Binary information transfer or binary digit. The basic unit of information in computer imagesetting; it represents a pulse, electrical charge or its absence. Each bit stands for one binary digit, 0 or 1. Bits are usually grouped together in blocks of eight to make bytes. Most computer operations work on byte-sized pieces of information.

bitmap image An image arranged according to bit location in columns. Resolution of a PostScript file processed through a RIP will have a bitmap image with the characteristics and resolution of the particular output device, e.g. laser printer at 300dpi up to 2400dpi, imagesetters at 1270dpi up to 5080dpi.

blanket cylinder On an offset litho printing machine, the cylinder that carries the blanket (fabric coated with a rubber or synthetic compound); it takes the printing image from the plate and transfers it to the substrate.

bleed Printed matter which runs off the edge of the substrate. Also used by bookbinders to describe overcut margins and mutilated print.

blind A blind plate is a litho plate that has lost its image. Blind book covers are blocked or stamped without using ink or a metallic effect.

blind blocking Blank impression made on book covers by binder's brass, without gold leaf, foil or ink.

blister packaging Method of packaging where an object is placed in a preformed, clear plastic tray and backed by a printed card.

block In binding, to impress or stamp a design on a cover. The design can be blocked in coloured inks, gold leaf or metal foil (see blind). In printing, a letterpress block is the plate from which an image is printed.

board, chip Inexpensive board made from mechanical wood and waste materials. It is used unlined for binding cases, rigid boxes, show cards, and white lined for cartons.

board, mill A high-grade board, brown in colour, made from rope and other materials, very hard, tough and with a good finish. It is mainly used for case-bound book covers.

board, paste Board which contains two or more laminations of paper having a middle or lower quality.

board, pulp Board manufactured from pulp as a homogeneous sheet on a cylinder machine, in a similar manner to paper.

board, straw Board made from straw and used principally for the covers of cased books and cheap account books.

bond Similar to bank paper but heavier, usually supplied in 63gsm and above.

bound book A book in which the boards of the cover have first been attached to it; the covering of leather, cloth or other material is then affixed to the boards. Bound books are more expensive to produce and much stronger than cased books.

broadband internet A high-speed internet connection.

broadsheet Any sheet in its basic size, i.e. not folded or cut; a newspaper size.

bromide A photographic paper used in graphic reproduction, phototypesetting and imagesetting on which a photographic image is created.

browser A computer program that retrieves and displays information from online services.

bulk Relative thickness of a sheet or sheets. Two papers may have the same weight but different bulk; one may be thin and one may be bulky.

bullseye Printing defect caused by particles of paper, board, dust or ink skin holding the paper or board away from the printing surface by forming a small solid dot in the centre of a clear circle surround on the affected printed area. Also known as a hickey.

burst binding A type of adhesive binding where the back of the book block is not sawn off, but is slit or slot punched in selected areas to allow glue penetration.

byte The standard measure of computer information and memory, consisting of eight bits. *See also* bit.

C sizes The C series within the ISO paper size range that is mainly used for envelopes or folders suitable for enclosing stationery in the A sizes.

calibration bar A strip of tones and solids used to check print-related quality throughout the printing process. *See also* colour control bar.

caliper The thickness of a material.

camera-ready artwork (CRA) Finished artwork that is ready to be photographed or reproduced digitally without further preparation.

carbonless paper Paper stock coated on the back and/or front with chemicals that react to form an image when written or typed on.

carton A container generally made from paper or board, but sometimes partially or totally from plastic. The printer or carton manufacturer generally delivers it to a user, either in flat or collapsed form, for assembly at the packaging point.

cartridge paper Tough, opaque paper with a rough surface. Principally used for guard books, large envelopes, drawing and offset printing.

case The cover of a book prepared in advance then affixed to the book.

case binding The binding of printed books; case bindings may be leather, cloth and other forms of covering.

CD-Rom Permanent medium for storing digital data.

chemical wood pulp Pulp that is prepared from chipped wood by treating with chemicals to remove the non-cellulose material, including lignin. It is used in the better grade of wood pulp papers and boards, and improves the qualities of mechanical pulp when the two are mixed. Also called wood-free.

cheque paper Paper chemically treated to highlight any tampering with writing on completed cheques.

china clay A fine white clay used in papermaking for loading and coating.

chip The basic building block for computers, made from silicon.

choke A specific adjustment or distortion where all or part of an element's perimeter is slightly pulled in towards the centre of the element. Choking of an element is normally used in conjunction with the spreading (*see* spread) of a neighbouring element to achieve colour registration standards. Choking may be performed in several ways: manually, photomechanically or digitally using a computer program.

client Any computer or workstation that uses the resources of another computer. *See also* server.

clip art A collection of graphics, such as drawings, photographs and logos, for use in a separately prepared design or piece of artwork.

CMYK Letters indicating the subtractive primary colours used in printing: cyan, magenta, yellow and black.

coated paper Paper that has received a coating on one or both sides. Art papers are coated papers, cast-coated papers are high-gloss papers on which the coating has been allowed to harden in contact with a highly finished casting surface. In addition there are brush-coated papers, chromo papers, roller-coated papers and machine-coated papers. Chromo papers are clay-coated in a separate operation from papermaking and machine-coated papers are coated during the papermaking process. Similar qualities are available in board weights.

coldset drying Web offset litho printing process where the printed web dries naturally – there is no assisted drying. It is used extensively for newspaper production and newspaper-type products. Coldset inks dry by penetration or absorption on soft absorbent substrates. *See also* heatset drying.

collating Checking through the signatures or pagination of book sections to ensure they are complete and in the correct sequence for binding. *See also* gathering.

collating marks Black step marks (usually 6pt rule) printed on the back folds or sections and in progressively different positions so that any displacement of sections may be checked after gathering.

colour control bar A coloured strip on the margin of the sheet which enables the platemaker and printer to check by eye or instrument the printing characteristics of each ink layer. *See also* calibration bar.

colour proofing techniques A wide range of techniques to reproduce full-colour images from film or digital data before the actual print run. They allow the client, colour separation house and printer to view the proofed result before the actual print run.

colour separation In colour reproduction the process of separating the colours of an original into a required colour form, e.g. C, M, Y, K.

compression Compacting data to reduce the size of image files. *See also* decompression.

computer-to-plate (CTP) Generating a printing plate directly from digital data. *See also* platesetter.

computer-to-press (CTPr) Imaging directly on to a plate carrier system on the press from a computer front end.

continuous tone Images that contain an apparently infinite range of shades and colours smoothly blended to provide a faithful reproduction of natural images. Often shortened to contone.

contract proof A coloured, hard-copy representation of the printed image, made from films or digital data, and used to create the final printing plates. The word 'contract' comes from the fact that, when signed by the client, a contract is formed, which states that the final printed job should be a close match to the contract proof.

control target Quality aid containing elements to highlight any variation in reproduction or printing quality. Can be used in digital printing and analogue (film) printing.

convertible press A press able to print on one or both sides of a sheet or web.

covering The process by which a cover is affixed fully to the spine and both sides of a book.

crease To mechanically press a rule into heavy paper or board, creating a channel to enable folding without cracking. *See also* score.

customisation Personalisation of printed matter using a digital printing system.

cut-in index An index where the divisions are cut into the edge of the book in steps. *See also* step index.

dandy (laid, spiral, wove) A cylinder of wire gauze on the papermaking machine that comes into contact with the paper while it is in a wet and elementary stage. The dandy roll impresses the watermark.

database A collection of data used by computer programs.

deckle The web width, i.e. the machine width, to which a papermaking machine can produce paper and board. It is limited by the deckle straps, which were originally the movable wooden frame on the hand-mould used for papermaking.

deckle edge The feathery edge around the borders of a sheet of hand-made or mould-made paper or board, due to the deckle or frame of the mould. Double deckle edging means that two sides of a machine-made sheet are rough-edged or feathered.

decompression Expansion of compressed data normally back to its original size. *See also* compression.

densitometer A device for measuring film or a printed product by reflected or transmitted light. Densitometers vary in their sophistication and their features, such as colour, black and white, read-out memory, computer printout.

desktop colour separation (DCS) An image format that consists of four separate CMYK separation files at full resolution, plus an EPS file for placement only. Also known as EPS 5.

desktop publishing (DTP) Using personal computers (PCs) for typesetting, page composition and image handling. The combination of all these functions gives electronic control within a single system of what was traditionally a sequence of specialist operations.

diestamping An intaglio printing process where the impression stands out in relief above the surface of the stamped material, either coloured (using inks) or blind (without colour).

digital Digital pulses, signals or values represent data in computer graphics, telecommunications systems and word processing.

digital asset management (DAM) Archiving and indexing digital content for reuse in print or other media.

digital font An electronically stored type font with characters stored as a series of digital signals.

digital page composition (DPC) A system designed to take a range of page elements, text, linework and images then integrate them into a user-specified format such as PostScript. Also known as electronic page composition system (EPCS), colour electronic page system (CEPS) and digital artwork and reproduction (DAR).

digital printing Taking digital data from a front-end computer system and outputting via a digital printing system directly on to a substrate.

digital workflow An all-digital workflow represented by data being created, manipulated and processed digitally to its final destination, such as CTF, CTP, CTPr, CD-Rom and internet.

distributed printing Printing a document or series of documents to different locations by using a linked network of computers and output devices, such as laser printers and digital printing systems.

dot gain The percentage size change of a halftone dot when it goes from its original state, either in analogue (film) form or digital form, to the printed substrate. Dot gain depends on the type of original, the method of printing and the choice of substrate. The press dot gain must be calculated before the print run and the dot size must be reduced accordingly, to counteract it. Dot gain is not a linear change; it varies with the size of the original dot.

download The transfer of digital data from one computer to another.

drawing program Design software that generates outline or vector-based images which are editable and do not deteriorate when enlarged.

drawn-on cover A paper book cover attached to the sewn book by gluing the spine.

driver A program or routine that allows a computer to communicate with and control a peripheral device such as a printer or scanner.

dummy A sample of a proposed job made up with the actual materials and cut to the correct size to show bulk, style of binding, etc. Also a complete layout of a job showing position of typematter, illustrations, margins, etc.

duotone A two-colour halftone produced from two halftone images of the same original. Different visual effects can be obtained by using different screen angles, contrast ranges, special screens, etc.

duplex paper or board Paper or board in two material qualities or two colours combined in the wet state on the papermaking machine, or created as a sandwich by gluing the different pieces together.

duplex printing Printing or copying on both sides of the substrate in one complete cycle of the operation. Often applied to copiers and digital printing systems. *See also* perfecting.

dye sublimation Printing and proofing where coloured dyes on plastic film carriers are heated so they vaporise and fuse on to the substrate as required.

edges, sprinkled The spattering of book edges from a brush charged with liquid ink; used for decoration. May also be done with an airbrush.

edition A number of copies printed a given time when some change has been made in type or format.

electron beam *See* radiation drying.

electronic book (e-book) Digital version of a book, which will normally include hyperlinks and possibly some multimedia elements.

electronic data interchange (EDI) Any commercial data transfer.

electrophotography The printing process used by many digital printing systems where a laser or light-emitting diode (LED) and photoconductive drum create charged image particles of toner that are transferred and fused to the substrate, where they form the printed result.

electrostatic printing Where the printing plate, drum or belt is charged overall with electricity and light is reflected from the non-image areas of the original being copied, destroying the charges in these areas. Toner powder is then applied, which adheres only to the charged areas; the toner is fused to the substrate using heat. *See also* laser printing.

embossing Using a relief block to create raised letters or designs on a substrate.

Encapsulated PostScript (EPS) A file format used to transfer PostScript image information from one program to another. An EPS file has two parts: a 72dpi PICT file used to display the file on a monitor and the PostScript code that describes the page.

encoder A mechanism for converting data in one format to data in another, e.g. RGB to CMYK.

encryption Encoding data to make it more secure.

endpapers Lining sheets at each end of a book that are used to attach the end sections to the cover.

Ethernet A networking system for high-speed data transfer between computer systems and peripherals over a coaxial link.

extranet Internet technologies that link groups of users, such as companies and their suppliers.

facsimile (fax) The transmission of copy, artwork or separations electronically from one location to another; a duplicate of an original; to produce a duplicate.

file A group of data created in the form of a document or application and stored under a unique name.

finishing All operations after printing. Also the hand operations of lettering and ornamenting the covers of a book.

first-and-third A printed sheet where the printed matter appears on pages 1 and 3 when folded.

flat back Bound sections having a square back, i.e. not rounded and backed.

flat wire stitching *See* stabbing.

flexography A relief process where printing is carried out using a photopolymer or rubber plate and a low-viscosity liquid-based inking system.

floppy disk A removable magnetic storage medium; the most common size is 3.5in and holds 1.44 megabytes of data.

flush A style of binding in which the covers and leaves are trimmed simultaneously as a final operation.

folioed Having consecutively numbered folios; compare with paged (q.v.).

font A set of type characters of the same design e.g. upper and lower case, numerals, punctuation marks, accents and ligatures. A typeface. Alternative spelling, fount.

foredge The edge of a book opposite the binding edge, spine or back.

format Repeated typographical instructions or other commands. Formatting is used in a computer to simplify repeated changes to text matter after it has been set and printed out, e.g. updating a price list.

for position only (FPO) A low-resolution image in a document showing the position and format of the final high-resolution image.

forwarding In case binding, the processes that come after sewing and before finishing.

fount *See* font.

four-colour process Colour printing using the three subtractive primary colours – yellow, magenta and cyan – plus black. The colours of the original are separated by an electronic or photographic process.

French fold A sheet of paper with four pages printed on one side and folded into four leaves without cutting the head. The inside four pages are then blank and printing appears on pages 1, 4, 5 and 8.

frequency modulated (FM) screening *See* stochastic screening.

front-end system The part of a computer system that controls input, correction, manipulation and storage. Compare with the back-end system, which is the output.

front lay *See* lay.

fugitive colour Ink that is not stable when exposed to certain conditions of light, moisture or atmosphere.

full-bound Style of binding in which the covering is one piece of material.

function codes Codes which control the functions of the setting system. Compare with input codes, which produce characters.

furnish The class and proportion of materials used in making paper or board.

gathering To take sections or sheets and place them in the correct order to make up a book.

generic mark-up A method of mark-up that describes the structure and other attributes of a document or print job in a rigorous and system-independent manner, so it can be processed for several different applications. *See also* Standard Generalised Markup Language

grain (in paper or board) *See* machine direction.

grammage The weight of a substrate such as paper; usually expressed in gsm.

grams per square metre (gsm) A unit for expressing the substance of paper or board as a weight per unit area.

Graphics Interchange Format (GIF) A cross-platform file format, particularly used for web images.

graphics tablet Used in computing and page make-up for layout or system control. A mouse, pen or puck on a drawing board controls movement on the video screen, traces in outlines or selects commands from a menu.

gravure printing An intaglio process where the printing areas are below the non-printing surface. The recesses are filled with ink and the surplus is cleaned off the non-printing area with a doctor blade before the paper contacts the whole surface and lifts the ink from the recesses.

greaseproof A wood pulp paper that is made translucent by prolonged beating of the pulp.

grey balance The condition in colour reproduction where the dot size values of the subjective primaries are balanced to give a visual neutral grey, e.g. cyan 60%, magenta 48% and yellow 46%.

greyboards Caseboards of a higher quality than chipboards; produced mainly in Holland.

greyscale Grey tones between black and white. A greyscale monitor is able to display grey pixels as well as black and white, but not colour pixels.

grid A regularly spaced set of lines in two dimensions to form a series of positional references. In electronic systems they may be used to position text and images accurately for on-screen page layout.

guard book A book with guards in the binding edge to prevent the back breaking when filled with cuttings, samples, patterns, etc.

guards Strips of paper sewn between the leaves of a book, on to which can be pasted maps, etc.

gutter The binding margin of a book.

half-bound Style of binding in which the back and corner coverings are made of one material and the rest is made of another.

half-sheetwork *See* work-and-turn, work-and-tumble.

halftone image An image which has had its tones translated into solids and various dot sizes. The human eye will see different tonal levels depending on the ratio of printed dot area to substrate background.

halftone screen The traditional name for a glass plate or film cross-ruled with opaque lines and having transparent squares; used to split up the image into halftone dots.

hard copy Typed or printed copy; an uncorrected proof; a final master copy.

hard disk A fixed magnetic storage medium in which the data-holding element cannot be removed. Hard disks have a very large storage capacity of several gigabytes, enabling data to be rapidly accessed and manipulated.

hard-sized paper Paper that has received maximum sizing. Lesser degrees of sizing are half-sized and quarter-sized.

hardware The electronic components of a computer; compare with software (q.v.).

headband Originally a narrow band of sewing round a strip of cane at the top and bottom of the spine on a hand-sewn book. It was there to strengthen the binding.

Imitation headbands made in long strips are sometimes glued to the head of a machine-sewn book to give it a better appearance.

heatset drying Web offset litho printing process where the printed web is dried by passing it through heating and chill drying units, which form part of the machine. Special heatset inks have to be used. *See also* coldset drying.

Hexachrome colours The four-colour set of yellow, magenta, cyan and black plus green and orange. Hexachrome colours are used to improve the printed colour gamut and reproduce around 90% of Pantone's special colours. *See also* HiFi colour.

HiFi colour A family of process options to improve on standard four-colour process inks and their traditional means of reproduction. New techniques such as Hexachrome inks and stochastic screening are very much associated with HiFi colour.

highlight The whitest part of a halftone when printed.

hollow The space in the back of the book between the two boards of the cover.

hot-foil technique A printing and finishing technique using very thin aluminium foil in a variety of metallic colours, such as gold, silver, red and blue. The metallic foil is released from the carrier base on to a substrate by applying heat and pressure from a metal printing plate, which bears the image to be hot-foiled.

house corrections Proof corrections that are not made by the author or copy originator.

hue The colour-defining component of a point in an image. A colour is fully defined by its hue and saturation.

hypertext A software system allowing extensive cross-referencing between related sections of text and associated graphic material.

Hypertext Markup Language (HTML) The language used to create text for the World Wide Web (WWW), including codes to define layout, fonts, embedded graphics and hypertext links. *See also* hypertext.

icons A symbol or graphic representation on a VDU screen of a program, option or window.

image The ink-carrying areas of a printing plate; the reproduction of an original in a new form.

imagesetter A system that can combine all the elements of a page – text, tints, graphics, etc. – directly on to paper or bromide, film or polyester plate material. Also known as a filmsetter.

impose To plan pages or images before platemaking and creating a montaged image master.

imposition scheme Planning the arrangement of the pages of a bound publication so they will follow in the correct sequence when folded.

India paper A very thin opaque rag paper used for books when extreme lightness or thinness is desired.

infrared (IR) *See* radiation drying.

inkjet A non-impact printing process where droplets of ink are projected on to paper or other material in a computer-determined pattern.

inner An imposition containing the pages that fall on the inside of a printed sheet in sheetwork; compare with outer (q.v.).

input Data for processing by a computer before outputting.

insert A piece of paper or card laid between the leaves of a book and not secured in any way.

insetting Placing one section inside another to create insetted work.

input device Any device that can apply an input to the computer. This includes the keyboard, disk drive, tape unit, voice recognition and any other peripherals that supply input signals.

Integrated Services Digital Network (ISDN) A telephone network service that carries data and voice transmissions by digital means, not analogue.

interface The method by which two independent systems communicate with each other. It usually refers to two electronic systems, but it may also describe communication between a user and a system.

interleaving In printing, placing sheets of paper between printed sheets as they come from the machine to prevent set-off; also known as slip sheeting. In bookbinding, taking a paper that is different from the one used in the general body of the book, e.g. writing paper and blotting paper, and insetting into and folding it around the sections of the book; the alternating of processed and plain sheets, such as in a duplicate book.

international paper sizes The standard range of metric paper sizes as defined by the International Organisation for Standardisation (ISO) and the British Standards Institution (BSI).

internet A worldwide network of computers.

interpolation Generating intermediate values between known values; it is often adopted in scanning applications, image manipulation and printer software to create intermediate pixels between the existing ones.

ion deposition Non-impact printing process where ions are projected from a replaceable print cartridge on to a rotating drum to form a latent dot matrix image.

justification The even and equal spacing of words to a predetermined measure. To justify a line is to space out a line of type to the required measure.

kettle stitch In binding, the stitch at the top and bottom of the spine that connects each signature to the following one.

key The outline of a drawing that is transferred or used as a guide when producing printing plates so the various colours will register with each other; the design which acts as the guide for position and registration of the other colours; the character key on a keyboard; to set via a keyboard.

knocking up To make the edges of a pile of paper or board straight, regular or flush.

laminating Applying transparent plastic film, with a gloss or matt finish, to the surface of printed matter to enhance its appearance and increase its durability.

landscape Oblong loose or folded printed sheet, or book, having its long sides at head and foot.

laser beam A fine beam of light, sometimes with considerable energy, used in colour scanning, copy scanning, imagesetting and platemaking. Laser stands for light amplification by stimulated emission of radiation.

laser engraving Engraving an image on to a printing plate, or a printing cylinder coated with rubber, using an intense laser beam. Used to produce gravure cylinders and flexo plates mainly for packaging.

laser printing Electrostatic printing where the image is not created by reflection from an original, such as electrostatic copying, but by switching a laser on and off according to digital information from a computer system.

lay The position of the print on a sheet of paper or board. Lays, front and side, are the guides to which paper or board is fed before being printed or otherwise processed on a machine, e.g. folding. Lay edges are the edges of a sheet that are laid against the front and side lays.

leaf A sheet of a book, containing two pages one on each side. A section of a book containing 32 leaves has 64 pages.

letterpress printing A relief process where the printing surface of metal, plastic, photopolymer or rubber is raised above the non-printing surface. The ink rollers and the substrate touch only the relief printing surface.

light-emitting diode (LED) A semiconductor that produces a light when a voltage is applied.

light pen A light-sensitive stylus used with certain VDUs for design or editing.

limp cover A flexible book cover; compare with a stiff board cover.

line art Artwork without any gradations of tone. In digital workflows, line art describes images containing only black and white pixels; also known as bilevel.

linen finish A surface impressed on paper or board to make it resemble linen, usually produced by passing the web between engraved cylinders. Other patterns can be given to paper or board after printing.

lithographic printing A planographic process where the printing and non-printing surfaces are on the same plane and the substrate makes contact with the whole surface. The printing part of the surface is treated to receive and transmit ink to the paper via a blanket cylinder. The non-printing surface is treated to attract water, hence to reject ink from the ink roller, which touches the whole surface.

loading Clay or other mineral included in the furnish of a paper or board to produce a more solid, opaque and smoother sheet; also known as filler.

look-through The appearance of paper or board when held up against a strong light.

machine direction The long direction of the paper web or board and the direction in which the cellulose fibres lie due to the motion of the papermaking machine. The sheet has stronger physical properties in the machine direction and shows less dimensional variation when subjected to changes in humidity. The direction in which a product is printed in a reel-fed printing machine, e.g. the head of the label first along the web, the foot of the label first along the web, wide edge of the label leading along the web, narrow edge of the label leading along the web.

manifold A thin, strong, smooth paper, substance under 45gsm, used for duplicating or copying.

matt art An art paper or board with a dull eggshell finish.

mechanical printing Any paper containing a proportion of mechanical wood pulp.

mechanical wood pulp Produced by grinding wood mechanically but retaining the lignin in the fibre. It is used substantially in cheaper grades of paper, such as newsprint, and combined with larger proportions of chemical wood pulp for better qualities.

menu The choice of operations displayed on a VDU.

mesh (screen printing) The weave dimension and fabric angle of material used for preparing silk screen stencils.

MF (paper) Machine finished or mill finished. Paper finished on the papermaking machine but not supercalendered.

MG (paper) Mill glazed or machine glazed. Process applied to a large range of papers that are characteristically rough on one side and highly glazed on the other, such as kraft paper.

microprocessor The chip that forms the central processing unit of a computer.

modem (modulator demodulator) A device that accepts a digital signal from a computer and adapts it for transmission over an analogue channel such as a telephone line.

modulator demodulator *See* modem

moiré pattern In colour printing, using traditional halftone screening, an irregular and unwanted screen clash patterning over the whole image in certain combinations or in specific areas of an image.

montage Mounting several colour separation films of one printing colour in register for subsequent transfer to the printing plate. Page montage is combining pages during page make-up. Photomontage is combining and blending images.

mull An open net fabric that is fixed to the backs of case-bound books, slightly overlapping front and back cover boards, to give strength.

multicolour machine A printing press that prints two or more colours in one press pass or operation.

multitasking Doing more than one task at a same time. Of a computer, running more than one program at a time.

numbering at press To number a job on the printing machine, normally by numbering boxes.

oblong *See* landscape.

offset printing A lithographic method of printing where the ink is first transferred from the image to an offset blanket and then to the stock, which may be paper, card, metal or other material.

Open Prepress Interface (OPI) Allows low-resolution images to be automatically replaced by high-resolution images at the output stage.

operating system Software that directs and controls the basic functions of a computer, such as storing files, linking with peripherals. OS X for Mac and Windows XP for PC are two operating systems.

optical character recognition (OCR) Reading typewritten or printed matter optoelectronically using a scanner and creating digital data for subsequent processing.

original Artwork that is to be reproduced.

outer An imposition containing the first and last pages of a printed sheet in sheetwork; compare with inner (q.v.).

overlap cover A cover of a paper-bound book that extends beyond the edges of the pages.

overs The production quantity, e.g. books and sheets, delivered to the customer above the net amount ordered, usually charged at a run-on rate; allowance to cover wastage.

paged Having consecutively numbered pages, compare with folioed (q.v.).

page description language (PDL) A language that identifies the parameters of a page as a set of coordinates. A raster image processor uses a page description language to translate page data into a suitable form for outputting. PostScript (q.v.) is a page description language.

paint program Design software that generates bitmapped images; compare with drawing program (q.v.).

palette A range of colours used for a specific job, accessed on electronic systems from a colour database and displayed on-screen. Colours in a palette may be classified according to Pantone or other colour systems and they can be changed in seconds.

panchromatic A photographic film or plate sensitive to all visible colours of the spectrum.

Pantone Pantone is a registered trademark of Pantone Inc. for colour standards, colour data, colour reproduction and colour reproduction materials, and other colour-related products and services, meeting its specifications, control and quality requirements. Also called the Pantone Matching System (PMS).

pasteboard Board made of two or more laminations of paper or board.

paste-up Any matter pasted up as copy for reproduction.

perfect binding *See* adhesive binding.

perfected sheet A sheet printed on both sides.

perfecting Printing the second side of a sheet or web; backing up.

perfector (press) A printing machine that prints both sides of the sheet as it passes through the machine. *See also* duplex printing.

perforating at press To perforate a job on the printing machine by using a perforating rule.

pigment Particles that absorb and reflect light and appear coloured to the eye; a substance that gives ink its colour.

pixel A picture element; the smallest part of a picture on a computer screen.

plate An image carrier for a printing process; an illustration of a book printed separately from the text and usually on different paper.

plate cylinder On a rotary printing press, the cylinder that carries the printing surface.

plate hooking Securing a plate into a book by folding the margin of the back edge in or around a section and sewing it with the section.

platen (press) A small direct impression printing machine, sometimes called a jobbing platen.

platesetter An advanced development of the imagesetter where a printing plate is produced from digital data without making a film. *See also* computer-to-plate (CTP).

point system A typographic system where all measurements are with respect to a 12pt pica of 4.217mm.

Portable Document Format (PDF) A format that allows a document to be saved, opened and viewed without needing the application which created it. PDF files are independent of operating systems, working equally well on Macs and PCs. Adobe Acrobat is the best popular software for creating PDF files.

PostScript A PDL developed by Adobe that describes the contents and layout of a page. PostScript also serves as a programming language that can be executed by a PostScript RIP in the output device to produce a printout or film containing the page. *See also* page description language.

preflighting Checking and monitoring digital data to ensure smooth running through an entire digital workflow by eliminating problems at source. Preflighting software examines features such as page geometry, graphics file formats, blends, trapping, fonts, text and output control settings.

presensitised plate A printing plate precoated for direct exposure, made in positive or negative form.

printing cylinder *See* plate cylinder.

process colours The printer's subtractive primary colours: cyan, magenta, yellow and black.

program Software instructions that enable a computer to perform a task.

progressive proofs A set of proofs that guide the printer by showing each plate printed in its appropriate colour and in registered combination.

proof A version of a document or colour illustration produced specifically for review before reproduction.

protocol An agreed set of rules or standards that allow computers to communicate with each other.

quarter-bound Style of binding in which the back covering is made of one material and the sides are made of another.

radiation drying Accelerated drying of specially formulated inks and varnishes by infrared (IR), ultraviolet (UV) or electron beam radiation.

random access memory (RAM) Used by a computer to store and access programs plus other data; it is erased when the computer is switched off. Also known as main memory.

raster The method used in most imagesetters, platesetters and VDUs to 'draw' the image. Each image consists of a series of parallel or rastered lines that are switched on and off as they cross the image area. The alternative is to use vectors.

raster image processor (RIP) Graphic workstations, including Macs and PCs, usually produce files in a very compact form based on vector definitions. However, these are not directly suitable for output, as all plotters and scanning systems need raster data to operate. RIP technology provides the link between vector and raster systems. PostScript is an example of a vector data generator.

read-only memory (ROM) A type of memory chip where the contents cannot be altered by writing data, or by switching off power. ROM is used for storing operating systems so that the system is available as soon as the machine is switched on.

recycled paper or board Paper or board made wholly or partly from recycled pulp.

recycled pulp Pulp made from waste, previously used paper and board. Fibre quality deteriorates during recycling, so paper cannot be recycled indefinitely.

register Printing two or more plates in juxtaposition so they complete an image or montage of images if printed on the same side of the sheet or web, or they back up accurately if printed on opposite sides of the sheet or web.

register marks Marks placed in the same relative position on sets of printing plates so that when the marks are superimposed during printing, the work falls into the correct position, assuming the plates have been made correctly.

repurposing Reusing content for a new purpose, e.g. PDF files prepared for print may be repurposed into an e-book.

retouching Manipulating a digital image, photographic negative or positive to modify tonal values or to compensate for imperfections.

reversing Altering the original from left to right in the reproduction, and vice versa.

RGB Letters indicating the additive primary colours: red, green and blue. *See also* CMYK.

right-reading Plate, paper or film, positive or negative from an imagesetter that can be read in the usual way, i.e. left to right.

rip once, output many (ROOM) A concept contained in most modern prepress workflows, where once the files are prepared and RIPped, they will retain their integrity, transporting or printing to any output device, without any change or deviation from its master state.

rosette The pattern created when all four-colour halftone conventional screens are placed at the traditional angles. The rosette pattern is clearly visible under a magnifying glass.

rounding and backing The hand or machine operation of shaping a book after sewing so that the back is convex and the foredge concave, and the formation of a shoulder against which to fit the cover boards.

run-through In ruling, where the lines run from one edge of the paper to the opposing edge without a break.

saddle-wire stitching To stitch with wire through the back of folded work.

SC (paper) *See* supercalendered.

scanner An input device that reads and captures data in a colour-separated form to produce a designated result, such as an RGB record of the original.

screen printing A stencil process where the printing and non-printing areas are on one surface. The printing image area is open or clear and produced by various forms of stencil. The substrate is placed under the screen then ink is passed across the top of the screen and forced through the open printing areas on to the substrate. It is often known as silk screen printing because the meshes were once made of silk.

screen ruling The number of halftone dots or lines per inch or per centimetre.

score To partially cut or crease with a rule into heavy paper or board, breaking the grain and making it easier to fold. *See also* crease.

search engine Software that searches sites on the internet.

section A folded sheet of paper forming part of a book; sections are sometimes made of insetted folded sheets of 4, 8, 16 or more pages.

server A computer that provides a service or supplies resources to other computers. *See also* client.

service provider An organisation that provides connections to the internet.

set-off Marking on the underside of a printed sheet due to ink transfer from the sheet on which it lies.

sew To fasten the sections of a book together by passing thread through the centre fold of each section to secure it to the slips; compare with stitch (q.v.).

sheetwork A certain number of pages are imposed in two formes; the inner forme is printed on one side and the outer forme is printed on the reverse side. Each backed-up sheet produces one perfect copy, sometimes known as work-and-back.

shrink-wrapping Method of packing printed products by surrounding them with plastic then shrinking by heat.

side stitching To stitch through the side from front to back at the binding edge with thread or wire. *See also* stabbing.

signature The number or letter printed at the foot of the first page in a section so the binder can check the position and completeness of the sections. Signatures are often indicated by printing a rule at the back of each section so that when the sections are folded and gathered, the signatures appear stepped on the back fold.

size Resin or other sizing material included in the furnish of a paper or board to bind the fibres and loading together, and to provide greater resistance to ink and greater strength in the sheet.

skiver An inexpensive leather made of split skins; the outer or grain side of this leather.

slitting Cutting a sheet or web into two or more parts after printing and before delivery.

slot Any pattern of hole, other than round, punched in paper or board.

soft proof Proof or image created and viewed on a monitor as against a hard-copy proof.

software Programs that enable a computer to perform its tasks.

spine *See* back.

spoilage Unprofitable materials and labour; spillage costs cannot be charged to a specific customer.

spot colour Any area of colour that is not printed using a CMYK process set, such as Pantone premixed inks. Also known as special colours.

spread The process generally carried out to enlarge the width of linework. The inverse function, choke (q.v.), is used to reduce the width of linework. This is done to ensure there is no gap between the linework and the surrounding area. The enlarged linework spreads over from its original area to give an overlay, simplifying the printing process by reducing the need for absolute accuracy of the press. It also compensates for shrinkage and stretch in the substrate to be printed.

spring back Pieces of strawboard or millboard rolled to the shape of the back.

square back *See* flat back.

squares Protective projections of the cover of a book beyond the edges of the leaves.

stabbing To stitch with wire through the side of gathered work at the binding edge.

Standard Generalised Markup Language (SGML) A versatile code used to mark up and identify the various elements of a document for outputting text.

standing matter Printing material such as planned film or plates used on a previous job that are retained pending possible reprint.

step index *See* cut-in index.

stitch To sew, staple or otherwise fasten together by thread or wire the leaves or signatures of a book or pamphlet.

stochastic screening With conventional halftone screening, the varying dot size creates an optical illusion of tonal values; however, the dot centre pitch distance is constant. In FM screening, the dots are randomly distributed to create this tonal change illusion. The greater the number of dots located within a specific area, the darker the resultant tone. The dots produced in this way are usually smaller than conventional halftone dots, giving improved definition, although it requires greater care and attention to detail during platemaking. Also known as frequency modulated (FM) screening.

stringing To insert and tie string on hanging cards, catalogues and other work, either singly or in batches.

strip gumming To take paper strips and apply water-soluble gum by hand or machine and then leave to dry.

stripping To glue a strip of cloth or paper to the back of a paperbound book or pad as a reinforcement; also to remove the waste material from between cartons and other shaped work.

substance *See* grammage.

sulphate Wood pulp prepared by chemical means using sodium hydroxide and sodium sulphide.

supercalendered (SC) Paper that has been given a smooth glazed surface by passing between the calender rolls under heavy pressure.

Tagged Image File Format (TIFF) A popular file format for exchanging bitmapped images, often scans, between applications.

Tagged Image File Format for Information Technology (TIFF/IT) A universally accepted file format specification developed from the standard ISO 12639.

taping Pasted strips of linen, calico or other suitable material attached inside or outside of sections to strengthen the paper, usually 10–12mm wide, also between sections to prevent breaking away.

template Time-saving master style that contains all the required descriptions and formatting for use as a guide or basis when creating additional related files or pages with some if not all the common features of the template.

thermal printing Non-impact printing process where heat is transferred from a digitally controlled printhead to a substrate, causing a change in colour.

thumb index Style of index where the divisions are cut into the edge of the book but not stepped; compare with cut-in index (q.v.).

tint laying Preparing the many patterns of mechanical shading.

tints Mechanical shading in line areas, normally available in 5% steps from 5% to 95%.

Transmission Control Protocol/Internet Protocol (TCP/IP) The procedure set up to regulate transmission on the internet.

turned in When the material used on the cover of a book is turned in round the edges, so as not to leave the edges of the cover boards exposed. *See also* flush.

twin-wire paper Even-sided paper produced from two webs joined together while still wet with their undersides at the centre.

type-high A traditional flatbed letterpress printing plate is said to be type-high, 23.317mm, when it is mounted to the correct height for machine printing.

ultraviolet ink (UV ink) Ink specially formulated to remain in liquid form until it is exposed to the correct wavelength of UV radiation, which cures it to a relatively solid, dry state. Depending on the amount of photoinitiators in the ink, which react to the UV radiation, the printed work may need to stand for a short time before further handling and processing. *See also* radiation drying.

undercolour removal (UCR) In four-colour printing, removing part of the cyan, magenta and yellow, while adding extra black. It reduces the total quantity of ink used.

underside (of a sheet) The surface of a paper web that receives the impression of the machine wire on the papermaking machine; often known as the machine wire side.

uniform resource locator (URL) The address of a web page.

unsewn binding *See* adhesive binding.

varnishing To apply oil, synthetic, spirit, cellulose or water varnish to printed matter by hand or machine to enhance its appearance or to increase its durability.

vegetable parchment A greaseproof paper, usually thicker and of better quality than ordinary greaseproof paper.

vehicle (of ink) Medium or varnish in which the pigment of a printing ink is carried or suspended.

vellum finish A finish applied to paper and smoother than parchment.

vignette A single dot pattern that may start at 50% dot and smoothly decreases to say 5%.

visual The design concept drawn either manually or electronically in colour to provide an impression of the final image.

visual display unit (VDU) or visual display terminal (VDT) A display unit, which consists of a cathode ray tube on which characters may be displayed, representing data read from the memory of a computer. The unit also incorporates a keyboard online to the computer.

volume basis Used mainly in book printing to denote the thickness (bulk) of 100 sheets of a given paper in 100gsm.

waterless litho A method of offset litho printing that does not use water. The process uses a special plate processed to have ink-repellent silicone non-image areas and ink-receptive photopolymer coating areas. To work correctly, the printing press needs to have a cooling system. The process is environmentally friendly and the printed result has a very high quality.

web During its manufacture, paper or board is wound on a roll or web. The phrase 'in the direction of the web' means in the direction of the run of the papermaking machine when the substrate is made. The direction of the web is important in work printed to register, as paper and board have greater stretch across the web than in the direction of the web.

web-fed press A press that is with substrate from a reel instead of in separate sheets.

web offset reel-fed offset litho printing There are three main press systems. Blanket-to-blanket systems have two plate and two blanket cylinders per unit that print and perfect the web of paper or board. In three-cylinder systems, plate, blanket and impression cylinders operate as in sheet-fed printing to print one side of the paper or board. Satellite or planetary systems have two, three or four plate and blanket cylinders arranged around common impression cylinders to print one side of the web in several colours.

what you see is what you get (WYSIWYG) The representation of text on-screen in a form exactly corresponding to its appearance on a printout.

whole-bound Style of binding in which the covering is one piece of material.

wire mark The impression of the machine wire imparted to the underside of the web of paper on a papermaking machine.

wood-free paper Any paper made from chemical wood pulp and containing no mechanical wood pulp. *See also* chemical wood pulp.

work-and-back *See* sheetwork.

work-and-tumble When matter is printed on both sides of a sheet by using a different gripper on backing up the sheet.

work-and-turn When matter is printed on both sides of a sheet by using the same gripper edge on backing up the sheet.

World Wide Web (WWW) A hypermedia system consisting of millions of websites forming the publishing heart of the internet.

wove Paper which shows an even texture instead of parallel lines.

wrappering Attaching a paper or board using a strip of glue at the spine of gathered work, stabbed or sewn.

xerography A form of electrostatic printing used in the Xerox DocuTech Production Publisher.